CONTRACTING WITH SOVEREIGNTY

The application of international law to state contracts with foreign private companies was the cause of continuing controversy throughout much of the twentieth century. State contractual undertakings with foreign investors raise a number of legal issues that do not fit well into the traditional pattern of international law as a law between states, but which also cannot be satisfactorily resolved by the exclusive application of the municipal law of the contracting state. In recent years the controversy has gained new prominence as a result of the advent of a new form of international dispute settlement, namely the mechanism of investment treaty arbitration. The main feature of this model of dispute resolution is that foreign investors are entitled to bring claims against states directly before international arbitral tribunals. This model, which emerged strongly in the late 1990s, has generated a rapidly expanding body of arbitral case law and in the process become one of the most significant new developments in modern international law Many of the disputes subject to investment treaty arbitration have their origin in contractual commitments made by states toward foreign investors. At the same time international commercial arbitration continues to be the preferred means of dispute resolution in contracts between foreign investors and states or state entities. This book explores how contract claims against states are dealt with in the two parallel processes of treaty-based and contract-based arbitration. The book charts the development of commercial arbitration into an international legal remedy in this field, discusses the theoretical problems which it creates for international law, and outlines the most significant substantive features of the international law applicable to contract claims as developed by arbitral tribunals on the basis of treaty standards and customary law.

Volume 31 in the series Studies in International Law

Studies in International Law

Volume 1: Between Light and Shadow: The World Bank, the International Monetary Fund and International Human Rights Law
Mac Darrow

Volume 2: Toxics and Transnational Law: International and European Regulation of Toxic Substances as Legal Symbolism
Marc Pallemaerts

Volume 3: The Chapter VII Powers of the United Nations Security Council
Erika de Wet

Volume 4: Enforcing International Law Norms Against Terrorism
Edited by Andrea Bianchi

Volume 5: The Permanent International Criminal Court
Edited by Dominic McGoldrick, Peter Rowe and Eric Donnelly.

Volume 6: Regional Organisations and the Development of Collective Security
Ademola Abass

Volume 7: Islamic State Practices, International Law and the Threat from Terrorism: A Critique of the 'Clash of Civilizations' in the New World Order
Javaid Rehman

Volume 8: Predictablity and Flexibility in the Law of Maritime Delimitation
Yoshifumi Tanaka

Volume 9: Biotechnology and International Law
Edited by Francesco Francioni and Tullio Scovazzi

Volume 10: The Development of Human Rights Law by the Judges of the International Court of Justice
Shiv Bedi

Volume 11: The Environmental Accountability of the World Bank to Third Party Non-State Actors
Alix Gowlland-Gualtieri

Volume 12: Transnational Corporations and Human Rights
Edited by Olivier De Schutter

Volume 13: Biotechnologies and International Human Rights
Edited by Francesco Francioni

Volume 14: Human Security and International Law: Prospects and Problems
Barbara Von Tigerstrom

Volume 15: The Arms Trade and International Law
Zeray Yihdego

Volume 16: Africa: Mapping New Boundaries in International Law
Edited by Jeremy Levitt

Volume 17: Forced Migration, Human Rights and Security
Edited by Jane McAdam

Volume 18: The Use of Nuclear Weapons and the Protection of the Environment during International Armed Conflict
Erik Koppe

Volume 19: The Shifting Allocation of Authority in International Law: Considering Sovereignty, Supremacy and Subsidiarity
Edited by Tomer Broude and Yuval Shany

Volume 20: Counterterrorism: Democracy's Challenge
Edited by Andrea Bianchi and Alexis Keller

Volume 21: Amnesty, Human Rights and Political Transitions
Louise Mallinder

Volume 22: Property Rights and Natural Resources
Richard Barnes

Volume 23: Human Dignity and the Foundations of International Law
Patrick Capps

Volume 24: Sovereignty and the Stateless Nation: Gibraltar in the Modern Legal Context
Keith Azopardi

Volume 25: The International Court of Justice and Self-Defence in International Law
James A Green

Volume 26: State Liability in Investment Treaty Arbitration: Global Constitutional and Administrative Law in the BIT Generation
Santiago Montt

Volume 27: Reappraising the Resort to Force: International Law, *Jus ad Bellum* and the War on Terror
Lindsay Moir

Volume 28: International Law and Dispute Settlement: New Problems and Techniques
Edited by Duncan French, Matthew Saul and Nigel White

Volume 29: The Democratic Legitimacy of International Law
Steven Wheatley

Volume 30: Reflections on the UN Declaration on the Rights of Indigenous Peoples
Edited by Stephen Allen and Alexandra Xanthaki

Volume 31: Contracting with Sovereignty: State Contracts and International Arbitration
Ivar Alvik

Contracting with Sovereignty

State Contracts and International Arbitration

Ivar Alvik

·HART·
PUBLISHING

OXFORD AND PORTLAND, OREGON
2011

Published in the United Kingdom by Hart Publishing Ltd
16C Worcester Place, Oxford, OX1 2JW
Telephone: +44 (0)1865 517530
Fax: +44 (0)1865 510710
E-mail: mail@hartpub.co.uk
Website: http://www.hartpub.co.uk

Published in North America (US and Canada) by
Hart Publishing
c/o International Specialized Book Services
920 NE 58th Avenue, Suite 300
Portland, OR 97213-3786
USA
Tel: +1 503 287 3093 or toll-free: (1) 800 944 6190
Fax: +1 503 280 8832
E-mail: orders@isbs.com
Website: http://www.isbs.com

British Library Cataloguing in Publication Data
Data Available

ISBN: 978-1-84113-657-8

Typeset by Hope Services, Abingdon
Printed and bound in Great Britain by
Lightning Source UK Ltd

To my parents

Preface

This book is the result of my four years as a research fellow with the Institute of Public and International Law at the University of Oslo. It was submitted for the degree of dr juris at the Faculty of Law in November 2006 and defended for the same degree in August 2007. For a young scholar with an academic interest, writing a doctoral dissertation is probably one of the most intellectually rewarding things one can do. It is, however, also an exhausting experience, and it has therefore taken some time to prepare the script for publication. Especially investment treaty arbitration is a new and rapidly developing field of law, and there have been significant developments in relation to certain of the issues that I discuss in the book. I have attempted to take account of the most significant new developments in arbitral practice. To the best of my abilities the book is therefore up to date as of January 2010. This nevertheless cannot fully hide the fact that the most rigorous and thorough review of the literature and cases underlying the general analysis of the book relates to developments before November 2006. Fortunately, I should add, I have found most developments in practice since the book was initially written to have strengthened the main lines of reasoning in the book. Thus, it has not been necessary to substantially revise the general structure of the analysis made.

When that is said, it is only right to add that the structure of the presentation in the book has undergone some significant changes from the originally submitted manuscript, to a large extent thanks to the insightful comments and critique received from my opponents, Professor James Crawford, Professor Jan Paulsson and Professor Giuditta Cordero Moss, both in the written evaluation and in their 'opposition' at the public defence of the dissertation. I owe them all great thanks, both for their positive and constructive comments and critique, and for having taken time out of their busy schedules to take on the job in the first place. Similar great thanks go to Richard Hart in Hart Publishing, both for his insightful comments on how to make a good dissertation into a good book, and for agreeing to print the book. In this regard I would especially like to thank both him and the others at Hart Publishing for their constructive, welcoming and friendly approach throughout the revision process. The greatest thanks and the most credit for their contributions to the book nevertheless go to my two supervisors, Professor Geir Ulfstein and Professor Ola Mestad, who provided continuing academic guidance and personal support throughout the writing of the original dissertation, and who with gentle prodding and constant replenishment of academic inspiration, both in their own way, proved to be the perfect combination of supervisors. Marius Emberland deserves special mention and great thanks for his constant support throughout the project and for having read and commented on an early version of the manuscript. I also owe thanks to the Faculty of Law at the University of Oslo, and specifically the Institute of Public and International Law, which made it possible for me to write the book in the first place. Having had quite extensive contacts with researchers from other countries throughout the writing of the dissertation, the Norwegian system of employing aspiring doctoral researchers as Research Fellows at the university with almost complete freedom, a decent salary and great office facilities always seemed to me a great privilege. Special thanks go to my fellow stipendiary colleagues at the Institute of Public and International Law, as well as in other departments of the Faculty, for having contributed to create such a great social and academic environment during the four years I spent writing this book. As part of my research for this book I spent a few rewarding months at the Lauterpacht Research Centre for International Law at the University of Cambridge, and at the Institut des Hautes Etudes Internationales at the Université de Paris II (Panthéon-Assas). Thanks are owed to both these great institutions and to the people I met there for inspiration and a friendly welcome. I would finally like to add my thanks to the Faculty of Law at the University of Oxford and to Somerville College, where I spent a formative year before I started writing this book and where I first came into contact with this fascinating field of law.

On a more personal note, I would like to extend my thanks to the many people close to me who have in an extended sense contributed to this work, probably more than they might know. Submitting and defending this doctoral dissertation has in a sense represented the 'crowning achievement' of my education and upbringing, and the stepping-stone into professional adulthood. The publication of this work thus represents the culmination of a long journey, from childhood, school and university, and onto being an academic and researcher and, currently, a practising lawyer. First and foremost among those who deserve thanks are naturally my parents, whose unwavering love, support and trust in their children have given me the best basis in life. This book is dedicated to them. I would also like to express my thanks to my sparring partners throughout childhood and into adulthood, my sister and brother, who, each in their own way, are always there to remind their older brother about the proper perspectives in life. My final thanks naturally go to my dear Ane and to my little daughter Martha, who give meaning to this and to everything else.

Oslo, 1 March 2010

Table of Contents

List of Abbreviations

AJIL	American Journal of International Law
Ann IDI	Annuaire Institut de Droit International
Arb Int'l	Arbitration International
BIT	Bilateral Investment Treaty
BYIL	British Yearbook of International Law
ECHR Reports	European Court of Human Rights: Reports of Judgments and Decisions
EJIL	European Journal of International Law
GA Res	General Assembly Resolution
Harv Int'l L J	Harvard International Law Journal
Harv L Rev	Harvard Law Review
ICC	International Chamber of Commerce
ICJ	International Court of Justice
ICJ Reports	International Court of Justice: Reports of Judgments, Advisory Opinions and Orders
ICLQ	International and Comparative Law Quarterly
ICSID	International Centre for Settlement of Investment Disputes
ICSID Reports	Reports of Cases decided under the Convention on the Settlement of Investment Disputes between States and Nationals of other States
ICSID Rev-FILJ	ICSID Review – Foreign Investment Law Journal
ILC	International Law Commission
Int'l Law Forum	International Law Forum: Journal of the International Law Association
ILM	International Legal Materials
ILR	International Law Reports
Iran-US CT Rep	Iran-US Claims Tribunal Reports
J Dr Int'l	Journal de Droit International
J Int'l Arb	Journal of International Arbitration
JWIT	Journal of World Investment and Trade
La Fontaine	La Fontaine, H: Pasicrisie Internationale 1794-1900: Histoire Documentaire des Arbitrages Internationaux
NYU J Int'l Law and Politics	New York University Journal of International Law and Politics
PCIJ	Permanent Court of International Justice

PCIJ Series	Permanent Court of International Justice: Judgments, Orders and Advisory Opinion
Recueil des Cours	Recueil des Cours: Collected Courses of the Hague Academy of International Law
Rev Arb	Revue d'Arbitrage
Rev B Dr Int'l	Revue Belge de Droit International
Rev Cr Dr Int'l Privé	Revue Critique de Droit International Privé
Rev G Dr Int'l Privé	Revue Générale de Droit International Privé
RIAA	Reports of International Arbitral Awards
Series A	European Court of Human Rights: Series A: Judgments and Decisions
Stockholm Int'l Arb. Rev.	Stockholm International Arbitration Review
TDM	Transnational Dispute Management
Tex Int'l L J	Texas International Law Journal
TfR	Tidsskrift for Rettsvitenskap
Trans Grot Soc	Transactions of the Grotius Society
UNCTAD	United Nations Conference on Trade and Development
UNCITRAL	United Nations Commission on International Trade Law
Va J Int'l Law	Virginia Journal of International Law
YbCA	Yearbook of Commercial Arbitration

Table of Cases

ICSID

Investment Treaty cases (ad hoc)

International Chamber of Commerce

Other International Arbitral cases

Iran-US Claims Tribunal

Permanent Court of International Justice (PCIJ)

International Court of Justice (ICJ)

European Court of Human Rights

UK cases

US cases

French cases

Canadian cases

Swiss cases

Table of National Legislation, International Agreements, Conventions and Treaties

Bilateral Investment Treaties

Other International Treaties

National Legislation

Miscellaneous International Resolutions, Codifications etc

. . . though so great a quantity of gold and silver is thus sent abroad, we must not imagine that it is sent abroad for nothing, or that its proprietors make a present of it to foreign nations.

Adam Smith, The Wealth of Nations (1776),
Book Two, Chapter II

1

Introduction

1.1 THE TOPIC

THE NOTION THAT a state can make contracts just as private persons and that private persons can contract with the state, raises complex legal issues. Particularly more so is this the case where some element of restriction of public power or administrative authority is involved. Bringing different legal, political and administrative philosophies and even mindsets head to head, this is a topic straddling such diverse areas as contract law, administrative law and constitutional law.[1] It is also a topic which, according to convention, at least until very recently, has been confined almost exclusively to the domain of municipal law. Indeed, a majority of public lawyers in the national domain might react with astonishment to the idea that international law should have anything to say about this subject, being situated at the core of constitutional and administrative law.

In this book I nevertheless examine a significant practice-driven response to this issue under international law, having developed in relatively recent years through two distinct dispute resolution processes, international commercial arbitration and the 'new' invention of investment treaty arbitration. This law is not to be found in developed codifications, but in a mass of international arbitral practice relating to what are essentially contractual disputes between states (or state entities) and foreign investors, usually in some manner concerning a contractual commitment made by the state in order to attract private capital and resources.[2] The addressee of such commitments is usually a multinational corporation, seeking opportunities to make use of its acquired capital and

[1] See eg Turpin, 'Public Contracts' in K Zweigert and K Drobnig (eds), *International Encyclopedia of Comparative Law* (Mohr Siebeck & Martinus Nijhoff, 1982); and Hadfield, 'Of Sovereignty and Contract: Damages for Breach of Contract by Government' (1998–99) 8 *Southern California Interdisciplinary Law Journal* 467.

[2] See eg the UNCTAD study on *State Contracts*, UNCTAD Series on issues in international investment agreements (UNCTAD/ITE/IIT/2004/11). Literature on the nature and forms of such agreements in different fields is abundant, see for a general account Sornarajah, *The Settlement of Foreign Investment Disputes* (Kluwer, The Hague, 2000) 25.

expertise in the most profitable location,[3] but it may also be smaller companies, or even individuals, having embarked on an economic venture abroad. The nature of the undertaking will often be a promise of certain benefits and guarantees of stability,[4] which may be combined with a concession or licence to exploit a natural resource or operate a public service.[5]

This form of agreement between a state and an investor is commonly known as an 'investment contract' (or agreement).[6] In earlier doctrine it was often encapsulated in the much-debated concepts of 'state contracts' or 'economic development agreements', being the subject of a stark theoretical controversy about whether international law could apply at all to such undertakings.[7] Today this phenomenon is a subject of renewed significance, mostly by virtue of the development of what is now known as investment treaty arbitration. This development has produced a mass of arbitral practice where previously there was merely a dozen or so prominent arbitral cases presided over by well-known professors of international law. The underlying problem involved and the main subject of this book, remains, however, essentially the same.

Thus, it is a noted and well-known dilemma that when such a contract is concluded, usually before the investment is made, the investor will be in a particularly advantageous negotiating position, offering the prospects of jobs, capital and technology, and with that general economic development, to a country or region where this may be sorely needed.[8] After the investment has been made, and if it proves to be successful, the situation in many ways is reversed. The investor is bound to a lasting engagement within the state in order to reap the promised return on its investment. If the government now, for political or other reasons, wishes to modify or terminate its original undertaking, the investor finds itself in a vulnerable position, since the government may use its executive and legislative

[3] The surge in foreign investment is obviously a key factor in the development of the multinational corporation as the main vehicle of business enterprise in today's world; see the standard treatise of Muchlinski, *Multinational Enterprises and the Law* (Blackwell Publishers, Oxford, 1999) 9–10 and 25 et seq.

[4] See eg Wälde and Ndi, 'Stabilizing International Investment Commitments: International Law versus Contract Interpretation' (1996) 31 *Tex Int'l LJ* 215, 220.

[5] In the natural resources sector this has seen a development from early long-term concession contracts to more modern variants of contracts, see eg Gao, *International Petroleum Contracts: Current Trends and New Directions* (Graham & Trotman, London, 1994); and Barberis, *Negotiating Mining Agreements: Past, Present and Future Trends* (Kluwer, The Hague, 1998) especially 141 et seq; and see also Maniruzzaman, 'The Relevance of Public International Law in Arbitrations concerning International Economic Development Agreements' (2005) 6(2) *JWIT* 263.

[6] See eg Sornarajah (2000), 25.

[7] See generally Leben, 'La théorie du contrat d'état et l'évolution du droit international des investissements' (2003) 302 *Recueil des Cours* 197.

[8] See eg Guzman, 'Why LDCs Sign Treaties That Hurt Them: Explaining the Popularity of Bilateral Investment Treaties' (1997–98) 38 *Va J Int'l Law* 639, 660.

authority to achieve its political aims.[9] In other words, in addition to ordinary commercial risk factors, the contract is subject to political risk. This creates a vicious circle. The investor may use its initial leverage to demand a particularly lucrative bargain in order to compensate for the political risk. But this only makes it more imperative for the state to get out of the arrangement when the investment has proved successful, and the investor reaps what may now appear from the state's perspective to be excessive gains. To break the vicious circle and mitigate political risk, a reliable concept of state commitment seems elemental.

The underlying substantive issue consequently addressed in the following is simple: what is the legal and structural basis for any such concept of contractual commitment under international law? The particular legal response to this issue provided by international law operates under certain complicating structural premises. International law is a decentralised legal system, without an effective procedural apparatus and enforcement mechanism. In realistic terms, having a legal claim is, however, inextricably linked to procedure, and the ability to invoke an effective and reliable remedy. Conversely, a crucial element of effective commitment is whether it can give rise to a claim ascertained by a competent authority that can also be enforced. In international investment law this function is served by what can be termed a 'hybrid' process of arbitration, so termed here because it does not operate strictly according to a traditional distinction between municipal and international law as mutually exclusive and separate spheres. Instead it straddles and combines the two in mutual reliance. Part of the reason for this is that a state commitment towards a foreign investor does not, according to convention, exclusively or even primarily invoke international law. A private investor is not a 'subject' of international law in the normal sense. In making an investment it submits to the municipal legal system of the host state.

A realistic approach to state commitment in the field of investment needs to address these procedural and structural premises of the law. The book accordingly consists of five main chapters, which loosely fall into three parts. The first part (chapters two and three) is concerned with the development and conceptualisation of the applicable international law on this subject, and how it has evolved through a distinct arbitral process assuming the function of an international legal remedy in relation to contract claims against states. In chapter two I examine the roots and development of this arbitral process in legal practice, whereas in chapter three I critically examine the doctrine conceptualising this practice in terms of international law. The second part (chapter four) concerns the

[9] This is what is sometimes termed the obsolescing bargain; see eg Inadomi, 'Independent Power Projects in Developing Countries: Legal Investment Protection and Consequences for Development' (Phd thesis, University of Oslo, 2005, unpublished) 44.

procedure whereby contract claims are made proper subjects of international adjudication. Here I particularly examine the diverse rules, practices and distinct concepts underlying and justifying the assertion of jurisdiction and the exercising of authority by arbitral tribunals over contract claims. The third part (chapters five and six) then addresses the substantive international law developed in arbitral practice regarding state contractual undertakings. In chapter five I first examine the application of certain general standards of international law, as possible grounds for claims based on state contracts and similar commitments of states toward foreign investors. In chapter six I then examine how, more specifically, contractual restraints on public authority have received a distinct conceptualisation in arbitral practice through the introduction of certain new concepts of international law, at least partly borrowed from municipal law. I conclude with a final chapter (chapter seven) where I attempt to draw together the separate lines of reasoning that have run through the book, and offer some final observations. In the rest of this introductory chapter I explain further the approach and method of the book. First, I explain the 'process' approach adopted in the book (section 1.2). I then briefly discuss the basis for considering arbitral practice a source of international law (section 1.3), before I discuss the method of interpretation I adopt in the book (section 1.4), and finally explain my choice of materials (section 1.5).

1.2 APPROACH—INTERNATIONAL LAW AS 'PROCESS'

In the book I intend to approach international investment law as a distinct body of law emerging through a decision-making process. This may be taken to entail what can be called a 'process perspective' on the law.[10] It means maintaining a perspective of the law as an authoritative process displaying and cementing policies and values.[11] Superficially, such an approach may appear to stand somewhat in contrast to a more traditional perspective on legal analysis as a construction of rules determined by reference to formal sources methodology.[12] The following nevertheless

[10] I can probably not disclaim a certain affinity with the so called 'process school' of international law, which originated in US scholarship in the 1960s and '70s eg through the writing of Chayes, Ehrlich and Lowenfeld, see O'Connell, 'New International Legal Process' in Ratner and Slaughter (eds), 'Symposium on Method in International Law' (1999) 93 *AJIL* 334.

[11] A well known expression of this approach is that advocated by Higgins, *Problems and Process* (Oxford, Clarendon Press, 1994) especially 1–12.

[12] For a more 'traditional' discussion of the relevant authoritative sources of international investment law, see Sornarajah, *The International Law on Foreign Investment* 2nd edn (Cambridge University Press, Cambridge, 2004) 87; and see also for a useful discussion of the methodology of treaty interpretation employed by arbitral tribunals, Schreuer, 'Diversity and Harmonization of Treaty Interpretation in Investment Arbitration' (April 2006) 3 *TDM* No 2.

represents no grand ambition to introduce or defend a revolutionary or controversial theory about international law as such. The ambition of the book is quite simple, namely to analyse a field of international law, which—as it appears to this author at least—is simply best approached by examining the legal processes through which it is developed, applied and implemented in practice. As a living practice, this law exists through the process of international arbitration, receiving its legitimisation as 'law', so to speak, by the acceptance of states through the general recognition afforded to arbitral awards under municipal legal systems. This approach contains certain implications and assumptions, which I ought to justify and explain somewhat further.

The first aspect of this relates to the treatment in the book of the well-known distinction between municipal and international law. While it is impossible to address the topic in this book without a sharp conceptual appreciation of this distinction, it is equally impossible to uphold any principled notion that municipal and international law are functionally separate in this field. Adopting a perspective on the law as fundamentally a decision-making process means, for one, that I do not always in the following adhere strictly to the arbitral tribunals' own perceived distinction between municipal and international law. This means that I am sometimes less concerned with the formal legal grounds enlisted in favour of a decision, than with what constituted the decisive, underlying consideration, directing and, fundamentally, *justifying* the decision. Thus, I do not consider that there is necessarily anything inconsistent or remarkable about considering a certain tribunal's interpretation and application of a contract on the alleged basis of municipal law, as a manifestation of the same fundamental principle that is revealed by another tribunal's interpretation of standards in an investment treaty or international customary law. Moreover, this 'process perspective' also requires a realistic appreciation of how the process functions through an interaction between municipal and international law. Whether a claim realistically can be pursued outside the state's own municipal legal apparatus and ultimately be enforced against the state depends on an interaction between international law, arbitral practices and municipal laws, which is not sufficiently addressed by a sole focus on international law. The approach adopted here is mainly to focus on practice itself, and on the conditions under which it is recognised and implemented by municipal legal systems.

A second aspect of the book's fundamental approach relates to the methodological focus I adopt. The following is primarily an analysis of practice, and of tendencies in practice, and not as such a 'traditional' legal analysis drawing out rules from all the relevant legal sources. One reason for this approach is the fragmented nature of international investment law, which is not set up as a coherent and integrated treaty regime, such as the EU, the WTO or the ECHR, but is instead encompassed in a vast and fragmented system of bilateral and multilateral investment treaties and customary practices.[13] This means that the actual applicability, basis and content of authoritative sources and concrete rules may differ from case to case. To give a full and systematic account of all the different rules and instruments that may be applicable in a given case has not been my aim here. Instead my aim is to say something about the basic normative structure of the law in question, and to analyse the main principles or at least tendencies of the law such as it is applied. This is not meant to disparage the significance of the formal and authoritative sources that ultimately apply in a concrete case, only to make clear that a detailed account in this regard is beyond the scope of the book. Instead, the following represents an account of applicable sources mainly as regarded from the focal point of each individual case, with the aim of drawing out and analysing the general normative structure reflected and cemented in case law. The value of this from a practical standpoint lies mainly in that this normative structure naturally superimposes itself on the sources applicable in a given case, as general principles somehow intrinsic to the legal process as a whole. This explains why different formulations in treaties are customarily interpreted in the same way, more or less as reflections of general standards, such as for instance is the case with different formulations of the ubiquitous umbrella—fair and equitable treatment—or expropriation clause in bilateral investment treaties.[14]

1.3 ARBITRAL PRACTICE AS A SOURCE OF LAW

While I do consider it relatively obvious that case law is a significant source of the law in this field, it is nevertheless a question on which it would have been possible to spend much more energy and theoretical effort than I do in this book. For the purposes of this book, I consider it mostly sufficient to observe that tribunals do tend to rely on the tendencies of prior cases as, at least, persuasive precedent.[15] To problematise this somewhat further, it may, however, be noted that, as is well known, there is no coherent doctrine of precedent in international law even in respect of decisions from authoritative standing adjudicative bodies such as the International Court of Justice. Arbitral tribunals residing over individual

[13] According to UNCTAD there were 2495 BITs entered into by the end of 2005, see UNCTAD: *World Investment Report 2006* 26. And see also generally Sornarajah (2004) 87 et seq.

[14] See ch 5.

[15] See further Schreuer, 'Diversity and Harmonization of Treaty Interpretation in Investment Arbitration' (April 2006) 3(2) *TDM* 10, and Kaufmann-Kohler, 'Arbitral Precedent: Dream, Necessity or Excuse' (2007) 23 *Arb Int'l* 357, 368 et seq.

cases have no authority beyond the single case. This means that it is clearly difficult to place any authoritative source value in individual cases. In arbitral practice it has instead been suggested that a heavy and consistent case load (a '*jurisprudence constante*') may be considered an expression of customary law, and as such would be binding for subsequent cases.[16] In the recent decision on the merits in *Saipem v Bangladesh*, the following view was set forth, which in my mind may serve as a concise expression of the approach generally reflected in arbitral practice:

> The tribunal considers that it is not bound by previous decisions. At the same time, it is of the opinion that it must pay due consideration to earlier decisions of international tribunals. It believes that, subject to compelling contrary grounds, it has a duty to establish solutions established in a series of consistent cases. It also believes that, subject to the specifics of a given treaty and of the circumstances of the actual case, it has a duty to seek to contribute to the harmonious development of investment law and thereby to meet the legitimate expectations of the community of States and investors towards certainty of the rule of law.[17]

Interestingly, this decision justifies its approach to precedent by referring to the harmonious development of investment law as a means to further the 'legitimate expectations' of states and investors towards the main goal of 'certainty of the rule of law'. No doubt, this provides an additional justification in the specific context of international investment law for considering a line of decided cases as authoritative precedent, and one that may be seen to be reflected in the increasing coherence of arbitral case law in this field.[18] Beyond this, it is difficult to say anything more concrete, especially about the relative source value of arbitral practice as measured against other sources. While the following presents an analysis of arbitral practice conceived as potential precedent for future cases, I therefore consider it difficult and largely futile to posit a more precise criterion of the value of arbitral practice as precedent. In a concrete case, this obviously depends on what other authoritative sources are applicable, and to my mind it is also more than anything else closely interlinked with the interpretation of the individual case. In practice, the value of a single case as precedent is likely to depend more than anything on its argumentative value. I shall therefore refrain from further discussion of this in the abstract and go on to explain my choice of materials and my approach to interpretation of the concrete cases.

[16] *SGS Societe Generale de Surveillance SA v Republic of the Philippines* (Decision on Jurisdiction, 2004) para 97.

[17] *Saipem SpA v People's Republic of Bangladesh* (Award, 2009) para 90. See also *Duke Energy Electroquil Partners and Electroquil SA v Republic of Ecuador* (Award, 2008) para 117.

[18] Kaufmann-Kohler (2007) 376.

1.4 INTERPRETATION—APPLIED AND CONSTRUCTED RATIO

There is a distinction between interpretation of cases handed down by a supreme court presiding over a certain municipal legal system, and cases which are the product of the less stringent system of international law and the international arbitral process. In the former instance there may be reasons for taking at face value expressions of principle uttered by the court, which are not similarly present with regard to decisions of ad hoc arbitral tribunals with no clear responsibility for the fundamental content and development of the law in question. This lies beneath the fundamental approach to interpretation adopted in this book.

Essentially, I look for the decisive ratio of the individual case, viz the rule or consideration which swayed the decision on the basis of its individual facts.[19] It is of course elemental to interpretation as such that it is not an exact science. In relation to interpretation of cases this fundamental approach nevertheless has certain more concrete implications, which I shall describe further. First, it means not necessarily taking at face value what the tribunals expressly state as the reasons for their award. The value of a decided case lies not primarily in the authority of the tribunal as such,[20] which concerns only the individual parties to the case, but in its actuality and responsiveness to individual facts.[21] What the tribunal actually states as the authority for its award is thus less interesting than the underlying reasons which actually compelled it to decide in a certain manner. I assume here that the compelling reasons behind an award may have been only partly, or incompletely, conceptualised through the pen or in the minds of the individual arbitrators. This approach means constructing a *potential* rationale of the decision, based on its individual facts. I nevertheless consider it clear that the authority of a 'constructed ratio' is derived from its demand to correspond with the actuality of the legal decision. An interpretation claiming such correspondence cannot go beyond what realistically swayed the decision in a

[19] MacCormick, *Legal Reasoning and Legal Theory* (Clarendon Press, Oxford, 1978) 215.

[20] This is different in the face of a formal doctrine of precedent. No such doctrine is recognised in the decentralized system of international law, and clearly even less so in respect of cases decided by *ad hoc* arbitral tribunals.

[21] This has been aptly formulated by some of the giants of international law. See eg Jennings, 'What is international law and how do we know it when we see it?' in *Collected Writings of Sir Robert Jennings* (Kluwer, The Hague, 1998) 730, 744 (originally published (1981) XXXVII *Swiss Yearbook of International Law* 59): 'The great value of decided cases for the development and clarification of the law is largely because truth is stranger than fiction, and real life throws up circumstances which the most imaginative writers never thought of'. And see also Fitzmaurice, 'Some Problems Regarding the Formal Sources of International Law' in (1958) *Symbolae Verzijl* 153, 172: 'a decision, if relevant to the case under discussion, has an actuality and a concrete character that causes it to impinge directly on the matters at issue, in a way that an abstract opinion, however good, can never do'.

concrete case, if only conceivably so in case of a ratio claimed to be implicit. In other words, I assume that a case cannot be held to support a ratio that it *might* have supported based on its individual facts, if it can be considered reasonably clear that the tribunal *did not* feel compelled by this in any way.

A second point to make is that while in the following I programmatically construct the ratio decidendi of cases, where, admittedly, it is not always evident in the stated reasons of the award, I nevertheless take as a starting point that the entry to discerning the rationale of a case must necessarily be the tribunal's own reasoning. I will naturally assume that tribunals do not consciously attempt to camouflage the real reasons of an award behind a fictitious rationale.[22] Thus, I assume that tribunals mean what they say, and say what they mean. Consequently, I attempt not to disregard the stated reasons of a case, either out of some conviction that alternative reasons ought to have been summoned, or any suspicion that the tribunals may have had ulterior motives.[23] This assumes a distinction, albeit a fine one, between reading alternative or ulterior ratios into a case irrespective of its stated reasons, which I seek to avoid, and critical reconstruction, which I consider a main objective of analysis. Thus, I allow myself sometimes to question quite freely whether what the tribunals say, and consequently mean, might not have been conceptualised quite differently to coincide with an alternative ratio. From this perspective, the requirement of textual veracity does not prevent quite radical contextual reconstructions, but indicates that an alleged ratio, if not fully conceptualised in the award, nevertheless ought to find some evident trace in its stated reasons to constitute a plausible interpretation.

1.5 MATERIALS

As will have become clear by now, the main source material addressed in this book is international arbitral awards. Two main kinds of awards are addressed.[24] The first are ordinary international commercial arbitral

[22] I am indebted here to the discussion in Høgberg, *Kontraktstolkning: særlig om tolkningsstiler ved fortolkning av skriftlige kontrakter* (Universitetsforlaget, Oslo, 2006) 86–7.

[23] *ibid*, 87.

[24] I have mostly relied on public journals, compilations of materials and case reports, such as the ILR (International Legal Reports), ILM (International Legal Materials), ICSID Reports, ICSID Rev-FILJ (ICSID Review—Foreign Investment Law Journal), and YbCA (Yearbook of Commercial Arbitration). In addition I have found immensely valuable certain internet sites and databases which routinely publicise arbitral awards and other relevant source material. Especially the University of Victoria (Canada) hosted website on 'Investment Treaty Arbitration' and the 'Investment Claims' website edited by Todd Weiler and Ian Laird deserve mention. They can be visited respectively at: ita.law.uvic.ca/ and www.naftaclaims.com. Additional to this, I have also had much use of the Kluwer Law internet database on arbitration, which is a subscription based service. This can be visited at: www.kluwerarbitration.com/arbitration/arb/default.asp.

awards based on contractual arbitration undertakings, which are in most instances comparable to awards rendered in normal contractual disputes between private parties. The second are investment treaty awards, based on provisions for investor-state jurisdiction in investment treaties.[25] ICSID awards, ie awards rendered under the ICSID Convention,[26] which make up a considerable part of the cases addressed, may fall into both categories, depending on the nature of consent involved (ie whether it is based in treaty or contract). UNCITRAL awards, ie awards based on the UNCITRAL arbitration rules,[27] which make up another considerable part of the cases addressed, may also fall into both categories according to the same distinction. Finally, the same applies to a number of cases decided under the framework of arbitration institutions such as the ICC Court of Arbitration, the Stockholm Court of Arbitration, or the London Court of International Arbitration. My choice of cases has not in principle been limited to any institution or procedure, however, but made on the basis of the issues addressed, as well as the function of the arbitral procedure in the concrete case. The latter means that I primarily focus on cases decided within the framework of a purpose to protect private rights and investments against public power, either a particular investment or foreign investment in general.

In addition to arbitral practice, I also refer in the book to rules of municipal and international law which govern the function of the arbitral process, such as arbitration rules, municipal arbitration laws, international conventions on arbitration, and principles of state immunity. My ambition here is for the most part to provide a broader insight into how the arbitral process realistically functions on the basis of an interaction of such rules, and not to provide an in-depth analysis of these rules as such. I also refer extensively in the following to source material employed by arbitral tribunals to reach substantive conclusions, such as investment treaty provisions, general principles, and state practice. However, as stated above, the following is mainly an analysis of arbitral practice, and does not pretend to give a comprehensive account of the law beyond that. When I refer in the following to treaties and authoritative sources other than arbitral practice, it is thus, with some fairly obvious exceptions, mostly by way of example, and as the raw material of arbitral practice in concrete cases.

There is an abundant literature on state contracts, diplomatic protection, general issues of state responsibility, international arbitration (commercial,

[25] Particularly in respect of the latter, another distinction can be made between *decisions on jurisdiction* and *awards*, where the former are preliminary decisions on whether the tribunal has jurisdiction under the treaty, and the second are decisions on the merits of a claim.

[26] Convention on the Settlement of Investment Disputes between States and Nationals of other States, (Washington, 1965) (1965) 4 ILM 524.

[27] United Nations Commission on International Trade Law (UNCITRAL) Arbitration Rules, adopted by the UN General Assembly in GA Res 31/98 (A/RES/31/98).

mixed and public), and, increasingly, also modern international investment law and arbitration based on investment treaties. I seek to be up to date on the most recent and significant contributions in the field, as well as the most significant tendencies of opinion in traditional literature, but I can lay no claim to having exhausted the vast mass of relevant literature.

Finally, a word about referencing: when I refer to cases in the following, I refer to them with the names of the parties (in full on the first mention and thereafter in shortened form), type of decision and year, where an award is openly available at one of the two open internet sites referred to above. If it is not, I also refer to the source from which I have obtained access to it. When referring to literature, the full reference is used when I first refer to the book or article in each chapter, thereafter I only refer to author name and year of publication.

2

History and Development—A Hybrid Genealogy

2.1 INTRODUCTION

IN THIS CHAPTER I describe how contract claims of foreign investors against states have emerged as a subject of international arbitral practice, and eventually international law. This is also the story of what has been termed an arbitral process of hybrid foundations, straddling the traditional divide between municipal and international law.[1] In the following, I cursorily examine the history and development of this process, and its origin in certain fundamental concerns related to protection of foreign investment, invariably effected through various means of distancing or detaching the host state's commitment from its own legal system.[2] I shall proceed in the following by first describing 'diplomatic protection' as the conventional modality of international law in this field, and secondly explaining its exceptional unsuitability in the context of foreign investment protection (section 2.2). I then discuss an early 'precursor' to modern investment arbitration, namely the practice of international claims commissions and its function up until the present in the Iran-US Claims Tribunal (section 2.3), before accounting for the main precursor to modern investment arbitration, that of international commercial arbitration, and its application to investment-contract disputes (section 2.4). Lastly, I describe modern investment arbitration on the basis of the ICSID Convention[3] and investment treaties as the now standard modality for settling investor-state contract disputes (section 2.5).

[1] Douglas, 'The Hybrid Foundations of Investment Treaty Arbitration' (2003) 74 *BYIL* 151.

[2] An account of the development of 'mixed arbitration' through so-called delocalisation from municipal law is also provided by Toope, *Mixed International Arbitration* (Grotius Publications, Cambridge, 1990).

[3] Convention on the Settlement of International Disputes between States and Nationals of Other States (Washington, 1965) 4 ILM 524.

2.2 INVESTMENT PROTECTION UNDER CLASSICAL INTERNATIONAL LAW—THE DOCTRINE OF DIPLOMATIC PROTECTION

Under a classical view of public international law, individuals and private, non-state entities were inhibited from advancing individual claims against states by a fundamental lack of standing under international law. While perhaps somewhat stricter in retrospect than in reality,[4] a prevailing view in mainstream doctrine was (and to some extent still is) that individuals lacked fundamental legal capacity under international law.[5] The law in this respect was cast out of a strong concept of state sovereignty, which appeared mainly in two guises. First, there was the doctrine of sovereign immunity, which ruled out the possibility of bringing claims against other states before municipal courts.[6] Secondly, and in many ways complementary to this, was the exclusive right of states to espouse the claims of their nationals against other states by exercising diplomatic protection.[7] The subject of this section is the fundamental lack of efficacy of diplomatic protection as a means of investment protection, something which eventually led to the development of other and alternative practices and remedies to secure foreign investments under international law. I first discuss the general features of the doctrine, before examining the amplification of these features in relation to contract claims.

A. General Characteristics and Unsuitability for Investment

Under international law, a state whose nationals are maltreated by another state has a right to make complaints and enact certain measures against the state in question. The exercise of this right is called 'diplomatic

[4] Cf the *North American Dredging Company Case* (US-Mexican General Claims Commission, 1926), IV RIAA 26, 28 (paras 6–7).

[5] See eg Borchard, *Diplomatic Protection of Citizens Abroad* (The Banks Law Publishing Co, New York, 1916) 16–17: 'Using the term "subjects" of law to connote those upon whom the law confers rights and imposes duties, the weight of authority considers states alone as the subjects of international law, and individuals as objects of international law. This conclusion is based on the theory that international law cannot ascribe rights and duties to individuals directly, and that individuals cannot invoke for their protection a rule of international law which has not been incorporated in municipal law'.

[6] The law of state immunity can in many ways be said to have undergone a similar development to that described here in relation to diplomatic protection, from an absolute to a relative principle more responsive to underlying individual interests, see eg Badr, *State immunity—An Analytical and Prognostic View* (Martinus Nijhoff, The Hague, 1984); Schreuer, *State Immunity: Some Recent Developments* (Groitus Publications, Cambridge, 1988); and Fox, *The Law of State Immunity* (Oxford University Press, Oxford, 2000).

[7] The classical work on the right of diplomatic protection is Borchard, *Diplomatic Protection of Citizens Abroad* (The Banks Law Publishing Co, New York, 1916).

protection', and its rationale has been said to follow from the function of states as guarantors of the welfare and security of individual citizens.[8] When exercising diplomatic protection, a state intervenes in a dispute between one of its nationals and another state, and extends in a sense its protective function over the individual into its external relation with the other state.[9] Crucial to the doctrine of diplomatic protection is that the state is exercising its own right, and not a right belonging to its national.[10] The underlying construction is that states are entitled to have their citizens treated by other states according to certain minimum standards,[11] and that the complaint of the individual citizen is transformed into a claim under international law only when it is taken up by the citizen's home state.

In realistic terms, diplomatic protection as such denotes nothing more than a process of elevating an originally private claim into an international claim between states. In the terminology of the International Law Commission, it describes the procedural capacity of states to invoke the responsibility of another state in respect of injury to its nationals.[12] There is no one procedure in this regard; a state may take advantage of all remedies generally available to it under international law to pursue a claim, such as diplomatic protest and negotiations,[13] countermeasures,[14] or (subject to jurisdiction) proceedings before international courts,[15]

[8] See Vattel, *Le droit des gens—ou principes de la loi naturelle appliqués a la conduite et aux affaires des nations et des souverains* Nouvelle Édition (Librairie de Guillaumin, Paris, 1863) Vol 1 Livre 2 §71, 47–8; and Borchard (1916) 30 et seq.

[9] Borchard (1916) 31.

[10] *Mavromattis Palestine Concessions case,* PCIJ Rep Series A No 2 (1924) 12: 'By taking up the case of one of its subjects and by resorting to diplomatic action or international judicial proceedings on his behalf, a state is in reality asserting its own rights—its right to ensure, in the person of its subjects, respect for the rules of international law'.

[11] *Case concerning the Barcelona Traction Light and Power Company (Belgium v Spain)* [1970] ICJ Rep 3, 46.

[12] Cf the official commentary to Art 42 of the ILC Draft Articles on Responsibility of States for Internationally Wrongful Acts, in the Report of the International Law Commission on the work of its 53rd session, GAOR 55th session, supp No 10 (A/56/10) (2001), see also Crawford, 'The ILC's Articles on Responsibility of States for Internationally Wrongful Acts: A Retrospect' (2002) 96 *AJIL* 874, 881. In this respect some might distinguish it from diplomatic *representation*, which can be considered to encompass the widest range of communications from one state to another, without necessarily alleging unlawful conduct, see Warbrick, 'Diplomatic Representations and Diplomatic Protection' (2002) 51 *ICLQ* 723, 724.

[13] See eg the famous communication between the US Secretary of State Hull and the Mexican authorities pursuant to the Mexican agrarian reforms from 1917 onwards, as reproduced in Lowenfeld, *International Economic Law* (Oxford University Press, Oxford, 2002).

[14] See eg the ILC Draft Articles on State Responsibility, esp Arts 49 and 52.

[15] There are several examples of inter-state disputes before the PCIJ and the ICJ that involved both investment claims in general, and claims related to contractual relationships in particular; before the PCIJ eg the *Mavromattis Palestine Concessions case*, PCIJ Rep Series A No 2 (1924); *Serbian and Brazilian Loans cases* (1930) PCIJ Series A No 20/21; *Lighthouses case* PCIJ Rep Series A/B No 62 (1937); *Panevezys-Saldutskis Railways case* PCIJ Rep Series A/B No 76 (1939); and the *Losinger case* PCIJ Rep Series C No 78. And before the ICJ eg the *Anglo-Iranian Oil Company case* [1952] ICJ Rep 93; and *Norwegian Loans case* [1957] ICJ Rep 9, both of

arbitral tribunals[16] and, subject to agreement with the respondent state, the establishment of individualised claims commissions providing aggrieved individuals with individual standing to pursue their claims, which I return to below.

The exclusivity of the home state's right in this regard essentially means that the aggrieved individual has no independent right to be protected by its home state; in other words, the home state has no *duty* to exercise diplomatic protection.[17] Whether it also means that the substantive right invoked truly can be said only to exist on the inter-state level is a more complex, theoretical question to which I return in chapter three below.

As a result of the inter-state functionality of diplomatic protection, one of its inevitable consequences is that relatively low-key disputes between states and foreign private persons are intrinsically politicised. This has two components, both of which combine to make the institution relatively ill suited for international investment disputes.

First, diplomatic protection means that the state identifies with the cause of its national. As a result the dispute escalates into an inter-state affair and takes on a political significance which most likely is far beyond its real impact on the actual economic and political interests of the states involved. The point has been made poignantly by Thomas Franck (in relation to the *Mavromattis Palestine Concessions case*):

which concerned claims relating to contractual relationships; and *the Nottebohm case* [1955] ICJ Rep 4; *Interhandel case* [1959] ICJ Rep 6; *Barcelona Traction case* [1970] ICJ Rep 3, and the *ELSI case* [1989] ICJ Rep 15, all of which have been concerned with more traditional investment matters.

[16] From the extensive survey of inter-state arbitrations in Stuyt, *Survey of International Arbitrations 1794–1989* (Martinus Nijhoff, Dordrecht, 1990), see eg award no 63 from 1859 between Britain and Honduras concerning claims and concessions of British nationals who 'have by grant, lease or otherwise, heretofore obtained from the Mosquito Indians, interests in various lands'; award no 36 between Great Britain and 'the Two Sicilies' concerning a 'sulphur monopoly' (1840), award no 164 between Great Britain, the USA and Portugal concerning a railway concession-contract (*the Delagoa Bay Railway Company case* (Award, 1900) Lafontaine 398), award no 201 between Colombia and Great Britain concerning a railway concession-contract (*Tribunal Arbitral International du Chemin de Fer d'Antioquia*) (1896), award no 202 between Chile and France concerning a contract for transportation of immigrants (1897), award no 214 between Siam and the USA concerning forest concession-contracts (1897), award no 232 between Guatemala and the USA concerning certain railway contracts (1900), award no 250 between Austria-Hungary and Turkey concerning certain contracts of the Oriental Railway Company (1903), award no 272 between France and Haiti concerning concession-contracts (1904), award no 292 between the USA and Venezuela concerning a river-steamship concession-contract (the *Orinoco Steamship Company case* (1910) XI RIAA 227), award no 316 between Morocco and the Netherlands concerning mine concession contracts (1914), award no 342 between Costa Rica and Great Britain concerning certain concession contracts granted by an interim administration (the *Tinoco case* (Award, 1923) 1 RIAA 369), and award no 396b between France and Greece concerning the so-called Lighthouses concessions (see also the case before the PCIJ, above n 15).

[17] *Barcelona Traction case* [1970] ICJ Rep 3, 44: '[W]ithin the limits prescribed by international law, a State may exercise diplomatic protection by whatever means and to whatever extent it thinks fit, for it is its own right that the state is asserting'.

> [W]hen this dispute appeared before the World Court, it was at once transformed into something quite different . . . What had been a quarrel between a businessman and an administrator became a dispute pitting Britain against Greece, kingdom against kingdom, national pride against national pride; for the rules of the International Court demand that the plaintiff must be all Greece, and not just Mr. Mavromattis, and the defendant must be Great Britain and not merely a Palestinian bureaucrat.[18]

Making an inter-state dispute out of an investment dispute is thus effectively, again in the words of Franck, to

> [reverse] the biblical formula. Instead of the full fury of the dispute between all the Israelites and all the Philistines being sensibly delegated to a single battle between David and Goliath, a simple quarrel between David and Goliath is senselessly expanded into a conflict between all the Philistines and Israelites.[19]

Secondly, this is inevitably combined with the home state's political discretion in respect of whether to pursue the dispute. The interest of the investor to pursue its claim is placed at the mercy of the political discretion of its home state government. This is not merely an unfortunate weakness; it is a functional pre-requisite of the doctrine. To make a dispute into an inter-state matter *requires* taking into account the broader political situation of which it is part. The home state government is bound to screen claims in the light of its broader interests and policies before deciding whether to pursue them.[20] This lack of certainty for individual investors is exacerbated by the government's discretion when it comes to management and distribution of whatever funds it can recover from the delinquent state, perhaps best illustrated by the practice of lump-sum settlements, ie that several separate claims are settled by the single payment of an agreed sum to the home government.[21] Based on a political compromise, this is typically reached where the home state's desire to obtain some pretence of satisfaction is met by the delinquent state's willingness to give the pretence of justice. Usually, not only does this tend to leave most claimants without just compensation, it also precludes further pursuit of their claims.[22]

These inherent political aspects fundamentally undermine the functional and commercial value of diplomatic protection as a reliable remedy for individual investors against political risk and government abuse. When

[18] *Mavromattis Palestine Concessions case (Greece v United Kingdom)*, PCIJ Rep Series A No 2 (1924) 4. Franck, *The Structure of Impartiality: Examining the Riddle of one Law in a Fragmented World* (The Macmillan Company, New York, 1968) 214.

[19] *ibid*, 214.

[20] Political willingness apart, another politically contingent factor is of course that the situation of the investor clearly depends to a great extent on the *political strength* of its home state.

[21] See Kokott (2002) 25, and generally, Lillich and Weston, *International Claims: Their Settlement by Lump Sum Agreements* (University Press of Virginia, Charlottesville, 1975).

[22] Kokott (2002) 25.

applied to contractual claims these weaknesses are not merely present, they are greatly exacerbated, as I show in the next section.

B. Diplomatic Protection in Respect of Contract Claims

The relative futility of relying on diplomatic protection as a remedy for breach of contract is illustrated by the ambiguity of traditional state practice in this regard. A tendency would seem to be that while diplomatic protection might be extended to contractual claims, governments have been reluctant to do so, even when diplomatic protection was in the vogue, at the end of the nineteenth and the beginning of the twentieth century.

Tellingly, the practice of the United States was, apparently, formerly to refuse appeals from their nationals for diplomatic protection in respect of claims based on contracts entered into with foreign states.[23] The reluctance of the United States to extend such protection found expression as long ago as 1823 in a letter penned by then secretary of state, John Quincy Adams:

> With regard to the contracts of an individual born in one country with the government of another, most especially when the individual contracting is domiciled in the country with whose government he contracts, and formed the contract voluntarily, for his own private emolument and without the privity of the nation under whose protection he has been born, he has no claim whatsoever to call upon the government of his nativity to espouse his claim, this government having no right to compel that with which he voluntarily contracted to the performance of that contract.[24]

The main reason for US policy seems to have been the perception that someone entering into a contract with a foreign state voluntarily undertakes a risk by submitting to the legal order of that state.[25] The practice of other states seems to have been more variable though. According to Borchard it did not appear 'that the countries of continental Europe make any substantial distinction between claims arising out of contract and those arising out of other acts'.[26] It is also somewhat doubtful whether US

[23] Borchard (1916) 284.

[24] *ibid*, 287.

[25] This is framed as follows by Borchard (1916) 285: 'There are several reasons why governments are and should be less zealous in pressing the claims of their citizens arising out of a breach of contract than those arising out of some tortuous act. The first reason is that the citizen entering into a contract does so voluntarily and takes into account the probabilities and possibilities of performance by the foreign government. He has in contemplation all the ordinary risks which attend the execution of the contract. In the second place, by going abroad, he submits impliedly to the local law and the local judicial system. The contract or the law provides remedies for breach of contract. These he must pursue before his own government can become interested in the case'.

[26] *ibid*, 286.

policy stemmed from a clear conviction that diplomatic protection in the context of contract claims was legally excluded as a matter of law.[27] Thus, no conclusive state practice would seem to have excluded diplomatic protection in respect of contractual claims. Indeed, certain contemporary developments indicate that claims based on contracts *could* in principle be made the subject of diplomatic protection. The adoption in 1907 of the Drago-Porter Convention for the Limitation of Use of Force for Recovery of Contract Debts would seem to suggest that at least contractual debts were subject to a right of diplomatic protection.[28] More generally, the same is evidenced by the practice of Latin American states of inserting 'Calvo' clauses in their contracts with foreign investors.[29] A Calvo clause is a promise by the foreign investor whereby he agrees to waive the right to diplomatic protection from his home state. If there was no right of diplomatic protection in respect of contracts, there would not be much point in the insertion of a Calvo clause.

While this suggests that international law did not strictly exclude the possibility of diplomatic protection in respect of contract claims, it nevertheless illustrates how states typically may be less willing to endorse such claims for political reasons. Two factors would seem to be important. One is the investor's voluntary submission to the risk of breach, the other the lack of moral 'drama' and reproach connected with a commercial contract claim.[30]

This shows how the inherent political 'infection' of diplomatic protection as a legal process greatly reduces its value for individual investors, to the point of being near worthless in a contractual context. What the rest of this chapter will show is that diplomatic protection increasingly has been, and is, replaced as the relevant international remedy by various procedures of international arbitration that can be invoked independently by individual investors. An important objective of such procedures is precisely the *depoliticisation* of investment disputes.[31] This has an economic and

[27] *ibid*, 286.

[28] Cf Jennings, 'State Contracts in International Law' (1961) 37 *BYIL* 156, 160, and Weil, 'Problèmes relatifs aux contrats passés entre un État et un particulier' (1969-III) 105 *Recueil des Cours* 95, 120. Article 1 of the convention reads: 'The Contracting Powers agree not to have recourse to armed force for the recovery of contract debts claimed from the Government of one country by the Government of another country as being due to its nationals. This undertaking is, however, not applicable when the debtor state refuses or neglects to reply to an offer of arbitration, or, after accepting the offer, prevents any *compromis* from being agreed on, or, after the arbitration, fails to submit to the award'.

[29] See generally Borchard (1916) 792 et seq.

[30] Conversely, it has been claimed that it may in many instances be a powerful remedy in cases which at the outset are more tainted with political controversy, such as fundamental human rights violations invoking moral outrage and concern, see Dugard, 'First report on diplomatic protection', presented to the International Law Commission on its 52nd session (2000) A/CN.4/506, 7 et seq.

[31] See generally Shihata, 'Towards a Greater Depoliticization of Investment Disputes: the Roles of ICSID and MIGA' (1986) 1 *ICSID Rev-FILJ* 1.

commercial rationale, creating certainty for individual investors and thereby facilitating investment, but it also carries the political benefit of reducing the potential for tension created by identification of state interests with the economic interests of individual investors.

As I shall come back to in the next chapter, this does not mean that the traditional international law of diplomatic protection is wholly excluded in this field. But it is relegated to the role of last resort, of possible significance only where individual remedies granted to the investor have been exhausted.[32] Implicitly this means that diplomatic protection has become largely redundant, if not in law, at least in fact, as a means to protect foreign investment.[33] As I come back to below, this is, at least partly, a practical consequence of the new role of municipal courts in the process of investment dispute settlement. The point is that enforcement of arbitral awards through possible seizure of state assets and comparable measures by municipal courts provides a much more effective remedy than exertion of pressure through traditional diplomatic channels.

2.3 MIXED CLAIMS COMMISSIONS

The unsuitability of diplomatic protection as a means of investment protection did not prevent capital-exporting states from engaging in various legal practices to protect their investors abroad. While the evident benefits of legal rather than political settlement may explain the frequent resort to inter-state arbitral tribunals and courts as described above, the additional benefits of individualised settlement at the initiative of individual claimants also found expression in another, more distinct tradition, namely that of international 'mixed' claims commissions or tribunals.[34] In a sense, this now mostly historical practice can be seen as one important precursor of modern investment treaty arbitration.[35]

[32] Orrego VicuÀa, 'Interim Report on the Changing Law of Nationality of Claims' First report of the Committee on Diplomatic Protection of Persons and Property, International Law Association (2000) 28, 32.

[33] See also to this effect Kokott (2002) 27: 'The result is striking: the incompleteness of protection provided by DP gave rise to the development of the BIT network. The consequence of that network is, in broad terms, the exclusion of diplomatic protection from the arena of foreign investment. In addition, the BIT system better reflects modern international law and its increasing recognition of individual rights than does traditional diplomatic protection'.

[34] These can be distinguished from *national* claims commissions, ie domestic tribunals established eg to distribute a lump sum settlement among individual claimants, see Wilson, 'Some Aspects of the Jurisprudence of National Claims Commissions' (1942) 36 *AJIL* 56.

[35] See generally Bederman, 'The Glorious Past and Uncertain Future of International Claims Tribunals' in Janis (ed), *International Courts for the Twenty-First Century* (Martinus Nijhoff, Dordrecht, 1992) 161.

Such claims commissions were judicial arrangements established by agreement between two states to handle a group of individual claims by nationals of one or both states against the other state, often in the aftermath of a political crisis such as revolution or civil war.[36] Vested with competence to decide claims brought and argued by the individual claimants themselves, such tribunals provided each individual claimant with a form of limited and ad hoc international standing.[37] The use of claims commissions goes all the way back to the 1794 Jay Treaty between the USA and Britain,[38] which set up commissions of three or five members for resolution of individual claims by citizens of either state against the other, pursuant to the 1775–83 War of Independence.[39] Following the Jay Treaty a considerable number of claims commissions were established. The most famous are perhaps the two US-Mexican claims commissions which were set up after the Mexican revolution, not to mention the Iran-US claims tribunal, founded in 1981 and still working.[40]

While most claims commissions in practice were non-reciprocal, and only adjudicated on claims against one of the states involved, one should not jump to the conclusion that this necessarily affected the fairness of the proceedings in individual cases.[41] Substituting the political contingencies of diplomatic protection with a relatively neutral judicial procedure based on individual initiative clearly had benefits for both parties.[42] To this extent such claims commissions invoked some of the same concerns that underlie modern investment treaty arbitration, and several issues confronting the contemporary arbitral process have their counterparts in issues addressed by the old claims commissions. In the following I discuss how the commissions addressed the question of jurisdiction over contract claims in a manner largely portending the later practice of investment

[36] Bederman (1992) 163.

[37] Usually this would nevertheless be subject to some form of screening from the home state government, see further Hudson, *International Tribunals: Past and Future* (Carnegie Endowment, Washington, 1944) 68.

[38] Treaty of Amity Commerce and Navigation between His Britannic Majesty and the United States of America (London, 1794).

[39] Hambro, *Folkerettspleie* (Gyldendal, Oslo, 1956) 27.

[40] Another somewhat related example is the *United Nations Compensation Commission* established after the Iraqi invasion of Kuwait in 1991, which has dealt with about 2.6 million private claims against the Iraqi government after the Kuwait invasion. See Bederman, 'The United Nations Compensation Commission and the Tradition of International Claims Settlement' (1994–95) 27 *NYU J Int'l Law and Politics* 1.

[41] Bederman (1962) 166.

[42] *ibid*, 166: '[I]t should be obvious that such agreements were only made where both parties perceived a benefit to be gained or a hazard to be avoided. This is so even when the right of claims was bestowed on only one party. For weaker states, agreeing to the settlement of claims possibly averted political disaster, at least in the era before the advent of the Charter and the prohibition of the use of force as a reprisal for acts directed against a state's nationals. For stronger nations, international claims resolution provided a relatively cheap and certain way to vindicate the rights of their nationals, and at the same time, to reinforce the rule of law'.

arbitral tribunals. I first address some instances of pre-war practice, before examining the more contemporary Iran-US Claims Tribunal.

A. Jurisdiction over Contract Claims

Evoking here a comparison with modern investment arbitration, claims tribunals were largely established as neutral substitutes for municipal court proceedings for the purpose of addressing, inter alia, claims of foreign nationals related to confiscation and destruction of property and investments in the state concerned. A partly disputed issue, inviting comparison with the modern context, was whether the commissions had jurisdiction over 'contract claims'.[43]

Claims arising out of contracts were habitually considered encompassed by jurisdiction over claims for *loss, injury or damages to persons or property*, insofar as something comparable to a 'denial of justice' was involved.[44] In the 1868 *Pond case* the US-Mexican claims commission stated it as follows:

> [C]laims arising out of contracts come under the cognizance of the commission, but as these contracts are made voluntarily between the parties, the umpire thinks that the validity of the contract should be proved by the clearest evidence, and that it should also be shown that gross injustice has been done by the defendant.[45]

But jurisdiction also appears to have been exercised in some cases over purely contractual claims.[46] An instance is the *Illinois Central Railroad*

[43] See further below ch 4 (especially section 4.4).

[44] See for relevant decisions, De Beus, *The Jurisprudence of the General Claims Commission, United States and Mexico* (Martinus Nijhoff Publishers, S-Gravenhage, 1938) 19. Moore, *International Law Digest*, Vol VI (Government Printing Office, Washington, 1906) 718, summarises the practice as follows: 'International commissions have frequently allowed claims based on the infraction of rights derived from contracts where denial of justice was properly established. This was done under the convention between the United States and Mexico of April 11, 1939; by the Commission under the act of congress of March 3, 1849, to carry into effect the Treaty of Guadalupe Hidalgo; by the Commission under the Treaty between the United States and Great Britain of February 8, 1953; by the Commission under the Convention between the United States and Peru of January 12, 1863; by the Commission under the Convention between the United States and Mexico of July 4, 1868: and by the Commission under the Convention between the United States and Venezuela of December 5, 1885'.

[45] *Pond case*, in Moore, *Arbitrations* (Washington, 1898) 3647.

[46] *Illinois Central Railroad Company v United Mexican States* (US-Mexican General Claims Commission, 1926) (1926) 20(4) *AJIL* 794. Borchard (1916) 297, observes: 'Practically all international commissions, where the terms of submission in the protocol could be construed as sufficiently broad, have exercised jurisdiction over contract claims'. See also the *Orinoco Steamship Company case* (1910) XI RIAA 227, which concerned a claim arising out of a river-boat concession. The initial jurisdiction of the US-Venezuelan claims commission extended to: 'All claims owned by citizens of the United States of America against the Republic of Venezuela which have not been settled by diplomatic agreement or by arbitration between the two governments'.

Company case, which was decided by the US-Mexican General Claims Commission of 1923–34. Jurisdiction was defined as encompassing

> [a]ll claims . . . against [either government] of citizens of [the other] whether corporations, companies, associations, partnerships or individuals, for losses or damages suffered by persons or their properties . . . and all claims for losses or damages originating from acts of officials or others acting for either Government and resulting in injustice . . .[47]

Discussing whether this included claims based on a mere breach of contract by the government, the commissionaires reasoned as follows:

> It is entirely clear that on several occasions both the United States and Mexico expressly gave claims commissions jurisdiction over contract claims, showing thereby that in principle conferring on an international tribunal jurisdiction over contract claims is not contrary to their legal conceptions. The so called Porter Convention of the Second Hague Conference of 1907, to which both the United States and Mexico are parties, though having for its object the prevention of the use of force in collecting debts growing out of contract obligations until other methods, including arbitration, had been exhausted, nevertheless is a striking illustration of the recognition of contract claims as proper subjects for submission to an international tribunal.[48]

Significantly, the tribunal then separated the question of jurisdiction from the question of whether an allegation of international responsibility was involved, finding no reason to limit its jurisdiction to claims based on international law:

> Must [the] opening words of Article I be construed in the light of the closing words of paragraph (1) of the same article, reading that the claims should be decided 'in accordance with the principles of international law' etc., to the effect that 'all claims' must mean all claims for which either government is responsible according to international law? The conclusion suggested exceeds what is required by logic and in the Commission's view goes too far. If it be true that all the claims of Article I should be decided 'in accordance with the principles of international law,' etc., the only permissible interference is that they must be claims of an international character, not that they must be claims entailing international responsibility of governments.[49]

While seemingly innocuous, this argument represents an indirect circumvention of municipal judicial sovereignty, foreshadowing later developments in investment arbitration. It effectively allows the international tribunal to apply the municipal law of the state in question, in a similar manner as is expressly mandated today by article 42 of the ICSID Convention. Exploiting the well-known difference between 'law in books'

[47] General Claims Convention between the United States of America and the United Mexican States, (Washington, 1923) Art I.

[48] *Illinois Central Railroad Company case,* as reproduced in De Beus (1938) 17.

[49] *ibid*, 16–17.

and 'law in fact', this allows the international tribunal to fashion its own somewhat idealised version of the 'book-law' of the state in question, while at the same time shrouding its reasoning in the cloak of the legal sovereignty of that same state.

B. The Iran-US Claims Tribunal

The most recent highpoint of the practice of mixed claims tribunals established on a bilateral, inter-state basis is the so-called Iran-US Claims Tribunal.[50] This court-like institution located in The Hague, was established in the wake of the Iran-US hostage crisis of 1979 to handle the mass of disputes and claims arising from the Islamic revolution in Iran.[51] Having made more than 4000 awards, decisions and orders throughout its career, the tribunal can properly be termed one of the success stories in the history of international dispute settlement. In significant respects, its practice can be seen to have anticipated and probably even contributed to the development of modern arbitration between states and investors. This is particularly related to its strong commercial and contractual components in both constitution and function, and the developed practice of the tribunal, which shall be briefly examined in the following.

A first point to note is that in addition to claims based on expropriation or other infringements of property rights, the jurisdiction of the tribunal also expressly extends to debt and contract claims of individual nationals against the governments of the two involved states.[52] Secondly, the jurisdiction of the tribunal is not limited to claims concerned merely with breach of international law.

[50] See generally Brower and Brueschke, *The Iran-United States Claims Tribunal* (Martinus Nijhoff Publishers, Boston, 1998) and Aldrich, *The Jurisprudence of the Iran-United States Claims Tribunal* (Clarendon Press, Oxford, 1996), and see also Caron and Crook (ed), *The Iran-United States Claims Tribunal and the Process of International Claims Resolution* (Transnational Publishers, Ardsley (NY), 2000).

[51] The basis of the tribunal is the so called Claims Settlement Declaration mediated by the Government of Algerie in 1981 to end the hostage crisis in the US embassy in Teheran, see Collier and Lowe, *The Settlement of Disputes in International Law* (Oxford University Press, Oxford, 2000) 74.

[52] The Claims Settlement Declaration, Article II: 'An international arbitral tribunal (the Iran-United States Claims Tribunal) is hereby established for the purpose of deciding claims of nationals of [either state] against [the other state] . . . if such claims are outstanding on the date of this Agreement, whether or not filed with any court, *and arise out of debts, contracts . . . expropriations or other measures affecting property rights*' (emphasis added). In addition the competence of the tribunal encompasses certain claims of the governments of Iran and the USA against each other, which arise out of inter-government contractual arrangements, and disputes concerning the interpretation of the primary documents of the Algiers Accord, the General Declaration and the Claims Settlement Declaration; see generally Caron, 'The Nature of the Iran-United States Claims Tribunal and the Evolving Structure of International Dispute Resolution' (1990) 84 *AJIL* 104, 130.

The singular function envisaged for the tribunal in this respect is reflected in the applicable provision on choice of law:

> The tribunal shall decide all cases on the basis of respect for law, applying such choice of law rules and principles of commercial and international law as the tribunal determines to be applicable, taking into account relevant usages of the trade, contract provisions and changed circumstances.

In fact, a majority of the cases before the tribunal has been ordinary commercial contract claims.[53] A number of claims brought before the tribunal, have, moreover, been framed both as commercial contract claims, and claims under international law for confiscatory annulment.[54]

For this reason, it has been observed that the tribunal has a mixed, or hybrid, character.[55] It combines aspects of international law arbitration with aspects of international commercial arbitration, functioning both as a substitute for municipal courts and an international remedy against the states involved (in practice Iran). This is reflected by the stipulated procedural rules of the tribunal, which, with some modifications, are those of the UNCITRAL rules of international commercial arbitration.[56] It is also reflected in the developed jurisprudence of the tribunal, which is based on a conspicuous blend of municipal law, general principles of contract and commercial law, treaty law and general international law.[57]

These features of the Iran-US Claims Tribunal to a large extent prefigure later developments in investment treaty arbitration, combining in a sense the two constituent elements of an authoritative treaty arrangement based on international law, and the function and modality of international commercial arbitration.

2.4 INTERNATIONALISED COMMERCIAL ARBITRATION

Arbitral procedures that allow claims from individual investors on the basis of formal inter-state arrangements may challenge, but still be reconciled quite easily with conventional views on international law as a law between states.[58] Alongside this stands another tradition, however,

[53] Brower and Brueschke (1998) 636.

[54] See eg *Amoco Int'l Finance Corp v Iran* (1987) 15 Iran-US CT Rep 189; and *Philips Petroleum Co Iran v Iran* (1989) 21 Iran-US CT Rep 79.

[55] Collier and Lowe (2000) 77; see also Caron (1990) 104; and Lloyd Jones, 'The Iran-US Claims Tribunal: Private Rights and State Responsibility' (1983–84) 24 *Va J Int'l Law* 259.

[56] The Claims Settlement Declaration article III no 2.

[57] See further Brower and Brueschke (1998) 631; and Crook, 'Applicable Law in International Arbitration—The Iran-US Claims Tribunal Experience' (1989) 83 *AJIL* 278.

[58] See eg *Case Concerning the Factory at Chorzów (Indemnity)* (Judgment, 1928), PCIJ Rep Series A No 17 (1929) 4, 28: 'International law does not prevent one State from granting to another the right to have recourse to international arbitral tribunals in order to obtain the direct award to nationals of the latter State of compensation for damage suffered by them as a result of infractions of international law by the first State'.

which is more difficult to reconcile with traditional precepts of international law, while having played an equally, if not more, important role as a forerunner of the contemporary practice of ICSID and investment treaty arbitration. This is the practice of international commercial arbitration, which, through the crucial concept of 'internationalisation' of state contracts, entered the domain of international law and investment from its roots in the tradition and customs of international commerce.[59]

In the following I describe how this intrinsically contractual form of arbitration came to be conceived as an effective remedy for investors to invoke rights under international law. This is the history of a relatively consistent arbitral practice which, evading doctrinal concerns and relying on teleology and legal pragmatism, broke through established legal dogma by relying on a legal fiction, namely that a contract between a state and a private investor could be *made into* a binding agreement under international law through the parties' resolution to make it so. I leave the theoretical and critical scrutiny of this concept to the next chapter. Here I seek to concentrate instead on the practice itself, and how it essentially arose out of certain underlying concerns and interests butting against the main doctrinal precepts of international law at the time.

I first give a brief account of international commercial arbitration and party autonomy, as the conceptual and 'ideological' fundament of internationalisation. Following this, I examine the genesis of the concept of internationalisation in inventive contract drafting and certain significant early cases, before tracing the concept's eventual maturity as a justification for applying international law in combination with more typical contractual principles drawn from municipal law.

A. Party Autonomy in International Commercial Arbitration

International commercial arbitration is today probably the preferred method of settling contract disputes in international commerce.[60] The legal essence of commercial arbitration is an agreement to refer disagreements arising out of a specific contractual (or other) relationship to a third party for final decision. The legal basis of arbitration is thus the involved parties' contractual autonomy or freedom of contract. The underlying

[59] See for a historical and sociological perspective, Dezalay and Garth, *Dealing in Virtue: International Commercial Arbitration and the Construction of a Transnational Legal Order* (The University of Chicago Press, Chicago, 1996) especially 63 et seq.

[60] Of standard works on international commercial arbitration I have particularly made use of Redfern and Hunter (et al), *Law and practice of international commercial arbitration* (Sweet & Maxwell, London, 2004); Gaillard and Savage (eds), *Fouchard, Gaillard, Goldman on International Commercial Arbitration* (Kluwer Law International, The Hague, 1999); and Craig, Park and Paulsson, *International Chamber of Commerce Arbitration* (Oceana Publications, Dobbs Ferry (NY), 2000).

principle, usually denoted 'party autonomy',[61] is really that the parties may waive their right of access to the courts in favour of a decision of an arbitral tribunal, and with final and binding consequences as a matter of law.[62] As this concept also provides the central conceptual foundation of the internationalisation cases, I use this section to briefly outline its significance in the original and ordinary context of international commercial arbitration.

A central aspect of party autonomy is that the composition of the tribunal, its location, and all other aspects of the process, are all left to the complete discretion of the parties. This provides a flexibility and freedom of choice which does not exist in respect of national court proceedings. The most common manner of arbitration is nevertheless submission to a standing arbitral institution with a pre-existing set of rules and procedures.[63] The most well known is the Court of Arbitration of the International Chamber of Commerce in Paris (ICC),[64] but other frequently used institutions are the London Court of International Arbitration (LCIA) and the Arbitration Institute of the Stockholm Chamber of Commerce. In ad hoc arbitration outside any standing institution it is common to adopt a standardised set of rules, such as the UN-sponsored UNCITRAL arbitration rules, as procedural guidelines.[65] In addition to flexibility, the main benefit of arbitration is that arbitral awards are more easily enforceable than municipal court judgments, offering in consequence a greater measure of certainty in international transactions.[66] This is secured on the international level by the New York Arbitration Convention,[67] which essentially obligates municipal courts to recognise arbitral agreements and to recognise and enforce foreign arbitral awards.[68] It thus constitutes an international obligation for member states to accept and recognise a minimum of party autonomy in the context of international commercial arbitration.

For what can be called the common law of international commercial arbitration, the concept of party autonomy has wider and more fundamental connotations however. The notion itself springs from the simple idea that an arbitral tribunal owes its existence to the will of the parties,

[61] See generally about this concept Cordero Moss, *International Commercial Arbitration—Party Autonomy and Mandatory Rules* (Tano Aschehoug, Oslo, 1999) 57.

[62] See also Fox, 'States and the Undertaking to Arbitrate' (1988) 37 *ICLQ* 1.

[63] In addition to providing a set of tested rules, such standing institutions generally take care of logistics and administrative matters in relation to the arbitration. Certain permanent institutions, such as the ICC Court of Arbitration, also exercise some supervision of the proceedings, mainly in order to ensure the enforceability of awards.

[64] The main work of reference is Craig, Park and Paulsson (2000).

[65] See generally Caron, Caplan and Pellonpää, *The UNCITRAL Arbitration Rules* (Oxford University Press, Oxford, 2006).

[66] See for a further account of benefits and advantages, Cordero Moss (1999) 149 et seq.

[67] United Nations Convention on the Recognition and Enforcement of Foreign Arbitral Awards (New York, 1958).

[68] Cordero Moss (1999) 57.

and therefore has no competence beyond what the parties have willed.[69] The concrete legal significance of this is that it constitutes a fundamentally limiting factor for the competence of each constituted arbitral tribunal.[70] At the same time, the notion has more than anything served to bolster the freedom and relative autonomy of international commercial arbitration in relation to municipal law. Effectively it has extended the competence of arbitral tribunals in comparison with municipal courts, largely freeing the arbitrators from allegiance to idiosyncratic municipal rules and policies in the field of substantive law. The crucial legal factor in this connection is the rule that municipal courts lack competence to review arbitral awards on their merits,[71] in combination with the developing self-awareness of international commercial arbitral tribunals as distinct instruments of international commerce, independent of any particular municipal legal system.[72]

The most significant consequence of this is a less strict abidance with municipal rules relating to substantive law and the conflict of laws.[73] Instead, a distinct international and comparative outlook has developed, with a focus on the concerns and evolving practices and customs of international commerce, more than particular municipal legal traditions.[74] In theory, this has been described as the development of a *lex mercatoria*: an alleged body of international substantive contract law conceived as being directly applicable to international commercial transactions.[75] The theory of a completely autonomous *lex mercatoria* has nevertheless been severely criticised.[76] In practice it is an overstatement to consider this *lex mercatoria* an autonomous legal system on par with municipal legal

69 See Fouchard, Gaillard, Goldman (1999) 29–31.

70 Cf the New York Convention (1958) Art V(c).

71 See eg Cordero Moss (1999) 169.

72 Dezalay and Garth (1996) especially 33 et seq; see also for an analysis of its significant driving factors in the needs and interest of international commerce especially Goldstajn, 'The New Law Merchant Reconsidered' in Fabricius (ed), *Law and International Trade: Recht und internationaler Handel / Festschrift für Clive M. Schmitthoff zum 70. Geburtstag* (Frankfurt, 1973) 171.

73 See Cordero Moss (1999) 247 et seq.

74 See generally, De Ly, *International Business Law and Lex Mercatoria* (North Holland, Amsterdam, 1992); and see also Meidell, *An Anational Approach to International Contracts* (Cappelen, Oslo, 2007).

75 Classical works are those of Goldman; see eg Goldman, 'Frontières du droit et lex mercatoria' (1964) *Archives de philosophie de droit* 177; and Goldman, 'The applicable law: general principles of law—the lex mercatoria' in Lew (ed), *Contemporary Problems in International Arbitration* (Martinus Nijhof Publishers, Dordrecht, 1987) 113–25; and those of Schmitthoff; see eg Schmitthoff, 'International Business Law: A New Law Merchant' in Cheng (ed), *Clive M Schmitthoff's Select Essays on International Trade Law* (Martinus Nijhoff Publishers/Graham & Trotman, Dordrecht, 1988). See also Lando, 'The Lex Mercatoria in International Commercial Arbitration' (1985) 34 *ICLQ* 747.

76 The classic critiques here are Mann, see eg Mann, 'England Rejects Delocalized Contracts and Arbitration' (1984) 33 *ICLQ* 193, and Mann, '*Lex facit arbitrum*' in *Liber Amicorum for Martin Domke* (Nijhoff, The Hague, 1967) 157; and Mustill, 'The New Lex Mercatoria: the First 25 Years' (1988) 4 *Arb Int'l* 86.

systems and international law, as is sometimes ventured.[77] Most arbitral tribunals will be concerned to identify a municipal law as the governing law of the contract in dispute, if for no other reason, then at least because this provides for more certain and certifiable legal solutions than the somewhat mythical *lex mercatoria*. What remains is, perhaps, first and foremost a greater dedication to the pre-eminence of the contract and the intention of the parties than would be possible under a strict municipal law perspective. While open to criticism on theoretical grounds, it is difficult to explain away the prevailing notion of the process of international commercial arbitration as largely autonomous, with no allegiance to any particular municipal law, and governed par excellence by party autonomy.[78]

This relative autonomy of international commercial arbitration is epitomised in the concept of 'delocalisation'.[79] This is essentially another word for the idea that the source of authority for an arbitral tribunal is party autonomy and not a particular municipal law.[80] Again, as an idea

[77] See also to this effect Cordero Moss (1999) 270–71.

[78] Cf eg the US Supreme Court, in *Mitsubishi Motors Corp v Soler Chrysler-Plymouth*, 47 US 614 (1985) 636: '[T]he international arbitral tribunal owes no prior allegiance to the legal norms of particular states; hence it has no direct obligation to vindicate their statutory dictates'. See also generally the classical study of Lew, *Applicable Law in International Commercial Arbitration: a study in commercial arbitral awards* (Oceana, Dobbs Ferry (NY), 1978); and the account of Lowenfeld, 'Lex Mercatoria: an Arbitrator's View' in Carbonneau (ed), *Lex Mercatoria and Arbitration* (Juris Publishing, Yonkers (NY), 1998) 71.

[79] See eg Paulsson, 'Arbitration Unbound: Award Detached from the Law of its Country of Origin' (1981) 30 *ICLQ* 358; Paulsson, 'Delocalisation of International Commercial Arbitration: When and Why it Matters' (1983) 32 *ICLQ* 53. See also Cordero Moss (1999) 178 et seq for a more critical perspective.

[80] The concept comes in many versions and makes different claims, but its essence is that the source of authority of international arbitration is an international or transnational concept of party autonomy independent of municipal law, which is merely recognised and implemented by municipal law when an arbitral award is enforced. This has two possible consequences: first it entails that an award can be considered valid in the country of enforcement, even though it has been set aside by the courts of the place of the arbitration; second, it entails that the courts of the place of arbitration should decline to exercise judicial control over international arbitral proceedings. The former finds its classic expression in French law, where the *Cour de Cassation* in the *Hilmarton case* enforced an arbitral award which had been set aside in Switzerland, considering that the award was 'an international award, which was not integrated in the legal system of that State, so that it remains in existence even if set aside and its recognition in France was not contrary to international public policy' (as cited and translated in Fouchard, Gaillard, Goldman (1999) 914–15). The second has its origins in the so called *Götaverken case* (award published in (1981) 6 *YbCA* 133), also of French origin, decided by the Paris Court of Appeals in 1981, which declined to exercise jurisdiction to set aside an award by a tribunal sitting in Paris, in a dispute concerning a shipbuilding contract in Sweden between the Swedish shipbuilder and a Libyan state-owned company. This strict approach has now been abandoned in French law, but is espoused at least in the laws of Belgium, Switzerland and Sweden, see further Fouchard, Gaillard, Goldman (1999) 911 et seq) The delocalization doctrine stands in contrast to the jurisdictional theory of arbitration, according to which arbitration is said to derive its judicial authority from the municipal law of the seat of the arbitration (*the lex loci arbitri)*. Under this view an award ought principally to be challenged under the *lex loci*, and an award

with affinities to *lex mercatoria* orthodoxy, the most zealous theories and ideas about delocalisation arguably overstate the point. Obviously, there is no such thing as a completely delocalised arbitration (at least not as an effective legal remedy). Successful arbitration is dependent on a venue for enforcement, and possibly for procedural assistance during the proceedings. The strength of international commercial arbitration as a legal remedy lies precisely in its extensive enforceability under the municipal legal apparatus of different countries. This necessitates the involvement of municipal courts and law, at least whenever an award is sought enforced or challenged. The crucial point is instead that municipal laws almost universally allow for and accept the fact that international commercial arbitration is based first and foremost on party autonomy, even as a notion to some extent unrestricted by ordinary municipal constraints and subject only to a limited measure of judicial control. This partly confirms the theory of delocalisation in matters of substantive law, in the sense that an arbitral tribunal is not necessarily bound by the same rules as a municipal court in the same place, though not as something necessarily inherent in the nature of international commercial arbitration, but as the preferred choice and common solution of municipal laws.

The concept of internationalisation of investment contracts is closely affiliated with the delocalisation theory.[81] It probably even constitutes the prime example of its effective application. It is founded in the notion that the authority of international arbitration as a judicial process does not derive from a specific municipal law, but rests in 'the autonomous will' of the parties, [82] underpinned by international policies and concerns.[83] Thus, international law may be made directly applicable to the contract, either by virtue of its direct submission to the international source of authority of the tribunal, or solely by virtue of the parties' intention to submit it to international law. These theoretical assumptions, as well as the presumed legal consequences of the concept, are questionable, an argument I return to in the next chapter. But at the same time the strength and consistency of the practice in question is difficult to deny. Elsewhere in this book I argue that the practice of internationalisation, at least to some extent, is based on sound and pragmatic legal concerns, but employs largely fictitious legal

which is invalid under the *lex loci* is necessarily invalid also under all other municipal laws. In support of this see eg Mann (1967) and Goode, 'The Role of the Lex Loci Arbitri in International Commercial Arbitration' (2001) 17 *Arb Int'l* 19, see also Cordero Moss (1999) 187 et seq; and Brækhus, 'Lokaliseringsproblemer i internasjonal kommersiell voldgift' *Lov og Rett* (1995) 641.

[81] See especially Toope (1990) 17 et seq.

[82] See eg Mayer, 'Le mythe de 'l'ordre juridique de base' (ou grundlegung)' in *Le droit des relations économiques internationales. Etudes offertes à Berthold Goldman* (Litec, Paris, 1982) 199, 215.

[83] See eg Weil, 'Droit international et contrats d'Etat' in *Mélanges offerts à Paul Reuter* (Pedone, Paris, 1981) 549, 576 et seq.

arguments to reach its desired end. The point here has been to draw attention to certain characteristics of the legal process in which the cases were anchored, and to examine how this provided the tribunals with the roots of a burgeoning self-awareness as to their function. I now turn to the more specific process of this transformation.

B. The Genesis of 'Internationalisation'

The contractual practice underlying the concept of internationalisation as it evolved in arbitral case law goes back to the interests in extraction of oil and mineral resources acquired by western companies in developing countries in the early twentieth century and later in the 1950s and '60s. According to traditional doctrine of the time, a private company making an investment in the territory of a foreign state did so largely at the mercy of the future policies, ideologies and interests of that state. As described above, the applicable response of traditional international law to interference with the investment would be diplomatic protection, raising the dispute to the inter-state level with all the political uncertainties involved in that process. In view of the enormous financial interests at stake, this did not provide the companies involved with satisfactory legal certainty.

One response to this was to enter into a contract with the host state disconnected from the legal system of that state and virtually 'inscribed' into the international legal order by virtue of the agreement of the parties.[84] The specific contractual mechanism was a reference in the contract to international arbitration, and the express choice of international law as directly applicable coupled with a stabilisation or 'freezing' of the host state's own law, ie a promise from the host state not to change the laws and regulations applicable to the contract, which by its own terms was made under or at least sanctioned by international law. A first, somewhat tentative precedent of this arrangement may have been a contract concluded by the Lena Goldfields Company with the Soviet government in 1925.[85] The contract involved a concession granted to the company for

[84] Cfr Berlin, *Contrat d'État, Répertoire Dalloz de Droit International* (Dalloz, Paris, 1998) 3: 'Par internationalisation, il faut comprendre le désir d'inscrire totalement la relation contractuelle dans l'ordre juridique international: En d'autres termes, de transformer le contrat d'État en un accord de droit international, source de droits et d'obligations sanctionnés par le droit international'.

[85] Certain other and older cases reeking of a somewhat 'colonial flavour' could also have been mentioned (see Gillis Wetter and Schwebel, *Some Little Known Cases on Concessions* (1964) 40 *BYIL* 183, 193). As far back as in 1864, an international arbitration was conducted between the Vice-Roy of Egypt and the Suez Canal Company, in the manner of an inter-state arbitration, and clearly envisaged to come within the sphere of international law. The arbitration concerned a concession that was construed as a reciprocal, contractual engagement, and which as a result could not, it was held, be unilaterally revoked by the government (Lafontaine 122: 'Sentence arbitrale rendue par l'Empereur Napoleon III, le

exploration, mining and transportation of gold and other minerals in vast areas of Eastern Siberia, the Urals and the Altai area. The contract was then revoked pursuant to the promulgation of one of Stalin's five-year plans in 1929, by a combination of government interference, confiscatory measures and raids by Soviet security forces, which reads like fiction, as does the whole story of the case.[86] Fortunately (apparently) for the history of arbitration, Article 90 of the contract set up an elaborate arbitration scheme, probably conceived and drafted from the start as a means of defence against the Bolshevik government.[87] The provision was invoked by the company, and arbitration proceedings were instigated in London, though eventually without the participation of the Soviet government, something which could not, however, due to another foresight of the contract, obstruct the conduct and fulfillment of the proceedings.[88] It produced an award against the regime of £13 million in damages, which equals about £500 million in modern (2005) money, giving an idea of the magnitude of the dispute at that time.

The award thus rendered constituted a precedent for ad hoc contract-based arbitration against governments in a number of ways. For the first time in this kind of case, the doctrine of the autonomy of the arbitration clause, and the competence of arbitrators to decide on their own competence was, at least implicitly, applied here. But the award is perhaps most notable because of the tribunal's reliance on general principles of law and international law to justify its decision, which it did in the following terms:

> It was admitted by Dr. Idelson, counsel for Lena, that on all domestic matters in the U.S.S.R the laws of Soviet Russia applied except in so far as they were excluded by the contract, and accordingly that in regard to performance of the contract by both parties inside the U.S.S.R. Russian law was 'the proper law of the contract,' i.e., the law by reference to which the contract should be interpreted.

6 juillet 1864 entre le Vice-Roi d'Egypte et la Compagnie universelle du canal de Suez'; interestingly the award is published by Lafontaine with the following comment: 'Cet arbitrage est á remarquer á raison de l'intervention directe, dans la contestation d'une compagnie financière. Dans les différents arbitrages, où des intérêts privés sont en jeu, les gouvernements, dont les intéressés sont les sujets, interviennent seuls dans le litige. Ici on pourrait justifier la participation directe de la Compagnie de Suez par le caractère de personne morale internationale que l'on pourrait lui attribuer'.) Another case is the *Compagnie du Katanga v The Colony of the Belgian Congo*, where the arbitral tribunal rendered an award based on 'general principles of law and equity'. The case concerned a concession granted by the then Congo Free State of King Leopold of Belgium, which gave the company ownership and exploitation rights for a period of 99 years over vast territories of Belgian Congo. However, given what is known of King Leopold's tyranny in the Congo, it is somewhat difficult to take seriously an award which refers to his running of the country as 'his glorious enterprise'. (See further about this case, Gillis Wetter and Schwebel (1964) 191).

[86] See for a historical account, Veeder, 'The Lena Goldfields Arbitration—the Historical Roots of Three Ideas' (1998) 47 *ICLQ* 747.

[87] *ibid*, 773.

[88] *ibid*, 773–4.

> But it was submitted by him that for other purposes the general principles of law such as those recognized by Article 38 of the Statute of the Permanent Court of International Justice at the Hague should be regarded as 'the proper law of contract' and in support of this submission counsel for Lena pointed out that both the Concession Agreement itself and also the agreement of June 1927, whereby the coal mines were handed over, were signed not only on behalf of the Executive Government of Russia generally but by the Acting Commissary for Foreign Affairs, and that many of the terms of the contract contemplated the application of international rather than merely national principles of law. *In so far as any difference of interpretation might result the Court holds that this contention is correct.*[89] (emphasis added)

This internationalisation of the legal issues was derived in part from article 89 of the contract, which provided that 'the parties base their relations with regard to this agreement on the principle of good will and good faith, as well as on reasonable interpretation of the terms of the agreement'.[90] The court took as its essential starting point that both the arbitration clause and this 'good will and good faith clause', had been significant premises for the company in entering into the agreement.[91] Their combined effect gave the company, without the formal assistance of its home state, a legal verdict against the Soviet Government for actions which might well have been in accordance with positive Soviet law at that time.

Clearly, the crucial aspect of this successful disconnection of the contract from Soviet law was the provision for arbitration. If the case had only been submitted to Soviet courts it is quite inconceivable that it would have been held to raise issues of international law. This is not to say that the Soviet judges necessarily would have shown a lack of respect for the validity and binding force of international law as such. They would just not have seen the relevance of international law in relation to the issue, which, involving as it did only a private subject, they would probably have considered a clear-cut matter of internal sovereignty. At the same time it was equally inconceivable for an arbitral tribunal, constituted for the sole purpose of judging the legality of the conduct of the Soviet government, to content itself with observing that such conduct was sanctioned by 'the law' of that country. The combined effects of the distance and neutrality of the individual judges in relation to the government—what Thomas Franck calls 'the impartiality syndrome'[92]—together with their no doubt strong

[89] *The Lena Goldfields case,* published in *The Times* (London) 3 September 1930, and reproduced in Nussbaum, 'The Arbitration between the Lena Goldfields Ltd. and the Soviet Government' (1950–51) 36 *Cornell Law Quarterly* 31, 42, para 22.

[90] *ibid,* para 6.

[91] *ibid,* para 6: 'It was proved to the satisfaction of the court in the course of the trial that Lena would not have entered into Concession Agreement at all but for the presence in the contract of this Arbitration Clause and of the preceding clause (Article 89) . . .'

[92] Franck (1968).

personal feeling of a manifest injustice having taken place, in a way compelled the tribunal to find a rule where perhaps no certain positive rule was to be found,[93] and to find a justification for this rule as a rule of law. The justification they found was what the parties had willed, and the law was 'the general principles of law' as manifested in international law. Thus the concept of internationalisation was born. One commentator enthusiastically describes the precedent set by the award in this respect as follows: 'As Lena Goldfields' counsel in the *Lena* arbitration, Idelson's internationalisation of a transnational contract was a gigantic first step for international commercial arbitration, almost equivalent to the caveman's discovery of fire'.[94] What international commercial arbitration discovered in the *Lena Goldfields* case was the possibility of applying international law directly in relation to a private entity, thus recreating itself as an independent private remedy against governments.

There is a clear line from the *Lena Goldfields* case to what may be the first 'clean' example of a consciously 'internationalised' contract. This was the contract entered into by the Anglo-Persian Oil Company with the government of Persia in 1933; a concession contract granting the company exclusive rights in large territories of Persia to 'search for and extract petroleum as well as to refine or treat in any other manner and render suitable for commerce the petroleum obtained by it'.[95] What is significant about the contract in this context is a mechanism specifically designed to insulate the contract from the legislative authority of the Persian government, which came to set a model for subsequent contractual practice. The key provision was article 22 of the concession, which in terms similar to the parallel provision in the *Lena Goldfields* contract made arbitration the exclusive means of dispute settlement in connection with the contract. But the Anglo-Persian Oil Company contract also contained an explicit choice of law clause, directing a tribunal to base its award on international law: 'The Award shall be based on the juridical principles contained in Article 38 of the Statutes of the Permanent Court of International Justice'.[96] Moreover, article 21 of the contract contained a clause whereby the

[93] At least most international lawyers at that time would presumably have disclaimed the possibility that international law could be invoked directly by a private subject against a state. See to this effect the classical statement of the PCIJ in the *Mavromattis Palestine Concessions case* PCIJ Rep Series A No 2 (1924) 12: 'In the case of the Mavromattis concessions it is true that the dispute was at first between a private person and a state . . . Subsequently, the Greek government took up the case. The dispute then entered upon a new phase: it entered the domain of international law, and became a dispute between two States . . . By taking up the case of one of its subjects and by resorting to diplomatic action or international judicial proceedings on his behalf, a State is in reality asserting its own rights—its rights to ensure, in the person of its subjects, respect for the rules of international law'.

[94] Veeder (1998) 772.

[95] Agreement between the Imperial Government of Persia and the Anglo-Persian Oil Company Ltd. (Teheran, 29 April 1933) Art 1, reproduced in the *Anglo-Iranian Oil Co case* (1952) ICJ Pleadings 21.

[96] *ibid*, art 22 para F.

government expressly promised not to annul, modify or amend the contract by legislation or other public acts in the future.[97] When the contract was subsequently revoked by the Iranian government in 1951, under a full-scale nationalisation of its oil industry (which essentially *was* the Anglo-Iranian Oil Co), the arbitration scheme set up by the contract was not pursued because the president and vice-president of the ICJ declined to act in place of the pre-war PCIJ and appoint an arbitrator.[98] Subsequent to this, the case was brought by the United Kingdom before the ICJ itself. But the ICJ ended up refusing jurisdiction for lack of sufficient consent from Iran under Article 36 of the ICJ statute.[99] Thus, the case produced no definitive judicial approval of the internationalisation scheme as such.

However, the contractual scheme did serve as a precedent for subsequent contractual arrangements, which eventually appeared in international arbitration practice.[100] One of the first cases to approbate the

[97] Article 21, section 3: 'This Concession shall not be annulled by the Government and the terms therein contained shall not be altered either by general or special legislation in the future, or by administrative measures or any other acts whatever of the executive authorities'. This was also re-emphasised in article 26, which essentially made any such revocation before 1993 subject to arbitration in the following terms: 'Before the date of December 31st, 1993, this concession can only come to an end in the case that the Company should surrender the Concession (Article 25) or in case that the Arbitration Court should declare the Concession annulled as a consequence of default of the Company in the performance of the present Agreement'.

[98] Veeder (1998) 770, see also Mann, 'State Contracts and International Arbitration' (1967) 42 *BYIL* 1, 280–84.

[99] *Anglo-Iranian Oil Company case* [1952] ICJ Rep 89, 113–14.

[100] Of other early post-war cases that supported some notion of internationalization, though not based on the strict contractual scheme of the Anglo-Persian case, two cases in particular stand out. In the *Abu Dhabi* case (*Petroleum Development Ltd v Sheikh of Abu Dhabi* (Award, 1951) 18 ILR 144), the sole arbitrator, Lord Asquith of Bishopstone, based his award in 'the good sense and common practice of the generality of civilised nations—a sort of modern law of nature' (*ibid*, 149). While he held that the contract normally at the outset would have been governed by the law of Abu Dhabi, the arbitrator held that: 'no such law can reasonably be said to exist. The Sheikh administers a purely discretionary justice with the assistance of the Koran; and it would be fanciful to suggest that in this very primitive region there is any settled body of legal principles applicable to the construction of modern commercial instruments' (*ibid*, 149). Substantive concerns are clearly implicit in this reasoning. To say that no law existed in Abu Dhabi might have been true from a conventional western point of view, in that no positive body of law applicable to this specific type of contract had been developed in Abu Dhabi. But to say that there was no law was untrue. The ruling law in Abu Dhabi at that time was Islamic law—the Sharia. And this law undoubtedly does include substantial principles of contract law that can be applied to commercial contracts, although probably not desirably so, from the western companies' point of view. In the later *Ruler of Qatar* case (*Ruler of Qatar v International Marine Oil Company Ltd* (Award, 1953) 20 ILR 534) this was put to the test. It seemed to be the case that if Islamic law should be applied to the contract, large parts of it would have been invalid. The conclusion drawn from this was that the Parties could not have intended that Islamic law should apply. Instead the tribunal held that the contract was governed by 'the principles of justice, equity and good conscience'. Thus the contract was conceived of as an autonomous contract, withdrawn from the sphere of the municipal law of Qatar. Clearly, the reason was not that there was no applicable law in Qatar, but that this law was not considered suitable for application to the

arrangement and give it a doctrinal justification was the *Sapphire* case.[101] The case is particularly interesting for underlining the significance of the arbitration clause in the internationalisation scheme. It concerned a joint venture contract for development of oil fields in Iran between the Canadian oil company Sapphire and the National Iranian Oil Company. Pursuant to disagreement regarding performance of the contract, a claim for damages was made by Sapphire and eventually referred to arbitration in Switzerland. The contract contained an arbitration clause, but no express choice of law. Finding nevertheless that the contract had been disconnected from Iranian law, the arbitrator referred to its particular objective as an investment contract in need of stability from legislative intervention,[102] and to the special role of the arbitration clause in this scheme:

> [I]f no positive implication can be made from the arbitral clause, it is possible to find there a negative intention, namely to reject the exclusive application of Iranian law. If in fact the parties had intended to submit their agreement to Iranian law and if the only significance of the arbitration was to deprive the Iranian authorities of jurisdiction in case of any dispute, the authors of the agreement—whom one must suppose were competent lawyers—would almost certainly not have failed to negative, by an expressive provision, any significance which such an arbitral clause normally carried as a connecting factor according to general doctrine.[103]

The substantial result of this, as perceived by the arbitrator, was to neutralise the legislative power of the Iranian government as far as the contract was concerned, essentially through the instrumentality of the provision in the contract for arbitration outside Iran.

Another important early case is that of *Saudi Arabia v Aramco*. While the tribunal in this case expressly rejected the possibility that the contract as such could be made subject to international law,[104] it relied heavily on a distinct notion of party autonomy, sanctioned by international law, to

contract. However, even if it is true that the parties did not intend Islamic law to apply, which all circumstances indeed seemed to indicate that they did not, the problem remains as to which law *permitted* them to make that choice. At least the prima facie applicable municipal law obviously did not. The answer can only be that the tribunal relied upon an objectively applicable notion of *party autonomy*, independent of any particular municipal law.

[101] *Sapphire International Petroleums Ltd v National Iranian Oil Company (NIOC)* (Award, 1963) 35 ILR 136.

[102] *ibid*, 171: 'Under the present agreement, the foreign company was bringing financial and technical assistance to Iran, which involved it in investments, responsibilities, and considerable risks. It therefore seems natural that they should be protected against any legislative changes which might alter the character of the contract, and that they should be assured of some legal security. This could not be guaranteed to them by the outright application of Iranian law, which it is within the power of the Iranian state to change'.

[103] *ibid*, 172.

[104] *Saudi Arabia v Arab American Oil Company (Aramco)* (Award, 1958) 27 ILR 117, 165: 'As the Agreement of 1933 has not been concluded between two States, but between a State and a private American Corporation, it is not governed by public international law'.

justify its authority.[105] Moreover, it contemplated the application of international law to specific issues relating to international responsibility, largely reminiscent of a strict internationalisation approach in terms of substance.[106]

Together these three cases provided important precedents for later cases to conceptualise the *possibility* of applying international law in contractual investment disputes, and thereby to recreate international commercial arbitration as an international law remedy.

C. Evolution of the 'Hybrid' Approach

Based on the earlier precedents of the *Lena Goldfields*, *Sapphire* and *Aramco cases*, the concept of internationalisation reached its peak with three cases known as the Libyan Oil arbitrations.[107] These cases definitively brought arbitration between states and foreign investors within the orbit of international law.[108] It has also later been noted how these big 'petroleum cases' were instrumental in establishing the prominence of arbitration more generally as the preferred means of dispute settlement in international commerce.[109]

The three cases sprang out of the Libyan nationalisation of a number of significant oil concessions belonging to three foreign oil companies, *Texaco Overseas Petroleum Co (TOPCO)*, *British Petroleum (BP)* and the *Libyan American Oil Company* (LIAMCO). The concessions all arose out of the same

105 *ibid*, 154–6.

106 *ibid*, 172: 'Lastly, the tribunal holds that public international law should be applied to the effects of the Concession, when objective reasons lead it to conclude that certain matters cannot be governed by any rule of the municipal law of any State, as is the case in all matters relating to transport by sea, to the sovereignty of the State on its territorial waters and to the responsibility of States for the violation of its international obligations'.

107 The first of the three cases is *BP Exploration Co (Libya) Ltd v Govt of Libya* (Award, 1973) (1979) 53 ILR 297, decided by Gunnar Lagergren, a Swedish Judge, the second is *Texaco Overseas Petroleum Co v Govt of Libya* (Award, 1977) 53 ILR 389, decided by Rene Jean Dupuy, professor of international law at the University of Paris; and the third and final case is *Libyan American Oil Co (LIAMCO) v Govt of Libya Libya* (Award, 1977) 62 ILR 141, decided by Dr. Mahmassani, a Lebanese scholar and expert on international law. The cases have been the subject of extensive commentary, see for instance; Fatouros, 'International Law and the Internationalized Contract' (1980) 74 *AJIL* 134; Greenwood, 'State Contracts in International Law—The Libyan Oil Arbitrations' (1982) 53 *BYIL* 27; Von Mehren and Kourides, 'International Arbitrations between States and Foreign Private Parties—The Libyan Nationalization Cases' (1981) 75 *AJIL* 476; Rigaux, 'Des dieux et des héros—Réflections sur une sentence arbitrale' (1978) *Rev Cr Dr Int'l Privé* 435; Stern, 'Trois arbitrages, un même problème, trois solutions' (1980) *Rev Arb* 3; Verhoeven, 'Droit international des contrats et droit des gens'(1978–79) *Rev B Dr Int'l* 209; and Weil, 'Droit international et contrats d'Etat' in *Mélanges offerts à Paul Reuter* (Pedone, Paris, 1981) 549.

108 See eg the treatment in Lowenfeld (2002) 417.

109 Dezalay and Garth (1996) 75.

generic contractual arrangement,[110] which was modelled on the scheme of the *Lena Goldfields* and *Anglo-Persian* cases. While arriving at their respective conclusions by quite different reasoning, the awards nonetheless, unanimously upheld the essential scheme of internationalisation, namely the effective withdrawal of the contract from the legal sovereignty of the state concerned. The key factor in this regard was the underlying conception by the tribunals of their own role, and that of international arbitration more generally, as a legal process divorced from the exclusive domain of municipal law. As I will return to elsewhere, a first crucial point of the cases was the reasoning of the tribunals to seise jurisdiction. All tribunals effectively upheld the contractually agreed arbitration arrangement over a subsequent Libyan annulment decree, relying expressly or implicitly on the concept of party autonomy, and a well-known concept of commercial arbitration law, usually known as the principle of the severability or autonomy of the arbitration clause.[111] When jurisdiction was thus established, the outcome of the cases was, as we shall see, to some extent given, illustrating the fundamental significance of the de facto internationalisation of the arbitral process as such.

The first of the awards to consider the contractual arrangement on the merits was the *BP award.* The sole arbitrator rejected both the argument of the claimant, that the ultimate governing law was public international law, and the argument of the respondent, that the case did not raise issues beyond Libyan law. Instead, the arbitrator chose to rely on 'the general principles of law', emphasising in this manner in effect the pre-eminence of the terms of the contract as the governing law.[112] The substantial outcome of this was a clear condemnation of the Libyan annulment as 'a fundamental breach of the BP Concession . . . on the basis of rules of applicable systems of law too elementary and voluminous to require or permit citation'.[113] In the next case, *Texaco v Libya*, the arbitrator also essentially relied on the contract as the fundamental law of the parties,[114] but was concerned to find a deeper justification for this as a matter of substantive law. This he did by

[110] The contracts were all based on the Libyan model concession, clause 16 of which stipulated inter alia that: 'The Government of Libya will take all steps necessary to ensure that the company enjoys all the rights conferred by this concession. The contractual rights expressly created by this concession shall not be altered except by mutual consent of the parties'. Together with this attempted neutralization of the legislative powers of the Government, the 'internationalization' of the contract was completed by clause 28 which made provision for international arbitration, and included the following choice of law clause: 'This concession shall be governed by and interpreted in accordance with the principles of the law of Libya common to the principles of international and in the absence of such common principles then by and in accordance with the general principles of law, including such of those principles as may have been applied by international tribunals'.

[111] See *BP v Libya* (Award, 1973) 53 ILR 297, 308; *Texaco v Libya* (Preliminary Award, 1975) 53 ILR 389, 407 et seq; and *LIAMCO v Libya* (Award, 1977) 62 ILR 141, 176–80.

[112] *BP v Libya* (Award, 1973) 53 ILR 297, 327–9.

[113] *ibid*, 329.

[114] *Texaco v Libya* (Award (Merits), 1977) 53 ILR 389, see especially at 445–6.

introducing a distinction between 'the law which governs the contract' and 'the legal order from which the binding nature of the contract stems'.[115] Only the latter, he held, could grant the parties the right to withdraw the contract from the control of municipal law as 'the law which governs the contract'.[116] What gave the parties this right in the case at hand was that the basic legal order was international law. The nature and objective of the contract in question, and the specific interests and policies involved, placed the contract directly 'within the domain of international law', according to the arbitrator,[117] thus empowering 'the parties to choose the law which was to govern their contractual relations'.[118]

A more realistic angle sees this reasoning as essentially serving to justify and rationalise what was evidently the main factor of the internationalisation, namely the submission to arbitration and its conception as an international remedy. In a way, the implicit assumption of the Texaco tribunal was also that it was really the nature of the arbitral process that induced the direct applicability of international law:

> [I]f it is appropriate for the tribunal to declare that this arbitration, for the reasons stated above, is governed by international law, it is because—the parties wanting to remove the arbitration from any national sovereignty—one cannot accept that the institution of arbitration should escape the reach of all legal systems and be somehow suspended *in vacuo*.[119]

The compelling image depicted is that of the judicial process as withdrawn from the bias of municipal law and, by virtue of this, drawn into the surrounding environment of pure international law, as universal law. The more realistic observation is that only this de facto delocalisation made the process susceptible to the potential demands of international law. Tellingly, also Dr Mahmassani in *LIAMCO v Libya* relied on a distinct conception of the arbitral process as independent of the local law, or any other municipal law.[120] This was even expressly set in the perspective of the nature of the concession arrangement, as a means to provide certainty and stability for the investment, and an effective remedy against the state independent of its own law.[121] In largely similar terms to the two foregoing cases, the arbitrator justified both the validity of the arbitral arrangement and the general ability of the parties to choose the governing law on the basis of a largely unrestricted conception of contractual autonomy as the fundamental basis of the proceedings.[122] This led the arbitrator to consider

[115] *ibid*, 443.
[116] *ibid*, 443.
[117] *ibid*, 449–50.
[118] *ibid*, 450.
[119] *ibid*, 436.
[120] *LIAMCO v Libya* (Award, 1977) 62 ILR 141, 180.
[121] *ibid*, 169–71.
[122] *ibid*, esp 170, 173, 175–6 and 178–80.

himself bound by the contract, primarily as conceived by principles of Libyan and Islamic law, but only to the extent 'common to international law', and complemented by general principles of law, as 'a compendium of legal precepts and maxims, universally accepted in theory and practice'.[123] More than in the other two cases however, this pointed the way to the later tendency of relying on a conditioned version of municipal law, instead of a strict internationalisation of the contract.

Leaving aside the different conceptions of what substantive law was applied, the most significant observation to be extracted from these cases is the commonality of approach to their basic function, as a contractual remedy independent of the legal system of the state. The operative fact clearly was the provision for arbitration. This was what drew the process out of the sphere of the de facto sovereignty of Libya. As in the *Lena Goldfields case,* the crucial point is that to deny the applicability of international law and implement the territorial law of the state party in accordance with conventional doctrine would have made a travesty of the arbitral process. It would have left the tribunals without any basis upon which to adopt the critical distance from both parties that is necessary for an independent judicial process.[124]

A number of subsequent awards more or less expressly adopted the 'internationalisation formula'.[125] Eventually, this could not, however, escape the exceptional impracticality of not being able to sufficiently conceptualise the essential role of the host state's legal system as the factual regulatory environment of the investment. Sensitive to this concern, a more recent trend of arbitral practice evinces what can be termed an indirect internationalisation approach,[126] relying on international law as an integrated part of municipal law, such as is also envisaged under Article 42 of the Convention on the Settlement of International Disputes between States and Nationals of Other States (ICSID Convention). This accepts that an investment contract primarily is subject to municipal law, but conditioned by international law.[127]

[123] *ibid,* 175–6.

[124] Franck (1968) 27–9.

[125] See eg *Revere Copper and Brass Inc v Overseas Private Investment Corp (OPIC)* (Award, 1978) 56 ILR 258; *AGIP SpA v Govt of the Peoples Republic of Congo* (Award, 1979), (1982) 21 ILM 726, para 88; *Elf Aquitaine Iran v National Iranian Oil Company (NIOC)* (1986) 11 *YbCA* 97, para 5; and *Deutsche Schachtbau- und Tiefbohrgesellschaft mbH v R'as Al Khaimah (United Arab Emirates) and The R'as Al Khaimah Oil Company (Rakoil)* (ICC Award Case No 3572, 1982) (1989) 14 *YbCA* 111, para 19.

[126] See also Lillich, 'The Law Governing Disputes under Economic Development Agreements: Reexamining the Concept of Internationalization' in Lillich and Brower (eds), *International Arbitration; towards Judicialization and Uniformity* (Transnational, Irvington (NY), 1994) 61, 92 et seq.

[127] A classical expression of this approach, which may also have inspired arbitral practice, is the separate opinion of Lauterpacht in the *Norwegian Loans case* [1957] ICJ Rep 9, 37: 'It may be admitted, in order to simplify a problem which is not at all simple, that an "international contract" must be subject to some national law: this was the view of the Permanent Court of

This approach can be illustrated by *Aminoil v Kuwait*. The case arose out of the Kuwaiti nationalisation of an oil-concession, which contained all the characteristics of an internationalised contractual arrangement, such as a reference to arbitration, a stabilisation clause and a reference to international law.[128] Thus, the investor claimed that the concession had been internationalised according to the *Texaco* formula. But instead of considering the contract disconnected from municipal law, the tribunal held that Kuwaiti law applied, but that international law and the general principles of law had to be considered part of the general law of Kuwait, *such as it was applicable* to the concession and the arbitral proceedings.[129]

Underlying this can be seen a clearer conception of the arbitral process as a hybrid, being transnational more than international in character, and invoking both municipal and international legal principles. The contract could not be considered subject solely to either international law or municipal law. Since it was a contract entered into with a private party it was at the outset subject to Kuwaiti law and sovereignty, but this again had to be applied from the neutral and disinterested perspective of an evolving international legal order:

> The different sources of the law thus to be applied are not—at least in the present case—in contradiction with each other. Indeed, if, as recalled above, international law constitutes an integral part of the law of Kuwait, the general principles correspondingly recognize the rights of the State in its capacity of supreme protector of the general interest. If the different legal elements involved do not always and everywhere blend as successfully as in the present case, it is nevertheless on taking advantage of their resources, and encouraging their trend towards unification, that the future of a truly international economic order in the investment field will depend.[130]

The tribunal thus rejected the notion of an autonomous or internationalised contract, and chose instead to remain within Kuwaiti municipal law, but as conditioned and complemented by international law as an integral part. In this case, the fundamental autonomy of the legal process in terms of substantive law was still maintained by relying on an essentially monistic conception of the relationship between municipal and inter-

International Justice in the case of the Serbian and Brazilian loans. However, this does not mean that national law is a matter which is wholly outside the orbit of international law. National legislation—including currency legislation—may be contrary in its intention or effects to the international obligations of the state. The question of conformity of national obligations with international law is a matter of international law'.

[128] For more about the background and facts of the case, see eg Tesón, 'State Contracts and Oil Expropriations: The Aminoil-Kuwait Arbitration' (1983–84) 24 *Va J Int'l Law* 323; and Hunter and Sinclair, '*Aminoil* revisited: Reflections on a Story of Changing Circumstances' in Weiler (ed), *International Investment Law and Arbitration: Leading cases from the ICSID, NAFTA, Bilateral Treaties and Customary International Law* (Cameron May, London, 2005) 347–81.

[129] *Aminoil v Kuwait* (Award, 1982) (1982) 21 ILM 976, para 6 et seq.

[130] *ibid*, para 10.

national law.[131] This tendency has been confirmed in several, more recent cases. In *Wintershall et al v Qatar*, the claimant company argued that a production sharing agreement, which bore all the hallmarks of a typically internationalised contract, had to be considered subject solely to international law.[132] As in the *Aminoil case*, the tribunal rejected this, determining instead the governing law to be 'the law of Qatar and, in case the Tribunal should determine that it is relevant to an issue, public international law'.[133] Similarly, in *SPP v Egypt (The Pyramids case)*, the ICC tribunal found that the applicable law was Egyptian law, but that international law had to be considered part of Egyptian law and have precedence in case of conflict.[134] Incidentally, this mirrors a parallel tendency of case law on the basis of article 42 of the ICSID Convention.[135]

The distinguishing common factor of this practice is the notion of arbitration as, on the one hand, a contractual phenomenon mainly dependent on party autonomy, and, on the other, a remedy in the service of an internationally sanctioned notion of the rule of law.[136] While this tendency in terms of significance has largely been overtaken by ICSID and investment treaty arbitration (to be explored below), there are also some recent examples which suggest a continued, if occasional showing in international commercial arbitral practice.[137]

2.5 CONVERGENCE OF PRACTICES—SHOWING THE WAY TO CONTEMPORARY 'INVESTMENT TREATY ARBITRATION'

The two ways of resolving claims by individual investors against states by arbitration that I have discussed above can together, with hindsight, be seen to have foreshadowed the more contemporary practice of investment

[131] See also Maniruzzaman, 'State Contracts in Contemporary International Law: Monist versus Dualist Controversies' (2001) 12(2) *EJIL* 309, 318.

[132] Lillich (1994) 91.

[133] *Wintershall et al v Qatar* (Award, 1988) (1989) 28 ILM 795, 802.

[134] *SPP v Egypt* (Award, 1983) (1983) 22 ILM 752, para 49.

[135] See especially (the ICSID award in) *SPP v Egypt* (Award, 1992) 3 ICSID Rep 189; *AMCO v Indonesia*, (Award (Resubmitted case), 1990) 1 ICSID Rep 569, para 37; and *LETCO v Liberia* (Award, 1986) 26 ILM 647.

[136] This has also received the approbation of the *Institut de droit international*, see the Resolution adopted at its Santiago de Compostela Session (1989) on 'Arbitration Between States, State Enterprises or State Entities, and Foreign Enterprises' in (1990) 63-II *Ann IDI* 324; and see Von Mehren, 'Arbitration between States and Foreign Enterprises: The Significance of the Institute of International Law's Santiago de Compostela Resolution' (1990) 5(1) *ICSID Rev-FILJ* 54; see also for a more critical perspective Shihata, 'The Institute of International Law's Resolution on Arbitration between States and Foreign Enterprises—A Comment' (1990) 5(1) *ICSID Rev-FILJ* 65.

[137] See especially *Himpurna California Energy Ltd (Bermuda) v PT (Persero) Perusahaan Listruik Negara (Indonesia)* (Award, 1999), (2000) 25 *YbCA* 13, para 41.

treaty arbitration under the ICSID Convention,[138] or occasionally even by reference to the 1958 New York Convention on the Recognition and Enforcement of Foreign Arbitral Awards. As I will come back to, the ICSID Convention is essentially a procedure for resolution of disputes between states and foreign investors, based on the model of international commercial arbitration, but providing an explicit basis of authority for the application of international law. By virtue of the habitual reference to ICSID in almost all bilateral and multilateral investment treaties, it is fair to say that this strengthened version of international commercial arbitration has become the standard procedural model of investment treaty arbitration.

A striking reflection of the arbitral modality adopted is the way in which investment treaty tribunals are routinely conceived not primarily as appellate bodies being hierarchically superior to municipal courts, but as virtual substitutes for municipal courts, in the sense that admission of a claim does not require exhaustion of local remedies, and may even preclude consecutive proceedings. Article 26 of the ICSID Convention expressly provides that consent to arbitration excludes recourse to other remedies, including the possibility of access to national courts, as set out in the following terms:

> Consent of the parties to arbitration under this Convention shall, unless otherwise stated, be deemed consent to such arbitration to the exclusion of any other remedy. A Contracting State may require the exhaustion of local administrative or judicial remedies as a condition of its consent to arbitration under this Convention.

Under the ordinary scheme envisaged under the ICSID Convention, where jurisdiction requires mutual consent in respect of the individual dispute between a state and an investor, this rule appears merely as a corollary of the normal modality of international commercial arbitration, where an agreement to arbitrate at the same time is a waiver of access to the courts.[139] By referring to ICSID however, the mechanism of investment treaty arbitration adapts this modality of international commercial arbitration to what is in reality a mandatory claims procedure based on international law. The result is an adjudicative process anchored in international law but side-stepping the usual requirement of exhaustion of local remedies, which usually is a requirement both for diplomatic protection and for proceedings before international human rights courts.[140] The underlying concern is to ensure the reliability of ICSID arbitration as a

[138] Convention on the Settlement of Investment Disputes between States and Nationals of other States (Washington, 1965). Reproduced with commentary in (1965) 4 ILM 524. See also generally Broches, 'The Convention on the Settlement of Investment Disputes between States and Nationals of other States' (1972-II) 136 *Recueil des Cours* 331.

[139] Fox (1988) 6.

[140] See Amerasinghe, *Local Remedies in International Law* 2nd edn (Cambridge University Press, Cambridge, 2004) especially 107 et seq.

commercially predictable and efficient remedy. This would be seriously undermined if it were subject to prior exhaustion of municipal court procedures. On the one hand, this means that an investor may go directly to investment arbitration, without awaiting or even attempting municipal court resolution.[141] On the other, it means that an investor is precluded from resorting to the municipal courts, once a definite consent in favour of ICSID has been made.

While ICSID Article 26 merely provides for a rebuttable presumption to this effect, and does not as such exclude prior recourse to municipal courts, what is known as a 'fork in the road' provision in a BIT may expressly lay down the mutual exclusivity of investment arbitration and national courts in this manner. Most BITs—at least those not expressly confining jurisdiction to treaty claims—contain such provisions. The BIT between Norway and Chile may provide an example. After having established the right of investors to submit claims either to national court proceedings or ICSID arbitration, it provides as follows:

> Once the investor has submitted the dispute to the competent tribunal of the Contracting Party in whose territory the investment was made or to international arbitration, the election of one or the other procedure will be final.[142]

This requires the investor to choose between arbitration and municipal courts; once a claim is filed the choice is final. In other words, in so far as a legal action is based on the same claim as that previously decided by a national court, the arbitral tribunal's jurisdiction is effectively excluded and confined to a possible claim for denial of justice.[143] Through this arrangement, conflicting decisions from municipal courts and investment arbitral tribunals are avoided. This would otherwise have been a practical problem, due to possibly overlapping competencies in relation to municipal law as well as international law.[144] The totality of this is not only to provide an exception to the principle of exhaustion of local remedies, but to stipulate the completely opposite requirement. In general, exhaustion is a requirement for invocation of international remedies; here instead it excludes the availability of the arbitral procedure.

Two conflicting priorities can be seen to have coincided in the conceptualisation of investment treaty arbitration in this manner as a substitute for municipal courts, according to the modality of international commercial arbitration. States have been, and are, sceptical about establishing

[141] Where jurisdiction is based on a separate BIT, it may even to some extent override exclusive jurisdiction clauses previously agreed to by an investor in a contract, see further below section 4.5.

[142] *Chile-Norway BIT* (1993) Art 8.

[143] *Pantechniki v Albania* (Award, 2009) see paras 67–8.

[144] As such it could also raise concerns under municipal constitutional law, eg under § 88 of the Norwegian constitution, according to which 'the Supreme Court pronounces judgment in the final instance'.

international courts or legal procedures which aim to function as appellate procedures over national courts. The reason is that this would endow the tribunals with a stronger international and moral status than if they were conceived merely to function as alternatives to national courts. At the same time foreign investors are sceptical towards litigation in national courts. This is not necessarily only because it is believed that the courts will be corrupt or unreliable or openly partisan as such. Even the most impartial national court may show greater understanding for the concerns of its home government than a neutral and detached international judge or arbitrator would. The result of this combination of interests is the submission of all legal aspects of the investment to arbitration, not as an appellate procedure above the national court process, but as an alternative to domestic litigation. More generally, this reflects the underlying hybrid character of investment arbitration. Partly, it is a consequence of its predominantly contractual and commercial origin, and partly of its characteristics as an international remedy which is at the same time directly binding under municipal law. The former encourages effectiveness and the finality of choice, after the model of international commercial arbitration; the latter encourages a finality of process to avoid conflicting jurisdictions and decisions under municipal law. This also shows how normal rules and procedures of international dispute settlement, designed to settle disputes between states, will not, and cannot, necessarily be relied on in this context.

3

A Theoretical Discourse—Conceptualising the Applicability of International Law to State Contracts

3.1 INTERNATIONAL LAW AND STATE CONTRACTS—CHALLENGING TRADITIONAL DOCTRINE

IN THE PREVIOUS chapter I described how international arbitration has assumed what I denoted a hybrid function, through application of international law to claims arising out of contracts between states and foreign investors. In this chapter I discuss the conceptualisation of this practice under international law. The essential problem involved is the applicability of international law to what can be termed 'vertical' relationships between states and private investors—ordinarily conceived as a relationship between 'sovereign' and 'subject'—which stands in contrast to the conventional applicability of international law to 'horizontal' inter-state relationships.[1] This is often regarded as concerning the incidence of legal personality or subjectivity under international law.[2] Specifically in relation to the present issue it has received much attention as a controversy over the applicability of international law to state contracts.[3] This has over the years surfaced as a relatively stark controversy between 'supporters' and 'opponents', somewhat along the lines of

[1] See also for the same terminology Spiermann, 'Applicable Law', paper submitted to the ILA Committee on Foreign Investment (2006) 6 and 8. (Note that I use 'horizontal' and 'vertical' applicability in a somewhat different sense here).

[2] See eg the classical treatment by Lauterpacht, 'The Subjects of the Law of Nations' in E Lauterpacht (ed), *International law: being the collected papers of Hersch Lauterpacht Vol II* (Cambridge University Press, Cambridge, 1975) 3, and see also the more recent and critical re-appraisal of the doctrine of subjects by Higgins, *Problems and Process: International law and How We Use It* (Clarendon Press, Oxford, 1994) 40 et seq.

[3] See for representative discussion in the more recent literature eg Leben, 'La théorie du contrat d'état et l'évolution du droit international des investissements' (2003) 302 *Recueil des Cours* 197, especially 299 et seq; Lankarani El Zein, *Les contrats d'etat a l'epreuve du droit international* (Bruylant, Bruxelles, 2002); Maniruzzaman, 'State Contracts in Contemporary International Law: Monist versus Dualist Controversies' (2001) 12(2) *EJIL* 309; and Lillich, 'The law Governing Disputes under Economic Development Agreements: Reexamining the Concept of Internationalization' in Lillich and Brower (eds), *International Arbitration; towards judicialization and uniformity* (Transnational, Irvington NY, 1994) 61.

the kindred *lex mercatoria* debate that I have previously alluded to. I should therefore start by clarifying a theoretical premise for the following discussion: a theoretical conceptualisation of the law must necessarily reflect and accommodate the law as it is practised (not meaning of course that it should surrender a critical distance for this reason). The relevant practice in our context, as I see it, and as described in the previous chapter, is that of a consistent tendency to apply what is conceived of as international law in individual investor-state disputes. Article 42 of the Convention on the Settlement of International Disputes between States and nationals of Other States (the ICSID Convention) makes express provision for such applicability. A mass of individual investment treaties provide individual rules and standards clearly applicable to vertical investor-state relationships. In addition there are the numerous contractual tribunals which have seen fit to apply international law without any express basis in treaty, as already described in some detail in the previous chapter. In the face of this, it would seem spurious to dispute that international law may and does apply, in some sense, 'vertically' to investor-state relationships. Instead, the real problem is how it applies and under what structural premises of international law. This is the subject of the present chapter, where I also attempt to trace the main lines of discussion and controversy up until the present.

The chapter maintains two main priorities. On the one hand I seek to show how doctrine has approached and dealt with the applicability of international law to state contracts as something quite problematic and exceptional, and how this is related to certain underlying ideas about the nature of international law and legal personality. On the other, I seek to show that what is problematical is not the notion of applicability as such, but certain assumptions about its consequences as a matter of substantive law. My fundamental argument in this regard is that the applicability of international law to defend private interests depends on the individual content of the substantive standards involved and not on a general preconception of legal personality. At the same time, I make the argument that international law and the manner in which it applies to protect private interests, such as a contractual position, is fundamentally structured by a concept of sovereignty as the basis of municipal law. This is reflected in the initial applicability of municipal law,[4] being a corollary of the essential nature of an investor-state relationship as a rapport between public authority and private rights and interests subject to municipal law, where municipal law at the same time may be conditioned or even superseded by applicable rules of international law. Finally, I maintain that it is necessary to distinguish this issue of substantive applicability from the

[4] This is a main point also of Douglas, 'The Hybrid Foundations of Investment Treaty Arbitration' (2003) 74 *BYIL* 151, 197 et seq.

separate issue regarding the authority of a given arbitral tribunal to apply international law. It is not inconceivable, though it may be a solution that should as far as possible be avoided, that a given rule of international law is substantively applicable to the subject at hand, but, for lack of sufficient consent from the respondent state, is nevertheless not within the authority of the arbitral tribunal to adjudicate upon. The remainder of the chapter is structured in the way that I first discuss the concept of internationalisation of state contracts, and the different theories attempting to justify this (section 3.2). I then discuss the question of applicability from the perspective of traditional doctrines of international law, and argue that the controversy is rooted in a traditional controversy between what I term monist and dualist perspectives on the nature of international law (section 3.3). Pursuant to this I propose a reconceptualisation of the question of applicability, and discuss in concrete terms whether relevant substantive rules and principles of international law may indeed be considered to apply 'vertically' to the relationship between a state and an investor (section 3.4). Finally, I discuss whether and to what extent arbitral tribunals rooted in the different existing regimes may indeed be considered vested with authority to adjudicate upon such applicable rules and principles of international law (section 3.5).

3.2 THE CONCEPT OF INTERNATIONALISATION

In chapter two above, I described how international commercial arbitration was used as a means to elevate contract claims against states into a subject of international law, and how the concept of 'internationalisation' was elemental to this practice. As a legal construct, this concept emerged and shaped itself in close interaction with international legal doctrine, represented by some of the most distinguished scholars at the time. The main doctrinal problem confronted was (or is) that an individual investor does not have international legal personality, and therefore has no ability to make a commitment under international law. This would also seem to deny the possibility of an investor securing a binding contractual commitment from a state under international law. If subject to the state's own law, as it would usually be, any such commitment would instead seem to be wholly at the mercy of the legislative authority of the state concerned. The practical phenomenon of 'internationalisation' evolved in arbitral practice as a response to this, rooted in the practical need for some concept of contractual commitment distanced from municipal law. The scholarly effort to develop the doctrine was, in its turn, a response to the challenge manifested by practice to established doctrine. In this section I show how two main approaches were adopted in legal doctrine; one essentially substantive, envisaging the contract as a separate legal order based on a priori validity; the other more formal, considering the contract transformed into an internationally binding agreement by virtue of submission to international law. This also exposes the critical inconsistencies and weaknesses of the doctrines and may lay the ground for a more realistic reconceptualisation of the essential problem involved.

A. A New Legal Order—The '*Contrat sans loi*'

One of the first attempts to describe the new practice of agreements detached from municipal law was what has been called the 'autonomous contract' (or 'Contrat sans loi') approach. Essentially, this approach regards the agreements in themselves as manifesting the positive law in force between the parties, binding by virtue of certain underlying principles of natural law, or 'general principles of law recognized by civilized nations'.[5] This approach is best illustrated by the writings of two well-known and distinguished scholars of international law, Lord McNair, and Alfred Verdross.

In 1957 Lord McNair wrote a now famous article in which he suggested that a special class of contracts, which he called 'economic development agreements', typically were governed by certain legal standards, which were neither municipal law nor public international law, but were instead encapsulated by what he called 'the general principles of law recognized by civilized nations'.[6] McNair argued that, because the contracts were typically referred to arbitration outside the territory of the state, they were made exempt from the automatic application of municipal law.[7] But since the parties were not both states, and therefore did not interact on the inter-state level, the contracts could not be governed by public international law.[8] Instead, he argued, the contracts were governed by 'the general principles of law', as a legal order related, but not similar to the '*jus inter gentes*' constituted by public international law:

[5] Cf the Statute of the International Court of Justice (1945) Art 38.1(c).

[6] McNair, 'The General Principles of Law Recognized by Civilized Nations' (1957) 33 *BYIL* 1.

[7] *ibid*, 6: 'In the case of the type of contract with which we are concerned in this article there is a special reason why the choice of a system of law should depend on the intention of the parties, expressed or implied, namely, that most of these contracts contain provision for arbitration . . . If it be true, as is generally recognized, that the submission of a dispute to the jurisdiction of a particular court amounts to an acceptance of the law of that court as the law governing the dispute, it would seem to follow that the submission of a dispute to a tribunal of arbitration involves the acceptance of such system of law as the arbitrator may decide to be the relevant one'.

[8] *ibid*, 10: 'One can truly infer from these contracts—both from what they do say and from what they do not say—that the parties are groping after some legal system which is not the territorial law of either party. The answer to these questions is not that these contracts are governed by public international law *strictu sensu*, for this system is an inter-State system—*jus inter gentes*'.

> Although it cannot be said that this type of contract is governed by public international law, it is public international law which has given birth to the legal system gradually being recognized as appropriate to it, for Article 38, paragraph 1 (c), of the Statute of the International Court of Justice which forms the title of this article, merely places on record one of the main sources of the rules of public international law. In other words, it is submitted that the legal system appropriate to the type of contract under consideration is not public international law but shares with public international law a common source of recruitment and inspiration, namely 'the general principles of law recognized by civilized nations'.[9]

A variation on the same theme is the theory developed by Verdross in a number of writings.[10] His theory has become known as the '*contrat sans loi*', which is to distort the essential content of Verdross's theory however. It does not picture a binding contract without any basis in a legal rule. What it depicts is really the lack of a positive and established legal order accommodating such contracts. Much like McNair, Verdross maintained that a contract disconnected from municipal law created a new positive legal order by itself, in the sense of constituting an exhaustive regulation of the relationship between the parties. The doctrinal rationale was similarly the effective detachment of the contract from the legal process of the contracting state, combined with the lack of an established international legal order befitting such contracts. Since this effectively withdrew the contract from any given positive law, the consequence, according to Verdross, was that it became subject to a limited number of universally accepted legal principles underlying all positive law, including the fundamental principle of the sanctity of contracts (*pacta sunt servanda*):

> [Q]uasi-international agreements normally contain special arbitration clauses providing that disputes concerning the interpretation and application of such agreements are to be submitted neither to a judicial or administrative authority of the contracting State, nor to private arbitral proceedings according to the internal law of the State but to special arbitral proceedings provided for by the *lex contractus* or by a special arbitration agreement and quite independent of the procedural laws of the contracting State. All this makes it clear that such an agreement inter pares is not a contract governed by the legal order of a State, but a new legal order established by the common will of the parties on the basis of the principle *pacta sunt servanda* and other general principles of law governing such contracts.[11]

[9] *ibid*, 6.

[10] See eg Verdross, 'Quasi-International Agreements and International Economic Transactions' (1964) *Yearbook of World Affairs* 230; and Verdross, 'Protection of Private Property under Quasi-International Agreements' in *Varia Juris Gentium* (Sijthoff, Leiden, 1959) 355.

[11] Verdross (1964) 234.

The leading notion of both Verdross and McNair is the same—that the contracts under consideration do not fit within the positive conception of either international or municipal law, but that they nevertheless draw legal validity from the general idea of 'the rule of law', and such principles as it is generally recognised to contain. Notably, for both McNair and Verdross the basis of the supposed internationalisation is thus a substantive principle—*pacta sunt servanda*, which is directly actualised through the disconnection of the contract from municipal law. This principle is considered a priori valid, in other words beyond the requirement of positive validation. As such it is able to ensure the substantive validity of the positive legal reality created by the contract, conceived as a self-evident first principle, existing above and beyond the positive legal orders constituted by either public international law or municipal laws. While on this view a de-nationalised contract does not fit within the positive body of rules constituting public international law, it is no less binding on the contracting states. It merely constitutes a different positive law, which nonetheless owes its life and strength to the same 'inexhaustible reservoir of legal principles from which tribunals can enrich and develop [the] law' in the words of McNair,[12] or, as stated by Verdross: 'It would be possible also to enlarge the term "international law", and to define it as the law governing all relations within the international community. All depends upon the initial definition of international law'.[13]

The argument developed by McNair and Verdross might therefore be described as essentially a substantive natural law approach, based on a notion of the transcendental validity of *pacta sunt servanda* as a legal norm. More recently a notion related to the *contrat sans loi* theory has been taken up in French legal doctrine as a more radical negation of the potential application of international law to state contracts, relying nevertheless on a notion of the sanctity of contracts as a conceived a-national legal principle.[14] It is not surprising that most theorists have not been willing to go that far. Especially Verdross's notion of the *contrat sans loi* has been criticised, the objection being that a contract cannot exist without a basis in some positive law.[15] Instead, a detour was invented to maintain the 'fiction' of an applicable positive law, namely that the contract might be expressly submitted to the positive legal order of international law.

[12] McNair (1957) 6.

[13] Verdross (1964) 232.

[14] See Mayer, 'La neutralisation de pouvoir normatif de l'Etat en matière de contrats d'Etat' (1986) *J Dr Int'l* 5; and Mayer, 'Le mythe de 'l'ordre juridique de base' (ou grundlegung)' in *Le droit des relations économiques internationales. Etudes offertes à Berthold Goldman* (Litec, Paris, 1982); and see also Verhoeven, 'Arbitrage entre États et entreprises étrangères: des regles specifique?' in 'Hommage à Jean Robert' (1985) *Rev Arb* 609.

[15] See eg Maniruzzaman, 'Choice of Law in International Contracts—Some Fundamental Conflict of Laws Issues' (1999) 16(4) *J Int'l Arb* 141, 145–9.

B. Making International Law Apply—The 'Choice of Law' Approach

Instead of *pacta sunt servanda* as a substantive principle, this approach relies initially on party autonomy as a principle of choice of law. The crux of the theory is that the choice of international law allegedly inscribes the contract into the international legal order as an internationally binding agreement immune from subsequent municipal legislation.[16] This express submission to international law is denoted 'internationalisation'.

The first to introduce this concept as a legal construct was FA Mann.[17] Mann suggested that contracts with states might be made subject to public international law, by virtue of the applicable conflict of laws rules. His main argument was that certain state contracts had international characteristics which constituted a bona fide reason for allowing them to be expressly submitted to international law.[18] The underlying rationale was that this would make the contract independent of and immune to the internal legislative powers of the state concerned:

> [I]f a contract with a state is governed by the law of such State it may, as a result of supervening legislation, be modified and destroyed. It would therefore be impossible to suggest as a general principle that a State, in entering into a contract, foregoes the right to change its terms. The right and power to do so depend on the proper law. If the proper law is public international law, that power and that right are necessarily excluded.[19]

Mann's reasoning contained the most crucial elements of the concept of internationalisation, such as it would come to be adopted in later practice and theory. The somewhat curious and idiosyncratic aspect of Mann's approach is, however, that he considered it essentially dependent on the municipal conflict of laws rules of the *lex loci arbitri* (ie the seat of the arbitration).[20] As later adopted and refined by doctrine and practice,

[16] Cf Berlin, 'Contrat d'État' in *Répertoire Dalloz de Droit International* (Dalloz, Paris, 1998) 3: 'Par internationalisation, il faut comprendre le désir d'inscrire totalement la relation contractuelle dans l'ordre juridique international: En d'autres termes, de transformer le contrat d'État en un accord de droit international, source de droits et d'obligations sanctionnés par le droit international'.

[17] Mann, 'The Law Governing State Contracts' (1944) 21 *BYIL* 11; and see also Mann: 'State Contracts and State Responsibility' (1960) 54 *AJIL* 572; and Mann, 'The Theoretical Approach towards the Law Governing Contracts between States and Private Persons' (1975) *Rev B Dr Int'l* 562.

[18] *ibid*, 19: '[I]f one party to a contract is an international person, particularly a state, there exists *ipso facto* a sufficient connection with super-national rules of law which, on any view of the proper law theory, may enable and justify the parties to de-localize their contract and to submit it to what may be called public international law, i.e. to internationalize it'.

[19] Mann (1975) 567.

[20] This must be seen in the perspective of Mann's general view of the arbitral process as strictly governed by the law of its seat, being an ardent supporter of the so called jurisdictional theory of arbitration, see eg Mann, '*Lex facit arbitrum*' in *Liber Amicorum for Martin Domke* (Nifhoff, The Hague, 1967) 157.

Mann's theory was grounded in an international or transnational concept of party autonomy,[21] usually explained as a 'general principle of conflict of laws'[22] or a 'principle of customary international law'.[23] The most sophisticated conceptualisations of the doctrine are found in French legal theory, most notably in the substantial contributions of Weil,[24] and more recently Leben.[25]

Weil seeks to explain internationalisation as something which itself is justified by international law, thus making the contract into a 'veritable international legal act' ('un véritable acte juridique international'[26]). The main invention in this regard is the concept of 'the basic legal order' ('l'ordre juridique de base'[27]), which is another term for 'the legal order from which the binding nature of the contract stems' introduced by the *Texaco* case.[28] Crucially, the role of this law is not conceived to be substantive; instead it has a 'dispatching' function by conferring on the parties' choice of law the required legal effect and validity.[29] It is accordingly supposed to be *objectively* applicable, that is, it must apply prior to and irrespective of the parties' choice. The presumption is that the basic legal order normally will be a municipal law, but that certain contracts may have their 'centre of gravity' within the international order, and therefore be prima facie subject to international law.[30] If such a contract contains a choice of international law, it is then both 'international' and 'internation-

[21] See especially *Texaco Overseas Petroleum Co v Govt of Libya* (Award (Merits), 1977) 53 ILR 389, para 25: 'Did the parties have the right to choose the law or the system of law which was to govern their contract? The answer to this first question is beyond any doubt; all legal systems, whatever they are, apply the principle of the autonomy of the will of the parties to international contracts'.

[22] See eg Maniruzzaman (1999), 151: 'It is thus party autonomy as a general principle of conflict of laws in which lies the binding force of the contract as well as the proper law of the contract . . . It is the agreement of the parties that provides the arbitrator with the springboard and not the seat of the arbitration'.

[23] *ibid*, 163, with further references.

[24] Weil, 'Problèmes relatifs aux contrats passés entre un État et un particulier' (1969-III) 128 *Recueil des Cours* 95; Weil, 'Les clauses de stabilisation et d'intangibilité insérées dans les accords de développement économique' in *Mélanges offerts à Charles Rousseau* (Pedone, Paris, 1974) 301; Weil, 'Droit international et contrats d'Etat' in *Mélanges offerts à Paul Reuter: le droit international: unité et diversité* (Pedone, Paris, 1981) 549; and Weil, 'Principes généraux du droit et contrats d'Etat' in *Le droit des relations économiques internationales: Etudes offertes à Berthold Goldman* (Litec, Paris, 1982) 387.

[25] Leben (2003); and see also Leben, 'Quelque réflexions théoriques a propos des contrats d'Etats' in *Souveraineté étatique et marchés internationaux à la fin du 20ème siècle; Mélanges en l'honneur de Philippe Kahn* (Litec, Paris, 2000); and Leben, 'Retour sur la notion de contrat d'Etat et sur le droit applicable à celui-ci' in *Mélanges offerts à Hubert Thierry* (Pedone, Paris, 1998) 247.

[26] Weil (1981) 562.

[27] *ibid*, 559.

[28] *Texaco v Libya* (Award, 1977) (1979) 53 ILR 389, 443.

[29] Weil (1981) 561: '[L]'ordre juridique de base . . . "grâce a son corps de règles de conflits", assure une fonction d'aiguillage, de dispatching si l'on préfère, vers les règles appelées à gouverner matériellement le contrat'.

[30] *ibid*, 572.

alised' in the sense that it is both anchored in and ultimately governed by international law.[31] Contrastingly, a contract lacking this international centre of gravity might still be internationalised, if allowed by the basic municipal legal order. In Weil's terms it would not be an 'international contract', however, for lacking the basis in international law as its ultimate source of validity and obligation:

> [C]eux des contrats d'Etat qui sont fondés dans l'ordre international constitueraient ainsi une catégorie spécifique d'actes juridiques internationaux, á côté des traités, des actes unilateraux des Etats et des organisations internationales et des actes judiciaires ou arbitraux. Le contrat simplement soumis á des règles de fond de droit international ne serait, au contraire, pas un acte juridique international.[32]

In this manner, the status of a true international legal act is reserved for contracts that are already objectively governed by international law. Thus, Weil escapes the criticism that a choice of international law can hardly invoke international law as international law in a true sense, if that choice itself is not in some manner touched by international law. The problem is, however, to explain why and how only certain contracts come to have their supposed centre of gravity in international law, and how this can take place independently of the parties' intention.[33]

This is in a sense where Leben's theory begins. His theory is similarly concerned with establishing a genuine link between state contracts and international law; between what he perceives as 'la notion nouvelle de contrat d'Etat',[34] and international law, as 'l'ordre juridique du contrat'.[35] Leben's main invention is to introduce a concept of the state as a double personality, with an external and an internal role.[36] This perceives the state as a Janus-like creature with two faces. One side is faced towards internal law, and is the state in its internal capacity, as 'l'Etat-Administration'.[37] The other side is faced towards the international community, and is the state in its external capacity, as 'l'Etat personne de droit international'.[38]

This provides the crucial criterion lacking in Weil's theory to explain which contracts are subject to international law.[39] According to Leben, contracts are subject to international law when they are entered into by the state in its external capacity, as a subject of international law:

[31] *ibid*, 566–7.
[32] *ibid*, 562
[33] See for critique, especially Mayer (1982).
[34] Leben (2003) 212.
[35] *ibid*, 263.
[36] The concept is borrowed from Pierre Mayer, who does not draw the same conclusions from it as Leben, see Leben (1998) 251, and Mayer (1986) 9 et seq. See also for a further theoretical discussion, Leben (2000); and Leben (2003) 322.
[37] Leben (2003) 327.
[38] *ibid*, 329.
[39] Leben (1998) 250.

> [C]e qui caractérisait ce type de contrat est la volonte d'égaliser la situation des deux contractants, c'est-à-dire de faire en sorte que le l'Etat ne soit pas à même d'utiliser ses prérogatives souveraines pour remettre en cause le contrat, sans qu'il soit redevable de quoi que ce soit au titre de la violation du contrat.[40]

In other words, a state contract subject to international law is characterised by the fact that the state has surrendered its sovereign prerogatives vis-à-vis its co-contractor. According to Leben, this is ensured by two crucial elements: first, a clause subjecting disputes to international arbitration, thereby displacing the competence of the host state's court; and secondly, a clause (or set of clauses) withdrawing the contract from the municipal law of the state concerned.[41] The latter is supposedly effectuated either by an express choice of international law, or a stabilisation (or freezing) of the host state's law.[42] Leben's theory is thus in a sense a development of the more typical choice of law approach. The state becomes bound by a contract on the international level essentially by agreeing to neutralise its own law and sovereign prerogatives under that law.[43]

Somewhat simplified, it may be said that these theoretical constructs, with some modifications and variations, are based on a set of shared critical assumptions, recognisable moreover in the application of the concept in arbitral practice. The crucial basis of internationalisation is thus the parties' expressed intention to internationalise the contract, ie to withdraw it from the control of municipal law, the legal effect of which depends on three assumptions. The first critical stage is the very definition of the problem as a conflict of laws issue, and the consequent assumption that conflict of laws methodology is applicable. This is a recurrent theme in both theory and practice, first self-evidently to define the problem as a choice of law issue, and then to go on and look for the applicable choice of law principle.[44] This was the express basis of Mann's theory, but it is also more or less implicit in the subsequent theories of Weil and Leben as explained above. It is, moreover, a recurrent feature and the necessary starting point of arbitral practice. When the problem is thus defined, the solution is to some extent self-evident, for the applicable principle can only be party autonomy. The international status (or not) of party autonomy is not necessarily in itself critical, since the near universal recognition of party autonomy is probably beyond doubt.[45] Thus, tribunals have

[40] Leben (2003) 258.
[41] *ibid*, 248 et seq.
[42] *ibid*, 249.
[43] *ibid*, 250.
[44] See thus eg Lalive, 'Contracts between a State or a State Agency and a Foreign Company' (1964) 13 *ICLQ* 987, 992: 'In order to find out the law of these contracts, the situation should first be examined in the light of the conflict rules and by applying the usual methods of interpretation available'. And see also Paasivirta, *Participation of States in International Contracts* (Lakimiesliiton Kustannus, Helsinki, 1990) 55 et seq.
[45] See generally Lando, 'The Conflict of Laws of Contracts' (1984-VI) 189 *Recueil des Cours* 225.

also accepted the internationalisation formula on the basis of municipal law.[46]

What is critical is the notion that international law can be invoked at all by conflict of laws methodology. This is linked to the second critical assumption, namely that the parties may choose any law to govern the contract, including a supranational law such as public international law or general principles of law.[47] The common argument is that the parties to an international contract are not prima facie bound by any particular municipal law; in other words no municipal law has a claim to application.[48] Why should they then not be able to choose a law without any municipal connection, such as a set of transnational rules or customs, to govern the contract? The more particular arguments are, as rehearsed above, that international law (or a set of transnational rules) is prima facie more suitable for the contracts in question, or that the contracts already have a natural connection with this law.[49]

In the two first stages of the argument, the question of withdrawing the contract from the control of the state's own municipal law is in this manner commonly presented as a preliminary issue without substantive connotations. The neutralisation of the state's sovereignty is presented as a formal and inevitable consequence of accepted conflict of laws methodology, which does not raise particular issues of substantive law. Only with the third critical assumption is the substantive issue finally confronted. But the principle now entering the picture appears self-evident, namely the principle that contracts must be observed (*pacta sunt servanda*). The status of this principle is commonly held to be 'indisputable',[50] or it is set out as

[46] See eg *BP Exploration Co (Libya) Ltd v Govt of Libya* (Award, 1973) 53 ILR 297, 326–7; and *Sapphire International Petroleums Ltd v National Iranian Oil Company (NIOC)* (Award, 1963) 35 ILR 136, 170–71.

[47] Cf eg the resolution of the *Institut de Droit International* at its 1979 session in Athens on 'The proper law of the contract in agreements between a state and a foreign person' (1979) 58-II *Ann IDI* 193–5 and 42–103. Art 2 of the resolution reads as follows: 'The parties may . . . choose as the proper law of the contract either one or several domestic legal systems or the principles common to such systems, or the general principles of law, or the principles applied in international economic relations, or international law, or a combination of these sources of law'. The supposed consequence of such a choice of law is further clarified in article 6 of the resolution, stipulating that it, inter alia, governs the state's 'exercise of its sovereign powers in violation of any of its commitments toward the contracting partner'.

[48] See eg Von Mehren and Kourides, 'International Arbitrations between States and Foreign Private Parties: the Libyan Nationalization Cases' (1981) 75 *AJIL* 476, 510–11: 'The international community fully recognizes that parties to a contract, including contracts between a state and foreign private enterprise, may choose the law to govern their contractual relations. It is also well established by international conventions and practice, general principles of law, and authoritative writings by commentators that, for purposes of such a choice, reference may be made to a body of law other than municipal law. Because the parties are not required to choose the law of their nationality or, indeed the law of any nationality, there is no compelling reason why they should not elect to have their contractual relations governed by principles and concepts that are not attached to any sovereign'.

[49] See eg Mann (1944) 19; and Weil (1981) 572.

[50] Von Mehren and Kourides (1981) 514.

'a fundamental principle of law'[51] or 'a fundamental principle of international law'.[52] Nobody would of course dispute that *pacta sunt servanda* is part of, and a fundamental rule of international law. Since the point of internationalisation is to make the contract subject to international law as its governing law, international law thus necessarily comes to recognise it as an agreement (or so goes the argument). An alternative and more sophisticated conceptualisation of this would be that of Leben: since the contract is entered into by the state in its external (or international) capacity, it is subject to the international legal capacity of the state to to make binding commitments. The essence of the internationalisation theory is thus in a way that having been subjected to international law (or the general principles of law), a contract is also made subject to the principle that it is binding.[53] Moreover, by being withdrawn from municipal law, the contract has become shielded from the effects of municipal legislation, allegedly on the basis of the general principle (of international law) that a state cannot escape international responsibility by referring to its own municipal law.[54]

C. Critique of the Concept of Internationalisation

This notion that a contract can be internationalised, and consequently made subject to the principle of international law that commitments should be upheld, essentially pretends to transform the contract from a 'vertical' into a 'horizontal' commitment for the state. The main problem with this notion is its fundamental failure to confront the substantive issue it addresses. It is tempting to say that it creates an illusion, which lies in its definition of the problem as a choice of law issue, and its idea of international law (or general principles of law) as just any other legal system which might be the subject of a choice of law. This conceals that the underlying issue which the theory seeks to confront is substantive; whether the state may bind itself not to repeal or modify the contract by subsequent legislation. The only objective of the choice of international law or general principles of law is to lift the contract into the sphere of application of the principle of *pacta sunt servanda* to neutralise the legislative sovereignty of the state concerned. Thus the detour around party autonomy and choice of law is really only a detour to get to the same result as is advocated by the *contrat sans loi* theory, namely the application to the contract of *pacta sunt servanda* as a standard external to the state.

[51] *Sapphire v NIOC* (Award, 1963) 35 ILR 136, 181.

[52] *Texaco v Libya* (Award (Merits), 1977) 53 ILR 389, para 51.

[53] See also Audit, 'Transnational Arbitration and State Contracts' (Hague Academy of International Law; Centre for Studies and Research, 1987) 77, 102–4.

[54] Mann (1975) 565.

The fundamental problem of the theory is that the obligatory character of this as a principle of international law can hardly follow from anything but itself. As remarked by Rigaux, the claim that a contract is binding under international law by reason of a choice of law is quite similar to the proof of legitimacy provided by ancient kings, who claimed to be descended from the gods.[55] In the same manner as the crucial point in respect of the latter is to identify when and how the gods first produced as their offspring a demi-god and human king, that of the former is to identify when and why the choice of law is touched by international law. While both the contract and the king claim to have been subject to the crucial event, the event itself remains a mystery. This does not disprove that the contract might be binding under international law, any less than the king's claim to be a god disproves his divinity. The point is merely that the claim does not make it any more likely; it does not validate itself. The concept of internationalisation seems to presuppose exactly what it seeks to achieve; that international law is applicable.

The theoretical conceptualisations examined above are essentially sophisticated attempts to get around this problem. Notable is Weil's notion of 'the basic legal order', which considers international law to be objectively applicable to certain investment contracts, to constitute a legal basis for the choice of law in such contracts. The fundamental objection to this in terms of theory is that it does not explain why a choice of law is necessary for internationalisation if the contract is already subject to international law.[56] A different perspective is to hold that the state's consent to internationalise the contract constitutes an implicit *recognition* of the private party as a subject of international law.[57] But also this assumes what it seeks to prove, that a contract between a state and a private entity *is prima facie binding* by the relevant standards of international law. If it is not, then how could it constitute any recognition of the personality of the investor? And if the investor did not have legal capacity in the first place, how could it gain rights from a contract in order to develop a 'limited personality' under international law?

The fundamental question is not whether the parties may choose international law as the governing law of their agreement, but whether international law substantively applies, to recognise the binding effects of a contract entered into between a state and a private subject. If it does, the choice of international law as a means of internationalisation would appear to be irrelevant (although it would of course be possible, if somewhat absurd, to hold that the relevant rule of international law in

[55] Rigaux, 'Des dieux et des héros—Reflexions sur une sentence arbitrale' (1978) *Revue critique de droit international privé* 435, 437.

[56] See generally Mayer (1982).

[57] See eg Seidl-Hohenveldern, *International Economic Law* (Kluwer, The Hague, 1999) 44. See also Leben (1998) 264 et seq.

itself requires a choice of international law before it becomes applicable.) If it does not, the choice would appear equally irrelevant because it is not touched by international law in the first place. As I shall revert to in chapter five below, a closer scrutiny of the internationalisation cases also reveals a clear substantive rationale which has nothing to do with choice of law as such.

3.3 CONFLICTING PERSPECTIVES OF INTERNATIONAL LAW

The concept of internationalisation can be seen as a doctrinal response to a deeper controversy; that of the fundamental applicability of international law to state contracts. However, as argued above, the attempt to dispel this controversy by having the contract proclaim its own attachment to international law does nothing to address the real and fundamental issue involved. As is clear from an abundant literature on the subject, the underlying controversy is therefore far from dispelled, but merely provoked by this. A confident strand of doctrine rejects the notion of the contract subject to international law, while an equally confident strand continues to affirm and embrace it. In this section I examine this discussion, and show how it can be traced back to a more fundamental conflict of perspectives on the nature of international law and international legal personality.

My argument below is that doctrine is split into two main directions of thought, which can be denoted respectively monist and dualist perspectives on the question of applicability.[58] It has been noted elsewhere that the monism/dualism controversy refers to a deeper theoretical schism within international legal doctrine, which again is closely related to different conceptions of international legal personality.[59] The dualist position in this regard is that the real and immediate subjects of international law are states, and that municipal and international law therefore are conceptually distinct and separate legal systems.[60] The monist position,

[58] This is not an original observation of mine; the terminology is borrowed from Maniruzzaman (2001).

[59] Nijman, *The Concept of International Legal Personality* (TMC Asser Press, The Hague, 2004) 115 et seq; and see also Lauterpacht (1975) eg 8 and 11. This split of doctrine into a dominantly positivist (and dualist), fact based approach on the one hand, and a more normative (and monist), functional-teleological or natural law based approach on the other, is a common enough observation; it is a main theme in Koskenniemi, *From Apology to Utopia* (Cambridge University Press, Cambridge, 2006), especially at 182 et seq; and see also Weil, 'Le droit international en quête de son identité' (1992-VI) 237 *Recueil des Cours* 9, 66–8.

[60] See eg for a classical representation of this position, Triepel, 'Les rapports entre le droit interne et le droit international' (1923) 1 *Recueil des Cours* 77, 83: 'Ce sont deux cercles qui sont en contact intime, mais qui ne se superposent jamais. Puisque le droit interne et le droit international ne régissent pas les mêmes rapports, il est impossible qu'il y ait jamais une "concurrence" entre les sources des deux systèmes juridiques'. And see also Fitzmaurice, 'The General Principles of International Law Considered from the Standpoint of the Rule of

conversely, claims that the real subjects of international law are ultimately individuals,[61] and that the conceptual distinction between municipal law and international law is merely a *creation* of international law.[62] Based on this I argue that absolute and mutually contradictory positions taken in the internationalisation controversy are dictated by respectively monist and dualist premises, which confound theories about the nature of international law with substantive arguments about its content. As an alternative I suggest a more pragmatic and functional approach, which sees applicability as a function of the content of individual rules. First, I review the dualist position; secondly, I discuss the contradictory perspective of the monist position; and thirdly, I suggest an alternative conceptualisation of the applicability of international law where I seek to reconcile monism as a formal perspective with dualism as a substantive principle of international law.

A. The Dualist Position

What I call the dualist position on applicability either endorses the strict primacy of the host state's municipal law, or maintains that the legal effect of a state contract depends on each municipal law with which it may come into contact. This is related to a dualist premise which rejects prima facie the possibility, or at least likelihood, that international law may apply to a state contract, irrespective of the subject-matter of the relevant rules. A strong reflection of the dualist perspective is a much-quoted statement of Sereni, where, refuting the applicability of international law to concession agreements, the author simply proclaims this to be an absurdity:

> Each legal system serves the purpose of regulating the status and relations of the social entities for which and among which it exists. An attempt at applying international law to private relations would be tantamount to seeking to apply the matrimonial laws of France or England to relations between cats and dogs.[63]

A more sophisticated version of this view is set forth by Mayer, who holds that the fundamental structure of international law precludes its

Law' (1957-II) 92 *Recueil des Cours* 5, 70: 'There is no common field, because two different sets of relations are involved'.

[61] See eg Kelsen, *General Theory of Law and State* (Harvard University Press, Cambridge, 1945) 342: 'International law regulates the mutual behaviour of States but this does not mean that international law imposes duties and confers rights only upon States, not upon individuals . . . All law is regulation of human behaviour. The only social reality to which legal norms can refer are the relations between human beings'.

[62] *ibid*, 351: 'Since the international legal order not only requires the national legal orders as a necessary complementation, but also determines their spheres of validity in all respects, international and national law form one inseparable whole'.

[63] Sereni, 'International Economic Institutions and the Municipal Law of States' (1959-I) 96 *Recueil des Cours* 129, 210.

application to a contract between a state and a private party. The reason is sovereignty, not as a substantive principle, subject to exceptions and so forth, but as an inherent feature of international law in its relation to municipal law:

> Imputable à la société des Etats . . . il n'a pour objet que les rapports entre composants de cette société: les Etats, et les personnes morales qu'ils créent (organisations internationales). Les individus lui échappent, pour la raison très simple que les Etats ont le monopole de la contrainte à leur égard.[64]

In other words, municipal sovereignty constitutes for each state a monopoly of constraint in relation to individuals. This excludes the application of international law to state contracts, because sovereignty provides the only possible source of law applicable to individuals.

A somewhat different version of this view is provided by Verhoeven. In his argument, international law is simply oblivious to a state's contracts with foreign nationals. His point is not that international law permits a breach of contract, but that it is indifferent to it:

> Il n'existe en effet présentement en droit des gens aucune règle qui interdise à un Etat de modifier ou de rompre le contrat qu'il a conclu avec un particulier étranger. Ce n'est point que le droit des gens autorise cette 'déstabilisation'. C'est simplement qu'il ignore de tels accords qu'il ne régit pas.[65]

International law simply does not touch the substance of a contract entered into by a state with a foreign national; it therefore has nothing to say about the state's subsequent conduct in relation to it.

Several other writers more traditionally confine the relevance of international law to the remote possibility of an inter-state claim based on diplomatic protection. Thus, for Bowett, international law is 'almost wholly irrelevant' to a state contract as such,[66] and where it might be relevant, it is so only on the inter-state level.[67] Wengler maintains that a contract does not concern the international legal order before it has been made the subject of a claim presented by the home state of the private contracting party.[68] Similarly, Amerasinghe takes as a premise that international law is only applicable if the home state decides to exercise diplomatic protection.[69] Affiliated but more politically charged arguments particularly aim to justify the primacy of the host state's law. Thus, Sornarajah has argued that state

64 Mayer (1986) 21.

65 Verhoeven (1985) 623.

66 Bowett, 'Claims between States and Private Entities: The Twilight Zone of International Law' (1986) 35 *Catholic University Law Review* 929, 936.

67 *ibid*, 936–7, and see also Bowett, 'State Contracts with Aliens: Contemporary Developments on Compensation for Termination or Breach' (1988) 59 *BYIL* 49.

68 Wengler, 'Les accords entre états et entreprises étrangères, sont ils des traités de droit international?' (1972) *Revue Générale de Droit International Privé* 313.

69 Amerasinghe, 'State breaches of Contracts with Aliens and International Law' (1964) 58 *AJIL* 881, 902.

contracts should be considered part of the 'reserved domain' of national sovereignty.[70] Maniruzzaman instead relies on a strict concept of party autonomy, maintaining that whether international law is applicable depends on eventual incorporation into the municipal law stipulated in the contract.[71] The most original dualist perspective is nevertheless that of Mann, whose theories I have already discussed above.[72] As already explained, the purpose of Mann's theory is to justify the application of international law. The position of Mann is, however, essentially dualist because of its implicit premise that the contract is subject either to municipal law or public international law, excluding to this extent any possibility of interaction and integration.

These standpoints may be seen to build upon the dualist conception of international law, ie, on the theoretical notion that international law and municipal law are mutually separate normative systems, where the former is conceived in principle as concerned only with relations between states. As a strictly theoretical position, this view emerged and flourished ancillary to positivist doctrine at the end of the nineteenth and the beginning of the twentieth century.[73] It is famously represented by Triepel, who formulated it as a relationship between 'deux cercles qui sont en contact intime, mais qui ne se superposent jamais'.[74] Theoretically aligned to a positivist or voluntarist tradition based on a 'personification of the state',[75] this has two particular aspects. First, it conceives sovereignty as a social fact outside the law, which transforms the collective of the state into a 'closed unit' under international law.[76] Secondly, it regards international law essentially as a positive creation emanating from this sovereignty, personified as will.[77]

As a theoretical position this maintains that international law may be concerned with the interests of individuals as beneficiaries, but does not therefore apply to these interests as such. If a private interest is protected by international law, what is protected is not the private interest as such, but the home state's interest in just treatment of its nationals.[78] This is conceptualised through a distinction between objects and subjects of

[70] See especially Sornarajah, 'The Myth of International Contract Law' (1981) *Journal of World Trade Law* 187; but see also Sornarajah, *The International Law on Foreign Investment* 2nd edn (Cambridge University Press, Cambridge, 2004) 402 et seq.

[71] Maniruzzaman (2001) 327.

[72] See especially Mann, 'The Theoretical Approach towards the Law Governing Contracts between States and Private Persons' (1975) *Rev B Dr Int'l* 562.

[73] See further Nijman (2004) 116 et seq.

[74] Triepel (1923) 83, as quoted above in note 60. See also Anzilotti, *Cours de Droit International* (Paris, 1929) 51: 'Emanant de normes fondamentales autonomes, le droit international et le droit interne sont, par suite, des ordres séparés'. And see also Fitzmaurice (1957) 68–85.

[75] Nijman (2004) 116.

[76] *ibid*, 118–19.

[77] *ibid*, 117.

[78] Fitzmaurice (1957) 70; Triepel (1923) 81.

international law. Individuals and private entities are considered objects in the sense that states have an interest in them, much as they may have in relation to land, boundaries and rivers. But they do not, any more than land, lakes or rivers, possess legal rights in their own capacity. They are not, therefore, subjects.[79] From a strict dualist point of view, even what may clearly appear to be individual rights—rights granted for instance under a human rights treaty (or a bilateral investment treaty)—are obligations fundamentally owed towards other states to respect certain standards of behaviour towards individuals.[80]

In a more qualified and contemporary version of dualist theory, individuals are not generally subjects of international law, but may nevertheless obtain a limited subjectivity to the extent expressly recognised by a particular rule to this effect.[81] If there is such a thing, this is probably what comes closest to a mainstream and orthodox doctrine of international law.[82] The dualist premise is not necessarily made redundant by this as a substantive claim about the law. It may function as a preconception imposed on relevant rules and principles; a strong presumption against any notion that such rules might be invoked by private individuals and entities in their own capacity. What remains is nevertheless that dualism is primarily a *theory* about the nature of international law as a creation of sovereign states.

B. The Monist Position

A striking difference in perspective is provided by what I denote the 'monist' position. In relation to state contracts, this perspective is distinguished by its functional orientation. It emphasises how the underlying needs and interests involved transcend municipal law, and consequently *require* the application of international law. At least two strands of monist perspectives on state contracts can be identified, one anchored in a pragmatic Anglo-Saxon tradition, and one anchored in a more teleological French legal tradition. Both, however, are characterised by a distinctly functional approach to international law.

[79] See eg Schwarzenberger, *A Manual of International Law* 4th edn (Stevens & Sons, London, 1960) 128 et seq.

[80] See eg Borchard, *Diplomatic Protection of Citizens Abroad* (The Banks Law Publishing Co, New York, 1916) 27: 'The resident alien does not derive his rights directly from international law, but from the municipal law of the state of residence, though international law imposes upon that state certain obligations which under the sanction of responsibility to the other states of the international community, it is compelled to fulfil'. And see also Wengler (1972) 315.

[81] See eg Schwarzenberger, *International Law as Applied by International Courts and Tribunals* Vol I (Stevens & Sons, London, 1957) 140–46. See for criticism Higgins (1994) 49.

[82] See eg Brownlie, *Principles of Public International Law* (Oxford University Press, Oxford, 2003) 57.

A clearly pragmatic and functional approach is reflected in the writing of Jennings, who expressly argues in favour of a monist perspective on state contract disputes.[83] According to Jennings, the principal question is whether 'a legal bridge' can be established 'between the contract and international law',[84] or whether 'an effective link [can] be forged between the principles of international law and the relevant municipal law, so that these two systems interact'.[85] Having framed the question as a choice between a monist and a dualist perception of international law, Jenning's argument is that the perception of international law as an exclusive inter-state system, which 'goes on in the department of state and should not be allowed outside',[86] is opposed to the 'reasonable development of international law as a vehicle of order for our time'. In respect of state contracts, this suggests a perspective where,

> the relationship between international law and municipal law must be regarded as a monist system and no longer can be explained on the basis of a dualist theory that international law and municipal law operate on different planes 'and never the twain shall meet'.[87]

According to Jennings, such a monist perspective is required by the quality of law as a social function. If international law were not considered applicable to a state contract, this would imply that no true obligation could arise from it, since it would be subject to 'the legislative competence' of the state, and therefore could be 'altered at will'.[88] Application of international law is required simply to make legal sense of the contract, irrespective of whether it is primarily governed by municipal law or not.[89]

A more formal monist perspective is that adopted by Lauterpacht, in his separate opinion in the *Norwegian Loans* case.[90] Norway had initially relied on the decision of the Permanent Court of International Justice in the *Serbian Loans* case, to contend that the loans owed by Norway to French bondholders were subject to the reserved domain of domestic sovereignty.[91] The

[83] See Jennings, 'Rules Governing Contracts between States and Foreign Nationals' in *Rights and Duties of Private Investors Abroad* (Matthew Bender, Albany (NY), 1965) 123; and Jennings, 'State Contracts in International Law' (1961) 37 *BYIL* 156.

[84] Jennings (1965) 127.

[85] *ibid*, 127.

[86] *ibid*, 128.

[87] *ibid*, 128.

[88] *ibid*, 124.

[89] *ibid*, 128: '[It is] difficult to make sense of the question of state contracts, unless we are prepared to recognise not only the primacy of international law over municipal law but also the primacy of international law as an element working within municipal law as applied by municipal courts'.

[90] *Case of Certain Norwegian Loans (France v Norway)* [1957] ICJ Rep 9.

[91] *Case concerning the Payment of Various Serbian Loans Issued in France (France v Serbia)*, PCIJ Rep Series A No 20 (1929) 5, 41: 'Any contract which is not a contract between States in their capacity as subjects of international law is based on the municipal law of some country. The question as to which this law is forms the subject of that branch of law which is at the present day usually described as private international law or the doctrine of the conflict of laws. The

following statement, where the judge distinguished this case, has become a prominent formulation of the primacy of international over municipal law on potentially any issue:

> It may be admitted, in order to simplify a problem which is not at all simple, that an 'international contract' must be subject to some national law: this was the view of the Permanent Court of International Justice in the case of the Serbian and Brazilian loans. However, this does not mean that national law is a matter which is wholly outside the orbit of international law. National legislation—including currency legislation—may be contrary in its intention or effects to the international obligations of the state. The question of conformity of national obligations with international law is a matter of international law. The notion that if a matter is governed by national law, it is for that reason at the same time outside the sphere of international law, is both novel and, if accepted, subversive of international law. It is not enough for a state to bring a matter under the protective umbrella of its legislation, possibly of a predatory character, in order to shelter it effectively from any control by international law.[92]

This statement asserts the co-applicability and inherent primacy of international law over municipal law irrespective of issue, and thereby refutes the notion that some issues by their very nature belong exclusively to municipal law. To this effect it represents monism as formal principle. It does not necessarily suggest that a state contract is binding under international law, only that international law necessarily applies to determine this as a substantive question.

The second monist strand, anchored in French legal theory, displays a clearer teleological orientation. In contrast to the co-applicability approach of Jennings and Lauterpacht, it relies on a monist premise to justify detachment of a state contract from municipal law, to become 'un véritable acte juridique international'.[93] A monist premise is arguably implicit in Weil's conception that a state contract may be objectively rooted in the international legal order.[94] The notion that it can be objectively determined by a legal criterion what legal system applies to a contract assumes a relationship of co-ordination, which again presupposes that international and municipal law are conceived as part of the same normative system in the first place. The monist premise of Weil's theory is revealed by the assumption that a contract is only prima facie subject to international law where particular economic and political interests are

rules thereof may be common to several states and may even be established by international conventions or customs, and in the latter case may possess the character of true international law governing the relations between States. But apart from this it has to be considered that these rules form part of municipal law'.

[92] Lauterpacht (dissenting opinion), *Norwegian Loans case* [1957] ICJ Rep 9, 37.

[93] Weil (1981) 562.

[94] See also for an implicit acknowledgment of this, Weil (1969) 121.

concerned that transcend municipal law.[95] This, again, is related to an essentially teleological conception of international law, because it assumes that international law is inherently responsive to economical and political needs and interests. A monist premise is furthermore explicit in the distinction introduced by Leben between contracts entered into by the state as internal government and as subject of international law, as already alluded to. As explained above, this is based on a monist conception of the state as a Janus-like creature, with one face towards international law and another towards municipal law. The purpose of this metaphor is that it provides the criterion of co-ordination between international and municipal law. The state transcends its own municipal law by invoking its capacity as a subject of international law. Ostensibly formal, this nevertheless eventually admits to be a teleological argument:

> On voit que cette analyse repose sur la volonté de donner un sens à la promesse de l'Etat. On pourrait partir sur une volonté tout autre. Par exemple, la volonté de protéger l'Etat contre des engagements jugés extravagants, ce qui pourrait aboutir à nier toute validité à ce type de clause. Il faut alors savoir qu'une telle attitude a pour conséquence l'impossibilité pour l'Etat de donner aux contractants privés les garanties que ceux-ci demandent.[96]

In other words, internationalisation is justified because it 'gives sense' to a state promise by providing it with a legal basis. A monist premise is again revealed by the open concept of international personality invoked to justify this. According to Leben, international personality is simply vested in 'tout personne capable d'entrer en litige directement avec an autre sujet du droit international en tant que tel et, éventuellement, d'attraire ce sujet devant une juridiction internationale'.[97] The model of internationalisation thus comes to stand as a confirmation and actualisation of the inherent capability of international law to accommodate individuals as subjects.

These doctrinal conceptualisations may be seen to build on the monist theoretical premise that municipal and international law form part of a singular social function, intrinsically responsive to the needs and interests running through the international community. This is affiliated with the more fundamental idea that international law is not merely a limited body of positive rules created by and for relations between states, but a grander social imperative for human society in its entirety, ultimately, and

[95] See Weil (1981) 580: 'Il est à peine besoin de préciser que ce ne sont pas tous les contrats d'Etats que l'on devra ainsi considérer comme relevant de l'ordre juridique international mais seulement ceux d'entre eux qui s'intègrent effectivement, par des liens objectifs d'ordre juridique ou politico-économique, aux relations entre Etats, c'est-à-dire essentiellement—mais non exclusivement—les accords de développement économique ou contrats d'investissements'.

[96] Leben (2003) 261.

[97] Leben (1998) 266.

necessarily, directed at the aims and interests of individual human beings.[98] From this stems an ideal conception of unity and co-ordination, as opposed to dualism and separation. This monist premise has found different theoretical expressions in international legal theory. It is possible to identify, at different ends of the scale, a distinctly formal and a distinctly teleological direction of monist thinking. A common factor is nevertheless the notion that the individual is the ultimate subject of international law. This may be illustrated with the theories of respectively Kelsen and Scelle.

For Kelsen, monism is a formal principle logically derived from the premise that international law is ultimately directed at individuals.[99] The argument is that two conflicting norms cannot both be valid from one and the same perspective, if no means exist for resolving the conflict between the two. In other words, something cannot both be validly permitted and prohibited at the same time.[100] If two potentially conflicting normative systems exist it is therefore necessary to establish the primacy of one or the other, something which, according to Kelsen, presupposes a relationship of co-ordination and therefore of unity. Since international law is premised on the principle of equal and sovereign states, this entails for Kelsen the choice of a monist perspective premised on the primacy of international law over municipal law.[101] This monist perspective is purely formal; it does not attempt to justify or premise that individuals have direct rights and obligations under international law. Its main point is to reveal the dualist personification of states as a function of international law,[102] whereby the law 'delegates' the regulation of individuals to national law.[103] This creates an apparent division between international and municipal law, where individual rights and obligations are directly

[98] Lauterpacht, 'The Grotian Tradition in International Law' in E Lauterpacht (ed), *International law: being the collected papers of Hersch Lauterpacht* Vol II (Cambridge University Press, Cambridge, 1975) 307, 336.

[99] Kelsen (1945) 342: 'All law is regulation of human behaviour. The only social reality, to which legal norms can refer are the relations between human beings. Hence, a legal obligation as well as a legal right cannot have for its content anything but the behaviour of human individuals. If then international law should not obligate and authorize individuals, the obligations and rights stipulated by international law would have no contents at all and international law would not obligate or authorize anybody to do anything'.

[100] *ibid*, 363: 'International law and national law cannot be different and mutually independent systems of norms if the norms of both systems are considered to be valid for the same space and at the same time. It is logically not possible to assume that simultaneously valid norms belong to different, mutually independent systems'.

[101] Although Kelsen admits that it is equally logical to postulate the supremacy of municipal law over international law, *ibid*, 388.

[102] *ibid*, 342.

[103] *ibid*, 348: '[P]resent international law obligates and authorizes individuals indirectly, through the medium of the various national legal orders. The norms of international law are mostly incomplete norms; they require completion by norms of national law. The international legal order presupposes the existence of the national legal orders . . . In this sense, the international legal order 'delegates' to the national legal orders the completion of its own norms'.

subject to municipal law. But since international law ultimately conditions individual rights and obligations through its primacy over national law, the divide is not absolute; it is merely a function of the law. Nevertheless, a crucial factor of the theory is that international law, as a matter of principle, will only provide individuals with direct rights or obligations in exceptional circumstances.[104] This reveals that Kelsen's theoretical monist perspective is precisely a theory, which does not necessarily differ from orthodox dualist doctrine in its claims about the substance of the law.[105]

A more distinctly teleological monist perspective, with consequent substantive demands about the content of international law, is that relied on by Scelle. As for Kelsen, a central premise for Scelle is that individuals are the ultimate subjects of the law, although for Scelle this comes as the more radical premise that individuals are the only real subjects of international law.[106] This is based on Scelle's conception of international law as an objective-normative imperative emerging from sociological and biological reality.[107] Central to this is a distinction between *droit objectif* and *droit positif*,[108] where the validity of positive law (*droit positif*) derives from and is conditioned by its correspondence with objective law (*droit objectif*), conceived as 'nécessités et possibilités biologiques'.[109] From this follows also necessarily a monist perspective. Because law is an objective emanation of *le fait social*,[110] as there is, ultimately, only one world community, so there is also only one law. International law is conceived as an inherent 'féderalisme juridique', where the law of every society is conditioned by the more universal community interest of which it is a part.[111] This can be seen to conceptualise as theory the premise underlying both Leben's and Weil's approaches, and, if to a lesser extent, Jennings's, that a matter which transcends municipal law in an objective sense, ipso facto becomes subject to international law as an international legal act.[112] It also

104 *ibid*, 348: 'It is, however, only in exceptional cases that international directly obligates or authorizes individuals. If this should become the rule, the borderline between international and national law would disappear'.

105 This of course, rather than detracting from it as a legal theory, attests to its clear and persistent qualities, at least in the eyes of this author.

106 Scelle denies that states can have legal personality in a real sense, because a state has no will or no conscious existence independent of the individuals of whom it is composed, see Scelle, *Précis de droit des gens* Vol I (Recueil Sirey, Paris, 1932) 9.

107 See also generally the chapter about Scelle in Koskenniemi, *The Gentle Civilizer of Nations* (Cambridge University Press, Cambridge, 2001) 327 et seq.

108 Scelle (1932) 5.

109 *ibid*, 4.

110 *ibid*, 31.

111 *ibid*, 32–34.

112 Perhaps not so surprisingly, we also find a strikingly comparable perspective to that of Leben in Scelle's own position on so called public debts, where he relied on a distinction between the *interior* and *exterior* debts of the state. Scelle, *Précis de droit des gens* Vol II (Recueil Sirey, Paris, 1934) 127: 'En matière d'emprunt public il faudra distinguer toutefois entre les emprunts intérieurs et les emprunts extérieurs, abstraction faite de la difficulté de savoir quel critérium permet de distinguer les uns et les autres. S'il s'agit d'emprunts intérieurs, on peut

shows how a teleological monist premise imposed on substantive law entails a presumption of international law as inherently responsive to what are conceived as the prevailing social and economic realities.[113] Thus, in relation to an internationalised state contract, the state is considered bound for the reason that it has pledged to be, and because it is considered 'eminently useful' that it should be able to do so.[114] Internationalisation is justified in order to 'make sense' of the state's guarantee.[115]

C. Reconciling the Monist and Dualist Premises

Although ostensibly carrying substantive implications, the above also shows how the internationalisation controversy stems from a theoretical question, namely whether international law is premised on states as its subjects. In this is, however, also contained the seed to untie the controversy. Monist and dualist perspectives ought to be regarded as what they are, namely theories seeking to explain the nature of international law from a certain doctrinal perspective. This essentially suggests that no substantive implication can be drawn from a monist or dualist premise. Conceived as statements of substantive law, both premises remain empty postulates until backed up by a relevant substantive legal argument.[116]

It is further suggested that neither a dualist nor a monist premise can be chosen to the exclusion of the other. On a broader scale, this recalls the structure of 'ascending' and 'descending' legal arguments revealed by Koskenniemi's now well-known critical analysis of international legal argument.[117] To retain legitimacy, a legal argument cannot be only normative (descending), or only based on fact (ascending).[118] While a further discussion of this critique is beyond the scope of the present book, it is suggested that it carries a comparable insight in relation to monist (prima facie descending) and dualist (prima facie ascending) premises imposed on the substantive law of state contracts. As a claim about the content of substantive law, both a singularly monist and a singularly dualist premise

admettre que le souscripteur ou le possesseur de titres s'est volontairement placé dans la même situation que le national et que, par conséquent, les garanties sont uniquement celles que fournit le droit constructif interne'.

113 In the words of Lillich, international law is considered a 'brooding omnipresence' always available to achieve a 'just resolution' of the dispute, Lillich (1994) 92.

114 *American Independent Oil Co (AMINOIL) v State of Kuwait* (Award, 1982) 21 ILM 976, para 90.

115 See Jennings (1965) 128; and Leben (2003) 261.

116 This is also recognised by representatives of both perspectives, see eg Kelsen (1945) 387; and Lauterpacht, 'International Law and the Law of the State' in E Lauterpacht (ed), *International law: being the collected papers of Hersch Lauterpacht* Vol I (Cambridge, 1970) 151, 152–3; and compare Fitzmaurice, below n 119.

117 Koskenniemi, *From Apology to Utopia: The Structure of International Legal Argument* (Reissue with new Epilogue) (Cambridge University Press, Cambridge, 2006).

118 See eg *ibid*, 17 et seq.

are doomed to fail. Monist and dualist perspectives realistically encapsulate complementary aspects intrinsic to the structure of international law in its relationship to municipal law. Dualist theory emphasises the state-centred quality of international law; its basis in state consent, and a notion of sovereignty as its main structural aspect. Conversely, monist theory emphasises the openness and intrinsic teleology of international law; it's ultimate concern with certain aims and interests transcending municipal law, and its functional justification as a response to these concerns, from a perspective superior to individual municipal laws.

Two propositions of particular relevance to the question of applicability can be extracted from this. First, international law must be conceived as inherently open, in the sense that it is potentially applicable in relation to any issue.[119] In this respect, monism with a primacy of international law must be accepted as formal principle (ie from the perspective of international law). This means that the 'vertical' applicability of international law to a state contract cannot be dismissed simply for the reason that international law is presumed to apply only to states. Ultimately this depends on a construction of the individual rule or principle involved. This is essentially the position articulated by Lauterpacht in the *Norwegian Loans* case. In other words, in order to determine whether international law applies, it is necessarily prima facie applicable. Secondly, accepting the notion that international law is prima facie applicable does not, however, necessarily mean it has anything substantial to say. A contract is not automatically binding merely because international law applies to it as a legal fact. Clearly, whether a state is bound by a contractual commitment made to a foreign investor depends on the applicable rules and standards of international law. As I discuss in the next section, it is, moreover, possible to consider the dualist premise (such as it is refined and conceptualised by Kelsen) to encapsulate an important structural premise of the vertical applicability of international law. It recognises that an individual or private entity is not a legal subject equal to a state, and insists on the still singular position of states as representatives of a municipal legal system based on internal sovereignty.

3.4 THE APPLICABILITY OF INTERNATIONAL LAW TO STATE CONTRACTS—A RECONCEPTUALISATION

That international law may apply to a contract between a state and an investor does not mean that the contract is necessarily disconnected from municipal law and host state sovereignty. In this section I discuss how, on

[119] See also to this effect, from a dualist perspective, Fitzmaurice (1957) 59: '[T]here is of course, in the ultimate sense, nothing which cannot be governed by international law—that is, nothing in the relations between States, which is not capable of being so governed'.

the contrary, the applicability of municipal law is an important premise of international investment law, which is intrinsic to the very structure of international law. In relation to contractual commitments to private investors, this has two aspects. First, although it has been held that international law is formally applicable to determine any issue, it is conceivable that the relevant rule of international law may be that a contractual commitment is fundamentally governed by the state's own municipal law. The notion that individuals and private entities lack international capacity is persistent in international doctrine; could it be that it has a substantive basis in a concrete rule of international law? I argue that it has, and that this rule is sovereignty conceived as empowerment of municipal law. Secondly, I argue that while this conditions the modality of application of international law to state contracts, it does not exclude it. A number of distinct standards of international law 'pierce the sovereign veil', both to protect distinct contractual positions, and to be invoked by an investor without the participation of its home state. To the extent that such standards protect interests created by contractual commitments, an investor acquires individual rights under international law by virtue of the contract. In the following, I discuss municipal sovereignty as a structural premise of the applicability of international law to individual rights, before I discuss and conceptualise the incidence of individual rights under current rules and standards of international law.

A. Sovereignty as Co-ordinating Principle—the Complementary Roles of Municipal and International Law

The fundamental structure of international law is premised on its function as a law between sovereign states, each of which sustains its own municipal legal system. International law thus presupposes a distinction between municipal and international law, and two distinct domains; an international domain primarily, or even exclusively, regulated by international law, and a municipal domain primarily regulated by municipal law.[120] The role of international law in relation to the latter is prima facie confined to delimitation of a legitimate sphere of jurisdiction. Within this sphere, municipal law is free to operate, although subject to state responsibility insofar as other substantive requirements of international law are disregarded.[121] This distinction between municipal and inter-

[120] Kelsen (1945) 349.

[121] Kelsen expresses this as follows, *ibid*, 350–51: 'The States . . . remain competent, even under international law, to regulate in principle all matters which can be regulated by an order limited in its territorial sphere; but they retain this competence only insofar as international law does not regulate a particular subject matter. The fact that a subject matter is regulated by international law has the effect that it can no longer be regulated arbitrarily by national law'.

national law constitutes a structural premise of the modality of application of international law to any subject-matter recognised as falling within the sphere of municipal authority. As reflected in the framework and practice of international arbitration in relation to contract claims against states, this can be seen to confirm that international law is not and cannot be invoked as a contract law per se, but may still apply to contractual rights. The main aspect of this is how municipal law is customarily considered to be initially applicable in cases dealing with contract claims under international law.

(i) The Initial Applicability of Municipal Law

As shown above, positions based on a strict dualist premise have rejected the applicability of international law to a state contract for the reason that private entities are considered to lack international legal capacity. As an implicit claim about substance, this assumes something more however, namely that international law contains a specific rule blocking or excluding its own applicability.[122] The rule upon which this is necessarily premised is sovereignty, conceived as the residue of legal authority over individuals and juridical persons within a certain territory. It is an essential corollary of sovereignty, as a structural premise of international law, that the immediate legal position of a private subject will depend initially on a municipal law, namely that produced by the domestic sovereignty to which it is presently subjected.[123] While this clearly does not exclude the applicability of international law, as shown above, it represents a significant co-ordinating principle suggesting a complementary relationship between municipal and international law.

The main significance of this is that it provides a conceptual basis for explaining how municipal law is initially applicable to define the essential subject-matter of an investment dispute, ie, the protected investment, whereas the role of international law in this picture is primarily to supplement and condition municipal law. To this effect it also justifies the hybrid function assumed by arbitral tribunals dealing with investment disputes, as described in chapter two above, where practice attests to the complimentary roles of municipal and international law in relation to contractual

[122] Some writers expressly claim that this is the case, see eg Sornarajah, 'Power and Justice in Foreign Investment Arbitration' (1997) 14 *J Int'l Arb* 103, 110 (claiming that international law applies only by way of a *renvoi* to municipal law); and Wolff, 'Some Observations on the Autonomy of Contracting Parties in the Conflict of Laws' (1959) 35 *Trans Grot Soc* 143, 150–51: 'The choice of the law of nations as the proper law of the contract includes the choice of all compulsory rules of that legal system, and therefore also the provision that only states can be subject to public international law'. See also for further references Paasivirta, 'Internationalization and Stabilization of Contracts versus State Sovereignty' (1989) 60 *BYIL* 315, 318.

[123] Kelsen (1945) 348.

investment disputes. The same is also expressly reflected in a number of the older cases dealing with contract claims. The classical statement is that of the Permanent Court in the *Serbian Loans* case, where it held that 'any contract which is not a contract between States in their capacity as subjects of international law is based on the municipal law of some country'.[124] As developed in other cases, this does not necessarily entail that international law is excluded; merely that it does not apply prima facie in the capacity of a contract law.[125] As such this does not of course exclude the possibility that international law could come to elevate a contractual obligation as such into an international obligation. This is, however, a substantive question, where it would be necessary to show such effect to follow, not merely from the contract's own preference for international law, but from a distinct rule of international law to this effect. One example of such a rule could be the so-called 'umbrella clause', often included in bilateral investment treaties. However, as I will come back to in chapter five below, not even this really excludes the initial applicability of some municipal contract law to interpret and determine the content of the contractual obligation involved. In the next section I turn to how arbitral practice has confirmed and developed this as a formal distinction, in order to co-ordinate the complementary roles of municipal and international law when determining whether a breach of contract also constitutes a breach of treaty.

(ii) The Distinction between Breach of Contract and Breach of Treaty

Since a contract relates primarily and initially to municipal law, the assumption would be that a breach of contract does not, of itself and as such, constitute a breach of international law. Not surprisingly, this is also reflected in arbitral practice. In the otherwise conflicting decisions in *SGS v Phillippines* and *SGS v Pakistan*, the two arbitral tribunals agreed it was 'well established'[126] that 'a violation of a contract entered into by a State with an investor of another State, is not, by itself, a violation of international law'.[127] This underlies a distinction between 'breach of contract' and 'breach of treaty' developed and repeatedly confirmed in investment

[124] *Serbian Loans case*, PCIJ Rep Series A No 20 (1929) 5, 41, (see above n 91 for full quotation); see also *Anglo-Iranian Oil Company case (United Kingdom v Iran)* [1952] ICJ Rep 93, 111–12.

[125] *Norwegian Loans case*, separate opinion of Lauterpacht [1957] ICJ Rep 9, 37 (see above note 91); *Saudi Arabia v Arab American Oil Company (Aramco)* (Award, 1958) 27 ILR 117, 165 et seq.

[126] *SGS Societe Generale de Surveillance SA v Republic of the Philippines* (Decision on Jurisdiction, 2004) para 122.

[127] *SGS Societe Generale de Surveillance SA v Islamic Republic of Pakistan* (Decision on Jurisdiction, 2003) para 167; see also Amerasinghe, *Local Remedies in International Law* 2nd edn (Cambridge University Press, Cambridge, 2004) 107 et seq.

treaty practice.[128] The distinction itself is generally agreed upon, but its significance has received two partly contradictory responses in practice. In practice, this primarily has significance with respect to the existence of jurisdiction, as I come back to in chapter four below.[129] The underlying fundamental issue is, however, whether investment treaty standards may be conceived to attach independently to the contract as a legal fact, ie whether international law applies directly, and how, to the contract.

One approach relies on a systemic separation of municipal and international law as legal orders, where the former is held to determine contractual issues with definitive effect for international law. A central case is *Azinian v Mexico*. The issue was whether the tribunal had jurisdiction under NAFTA[130] over a claim based on rescission of a concession contract. According to the claimant, this rescission constituted an unlawful expropriation of its contractual rights. The tribunal refused to assume jurisdiction over the claim, however, because the contract had been deemed invalid under Mexican law by the competent Mexican courts.[131] Two basic points can be extracted from the award. On the one hand, the tribunal distinguished a breach of the contract from a breach of NAFTA, holding that the latter did not in principle apply to a mere breach of contract as such.[132] On the other hand, the tribunal held that the contract, as an object of treaty protection, was also necessarily defined by its express submission to Mexican law and the jurisdiction of the Mexican courts:

> How can it be said that Mexico breached NAFTA when the Ayuntamiento of Naucalpan purported to declare the invalidity of a Concession Contract which by its terms was subject to Mexican law, and to the jurisdiction of the Mexican courts, and the courts of Mexico then agreed with the Ayuntamiento's determination?[133]

According to the tribunal, the issue was consequently not whether the rescission as such was unlawful, since this was determined by municipal law, but whether the decision of the competent Mexican courts constituted a denial of justice. The tribunal, in other words, refused to cast itself as an

[128] See eg *Bayindir Insaat Turizm Ticaret ve Sanayi AS v Islamic Republic of Pakistan* (Award, 2009) para 133 et seq; *Duke Energy Electroquil Partners and Electroquil SA v Republic of Ecuador* (Award, 2008); *TSA Spectrum de Argentina SA v Argentina* (Award, 2008) para 56, *Jan de Nul v Egypt* (Decision on Jurisdiction, 2006) para 79, *Bayindir v Pakistan* (Decision on Jurisdiction, 2005) para 148, *Impregilo v Pakistan* (Decision on Jurisdiction, 2005) para 210, *Salini Costruttori SpA v Hashemite Kingdom of Jordan* (Decision on Jurisdiction, 2004) para 152, *Joy Mining Machinery Ltd v Arab Republic of Egypt* (Award on Jurisdiction, 2004) para 71 et seq, *Occidental v Ecuador* (Award, 2004) para 51, *SGS v Philippines* (Decision on Jurisdiction, 2004) para 122 and *SGS v Pakistan* (Decision on Jurisdiction, 2003) para 147.

[129] See particularly sections 4.4 and 4.5.

[130] North American Free Trade Agreement (1994).

[131] *Azinian et al v United Mexican States* (Award, 1999) para 95 et seq.

[132] *ibid*, para 87: '[T]he Claimants' fundamental complaint is that they are the victims of a breach of the Concession Contract. NAFTA does not, however, allow investors to seek international arbitration for mere contractual breaches'.

[133] *ibid*, para 96.

appellate court, and instead held that it could only consider whether the court process as such was in breach of the NAFTA; beyond this it was bound to accept the judgment of the courts on the merits with respect to the validity of the concession contract under municipal law.[134] In adopting this second premise, the *Azinian* tribunal implicitly assumed that the contract, as a legal fact, had no independent legal consequences under the treaty, being a legal relationship systemically belonging to municipal law. In other words, its significance under international law was exhaustively determined by municipal law as conceived by the competent municipal courts.

This latter premise has also been accepted in a number of other decisions. In *Vivendi v Argentina*, in a decision which was later annulled for this reason, the initial tribunal dismissed the claims under the treaty on the merits, because they were contingent on contractual issues that had to be resolved by the local courts vested with jurisdiction under the contract.[135] Similarly, in *SGS v Pakistan*, the tribunal relied on what it apparently conceived as a split of functions between municipal courts and investment treaty tribunals; the former having exclusive competence over contract claims, the latter over treaty claims.[136] This line of cases in reality invokes a dualist premise reminiscent of the decision of the PCIJ in the *Serbian Loans* case, assuming that a state contract 'relates exclusively to a nexus of municipal law'.[137]

In a second and eventually more forceful tendency of case law a similar distinction between breach of contract and breach of treaty has, however, been relied on to contradict this premise of mutual exclusivity.[138] The distinction was first conceptualised as follows by the Annulment Committee in the *Vivendi* case:

> A state may breach a treaty without breaching a contract, and vice versa . . . whether there has been a breach of the BIT and whether there has been a breach of contract are different questions. Each of these claims will be determined by reference to its own proper or applicable law—in the case of the BIT, by

[134] *ibid*, para 99: 'Even if the Claimants were to convince this arbitral tribunal that the Mexican courts were wrong with respect to the invalidity of the Concession Contract, this would not per se be conclusive as to a violation of NAFTA. More is required; the Claimants must show either a denial of justice, or a pretence of form to achieve an internationally unlawful end'.

[135] *Compania de Aguas del Aconquija (CAA) and Compagnie Generale des Eaux (CGE) (later Vivendi) v Argentine Republic* (Award, 2000) paras 77–8.

[136] *SGS v Pakistan* (Decision on Jurisdiction, 2003) para 146 et seq.

[137] *Serbian Loans case*, PCIJ Rep Series A No 20 (1929) 5, 20.

[138] See eg *Jan de Nul v Egypt* (Decision on Jurisdiction, 2006) para 79; *Eureko BV v Poland* (Award, 2005) para 92 et seq; *Bayindir v Pakistan* (Decision on Jurisdiction, 2005) para 148; *Impregilo v Pakistan* (Decision on Jurisdiction, 2005) para 210; *Occidental Exploration and Production Company v Republic of Ecuador* (Award, 2004) para 51; and *SGS v Philippines* (Decision on Jurisdiction, 2004) para 122.

> international law; in the case of the Concession Contract, by the proper law of the contract.[139]

The committee related this to the general principle of state responsibility that whether an act is internationally wrongful is governed by international law, and not affected by the characterisation of the same act as lawful by internal law (or vice versa).[140] Crucially, by relying on this distinction, the annulment committee presupposed that only the question of contractual responsibility as such belonged to municipal law. But it also held that 'a state may breach a treaty without breaching a contract'.[141] In other words, the conceptual distinction between a breach of contract and a breach of treaty did not entail that the significance under the treaty of a contractual commitment was exhausted by its characterisation under municipal law by the municipal courts. For the annulment committee it meant precisely the opposite. The significance of the contract, and an eventual disregard or violation of it, under the relevant treaty standards was necessarily governed by 'the ICSID convention, by the BIT and by applicable international law'.[142] The committee did not dispute that municipal law 'might be relevant—as municipal law is often relevant—in assessing whether there has been a breach of the treaty'.[143] It admitted that interpretation of the contract might be crucial to determine whether a breach of treaty had occurred, necessitating recourse to its applicable municipal law.[144] But—and this is the main point of the decision—municipal law then is applicable by virtue of the relevant international legal standard, and is therefore also conditioned and determined by it. The opposite conclusion would effectively have entailed a primacy of municipal law over international law in matters prima facie governed by municipal law. This latter understanding has subsequently been relied on by an increasing number of tribunals to assert jurisdiction, without awaiting resolution based on contractual jurisdiction clauses in so far as parallel treaty claims are maintained.[145] What this tendency primarily emphasises is the purely formal and conceptual bearing of the distinction between breach of contract and breach of treaty. That municipal law applies does not mean that international law is precluded (and vice versa).

[139] *Compania de Aguas del Aconquija (CAA) and Vivendi v Argentine Republic* (Decision on Annulment, 2002) paras 95–6.

[140] This fundamental rule is set out in Art 3 of the International Law Commission (ILC) Draft Articles on Responsibility of States for Internationally Wrongful Acts, which reads as follows: 'The Characterization of an act of a State as internationally wrongful is governed by international law. Such characterization is not affected by the characterization of the same act as lawful by internal law'.

[141] *CAA and Vivendi v Argentina* (Decision on Annulment, 2002) para 95.

[142] *ibid*, para 102.

[143] *ibid*, para 101.

[144] *ibid*, para 105.

[145] I revert to this issue in chapter four below, see section 4.5.

International law may apply to condition and sanction municipal law, and municipal law may apply to complete and fill out the standards set by international law.

This formal significance of the distinction between 'breach of contract' and 'breach of treaty' can be phrased in terms of the doctrine of state responsibility, as signifying essentially that a contract does not itself constitute a 'primary obligation' under international law.[146] If a rule follows from a treaty or customary law, it constitutes ipso facto an international obligation, and a breach entails prima facie responsibility. No such status is afforded to a 'vertical' state contract under international law. What is material where a state disregards its contractual commitments to an investor is whether this violates a distinct rule, or obligation, under international law that is separate from and external to the contract.[147] As I return to in chapter five, there are a number of common treaty standards and certain generally accepted standards of customary law, which all have a bearing on performance of contractual undertakings of states toward foreign investors, all of which, however, generally seem to require something more than a breach of contract in order to apply. What follows is that it is usually meaningless to apply the law of state responsibility to a breach of contract as such. The law of state responsibility is not directly linked to the contract as obligation, only indirectly as a legal fact taken into account by the relevant international obligation.[148]

B. Do the Applicable International Rules and Standards create Individual Rights?

Another question is whether international rules and principles that do apply to foreign investment in general, and contractual commitments in particular, can be considered to create individual rights. The rules in

[146] The concept of primary obligations is derived from the distinction made by the ILC in its work on state responsibility, between primary and secondary rules. 'Primary rules' are the obligations incumbent on states to act or not to act in a certain manner. 'Secondary rules' are the rules of general application which shapes and conditions state responsibility. The law of state responsibility, as it is envisaged by the ILC, does not in itself contain primary rules but consists of these so called secondary rules of responsibility, see generally Bodansky and Crook, 'Symposium: The ILC's State Responsibility Articles, Introduction and Overview' (2002) 96 *AJIL* 773; and Crawford, *The International Law Commission's Articles on State Responsibility* (Cambridge University Press, Cambridge, 2002) 2, and 14–16.

[147] Cf ILC Draft Art 12: 'There is a breach of an international obligation by a State, when an act of that state is not in conformity with what is required of it by that obligation, regardless of its origin or character'.

[148] Cf *Noble Ventures v Romania* (Award, 2005) para 53: '[I]n normal circumstances *per se* a breach of a contract by the State does not give rise to direct international responsibility on the part of the State. This derives from the clear distinction between municipal law on the one hand and international law on the other, two separate legal systems (or orders) the second of which treats the rules contained in the first as facts'.

question are those stipulated by investment treaties, and certain generally accepted principles of customary law formerly and conventionally invoked by states exercising diplomatic protection. In an investment treaty context this problem has been framed as a question of the capacity in which an investor is acting when invoking protection under a treaty; whether it acts in a derivate (or representative) capacity of its home state, or instead acts in its own direct and immediate capacity.[149] In the context of customary law conventional orthodoxy more radically excludes any possibility of an investor invoking an international right, due to the often quoted '*Mavromattis* formula', which maintains that a state when exercising its diplomatic protection in reality is claiming its own right.[150] In the following I argue that this is mostly based on a fiction. I maintain two things; first, that the original modality of rules under both investment treaties and traditional customary law is to apply directly to individual investors in their relations with states; secondly, that the residual rights and interest of the home state in the matter are fundamentally derivative of this initial applicability to the vertical relationship between the state and individual private interest in question. Moreover, I maintain that this is the case both with regard to the law developed under investment treaties and under customary international law.

(i) Investment Treaty Standards

The standard model of an investment treaty is a catalogue of substantive treatment standards, which may be invoked by individual investors through specified arbitration procedures. It can hardly be denied that such treaties, at least in a conditional sense, grant individual rights to investors, in the sense of protecting the interests of individual investors also being individually entitled to invoke the protection afforded.[151] At the same time, no firm conclusions can be drawn from this alone as to whether the rights are 'direct' or 'derivative',[152] in other words, whether the 'original' right or interest is that of the investor or the state. This would seem to be largely a terminological question, where both perspectives in theory are possible.[153] The few relevant cases have espoused both perspectives. Thus, in *Loewen v USA* the tribunal held that the treaty (NAFTA) established 'a field of international law where claimants are permitted for convenience

[149] Douglas (2003) 162 et seq.

[150] *Mavromattis Palestine Concessions case (Greece v United Kingdom)*, PCIJ Rep Series A No 2 (1924) 4, 12.

[151] See eg also to this effect Douglas (2003) 181; Spiermann, 'Individual Rights, State Interests and the Power to Waive ICSID Jurisdiction under Bilateral Investment Treaties' (2004) 20(2) *Arb Int'l* 179; and Paulsson, 'Arbitration without Privity' (1995) 10 *ICSID Rev-FILJ* 232.

[152] The terminology is that of Douglas (2003) 160 et seq.

[153] Douglas (2003) 168.

to enforce what are in origin the rights of Party states'.[154] Contrastingly, in *CMS Gas v Argentina*, the tribunal held that the prevalent characteristic was that of 'recognizing the direct right of action by individuals'.[155] In respect of what is, primarily, a theoretical question and a matter of perspective, not much is in any case gained by perusing the differing views set forth by arbitral tribunals. What matters, is obviously the substance of the law such as it has grown out of a distinct mechanism for enforcement of claims under investment treaties.

In one sense rights under investment treaties are surely derivative or conditional, since applicability of the treaty to individual investors is determined by a criterion of nationality.[156] Moreover, a treaty entered into by two states can also normally be abrogated or suspended by the same states, and is subject to the ordinary principles of international law regulating the mutuality of rights and obligations between states. At least until a claim has been submitted to arbitration, one must assume that the individual rights are subject in principle to the normal continuance of the treaty relationship between the two states involved.[157] In another and more fundamental sense, however, the derivative scheme fails to explain

[154] *Loewen Group Inc v USA* (Award, 2003) para 233: 'Rights of action under private law arise from personal obligations (albeit they may be owed by or to a State) brought into existence by domestic law enforceable through domestic tribunals and courts. NAFTA claims have a quite different character, stemming from a corner of public international in which by treaty, the power of States under that law to take international measures for the correction of wrongs done to its nationals has been replaced by an *ad hoc* definition of certain kinds of wrong, coupled with specialist means of compensation. These means are both distinct from and exclusive of the remedies for wrongful acts under private law . . . It is true that some aspects of the resolution of disputes arising in relation to private international commerce are imported into the NAFTA system . . . But this apparent resemblance is misleading. The two forms of process, and the rights which they enforce, have nothing in common. There is no warrant for transferring rules derived from private law into a field of international law where claimants are permitted for convenience to enforce what are in origin the rights of Party states'.

[155] *CMS Gas Transmission v Argentina* (Decision on Jurisdiction, 2003) para 45: 'Diplomatic protection has been dwindling in current international law, as the State of nationality is no longer considered to be protecting its own interest in the claim but that of the individual affected. To some extent diplomatic protection is intervening as a residual mechanism to be resorted to in the absence of other arrangements recognizing the direct right of action by individuals. It is precisely this kind of arrangement that has come to prevail under international law, particularly in respect of foreign investment, the paramount example being that of the 1965 Convention'.

[156] See generally about the nationality criterion, Douglas (2003) 171 et seq.

[157] In principle this invokes two sets of rules which may condition the continued applicability of the treaty; on the one hand the law of treaties as reflected in the Vienna Convention of 1961, commonly held to manifest customary law, and on the other hand the various circumstances precluding wrongfulness under the general law of state responsibility, as set out in the ILC Draft Arts 20 et seq. Especially in relation to the latter, it is nevertheless not obvious that they apply without modification to rules such as investment treaties, which aim to protect individual and private interest. For instance, it is far from obvious that a home state may consent to suspend application of an investment treaty in relation to an individual investor of its nationality (at least if the investor has relied on the treaty), or even less so that breaches of an investment treaty may be justified as countermeasures.

essential characteristics of the rights and obligations under investment treaties. An investor has, as a rule, full functional control over its eventual claim, and is free to decide whether to pursue it or not by instituting arbitral proceedings. This has been held to apply even over the express opposition of the home state.[158] Moreover, the interests encompassed by the rights in question are those of individual investors alone. It is an evident aspect of both the substantive primary obligations involved, and the secondary standards of compensation relative to their breach, that once applicable they apply solely by reference to the individual circumstances of each investor. In this functional sense the legitimate interest of the home state is clearly a residual interest, derivative of and conditioned by the individual interests of investors. This is expressly reflected in the scheme contemplated under the ICSID Convention.[159] According to article 27, the right to exercise diplomatic protection is suspended where the state and the foreign investor have mutually consented to international arbitration.[160] The individual mechanism thus takes precedence over the normal rights of the state, which are only preserved to the extent that the other state fails to comply with a final award. To this extent, the right of the individual investor, although initially acquired by virtue of its derivative status as a national of its home state, is unquestionably its own direct, immediate and irrevocable right.

(ii) Customary Law and the 'Vattelian Fiction'—A Reconceptualisation

In contrast to the position under investment treaties, the orthodox position under international law is that customary law invokes an exclusive right of states,[161] without any correlation to substantive rights, or even interests, of individuals.[162] It may initially be noted that this stands in contrast to the quite consistent arbitral practice examined in chapter two, where international law was held to apply to contractual disputes between states and private companies without any basis in a treaty. My point here is not to claim that this in itself necessarily constitutes evidence of the applicability

158 See further and with references to relevant practice, Douglas (2003) 170.

159 Convention on the Settlement of International Disputes between States and Nationals of Other States (1965).

160 The ICSID Convention (1965) Art 27 para 1: 'No Contracting State shall give diplomatic protection, or bring an international claim, in respect of a dispute which one of its nationals and another Contracting State shall have consented to submit or shall have submitted to arbitration under this Convention, unless such other Contracting State shall have failed to abide by and comply with the award rendered in such dispute'.

161 See eg for a classical expression of this, Oppenheim (Lauterpacht (ed)), *International Law: A Treatise* 8th edn (Longmans, London, 1955) 640: '[I]f individuals who possess nationality are wronged abroad, it is, as a rule, their home State only and exclusively which has a right to ask for redress, and these individuals themselves have no such right'.

162 See also to this effect Douglas (2003) 167: 'A state bringing a diplomatic protection claim is not an agent of its national who has a legally protected interest at the international level; the state is rather seeking redress for the breach of an obligation owed to itself'.

of the norms in question. Essentially I maintain that this practice is supported by a constructive reading of the substantive norms involved, in other words, that the relevant norms of customarily international law apply by virtue of their own content to individual investors.

The orthodox position was formulated as follows in the *Mavromattis Palestine Concessions* case to defuse the objection that the dispute before it was not an inter-state dispute:

> By taking up the case of one of its subjects and by resorting to diplomatic action or international judicial proceedings on his behalf, a state is in reality asserting its own rights—its right to ensure, in the person of its subjects, respect for the rules of international law.[163]

The proposition that the state asserts its own right by protecting its national also echoes in the later practice of the ICJ, which reiterated and confirmed it both in the *Nottebohm* case[164] and the later *Barcelona Traction* case.[165] Its justification and rationale are commonly thought to be provided by what is often termed the 'Vattelian fiction';[166] the notion that an injury to a citizen constitutes a separate and direct injury to its home state.[167] This sees the material injury from the state's perspective of the individual as an object of its material interest.[168] While it is open to discussion whether it should be characterised as a fiction for this reason, it can however at least be shown that this proposition does not reflect the substantive rationale of the law involved. A closer scrutiny reveals precisely the opposite, namely that it provides a means to rationalise how a state may reasonably be conceived to have a legitimate interest even if it has no direct and material interest in the subject-matter. Two alternative angles can be invoked in this regard: first, that this is intrinsic to the

[163] *Mavromattis Palestine Concessions case*, PCIJ Rep Series A No 2 (1924) 12.

[164] *Nottebohm case (Liechtenstein v Guatemala) (second phase)* [1955] ICJ Rep 4, 24: 'Diplomatic protection and protection by means of international judicial proceedings constitute measures for the defence of the rights of the state'.

[165] *Case concerning the Barcelona Traction Light and Power Company (Belgium v Spain)* [1970] ICJ Rep 3, 44: '[W]ithin the limits prescribed by international law, a State may exercise diplomatic protection by whatever means and to whatever extent it thinks fit, for it is its own right that the state is asserting. Should the natural or legal persons on whose behalf it is acting consider that their rights are not adequately protected, they have no remedy in international law'.

[166] See eg Lillich, *The Human Rights of Aliens in Contemporary International Law* (Manchester University Press, Manchester, 1984) 1; and *Report of the International Law Commission on its 53rd session* (2001, A/56/10) 510.

[167] See eg Schwarzenberger (1957) 141; and for a more contemporary perspective Douglas (2003) 165: 'The notion of a vicarious injury caused to the state of the national is essential to the rationalization of diplomatic protection because it transforms damage done to private interests into an international delict opposable by one sovereign state to another. This transformation is not a procedural quirk or fiction as is sometimes maintained, but is instead fundamental to the compatibility of diplomatic protection with the traditional principles of state responsibility for international wrongs'.

[168] Schwarzenberger (1957) 141.

original rationale provided by the 'Vattelian fiction' itself, and secondly, that it is implicit to the rational core of the individual norms invoked.[169]

The notion that an injury to a national also constitutes a separate injury to its home state originates with Vattel, who classically explained the basic rationale of diplomatic protection as follows:

> Quiconque maltraite un citoyen offense indirectement l'Etat, qui doit protéger ce citoyen. Le souverain de celui-ci doit venger son injure, obliger, s'il le peut, l'agresseur à une entière réparation ou le punir, puisque autrement le citoyen n'obtiendrait point la grande fin de l'association civile, qui est la sûreté.[170]

The orthodox interpretation is that Vattel here asserts that injury to a national constitutes a *direct* injury to the state, and that the state therefore has a right under international law.[171] The statement has even been given the following translation into English:

> Anyone who mistreats a citizen directly offends the state. The sovereign of that State must avenge its injury, and if it can, force the aggressor to make full reparation or punish him, since otherwise the citizen would simply not obtain the main goal of civil association, namely, security.[172]

But on a closer reading, this is not what is said in the original French. The French statement expressly says that maltreatment of a national is an *indirect* offence to the state, 'which has to protect its national'. Reading this as a 'because' and not as a 'therefore' transforms the statement from an empty postulate into a sophisticated philosophical rationale of diplomatic protection.[173] In other words, an injury to an individual national constitutes an indirect offence to the state, 'because the state has to protect its national'. This understanding links the right of the state to exercise diplomatic protection under international law with the functional justification of the state as a social institution, namely to protect and maintain the interests of its individual constituent members. The state has an interest because an injury to its national strikes at the core of the state's ultimate function and justification as a social institution, to protect its citizens. Thus on a closer scrutiny, Vattel does not postulate that a state is directly and materially injured in the person of its national. Instead he rationalises why injury to an individual concerns its home state, even though it suffers no material injury. That diplomatic protection aims to protect the interests of individual citizens is not disputed by Vattel; it is his premise.

169 This is not an original observation of mine, see especially Bennouna, *Preliminary Report on Diplomatic Protection* (1998, A/CN.4/484) 7 et seq.

170 Vattel, *Le droit des gens—ou principes de la loi naturelle appliqués a la conduite et aux affaires des nations et des souverains*, Vol 1, Livre 2, §71, 47–8 Nouvelle Édition (Librairie de Guillaumin, Paris, 1863).

171 See eg Borchard (1916) 352; and Douglas (2003) 165–7; see also Bennouna (1998) 5 et seq.

172 See Bennouna (1998) 5; and Douglas (2003) 166–7.

173 This may also be the real tenor of Douglas' argument, see Douglas (2003) 166–7.

It is of course entirely possible that international law could have created its own Vattelian fiction based on a different understanding. A conceivable perspective might have been that foreign investment is essentially an extension of the national economy of the home state of the investor into another state; the investor being an agent of the national economy, and his capital, although invested abroad, a part of the national wealth.[174] This perspective is not devoid of reality. A state may, clearly, be directly, heavily and materially affected by interference with the investments of its national economic entities. It is conceivable that this could have been the singular interest protected by diplomatic protection. I show in what follows that this is nevertheless not the case. The substantive law clearly reveals an underlying rationale aimed at defending individual interests as such, irrespective of the state's own material interest.

This may be illustrated with two of the cases most often relied on to uphold the orthodox view, the *Barcelona Traction* case and the *Chorzow Factory* case. The first case concerned a claim by Belgian shareholders against Spain in relation to the alleged unlawful liquidation of a company in which they held a majority share. Belgium relied on the fact that the substantive economic interest in the company was Belgian, claiming a right to exercise diplomatic protection on that basis. This was rejected by the court, for the reasons, first, that the direct injury was suffered by the company and not the individual shareholders,[175] and, secondly, that the company was incorporated in Canada and therefore had to be considered a Canadian company.[176] The company had no significant ties with Canada beyond registration. The court nevertheless relied on an essentially formal criterion of nationality, which was also termed decisive for the right to exercise protection.[177] Both this and the concrete reasoning of the court suggest that the substantive rationale of the rule was held implicitly to be protection of the individual interest of the company.[178] If the real concern

[174] See to this effect Seidl-Hohenveldern (1999) 26; and the separate opinion of Judge Gros in *the Barcelona Traction case* [1970] ICJ Rep 3, 269: '[T]he economic world today exhibits phenomena of State intervention in and responsibility for the economic activity of the subject within the national territory or abroad which are so frequent and thoroughgoing that the separation of the interest of the individual from that of the state no longer corresponds to reality'.

[175] *Barcelona Traction case* [1970] ICJ Rep 3, 35–7.

[176] *ibid*, 42–5.

[177] *ibid*, 46.

[178] *ibid*, 46: 'The opinion has been expressed that a claim can accordingly be made when investments by a State's nationals abroad are thus prejudicially affected, and that since such investments are part of a State's national economic resources, any prejudice to them directly involves the economic interest of the state . . . Governments have been known to intervene in such circumstances not only when their interests were affected, but also when they were threatened. However, it must be stressed that this type of action is quite different from and outside the field of diplomatic protection. When a State admits into its territory foreign investments or foreign nationals it is, as indicated in paragraph 33, bound to extend to them the protection of the law. However, it does not thereby become an insurer of that part of another State's wealth which these investments represent. Every investment of this kind

had been the material interests of the state, the right ought naturally to have been shaped accordingly, and there would have been no reason to identify a single claimant state.[179] Similarly, in the *Chorzow Factory* case, the court took the following view of what was the governing principle of reparation:

> It is a principle of international law that the reparation of a wrong may consist in an indemnity corresponding to the damage which the nationals of the injured state have suffered as a result of the act which is contrary to international law.[180]

Thus, the injury for which reparation was due was equiparated with the individual interest. However, since by this one might be led to think that it was in fact the right of the national which was asserted, the court proceeded to clarify:

> The reparation due by one state to another does not however change its character by reason of the fact that it takes the form of an indemnity for the calculation of which the damage suffered by a private person is taken as the measure. The rules of law governing the reparation are the rules of international law in force between the two states concerned, and not the law governing the relations between the State which has committed a wrongful act and the individual who has suffered damage. Rights or interests of an individual the violation of which rights causes damage are always in a different plane to rights belonging to a State, which rights may also be infringed by the same act. The damage suffered by an individual is never therefore identical in kind with that which will be suffered by a state; it can only afford a convenient scale for the calculation of the reparation due to the state.[181]

This does not change the fact that the material interest involved, as a matter of principle, was considered a reflection of the individual interest.[182] Indeed, the crux of the court's reasoning would seem to be that the state interest was different in kind precisely because it was derivative of the individual interest, ie being as such by nature indirect.

While this shows that the right of diplomatic protection, such as it is recognised in practice, is a right to represent the individual interests of nationals in relation to other states, it does not in itself necessarily mean that the individuals have 'rights'. What it shows is that the underlying substantive norms are directly aimed at individual interests. In this respect it is possible to make a distinction between being the beneficiary of a right, and having the capacity to assert it.[183] To say that an obligation is

carries certain risks. The real question is whether a right has been violated, which right could only be the right of the state to have its nationals enjoy a certain treatment guaranteed by general international law'.

179 *ibid*, 48–50.

180 *Case Concerning the Factory at Chorzów (Germany v Poland)* (Indemnity), PCIJ Series A No 17 (1928) 27.

181 *ibid*, 28.

182 See also Bennouna (1998) 7, with further references.

183 Lauterpacht, *International Law and Human Rights* (Stevens & Sons, London, 1950) 27.

not owed to its beneficiary is theoretically possible, but it also neglects the immediate reality which it addresses. It is equally possible to say that the beneficiary indeed has a 'right', while accepting that it does not come accompanied with the capacity to assert it.[184] It all depends on the definition of 'right'. In the context of investment protection, this nevertheless suggests that the norms involved apply in a substantive sense to the relationships between states and investors. This is an implicit assumption of the provision on applicable law in the ICSID Convention. Article 42 stipulates that a tribunal shall apply 'such rules of international law as may be applicable.'

This article obviously does not make international law applicable in substance; it is intelligible only if seen as declarative of a presupposition to the effect that certain rules are substantively applicable. The same assumption was made explicit by the ICJ in the *Barcelona Traction* case:

> [W]hether in the form of multilateral or bilateral treaties between States, or in that of agreements between States and companies, there has since the Second World War been considerable development in the protection of foreign investments. The instruments in question contain provisions as to jurisdiction and procedure in case of disputes concerning the treatment of investing companies by the States in which they invest capital. Sometimes companies are themselves vested with a direct right to defend their interests against States through prescribed procedures.[185]

The court thus assumed that individual rights would exist ipso facto by virtue of direct access to an international remedy, created either by treaty or, significantly, by 'agreements between States and companies'.

What this all entails is that application to individuals as beneficiaries is not merely an incidental, but an intrinsic aspect of the customary substantive law underlying diplomatic protection. This means that nothing about the substantive content of the law necessarily confines it to that mechanism.[186] It suggests, as with investment treaties, that the home state interest is equally satisfied, or even more so, if an individual investor can make its own claim, since its interest is merely residual and derivative.[187] The

[184] See to this effect the *La Grande case (Germany v USA)* (Judgment (ICJ), 2001) para 77: '[T]he court concludes that article 36, paragraph 1, creates individual rights, which, by virtue of article I of the Optional Protocol, may be invoked in this Court by the national State of the detained person. These rights were violated in the present case'.

[185] *Barcelona Traction case* [1970] ICJ Rep 3, 47.

[186] A parallel is provided by the development of international criminal law pursuant to World War II. The Nuremberg tribunal invoked the functional rationale of the existing rules, to reject that they could only create state responsibility (as different from individual), cf *Re Goering and others* (1946) 13 ILR 203, 221: 'Crimes against international law are committed by men, not by abstract entities, and only by punishing individuals who commit such crimes can the provisions of international law be enforced'.

[187] Higgins (1994) 52.

corollary is, however, that the question of applicability in a concrete arbitration ultimately comes to depend on the tribunal's competence to apply international law. This has no easy either/or answer. It largely depends on the arbitral procedure invoked, and on the municipal legal order relied on to corroborate the arbitration. This is the subject of the next section.

3.5 THE AUTHORITY OF ARBITRAL TRIBUNALS TO APPLY INTERNATIONAL LAW

The competence, or authority, vested in an arbitral tribunal is, in terms of substantive law, closely linked to the basis of its jurisdiction. In investment treaty arbitration, where jurisdiction is based directly on a provision for investor-state arbitration in an investment treaty, the authority to apply international law is self-evident. It is inherent in the primary objective of the arbitral reference, to secure effective enforcement of the investment treaty of which it is part. The situation is different where the basis of jurisdiction is a contract between the state or state entity and a foreign company. Also here it is, however, necessary to distinguish between two different arbitral regimes. The basis of the arbitral tribunal's authority is markedly different pursuant to, on the one hand, the ICSID Convention, and on the other hand, ordinary commercial arbitration subject to the 1958 New York Convention on the Recognition and Enforcement of Foreign Arbitral Awards. This is, however, not to say that the content of the authority vested in arbitral tribunals in the end necessarily needs to be conceived so very differently, whichever is the basis of arbitral authority in the given case, as I show in the following.

A. The ICSID Convention Article 42—Inherent Competence to Apply International Law

As already discussed in chapter two above, the competence of an ICSID tribunal to apply international law follows directly from article 42 of the ICSID Convention, set out in the following language:

> The Tribunal shall decide a dispute in accordance with such rules of law as may be agreed by the parties. In the absence of such agreement, the Tribunal shall apply the law of the Contracting State party to the dispute (including its rules on the conflict of laws) and such rules of international law as may be applicable [188]

This initially makes clear that the jurisdiction of an ICSID tribunal is not limited to claims based on international law; it is not even its main function

[188] ICSID Convention (1965) Art 42(1).

to apply and interpret international law. According to the scheme originally conceived under the convention, an ICSID tribunal exercises a function similar to ordinary international commercial arbitration. A typical dispute thus envisaged would entail construction and interpretation of a contract between a state and an investor, naturally invoking primarily contract law and other relevant rules of municipal law affecting the contract. In this picture, international law mainly supplements and conditions the otherwise applicable law, and does not constitute the main frame of reference.

At the same time, this does not mean that the application of international law is secondary or conditioned in any sense by the applicable municipal law. The appropriate relationship of municipal to international law was expressed in this sense as follows by the final tribunal in *AMCO v Indonesia*:

> If there are no relevant host-state laws on particular matter, a search must be made for the relevant international laws. And, where there are applicable host-state laws, they must be checked against international laws, which will prevail in case of conflict. Thus, international law is fully applicable, and to classify its role as 'only' 'supplemental and corrective' seems a distinction without a difference. In any event, the tribunal believes that its task is to test every claim of law in this case first against Indonesian law, and then against international law.[189]

Thus, municipal law (or the contract) is primary in the sense that it provides the starting point for the legal resolution, but international law is primary in the sense that it provides the final test and prevails in case of conflict. In this sense an ICSID tribunal fulfills the role of an authoritative judicial organ under international law co-terminously with its role as a substitute for municipal courts in the manner of an international commercial arbitral tribunal.

Incidentally, one might have thought that this conception of the powers of arbitral tribunals as extending to municipal as well as to international law, would be limited to an ICSID arbitration based on an actual consent from the state relating to the individual dispute, where the analogy to international commercial arbitration is most appropriate. Prima facie, it might seem natural to consider the main function of an investment treaty tribunal, in contrast, to lie in interpretation and application of international law. However, recent arbitral practice has confirmed that the conception of the arbitral tribunals as having a distinctly hybrid function also applies to investment treaty arbitration under ICSID. In *Wena Hotels v Egypt*, the respondent state claimed annulment, on the ground that the tribunal had failed to apply Egyptian law as the primary law applicable.

[189] *AMCO Asia Corp v Republic of Indonesia* (Award (Resubmitted case), 1990) 1 ICSID Rep 509, para 40.

The annulment committee held that no law could claim exclusive prima facie application, distancing itself from former more absolutist views to either effect:

> Some of these views have in common the fact that they are aimed at restricting the role of international law highlighting that of the host State. Conversely, the view that calls for a broad application of international law aims at restricting the role of the law of the host State. There seems not to be a single answer as to which of these approaches is the correct one. The circumstances of each case may justify one or another solution . . . What is clear is that the sense and meaning of the negotiations leading to the second sentence of Article 42 (1) allowed for both legal orders to have a role. The law of the host State can indeed be applied in conjunction with international law if that is justified. So too international law can be applied by itself, if the appropriate rule is found in this other ambit.[190]

In other words, the tribunal could not picture itself solely as either a municipal law or an international law tribunal. Similarly, in *CMS Gas v Argentina*, the tribunal was faced with a dispute over a gas privatisation arrangement, involving a gas transmission contract and licence, and municipal regulation governing the privatisation. Relying on the *Wena Hotel* case, the tribunal explained its own approach as follows:

> More recently, however, a more pragmatic and less doctrinaire approach has emerged, allowing for the application of both domestic law and international law if the specific facts of the dispute so justifies. It is no longer the case of one prevailing over the other and excluding it altogether. Rather, both sources have a role to play . . . Indeed, there is here a close interaction between the legislation and the regulations governing the gas privatization, the License and international law, as embodied both in the Treaty and in customary international law. All of these rules are inseparable and will, to the extent justified, be applied by the Tribunal.[191]

This approach is, not co-incidentally, quite similar to the contractual arbitration practice relating to investment agreements maturing after the Libyan oil arbitrations. Tribunals are envisaged to apply and authoritatively interpret *both* municipal law *and* international law as independently applicable legal norms and standards.[192] The Libyan oil arbitrations and the other cases propounding the strong internationalisation formula ostensibly provide an exception to this. On a closer reading, a quite similar approach is, however, also implicitly attested by most of the internationalisation cases themselves. It is striking that none of these actually applied international law as a contract law, commonly referring instead

[190] *Wena Hotels Ltd v Arab Republic of Egypt* (Decision on Annulment, 2002) paras 39–40.
[191] *CMS Gas v Argentina* (Award, 2005) paras 116–17.
[192] See especially *AMINOIL v Kuwait* (Award, 1982) para 10.

to 'general principles of law' where merely contractual issues were involved.[193]

This approach, where arbitral tribunals assume powers to authoritatively determine issues belonging under both municipal and international law, stands in some contrast to the conventional learning on the status of municipal law before international tribunals. The conventional view maintains that rules of municipal law are facts to be established by evidence, and not law to be determined by interpretation.[194] A main feature of investment arbitration is that it deals with both municipal law and international law from the perspective of an integrated and hybrid process. The reason is that investments, as private rights, initially only exist under and by virtue of municipal legal rules. In order to do justice to the various interests deserving of protection under international law, in line with the purpose of the relevant international rules and standards, there is a need to be able to give independent and authoritative appreciation of these as legal facts initially determined under municipal law. Contractual commitments are obviously a prime example of this, as I also will come back to, especially in chapter five below. To this effect the conceived function of an investment arbitral tribunal is fundamentally comparable with that of a municipal court applying international law from its perspective in municipal law, while being at the same time in a sense the inverse of this. The difference is that an arbitral tribunal based on the ICSID Convention and/or an investment treaty is disconnected from the municipal legal process of the host state, and operates as an authoritative tribunal fundamentally sanctioned by international law. Elevating this to the level of fundamental principle means that an ICSID tribunal shall envisage itself in the role of the host state's municipal courts, but from a perspective of monism with a primacy of international law.

While this shows how an ICSID tribunal is ordinarily expected to apply international law, a different issue is whether an ICSID tribunal necessarily, and always, has such competence. In other words, may the parties exclude this competence by their express choice of a municipal law as the exclusively applicable law? While jurisdiction under ICSID is based on the treaty, it also requires the mutual consent of the parties in respect of the individual dispute. The authority of the arbitral tribunal thus appears as a function of the Convention and the contractual consent at the same

[193] See eg *Sapphire v NIOC* (Award, 1963) 35 ILR 136, 175; *Petroleum Development Ltd v Sheikh of Abu Dhabi* (1951) 18 ILR 144, *Petroleum Development (Qatar) Ltd v Ruler of Qatar* (1951) 18 ILR 161; *Ruler of Qatar v International Marine Oil Company Ltd* (1953) 20 ILR 534; *Texaco v Libya* (Award (Merits), 1977) (1979) 53 ILR 389, paras 49–52; and *Saudi Arabia v Aramco* (Award, 1958) 27 ILR 117, 169.

[194] Cf the classical statement of the PCIJ in *Certain German Interests in Polish Upper Silesia*, PCIJ Rep Series A No 7, 19: 'From the standpoint of international law and of the Court which is its organ, municipal laws are merely facts which express the will and constitute the activities of States, in the same manner as do legal decisions or administrative measures'.

time. This dual basis of authority creates a certain tension with respect to the authority of tribunals operating under the Convention, especially as it relates to the competence to apply international law. Thus, according to article 42, the arbitral tribunal shall primarily follow the choice of law of the parties, and only by default refer to international law as a supplement and corrective to the municipal law of the host state. This would indeed suggest that the parties can exclude application of international law through an exclusive choice of municipal law.[195]

This nevertheless stands in stark contradiction to some of the more fundamental premises of ICSID as a remedy based on international law.[196] Giving effect to an exclusive choice of municipal law would effectively turn it into a 'Calvo clause' under international law. The issues decided by an ICSID award are *res judicata*, and would therefore constitute an effective waiver of the investor's general rights under international law. This would contradict the relatively consistent tendency, reflected in the practice of old claims commissions, of refusing any such absolute effect to Calvo clauses.[197] It has also been rejected accordingly in more recent ICSID practice. This has instead emphasised the inherent competence and duty of ICSID tribunals to apply international law. The general concerns involved were explained as follows by the annulment committee in *AMCO v Indonesia*:

> [A]pplicable norms of international law must be complied with since every ICSID award has to be recognized, and pecuniary obligations imposed by such award enforced, by every Contracting State of the Convention (Article 54 (1), Convention). Moreover, the national State of the investor is precluded from exercising its normal right of diplomatic protection during the pendency of the ICSID proceedings and even after such proceedings, in respect of a Contracting State which complies with the ICSID award (Article 27 (1), Convention). The thrust of Article 54 (1) and of Article 27 of the Convention makes sense only under the supposition that the award involved is not violative of applicable principles and rules of international law.[198]

In *SPP v Egypt*, the tribunal employed a somewhat convoluted and formalistic argument to the same effect. Holding that international law applied to lacunae in municipal law, it extended this concept so as to

[195] Though less than conclusively, a few cases would seem to assume that an exclusive choice of municipal law should be given effect, see eg *Aucoven v Venezuela* (Award, 2003) paras 99–100; and *Liberian Eastern Timber Corporation (LETCO) v Republic of Liberia* (Award, 1986) 26 ILM 647, 657–8. See also to this effect Maniruzzaman: 'State Contracts in Contemporary International Law: Monist versus Dualist Controversies' (2001) 12(2) *EJIL* 309, 327; and Nassar: 'Internationalization of State Contracts: ICSID, the Last Citadel' (1997) 14 *J Int'l Arb* 183, 200–202.

[196] See also Leben (2003) 282 et seq.

[197] See eg the *North American Dredging Company Case* (US-Mexican General Claims Commission, 1926), IV RIAA, 26, 27; and see generally Summers, 'The Calvo Clause' (1932–33) 19 *Va L Rev* 459.

[198] *AMCO v Indonesia* (Decision on Annulment, 1986) 1 ICSID Rep 509, para 21.

encompass every issue where municipal law would lack capacity to conclusively regulate an issue.[199] This it framed as a rebuttal of a common premise of the parties, namely that application of international law depended on whether the first or second sentence of article 42(1) applied. The tribunal essentially held instead that it was bound to apply international law in any case where 'international law is violated by the exclusive application of municipal law'.[200]

It is nevertheless hard to deny that an exclusive choice of municipal law—at least to the extent that it expressly excludes the applicability of international law and no contrary interpretation is possible—reveals a certain tension between the consensual basis of jurisdiction, reflected in the concept of party autonomy in the first sentence of article 42, and the nature of ICSID arbitration as an international remedy. The dilemma of the tribunal is that if the state has consented to arbitration only on the condition of an exclusive choice of municipal law, there is no effective consent by the state to have the arbitral proceedings function as an international remedy. But, at the same time, it is inconceivable to vest an award disregarding applicable rules of international law with *res judicata* effect under international law and require it to be enforced by every member state. This mirrors the tension between excess of competence and the public policy exception in the general framework of international commercial arbitration, which shall be reviewed below. More forcefully than is the case for international commercial arbitration, however, the system and purpose of the ICSID Convention militates in favour of an inherent power (and duty) of ICSID tribunals to apply international law. The minimum standards of international law protecting foreign investment constitute the international *ordre public* restricting party autonomy in an ICSID context. Thus, a tribunal should rather decline jurisdiction than disregard rules of international law, at least insofar as they are mandatory and not subject to waiver by their own terms.

B. Application of International Law by Commercial Arbitral Tribunals

To consider an ordinary commercial arbitral tribunal vested with the same authority to apply international law as an ICSID tribunal may at first sight

[199] *SPP v Egypt* (Award, 1992) 3 ICSID Rep 189, paras 78–80: '[T]he Parties' disagreement as to the manner in which Article 42 is to be applied has very little, if any, practical significance . . . [E]ven accepting the Respondent's view that the parties have implicitly agreed to apply Egyptian law, such an agreement cannot entirely exclude the direct applicability of international law in certain situations. The law of [Egypt], like all municipal legal systems, is not complete or exhaustive, and where a lacuna occurs it cannot be said that there is agreement as to the application of a rule of law which *ex hypothesi*, does not exist. In such case, it must be said that there is absence of agreement' and, consequently, the second sentence of Article 42(1) would come into play'.

[200] *ibid*, para 84.

appear deeply problematic and even paradoxical. State contract arbitration depends on municipal law for recognition and enforcement, and to this effect finds its source of authority in municipal law. This would seem to presuppose a competence necessarily also circumscribed by municipal law. However, as already examined in chapter two above, such inhibitions are not reflected by arbitral practice relating to state contracts. Though controversial in theory, practice has relied on the concept of internationalisation as a proven basis for application of international law. I argue in the following that this should be seen as an assumed competence on the basis of an express or implicit choice of law, and that this is implicitly accepted, and even to some extent required, under the 1958 New York Convention on the Recognition and Enforcement of Foreign Arbitral Awards.

(i) Choice of Law as Express and Implied Powers

According to the internationalisation formula discussed above, international law can be made applicable to a state contract by virtue of the parties' choice of law. A not uncommon practice is accordingly to include choice of law clauses in investor-state contracts, referring to international law alone or in combination with general principles of law or a municipal law.[201] As held above (section 3.2), it is reasonably clear that a choice of international law is meaningless from a conflict of laws perspective. In contrast to municipal law, international law does not function by virtue of alternative spheres of jurisdiction, but conditions and controls municipal law and state power from a vantage point of all-encompassing primacy. Does this mean that a choice of international law serves no purpose? This would seem counter-intuitive in view of the considerable practice of arbitral tribunals placing reliance on an express or implied choice of international law.[202] A common feature of the cases is that they justify application of international law by referring to the express or implicit choice of law of the parties. According to one of the leading textbooks on the conflict of laws, it is 'clear that parties may choose public international law to govern the substance of their contract'.[203] The practical phenomenon that

[201] See generally Leben, 'La théorie du contrat d'état et l'évolution du droit international des investissements' (2003) 302 *Recueil des Cours* 197, 264.

[202] See *the Lena Goldfields case,* published in *The Times* (London), 3 September 1930 in Nussbaum, 'The Arbitration between the Lena Goldfields Ltd. and the Soviet Government' (1950–51) 36 *Cornell Law Quarterly* 31, para 22; *Sapphire v NIOC* (Award, 1963) 35 ILR 136, 172–6; *BP v Libya* (Award, 1973), 53 ILR 297, 327; *Texaco v Libya* (Award, 1977) 53 ILR 389, paras 31–5; *Revere Copper v OPIC* (Award, 1978) 56 ILR 258, 272–9; *LIAMCO v Libya* (Award, 1977) 62 ILR 141, 171 et seq; *AMINOIL v Kuwait* (Award, 1982) 21 ILM 976, para 8; *Deutsche Schachtbau- und Tiefbohrgesellschaft mbH v R'as Al Khaimah (United Arab Emirates) and Rakoil* (Award, 1982), (1989) 14 YbCA 111, para 18; *Elf Aquitaine v NIOC* (Award, 1982), (1986) 11 *YbCA* 97; *Wintershall et al v Qatar* (Award, 1988) 28 ILM 795 (p 8 of the award).

[203] Dicey, Morris, and Collins (eds), *The Conflict of Laws* (Sweet & Maxwell, London, 2000) 606.

arbitral tribunals apply international law pursuant to a choice of law cannot be neglected.

It must still be held that this choice of law does not invoke party autonomy in any sense as a conflicts rule.[204] What it does instead, it may be suggested, is to vest the arbitral tribunal with the necessary competence to apply applicable rules of international law.[205] The choice of international law must in other words be construed as an express authorisation of the tribunal to take account of relevant rules of international law. The ICSID Convention provides the most appropriate analogy here, insofar as issues relating to the applicability of international law are concerned. It is telling that article 42 on the applicable law is contained in a section on the 'powers and functions of the tribunal'. This provision clearly is not an ordinary conflicts rule, presuming as it does that rules of international law may be prima facie applicable, not to mention that it expressly refers to the conflicts rules of the host state. As held above, this envisages the ICSID arbitral tribunal in a role comparable to a national court, but with the additional independent authority to take account of international law, ie not dependent on whether the international rule is recognised by the municipal law in question.

Arbitral practice relating to a choice of international law in state contracts can be seen in a similar perspective. It is illustrative that no case seems actually to have applied international law as an alternative to a municipal contract law or 'general principles of law'.[206] One commentator, having examined the cases concerned, has noted that internationalisation or delocalisation of contracts commonly has been held to invoke 'general principles of law' to address traditional contractual issues such as interpretation and non-performance, whereas traditional rules of public international law primarily have been invoked to address issues transgressing the contract itself, such as annulment or expropriation of the contract through subsequent legislation.[207] It would, in other words, seem that 'the general principles of law' have been invoked as a kind of delocalised contract law (or *lex mercatoria*), which is not part of international law as such (ie as the law applicable to states in their capacity as such, whether in their relations to other states or to the exercise of power over individuals and private entities).

The three Libyan oil concession cases are illustrative here. While there are considerable differences in the respective approaches of the tribunals, all upheld the essential scheme of the concessions in one respect. It was agreed that the *lex contractus* in the first place was Libyan law in so far as

[204] See Cordero Moss (1999) 73 et seq.

[205] See also to this effect Paasivirta, *Participation of States in International Contracts* (Lakimiesliiton Kustannus, Helsinki, 1990) 114 et seq.

[206] With the possible exception of *BP v Libya* (Award, 1973) 53 ILR 297, see eg 328–9.

[207] See Paasivirta (1990) 105 et seq.

compliant with international law, and that the applicability of general principles of law, as the alternative *lex contractus*, was prompted only by such non-compliance.[208] Even in these archetypes of the internationalisation formula, the actual role conceived for international law in its conventional sense was thus one of conditioning and control of the relevant municipal law, rather than as a *lex contractus* itself. This is clearly how its role has come to be conceived in more recent state contract practice, where international law has been applied as complementary to the *lex contractus*, from the vantage point of the arbitral tribunal's transnational perspective, as a necessary part of the applicable municipal law in the manner stipulated under the ICSID Convention.[209]

Conceptualising a choice of international law as a competence vested in the arbitral tribunal, entails a different perspective on the conditions and consequences of such a choice of law. First, the choice of law is not merely a factor connecting the relationship at hand to an appropriate applicable law; the tribunal exceeds the very basis of its authority if it disregards the parties' directions as to choice of law. Secondly, this perspective may also explain and justify why tribunals to such a large extent have seen themselves competent to apply international law without any basis in an express choice of law.[210] It provides a perspective for understanding this as an affirmation by an arbitral tribunal of the autonomous source of its authority, and of its own relative autonomy from any particular municipal law. By applying international law, the arbitral tribunal asserts the international aspect of its jurisdiction, conceived in a sense as an implied power assumed by virtue of its perceived purpose as a judicial remedy independent of the state's own legal system.

From another angle however, this also means that a choice of law clause fundamentally delimits the reach of the state's consent to arbitration as a remedy under international law, or as put by Fox, 'a loss of liberty, an acceptance of constraints from which it is otherwise free'.[211] It means that an explicit and exclusive choice of the host state's law might have to be given effect by the tribunal, to the exclusion of otherwise applicable rules of international law. If the choice of law clause explicitly envisages exclusive application of the host state's municipal law, it effectively entails that the state has not consented to create an international remedy. This arguably requires that the exclusion of international law is explicit, however; a mere

[208] *BP v Libya* (Award, 1973) 53 ILR 297, 329; *Texaco v Libya* (Award (Merits), 1977) 53 ILR 389, 461–2; and *LIAMCO v Libya* (Award, 1977) 62 ILR 141, 173.

[209] See especially *AMINOIL v Kuwait* (Award, 1982) 21 ILM 976, para 6; and *SPP v Egypt* (Award (ICC), 1983) 3 ICSID Rep 46, 64–5.

[210] See especially *the Lena Goldfields case* (Award, 1930), *The Times* (London), 3 September 1930 in Nussbaum: 'The Arbitration between the Lena Goldfields Ltd. and the Soviet Government' (1950–51) 36 *Cornell Law Quarterly* 31, para 22; *Sapphire v NIOC* (Award, 1963) 35 ILR 136, 172–6; and *Revere Copper v OPIC* (Award, 1978) 56 ILR 258, 272.

[211] Fox (1988) 4.

choice of the host state's law without more is not sufficient. Something else would contradict the presumption clearly displayed in arbitral practice, in favour of considering application of international law as an *implied power* of arbitral tribunals. An intersecting concern is, however, that a failure to apply relevant rules of international law can also render the resultant award unenforceable as a violation of international public policy, as I come back to immediately below.

(ii) Limitations on Judicial Review

The effectiveness of an assumed competence to apply international law is largely ensured by the limited availability of judicial review and challenge of awards. To the extent that a tendency is cemented in arbitral practice, and is beyond the possibility of review and challenge by municipal courts, it is implicitly validated as effective law. The assertion in arbitral practice of competence to apply international law may to this effect be considered implicitly validated and sanctioned by the New York Convention.[212] The main rule under the Convention is that valid awards must be given effect without review on the merits.[213] Thus, the crucial issue is whether recognition and enforcement of an arbitral award can nevertheless be refused for the reason that it is based on international law (ie assuming that awards rendered against states in investment disputes in general are arbitrable under the *lex fori*). Under the system of the Convention, this could be based on one of two possible exceptions: either (i) that the tribunal by applying international law exceeded its competence; or (ii) that giving effect to the award for this reason could be held to violate the public policy of the *lex fori*.[214]

With respect to the first ground it is unlikely to provide a plausible defence. Application of international law pursuant to an express choice by the parties is clearly not an excess of competence in the sense contemplated by the New York Convention. The relevant provision requires that the award contain 'decisions on matters beyond the scope of the submission to arbitration'.[215] In relation to choice of law, this suggests that a municipal court may not superimpose its own views on the effects or validity of a choice of law made by the parties. It can only refuse to give effect to an award which manifestly disregards the parties' own choice of law, although even this is not unproblematic, since it may be hard to distinguish from a review on the merits.[216] On the other hand, it is conceivable

[212] See also the European Convention on International Commercial Arbitration (Geneva, 21 April 1961) 484 UNTS 364, Art VII.
[213] Van den Berg (1981) 269.
[214] The New York Convention article V, 2(b).
[215] The New York Convention article V, 1(c).
[216] See generally Cordero Moss, 'Can an Arbitral Tribunal Disregard the Choice of Law made by the Parties?' (2005) 1 *Stockholm Int'l Arb Rev* 1; but see also Cordero Moss (1999) 276 and 289.

that an application of international law without any basis in a choice of law by the parties could be set aside on this basis, if it were seen to disregard the intention of the parties. This would principally seem to be the case if the contract contains an exclusive choice of municipal law. A lack of express choice of international law would not seem to be sufficient, however. A municipal court cannot disregard the considerable practice supporting application of international law as an implicit competence,[217] especially where attempts have been made to neutralise the municipal law of the state party. The presumption is that arbitration in such circumstances is meant to constitute an effective remedy beyond the control of the host state. To set aside an award for application of international law in such circumstances would be to disregard the reasonable intentions of the parties. A tribunal's assertion of implicit competence to apply international law is thus unlikely to justify challenge of an award. ICSID practice nevertheless suggests that an award could be set aside for manifestly ill-founded application of specific rules alleged to be part of international law, if no plausible effort is made to verify the existence of the rules under accepted sources of international law.[218]

With respect to the second ground, relating to public policy, it will usually be equally unfounded. It is difficult to contemplate a state maintaining that an effective vindication of international law ipso facto should violate its public policy. It might not be in the state's interest to let its courts entertain certain types of claims against other states, and for this reason jurisdiction over such claims not deemed arbitrable under the *lex fori* may be refused. But if the claim is allowed, the application by an arbitral tribunal of relevant rules of international law is not in itself a matter of arbitrability.

Nor can awards based on international law be met with the objection sometimes launched against awards based on notions of 'abstract justice', or certain varieties of 'equitable principles', that it is not based on 'law' in the proper sense. Under English law it is deemed a principle of public policy that an arbitral award will not be recognised and enforced unless based on 'a fixed and recognisable system of law'.[219] Thus, an award will be refused if based on, 'some different criterion such as the view of the individual arbitrator or umpire on abstract justice or equitable principles'.[220] But it has also been held that this will not prevent recognition of

[217] See eg to this effect the decision of the English Court of Appeal in *Deutsche Schachtbau- und Tiefbohrgesellschaft mbH v R'as al-Khaimah Oil Co and Shell International Petroleum Co Ltd* [1987] 3 WLR 1023, 1035 (as quoted below n 222).

[218] See especially *Klöckner Industrie-Anlagen GmbH and others v United Republic of Cameroon* (Decision on Annulment, 1985) 114 ILR 243, 265.

[219] *Orion Compania Espanola de Seguros v Belfort Maatschappij voor Algemene Verzekgringeen*, [1962] 2 Lloyds Rep 257, 264.

[220] *ibid*, 264.

awards based on international law.[221] Moreover, in a later case, granting leave to enforce the above mentioned *Deutsche Schachtbau* award, the Court of Appeal even held that the tribunal's application of 'internationally accepted principles of law governing contractual relations' did not bar subsequent enforcement of the award under English law.[222]

More generally, it is recognised that the public policy exception needs to be interpreted narrowly.[223] The legislative history and purpose of the Convention, as well as subsequent municipal court practice, suggest that what is contemplated by the public policy exception is a narrower and more restricted concept than national *ordre public*.[224] US courts have confined the public policy exception under the New York Convention to 'the forum State's most basic notions of morality and justice'.[225] A more general trend is to distinguish between 'international' and 'domestic' public policy, restricting the public policy exception under the Convention to the former.[226] This clearly militates against the possibility of refusing enforcement of an award applying international law, even if held to violate particular public policies in the forum state opposed to international law. In a sense there is no better manifestation of true and objective international public policy than international law. While the international public policy exception as construed under the Convention is not the same as and clearly extends beyond international law,[227] this nevertheless suggests that it is close to absurd to consider the application of international law by an arbitral tribunal as contrary to international public policy under the Convention. On the contrary, it can plausibly be argued that failure to apply international law (if relevant) usually will constitute a legitimate ground for refusing recognition and enforcement of an award.

[221] *ibid*, 264: '[I]t may be, though perhaps it would be unusual, that the parties could validly agree that a part, or the whole of their legal relations should be decided by the arbitral tribunal on the basis of a foreign system of law, or perhaps on the basis of principles of international law; for example, in a contract to which a Sovereign State was a party'.

[222] *Deutsche Schachtbau- und Tiefbohrgesellschaft mbH v R'as al-Khaimah Oil Co and Shell International Petroleum Co Ltd* [1987] 3 WLR 1023 (CA) 1035: 'I am left in no doubt that the parties intended to create legally enforceable rights and liabilities and that the enforcement of the award would not be contrary to public policy. That only leaves the question whether the agreestems of law. I can see no basis for concluding that the arbitrator's choice of proper law—a common denominator of principles underlying the law of the various nations governing contractual relations—is outwith the scope of the choice which the parties left to the arbitrators'.

[223] See eg Van den Berg (1981) 359 et seq.

[224] *ibid*, 361–2.

[225] *Parsons & Whittemore Overseas Inc. v Societe Generale de L'Industrie du Papier* (RAKTA) 508 F 2d 969 (1974) 974.

[226] Van den Berg (1981) 362 et seq.

[227] Cordero Moss (1999) 308 et seq.

4

Procedural Aspects—Jurisdiction and Enforceability

4.1 INTRODUCTION

IN CHAPTER TWO above I argued that the crucial factor compelling the novel application of international law to state contracts was the subjection of the contracts to international arbitration, and thereby to a legal process detached from the municipal legal sphere. In this chapter I examine the legal criteria under which arbitral tribunals assert such authority over contract claims, as well as the main elements of the procedural framework shaping and giving force to this authority. Two relatively distinct but nevertheless interdependent procedural elements can be seen to shape and condition the authority exercised by international arbitral tribunals over contract claims against states, namely jurisdiction and enforceability. The following explores the conceptualisation of these procedural elements in arbitral practice, first under ordinary commercial arbitration based on a contractual consent (section 4.2), and secondly under the parallel regime specific to investment disputes established by the ICSID Convention (section 4.3). Following this, I address the specific jurisdictional issues arising in respect of so-called investment treaty arbitration, ie arbitration where the basis of jurisdiction is not an individual agreement with the host state but an investment treaty between the host state and the investor's home state (section 4.4). Finally, I address the question of overlapping jurisdiction, in the situation where a claim appears to be covered both by investment treaty arbitration and a contractual jurisdiction clause (section 4.5).

4.2 INTERNATIONAL COMMERCIAL ARBITRATION—DETACHING ARBITRAL AUTHORITY FROM MUNICIPAL LAW

Arbitration based on state contracts has long been employed as a remedy to invoke international law in investor-state relationships. As described in chapter two, this developed as a practice independently of international conventions and before the advent of modern investment treaty arbitration.

The ICSID Convention, which I will return to in the next part, provides an internationally sanctioned basis for jurisdiction in state contract disputes, but is limited to instances where there is an express reference to ICSID, and both the host state and the national state of the investor are members of the Convention. ICSID is, however, not the only viable option for contractual arbitration of investment disputes. Ordinary commercial arbitral mechanisms may be used in state contracts as a defence against political risk, especially in large-scale infrastructure projects involving state entities.[1] In this section I show how the procedural and conceptual framework of international commercial arbitration applies to provide an effective remedy in the context of international law and foreign investment. My main objective is to show how this comes about through assumption of international authority, together with its effective recognition—and consequent confirmation—by municipal law. The result is a process ultimately, although to a varying extent, dependent on municipal law, but still operating in relative independence of any particular municipal law, and functioning by virtue of this as an international remedy that may be invoked to enforce an investor's contractual rights pursuant to a state undertaking. This has two main aspects, the first being the assumption of jurisdiction based on an independent concept of party autonomy partly rooted in international law, and the second how this is implicitly buttressed through the municipal enforceability of the resultant arbitral awards.

A. Rooting Party Autonomy in International Law

In order for arbitration to constitute an efficient remedy against a state, it is necessary to assume a concept of party autonomy, which, at least to some extent, is independent of the underlying contract and the municipal law of the host state. This appears necessary in two main categories of circumstances: (i) where the action complained of is a government repudiation of the very contract in which the undertaking to arbitrate is contained; and (ii) where the state maintains that it did not have capacity under its own law to submit to binding arbitration. As I come back to in the next part of this chapter, the ICSID Convention uses an independent notion of consent rooted in the Convention itself to address this. However, as I show in this section, a comparable notion has also evolved under the general framework of international commercial arbitration, and is slowly finding its roots in international law.[2] Conceptually linked to the general principle of 'separ-

[1] See eg Inadomi, 'Independent Power Projects in Developing Countries: Legal Investment Protection and Consequences for Development' (Phd Thesis, University of Oslo, 2005, unpublished) 74.

[2] See also generally Gaillard and Savage (eds), *Fouchard, Gaillard, Goldman on International Commercial Arbitration* (Kluwer, The Hague, 1999) 197 et seq.

ability' in international commercial arbitration, a notion of party autonomy independent of any municipal law and partly rooted in international law has evolved as the source of authority in the international arbitral process.

(i) The Doctrine of Separability and Irrevocability of Consent[3]

When a claim has been brought against a state under an arbitration clause in a contract it is sometimes claimed by the state that the submission to arbitration has been made ineffective by its own subsequent repudiation of the contract. For a tribunal to claim jurisdiction in this circumstance, the crucial question is whether, and how, the arbitration clause may survive the alleged termination of the contract in which it is contained. How can the tribunal claim authority to decide that the state had a right to terminate the contract, without also undermining its own authority? In commercial arbitration the solution to this is generally provided by the doctrine of the 'autonomy' or 'separability' of the arbitration clause together with the doctrine of 'competence competence'.[4] The former maintains that consent to arbitration is severable from, and may survive the invalidity of, the main contract containing it. The latter maintains that an arbitral tribunal has prima facie competence to determine its own competence. The shared rationale is to give effect to the intention of the parties and facilitate the effectiveness of arbitration in the face of allegations of invalidity.[5] This is a general principle of international commercial arbitration, which is recognised by most significant arbitration rules and standards as well as national legislations.[6] In state contract arbitration, this has achieved another and more fundamental significance, however, as a separate basis for continued jurisdiction in the face of state repudiation or annulment of the contract containing the arbitration clause. Two cases in particular provide what are now classical expressions of this movement from separability to irrevocability.[7]

[3] See also Schwebel, *International Arbitration: Three Salient Problems* (Grotius Publications, Cambridge, 1987) 1–60.

[4] See generally Redfern and Hunter (with Blackaby and Partasides), *Law and Practice of International Commercial Arbitration* (Sweet & Maxwell, London, 2004) 251; and Fouchard, Gaillard, Goldman (1999) 197.

[5] See eg Schwebel (1987) 4.

[6] See eg Fouchard, Gaillard, Goldman (1999) 197, and Redfern and Hunter (2004) 251 et seq. The UNCITRAL Model Law of Arbitration, art 16(1), sets out the principle as follows: 'The arbitral tribunal may rule on its own jurisdiction, including any objections with respect to the existence or validity of the arbitration agreement. For that purpose, an arbitration clause which forms part of a contract shall be treated as an agreement independent of the other terms of the contract. A decision by the arbitral tribunal that the contract is null and void shall not entail *ipso jure* the invalidity of the arbitration clause'.

[7] The same assumption is also implicit in earlier cases where tribunals have exercised jurisdiction on the basis of arbitration clauses in contracts subsequently annulled by the respondent government. See eg *Lena Goldfields case* published in *The Times* (London), 3 September 1930, as reproduced in Nussbaum, 'The Arbitration between the Lena Goldfields

The first case is *Texaco v Libya*. Proceeding from the basis that a tribunal must determine its own jurisdiction (*competence competence*),[8] the arbitrator formulated the jurisdictional issue as follows:

> Supposing that the measures of nationalization could have had the effect of voiding the Deeds of Concession themselves, can this effect extend to the provisions of these Deeds relating to arbitration, and more specifically, to Clause 28 [the Arbitration Clause]?[9]

This was answered in the negative with reference to the principle 'of the autonomy or the independence of the arbitration clause'.[10] According to the arbitrator, the principle had 'the consequence of permitting the arbitration clause to escape the fate of the contract which contains it'.[11] Since, moreover, the contract itself provided for arbitration in case of termination,[12] this could not have the effect of depriving the tribunal of its jurisdiction.[13] By severing the arbitration clause from the rest of the contract to uphold jurisdiction, the tribunal effectively held the arbitration agreement not only to be independent of the rest of the contract, but also irrevocable and binding for the state irrespective of its subsequent repudiation.

The second case is *Liamco v Libya*, where the concept of irrevocability as a rule of international law was even more pronounced. While assuming that the initial capacity of the parties to submit to arbitration was confirmed by the municipal laws respectively applicable to them, the arbitrator then went on to discuss the effect of the undertaking under international law:

> It is widely accepted in international law and practice that an arbitration clause survives the unilateral termination by the state of the contract in which it is inserted and continues in force even after that termination. This is a logical consequence of the interpretation of the intention of the contracting parties, and appears to be one of the basic conditions for creating a favourable climate for foreign investment. This rule was adopted by decisions of the International Court

Ltd. and the Soviet Government' (1950–51) 36 *Cornell Law Quarterly* 31; *Losinger & Cie SA v Kingdom of Yugoslavia* PCIJ Series C No 78 (1936); *Sapphire International Petroleums Ltd v National Iranian Oil Company (NIOC)* (Award, 1963) 35 ILR 136, 166–7; *BP Exploration Co (Libya) Ltd v Govt of Libya* (Award, 1973) 53 ILR 297, 308; see also generally Delaume, 'State Contracts and Transnational Arbitration' (1981) 75 *AJIL* 784, 788.

[8] *Texaco Overseas Petroleum Co v Govt of Libya* (Award (Jurisdiction), 1977) 53 ILR 389, 404: 'It is for the Sole Arbitrator, and for him alone, to render a decision on his own jurisdiction by virtue of a traditional rule followed by international case law and unanimously recognized by the writings of legal scholars'.

[9] *ibid*, 407–8.

[10] *ibid*, 408.

[11] *ibid*, 408.

[12] *ibid*, 402, reproducing the relevant provision (clause 28, para 1 of the concession) as follows: 'If at any time *during or after* the currency of this Concession any difference or dispute shall arise . . .'

[13] *ibid*, 412.

of Justice (ex. in the *Ambatielos case* in 1952 and 1953) and of many arbitral tribunals (ex. in *Losinger & Co. v State of Yugoslavia*). Such decisions have confirmed the obligation of the State to arbitrate with a private party according to the terms of the contract despite the protest or default of the State and despite arguments that the agreement containing the arbitration clause had been terminated or come to an end.[14]

The arbitrator thus relied upon a supposed rule of international law to the effect that an arbitration agreement is binding and remains in force, independent of the fate of the contract of which it is a part, even its subsequent annulment by the state. This rule goes beyond the doctrine of severability as it is conceived by traditional arbitration rules and legislation. Its main significance is not that the arbitration agreement is separate from the rest of the contract, but that it is irrevocable once the state has first consented.

The significance of considering this a rule of international law may be illustrated by the *Himpurna* case, where this supposed rule of international law was considered by the tribunal to override the *lex arbitri*—in this case the municipal law of the host state. This case proceeded in an extraordinary manner. The Indonesian domestic courts issued injunctions against the proceedings (which concerned a claim of approximately US$ 4 billion), leading to the migration of the tribunal to The Hague to avoid what it saw as abusive exercise of court supervisory jurisdiction over the proceedings. The tribunal first held that government annulment of an undertaking to arbitrate had to be considered an 'abuse of rights' under international law, and therefore ineffective to restrain the proceedings.[15] It then refused to comply with the subsequent court injunction and discontinue the proceedings, considering the court injunction a 'denial of justice' under international law:

> The present arbitral tribunal considers that it is a denial of justice for the courts of a State to prevent a foreign party from pursuing its remedies before a forum to the authority of which the foreigner relied in making investments explicitly envisaged by that state . . . [A] state is responsible for the actions of its courts, and one of the areas of state liability in this connection is precisely that of denial of justice.[16]

The tribunal thus effectively held that both the Indonesian government and the Indonesian courts lacked authority under international law to restrain the proceedings, even though it did not dispute that the *lex arbitri* of the proceedings was rightfully Indonesian law. The implication of this argument is striking. The arbitral tribunal effectively cast itself as an

[14] *Libyan American Oil Co (LIAMCO) v Govt of Libya* (Award, 1977) 62 ILR 141, 178.

[15] *Himpurna California Energy Ltd (Bermuda) v PT (Persero) Perusahaan Listruik Negara (Indonesia)* (Award, 1999) (2000) 25 *YbCA* 13, paras 324–5.

[16] *ibid*, para 184.

international tribunal with independent competence to interpret international law, seemingly vested in it by the contract and international law itself. To say that the tribunal conceived itself as an agent of Indonesian law is clearly not feasible. Although it clearly conceived itself as bound by Indonesian law as the *lex arbitri,* it did so not as an element of the Indonesian legal system, but as an agent of the international community applying a conditioned version of Indonesian law, chastened and approved by international law.

This notion that a state is prevented by a particular rule of international law from revoking its consent to arbitration once given has also been confirmed by several other cases.[17] To say that arbitral practice based on these cases presents a conclusive picture in favour of an international principle of party autonomy may, nevertheless, be going a step to far. No doubt, the conventional view displayed by the weight of arbitral practice and literature is still that the consent to arbitrate needs to be rooted in some municipal law.[18] This nevertheless does not necessarily contradict or disprove the clear tendency of the cases discussed here. Thus, there is clearly a notable lack of cases upholding a state's annulment of its consent to arbitrate. Save for the ruling of the Swiss Federal Supreme Court in the case of *Société des Grands Travaux de Marseille v East Pakistan International Development Company (EPIDC),* which I discuss below, I have found none. Furthermore, it should be noted that upholding jurisdiction in most cases will simply appear as a straightforward application of the doctrine of separability under the *lex arbitri.* The *Himpurna* case was exceptional in that the host state's law at the same time was the *lex arbitri.* It therefore provides one of the few cases where it was necessary to assume the existence of an international rule in order to uphold jurisdiction.

(ii) Irrevocability of Consent as a Rule of International Law

While arbitral practice may be taken to support the notion that irrevocability of consent is a rule of international law, it is less clear whether this is reflective of a generally accepted principle of international law, or merely of certain self-assertive tendencies of the arbitral process. A ruling of the Swiss Federal Supreme Court in the case of *Société des Grands Travaux de Marseille*

[17] See eg *Elf Aquitaine v NIOC* (Award, 1982), (1986) 11 *YbCA* 97: 'It is a recognised principle of international law that a state is bound by an arbitration clause contained in an agreement entered into by the state itself or by a company owned by the state and cannot thereafter unilaterally set aside the access of the other party to the system envisaged by the parties in their agreement for the settlement of disputes'. See also *Benteler v Belgium* (Award, 1983), [1985] European Commercial Cases 185. And see Paulsson, 'May a State Invoke its Internal Law to Repudiate Consent to International Commercial Arbitration' (1986) 2(2) *Arb Int'l* 90.

[18] See eg Cordero Moss, *International Commercial Arbitration—Party Autonomy and Mandatory Rules* (Tano Aschehoug, Oslo, 1999) 178 et seq.

v EPIDC might suggest the latter. The case concerned a claim by a private French company (SGTM) against a Bangladeshi state owned corporation (EPIDC), which subsequently was decreed dissolved and had all its assets transferred to another state-owned company (BIDC) created by the same decree. The latter company was identical to the first in virtually all aspects, but the decree stipulated that it should not be bound by any arbitration agreements to which EPIDC was a party. Eventually also this company was dissolved and all its assets vested in the Bangladeshi government. The arbitral tribunal held that this was an unlawful revocation of the submission to arbitration, both under international law and Swiss ordre public.[19] This award was annulled by the Swiss Federal Supreme Court, on the basis that the arbitrator lacked competence over both BIDC, as a non-existing entity after having been dissolved, *and* the Bangladeshi government, since it was not a party to the contract and had not consented to arbitration in respect of itself. The court thus held that the arbitrator had exceeded its competence, since there was no positive basis for the jurisdiction exercised. With respect to the dissolution of EPIDC and BIDC and the resulting loss of their capacity to arbitrate, the court held that this was a matter governed by the law of the seat of the corporation, in other words the law of Bangladesh. The court nevertheless held that *ordre public* might be applicable, but only to exclude a foreign law, and not to vest capacity in an entity otherwise lacking under its own law.[20] The effective outcome of this was to uphold the government's rescission of the arbitration arrangement under its own law. This has, however, been severely criticised in the literature.[21]

The trend of state practice is equally inconclusive. First of all, as revealed by the cases already cited above, some governments not only prefer not to participate in such arbitral proceedings, but even routinely obstruct proceedings to which they are parties. By contrast, participation in arbitrations under the treaty-based ICSID regime is conspicuously high. This may clearly have something to do with the wider legitimacy enjoyed by this regime, as a treaty-based regime. On the other hand, cases of non-participation and obstruction have tended to evoke protests from the investor's home state, exercising in this respect its right of diplomatic protection.[22] Thus, in the *Anglo-Persian* case, the United Kingdom claimed

[19] *Société des Grands Travaux de Marseille v East Pakistan Industrial Development Company* (Award (ICC Case No. 1803), 1972), (1980) 5 *YbCA* 177, 182.

[20] *Société des Grands Travaux de Marseille v Republic of Bangladesh and Bangladesh Industrial Development Corp* (Tribunal Federal, 1976), (1980) 5 *YbCA* 217, 219: '[I]t cannot be denied that, in fact, their effect is to deprive the appellant from the possibility of presenting his claims in conformity with the arbitral procedure as provided in the contract . . . They have a discriminatory character because the appellant is practically the only one aimed at by these Orders . . . If these discriminatory measures have to be applied directly in a Swiss arbitral award and in respect of Swiss creditors, they must be opposed by virtue of Swiss *ordre public*'.

[21] See eg Delaume (1981) 789.

[22] Cf the statement of the ICJ in the *Nicaragua case (Nicaragua v USA)* [1986] ICJ Rep 14, para 186: 'In order to deduce the existence of customary rules, the Court deems it sufficient that

that Iran's obstruction of arbitral proceedings with the company constituted a denial of justice and used this as one basis for its claim before the International Court of Justice.[23] In the *Losinger* case before the PCIJ, Switzerland claimed that Yugoslavia's failure to participate in the proceedings in accordance with the arbitration clause constituted a violation of the acquired rights of the company, and 'an abuse of rights' by the Yugoslav government.[24] Similarly, the *Lena Goldfields* case was subject to protracted negotiations between the United Kingdom and the Soviet Union after the initial decision was rendered. These led to a settlement in 1935 whereby the Bolshevik government promised to pay part of its debt to the company.[25] Still, the NIEO[26] resolutions on permanent sovereignty adopted by the UN General Assembly in the '60s and '70s clearly reveal the scepticism at that time of developing states toward arbitral resolution of investment disputes.[27] While the first 'compromise' resolution of 1962 expressly supported arbitration in investment disputes,[28] the final Charter of Economic Rights and Duties of States referred such disputes to the exclusive domain of municipal courts, unless otherwise agreed 'by all states concerned'.[29] This constituted 'a concerted effort by the developing countries to repudiate a system of law in whose creation they had played little or no part',[30] but it was also highly controversial and most developed countries voted against it or abstained. Thus, it was clearly not reflective of

the conduct of states should, in general, be consistent with such rules, and that instances of state conduct inconsistent with a given rule should generally have been treated as breaches of that rule'.

[23] *Anglo Iranian Oil Company case*, ICJ Pleadings, 120: 'Even if it were possible for the Government of Iran to assert that the unilateral denunciation of the Convention for the purpose of nationalization was dictated by the vital interests of the State, it does not follow that these vital interests of the State demanded that the termination of the Convention be combined with the cancellation of the clause which is the proper instrument for providing a remedy . . . This refusal of the Iranian government to allow the clause of the Concession Convention providing for arbitration any effect whatever enhances the unlawfulness of the unilateral termination of the Convention and adds to it the element of another international delinquency, namely, denial of justice'.

[24] *Losinger case* PCIJ Series C No 78 (1936) 26 (as related by Schwebel (1987) 72 et seq).

[25] Only part of the promise was honoured, and the Lena Goldfields case continued to be a disputed issue between the UK and the Soviets until a final settlement in 1968, see Veeder, 'The Lena Goldfields Arbitration: The Historical Roots of Three Ideas' (1998) 47 *ICLQ* 747, 786–90.

[26] New International Economic Order.

[27] See generally Lowenfeld, *International Economic Law* (Oxford University Press, Oxford, 2002) 407 et seq.

[28] UNGA res. No. 1803 (XVII) on *Permanent sovereignty over natural resources*, para 4 (if): '[U]pon agreement by sovereign States and other parties concerned, settlement of the dispute should be made through arbitration or international adjudication'.

[29] UNGA Res 3281 (XXIX) *Charter of Economic Rights and Duties of States*, Art 2 (c) (if.): 'In any case where the question of compensation gives rise to a controversy, it shall be settled under the domestic law of the nationalizing State and by its tribunals, unless it is freely and mutually agreed by all States concerned that other peaceful means by sought on the basis of the sovereign equality of States and in accordance with the principle of free choice of means'.

[30] Lowenfeld (2002) 413.

anything resembling settled consensus. Nevertheless, it reflects, if nothing else, a lack of settled consensus at the time upon a system of protection of foreign investment underscored by international arbitration. This may have been overtaken by the more recent tendency of investment treaty arbitration. Most of the treaties referring to investor-state arbitration have come into existence after the attempts of developing countries to 'divorce international investment from international law'.[31] However, while investment treaty practice does appear to confirm and cement investment arbitration as a preferred model of dispute resolution in this field, it clearly does not itself conclusively settle the issue where no treaty exists.

The most crucial argument in favour of a distinct irrevocability rule under international law is perhaps that it is difficult to see any legitimate reason why a state should be able to submit to arbitration, and give the pretence of a reliable remedy to attract investment under a contract, only to withdraw its submission after realising the benefits. While there may be weighty objections against upholding contractual commitments placing restraints upon the exercise of public power, these concerns do not to the same extent apply to an arbitration undertaking, which at the same time may be crucial for the investor, having relied on this to make the investment in the first place.[32] This provides a compelling inner rationale to the supposed irrevocability rule asserted in arbitral practice, suggesting that it may be justified as part of a more fundamental concept of good faith under international law.

(iii) The Basis of Authority—Relative Autonomy

The irrevocability of a state's consent to arbitration under international law does not mean that the validity of consent is necessarily subject to international law.[33] The conventional approach would seem rather to be that it is subject to municipal law for its initial validity, and relies on international law (or *ordre public*) merely for its irrevocability.[34] This derives from the general acceptance that investment arbitration is a species of commercial arbitration subject to municipal arbitration law.[35] The law

[31] *ibid*, 413.

[32] Cf *Liberian Eastern Timber Corporation (LETCO) v Republic of Liberia* (Award, 1986) 26 ILM 647, 662: 'LETCO's right to arbitration is a guarantee that it will not have its long-term and costly investment arbitrarily rendered useless by the Government of Liberia. Inevitably, such a provision is considered fundamental to the foreign investor and is likely to be a condition of the investment itself'.

[33] By the term validity I intend to cover all conditions of initial validity, in other words, contractual and formal validity, arbitrability, and capacity to submit to arbitration, see eg Redfern and Hunter (2004) 134 et seq.

[34] See eg Mann, 'State Contracts and International Arbitration' (1967) 42 *BYIL* 1, 6–7.

[35] This has been held to apply even in relation to investment treaty arbitration outside ICSID, see Z Douglas, 'The Hybrid Foundations of Investment Treaty Arbitration' (2003) 74 *BYIL* 151, 213.

governing the consent must be identified through the conflict of laws rules of the relevant municipal jurisdiction. Most municipal laws will in this regard make a distinction between contractual validity, arbitrability, and capacity to submit to arbitration.[36] The common rule would seem to be that contractual validity must be determined either by the law chosen by the parties or by the *lex arbitri*.[37] Arbitrability, which is mainly an issue of public policy,[38] presumably has to be governed by the *lex fori* directly,[39] although it may be difficult to separate in all instances from the issue of capacity.[40] And capacity will be determined by the parties' respective national laws.[41]

It is the latter rule that in particular, if strict, is likely to create problems for investor-state arbitration. The domestic law of the state party might contain restrictions on the capacity of either the state or state entities to submit to arbitration.[42] Such restrictions need not necessarily be explicit: they may be implicit in the general scheme of the state's constitutional or administrative structure, for instance as a general prohibition against contracting with public power unless expressly authorised. In the context of international investment it would often seem unreasonable to allow a state to avoid a prior submission to arbitration on the basis of its own law, whose workings and application it would clearly be closer to appreciate than the foreign investor.[43] The same consideration applies to a public entity such as a state enterprise, which is typically established for the specific purpose of entering into relations with foreign commercial parties,

36 Redfern and Hunter (2004) 134 et seq.

37 See eg the United Nations Convention on the Recognition and Enforcement of Foreign Arbitral Awards (New York, 1958), Art V 1(a): 'Recognition and enforcement of the award may be refused . . . only if . . . the [arbitration] agreement is not valid under the law to which the parties have subjected it or, failing any indication thereon, under the law of the country where the award was made'. See also the UNCITRAL Model Law (1985) Art 36: 'Recognition or enforcement of an arbitral award, irrespective of the country in which it was made, may be refused only . . . [if] the [arbitration] agreement is not valid under the law to which the parties have subjected it or, failing any indication thereon, under the law of the country where the award was made'.

38 Redfern and Hunter (2004) 139.

39 The *lex fori* may however consider arbitrability an aspect of validity, and therefore refer to the law governing the arbitration agreement. For the arbitral tribunal itself the issue may appear somewhat more complex; it may want to ensure both that the award will not be challenged of the courts of the *situs* and that it will be enforceable under the most relevant national jurisdictions. This may require that account is taken of rules impinging on arbitrability from either jurisdiction. See further, Hanotiau, 'What Law Governs the Issue of Arbitrability' (1996) 12(4) *Arb Int'l* 391.

40 Redfern and Hunter (2004) 147–8.

41 Cf the New York Convention (1958) Art V 1(a): 'Recognition and enforcement of the award may be refused . . . only if . . . the parties to the agreement referred to in article II were, under the law applicable to them, under some incapacity . . .'. And see also *LIAMCO v Libya* (Award, 1977), (1982) 62 ILR 141, 177–8.

42 Redfern and Hunter (2004) 146–7.

43 See eg Böckstiegel, *Arbitration and State Enterprises* (Kluwer Law and Taxation Publishers, Deventer, 1984) 14.

and consequently under the natural assumption that it has general authorisation to enter into arbitral arrangements. Having already invoked the irrevocability of consent as a mandatory rule of international public policy, in order to neutralise attempts at subsequent repudiation, the step is not far, moreover, from inferring even the initial validity of the arbitration agreement from an independent concept of party autonomy.[44] This is reflected in a number of cases, where jurisdiction was inferred from the parties' 'raw' intention, without interposition of the more conventional conflict of laws approach.

This is firstly explicit in some of the classical internationalisation awards. In both *Aramco v Saudi Arabia* and *Texaco v Libya*, the awards expressly excluded the applicability of municipal law to any part of the procedure. The tribunal in the former case consequently held that it derived 'all its powers from the Arbitration Agreement',[45] and that the arbitration was therefore governed by international law.[46] The tribunal in the latter also had to assume that the arbitration clause was prima facie valid and binding irrespective of any municipal law.[47] The reasoning of the tribunal elsewhere suggests that the essential basis of jurisdiction was inferred from international law, in the same manner as the validity of the contract in general, as 'the legal order from which the binding nature of the contract stems'.[48] The approach adopted in these two cases effectively meant that the consent of the two states involved was derived from their supposed capacity to commit to dispute settlement on the level of international law, almost in the same manner as if an arbitration agreement had been concluded with another state.[49] The sovereignty of the state involved was deemed to preclude submission of the proceedings to another municipal law. This analogy is somewhat problematic, however, from the point of view of the purpose of arbitration as a legal remedy in this context. It disregards the commercial and hybrid nature of state contract arbitration, which lies in its combination of municipal enforceability and international authority.[50] By taking this approach to its ultimate consequence, depicting the arbitral award as an 'international' award, it might in effect fail to be recognised under the 1958 New York Convention, as I will come back to below. Other cases consequently have taken a more sceptical view of the

44 Fouchard, Gaillard, Goldman (1999) 197.

45 *Saudi Arabia v Arab American Oil Company (Aramco)* (Award, 1958) 27 ILR 117, 146.

46 *ibid*, 155–6.

47 *Texaco v Libya* (Award (Jurisdiction), 1977) 53 ILR 389, 412.

48 *ibid*, 443.

49 Cf especially *Aramco v Saudi Arabia* (Award, 1958) 27 ILR 117, 152–3.

50 See to this effect also Fox, 'States and the Undertaking to Arbitrate' (1988) 37 *ICLQ* 1, 10: 'Clearly if the undertaking to arbitrate rests solely on consent of the parties and that consent is interpreted in the same way as a State's undertaking to arbitrate in inter-State arbitrations, it deprives the proceedings, the arbitrator and the award of the support and enforcement procedures of local courts'.

desirability of dislocating the process altogether from an initial basis of validity under a municipal law, adopting rather a second and alternative hybrid approach, based neither exclusively in international nor in municipal law. The case of *BP v Libya* is illustrative.[51] The arbitrator seemingly inferred his authority in the first place from the contract without any interposition of a municipal law.[52] Significantly however, he then distinguished himself from the *Aramco* tribunal's approach with exclusive reliance on international law, explaining instead that he would make his decision as far as possible a 'Danish award' based on the *situs* of the proceedings in Copenhagen.[53] The rationale was that only an award anchoring its authority in a municipal law would be an 'effective remedy':

> The Tribunal cannot share the view that the application of municipal procedural law to an international arbitration like the present one would infringe upon such prerogatives as a State party to the proceedings may have by virtue of its sovereign status . . . By providing for arbitration as an exclusive mechanism for resolving contractual disputes, the parties to an agreement, even if one of them is a State, must, however be presumed to have intended to create an effective remedy. The effectiveness of an arbitral award that lacks nationality—which it may if the law of the arbitration is international law—generally is smaller than that of an award founded on the procedural law of a specific legal system and partaking of its nationality.[54]

This provides an approach both distinct from the normal conflict of laws approach in international commercial arbitration, and the exclusive international law approach of the *Texaco* and *Aramco* cases. The image is that of the tribunal's authority as an essentially free-floating creation of the contract, but susceptible to recognition and enforcement by different municipal laws as a contractual remedy. Compliance with the chosen *lex arbitri* is seen as a matter of convenience, to 'partake of its nationality' and ensure the award's enforceability as a private and commercial contractual award on the level of municipal law; not as something objectively imposed on the tribunal.

[51] But see also for earlier cases, the *Alsing* case *(Alsing Trading Co and Svenska Tändsticks AB v Greece)* (Award, 1954) 23 ILR 633; and *Sapphire v NIOC* (Award, 1963) 35 ILR 136.

[52] *BP v Libya* (Award, 1973), (1979) 53 ILR 297, 308, and see also 326: 'In contradistinction to all national courts, the *ad hoc* international arbitral tribunal created under an agreement between a State and an alien, such as the present Tribunal, at least initially has no *lex fori* which, in the form of conflicts of law rules or otherwise, provides it with the framework of an established legal system under which it is constituted and to which it may have ultimate resort'.

[53] *ibid*, 309: 'The Tribunal is not competent to establish conclusively the nationality of its Award, for this can only be decided by the Courts of Denmark and of other jurisdictions in which enforcement of the Award may be sought. However, the tribunal deems this award to be Danish, and the proceedings have been conducted in a manner designed to be consistent with this view and intent'.

[54] *ibid*, 309.

This approach is also reflected in several other cases subsequent to the *BP award*.[55] In the *Deutsche Schachtbau* case the tribunal held that the proceedings were governed by Swiss law, as the procedural law of the arbitration, but considered the validity of the arbitration clause governed by 'internationally accepted principles of law governing contractual relations'.[56] In a more recent ICC case from 2001, the tribunal formulated the same basic approach cogently as follows:

> An international arbitral tribunal is not an organ of the state in which it has its seat in the same way that a court of the seat would be. The primary source of the Tribunal's powers is the parties' agreement to arbitrate. An important consequence of this is that the Tribunal has a duty vis à vis the parties to ensure that their arbitration agreement is not frustrated. In certain circumstances, it may be necessary to decline to comply with an order issued by the court of the seat, in the fulfilment of the Tribunal's larger duty to the parties . . . Of course, this is not to say that a contract, including an arbitration agreement, has a validity that is independent of any legal order. Indeed a contract derives its binding force from its recognition by one or more legal orders. However, an agreement to submit disputes to international arbitration is not anchored exclusively in the legal order of the seat of the arbitration. Such agreements are validated by a range of international sources and norms extending beyond the domestic seat itself.[57]

The source of authority is thus conceived in terms of a relative independence from municipal law, dependent on municipal law for practical enforceability and recognition, but not dependent on or standing in any immediate relationship to a particular municipal law.

This approach is then often conspicuously complemented by reliance on distinct rules of international law or international public policy, which, irrespective of municipal law, may presume validity specifically where the undertaking of a state or state entity is in question. It is particularly reflected in cases where the state party claims to have been inhibited by its own law from submitting to arbitration. In the case of *Benteler v Belgium*, a claim by the Belgian state that it lacked capacity to submit to arbitration was rejected by the tribunal. It held that the dispute in question was a 'commercial dispute' within the scope of the Geneva Arbitration Convention, article II of which then expressly provides that

[55] See eg *Deutsche Schachtbau- und Tiefbohrgesellschaft mbH v Rakoil and R'as Al Khaimah (United Arab Emirates)* (Award, 1982) (1989) 14 *YbCA* 111; *Elf Aquitaine v National Iranian Oil Company (NIOC)* (Award, 1982) (1986) 11 *YbCA* 97; *Framatome SA v Atomic Energy Organization of Iran* (ICC Case No 3896, 1984) (1983) 8 *YbCA* 94; and *S v State X* (ICC Case No 10623, 2001) (2003) 21(1) *ASA Bulletin* 82, paras 128–9; see also generally, and with further references, Fouchard, Gaillard, Goldman (1999) 234–6.

[56] *Deutsche Schachtbau v Rakoil and R'as Al Khaimah* (Award, 1982) (1989) *14 YbCA* 111, para 12.

[57] ICC Case No 10623 (Award, 2001) (*S v State X)* (2003) 21(1) *ASA Bulletin* 82, paras 128–9.

legal persons of public law have the right to conclude valid arbitration agreements.[58]

This provided an international basis of validity for the jurisdiction of the tribunal.[59] However, although not necessary to reach its conclusion, the tribunal then went beyond the treaty to refer to what it considered a general principle of international arbitration, holding that 'a State which has subscribed to an arbitration clause or an arbitration agreement would act contrary to international public order in later invoking the incompatibility of such an obligation with its domestic legal order'.[60] In both the *Elf Aquitaine* case and the *Framatome* case, conspicuously without distinguishing between initial validity and subsequent annulment, the tribunals similarly dismissed the contention of Iran that the arbitration clause was null and void from the outset, pursuant to a provision of the Iranian constitution requiring the approval of Iran's Council of Ministers.[61] This may be seen as related to the rationale of the rule involved, as an aspect of a broader principle of good faith.[62]

This principle of assumed capacity to enter into valid arbitration agreements does not necessarily mean that the municipal law of the state is of no consequence. An evident lack of capacity to submit to arbitration will presumably prevent jurisdiction, also in case of a state or state entity, at least in so far as it had to appear evident to the other party. Essentially, a reasonable interpretation of the rule would seem to suggest that the state is barred from invoking lack of capacity under its own law if its co-contractor had a legitimate reason to believe the submission was valid; effectively, a state will be presumed competent under its own law.[63]

A related rule of international law has been relied on to reject the claim that a dispute is non-arbitrable for violation of the state's sovereign

[58] See the European Convention on International Commercial Arbitration (Geneva, 21 April 1961) 484 UNTS 364 (The Geneva Convention), Art II, No 1: 'In cases referred to in Article I, paragraph 1, of this Convention, legal persons considered by the law which is applicable to them as 'legal persons of public law' have the right to conclude valid arbitration agreements'. As not many states have ratified it, the convention's scope of application remains relatively limited.

[59] *Benteler v Belgium* (Award, 1983) (1984) 1(2) *J Int'l Arb* 184, 185–8.

[60] *ibid*, 189; and see also *Italian Company v African State Entity* (ICC Case No 1939), (Award, 1971), as cited and translated in ICC Case No 10623 (Award, 2001) (*S v State X)* (2003) 21(1) *ASA Bulletin* 82, para 161; 'International public policy would be strongly opposed to the idea that a public entity, when dealing with foreign parties, could openly, knowingly, and willingly, enter into an arbitration agreement, on which its co-contractor would rely, only to claim subsequently, whether during the arbitral proceedings or on enforcement of the award, that its own undertaking was void'.

[61] *Elf Aquitaine Iran v National Iranian Oil Company (NIOC)* (Award, 1982), (1986) 11 *YbCA* 97; and *Framatome SA v Atomic Energy Organization of Iran* (Award (ICC Case No 3896), 1982) (1983) 8 *YbCA* 94.

[62] See eg ICC case No 6474 (Partial Award, 1992), (2000) 25 *YbCA* 278, para 12.

[63] An analogy to Art 46 of the Vienna Convention may be appropriate in this regard, see Castberg, 'International Law in Our Time' (1973-I) 138 *Recueil des Cours* 1, 6.

immunity. According to the principle of state immunity for public acts (*acta jure imperii*), which applies to claims against a state (or state entity) before the municipal courts of other states, it could be argued that an arbitral tribunal depending on municipal courts for recognition and enforcement of its award must respect sovereign immunity, or else accept to conceive itself by analogy with inter-state arbitration to lack the remedial power of private commercial arbitration.[64] Instead it has been held that a state waives its sovereign immunity by submitting to arbitration.[65]

All this reveals a tendency in arbitral practice to conceive the initial source of its authority in terms of a relative independence from municipal law, dependent for its effectiveness as a remedy on municipal law, but lacking an immediate relationship to any particular municipal law. This has proved a pervasive notion also outside the confines of arbitral practice itself. In its 1990 resolution on '*Arbitration between States, State Enterprises or State Entities, and Foreign Enterprises*'[66] the Institut de Droit International gave its scholarly stamp of approval to such a concept of relative autonomy. The resolution proclaims the pre-eminence of party autonomy,[67] and sets out the so-called *in favorem validitatis* principle as the main rule of validity. It thus promulgated a distinctly liberal and international concept of party autonomy, confirming aforesaid tendencies in arbitral practice. The resolution inter alia maintains that validity might be inferred from both municipal and international legal standards,[68] allowing for invalidity

[64] See especially *Aramco v Saudi Arabia* (Award, 1958) 27 ILR 117, 155.

[65] See especially ICC Case No 2321 (Award, 1974), (1976) 1 *YbCA* 133, 134: 'A sovereign State must be sovereign enough to make a binding promise both under international law and municipal law. As to the latter aspect of the question I was informed by the Counsel of the First Defendant that according to both [the law of the respondent state] and English law the capacity of the state to enter into arbitration clauses was not restricted as such and that also the State could be sued in its own courts. To require or assume then that a promise of a State to submit to arbitration, in order to be binding has to be confirmed in the face of the arbitrator would probably impair the sovereignty of a State and its dignity more than the arbitrator's performance of his task, conferred upon him in accordance with what the parties once have agreed upon. The issue whether the subject matter of the present dispute is a matter *jure gestionis* or *jure imperii* has also been argued by the parties on each side. From what I have said above it follows that this distinction is of no relevance once the parties have agreed upon arbitration'.

[66] Resolution adopted by the Institute of International Law at its Santiago de Compostela Session (1989) on *Arbitration Between States, State Enterprises or State Entities, and Foreign Enterprises* (1990) 63-II *Ann IDI* 324.

[67] *ibid*, art 1: 'Arbitrators derive their authority and powers from the parties' agreement providing for arbitration. An arbitrator shall neither exceed his powers nor do less than is required to exercise his authority completely; and he shall exercise his functions impartially and independently'. This provision abandons the so called jurisdictional theory of arbitration, which regards arbitration as essentially a substitute for municipal courts, operating by license of the territorial, sovereign power: see the draft report by Von Mehren and Jiménez de Arechaga, in (1989) 63-I *Ann IDI* 100.

[68] The Santiago de Compostela Resolution (1989), Art 4: 'Where the validity of the agreement to arbitrate is challenged, the tribunal shall resolve the issue by applying one or more of the following: the law chosen by the parties, the law indicated by the system of private international law stipulated by the parties, general principles of public or private

only in the case of violation of 'international public policy'.[69] The resolution also dismisses lack of capacity as a valid reason for states and state entities to resist arbitral proceedings.[70] According to the rapporteur, the resolution was meant precisely to emphasise the arbitral process as a system of dispute resolution, whose authority 'does not emanate from a discrete sovereign but rather from an international order'.[71]

More significant than arbitral practice and scholarly opinion is perhaps the fact that a concept of relative autonomy is also widely accepted by significant municipal laws. Such acceptance may be explicit or merely implicit, but is often reflected in a distinctly liberal approach to commercial arbitration conceived as international (as distinct from domestic). Most explicit is the liberal approach of French courts. Under French law the validity of a clause referring to international arbitration (as distinct from domestic) may be inferred directly from a substantive rule of autonomy applicable to international arbitration.[72] The main rationale of this approach is precisely to sustain the validity of arbitration agreements in the face of alleged restrictions in the municipal law otherwise applicable, in so far as no principle of international *ordre public*, as conceived by French law, is violated.

Less explicit but equally effective is the more common *in favorem validitatis* rule relied on by other municipal laws. According to Swiss law, an agreement to arbitrate is valid if it

> conforms either to the law chosen by the parties, or to the law governing the subject matter of the dispute, in particular the law governing the main contract, or if it conforms to Swiss law.[73]

international law, general principles of international arbitration, or the law that would be applied by the courts of the territory in which the tribunal has its seat. In making this selection, the tribunal shall be guided in every case by the principle *in favorem validitatis*'.

[69] *ibid*, Art 2: 'In no case shall an arbitrator violate principles of international public policy as to which a broad consensus has emerged in the international community'.

[70] *ibid*, Art 5: 'A State, a state enterprise, or a state entity cannot invoke incapacity to arbitrate in order to resist arbitration to which it has agreed'.

[71] Von Mehren, 'Arbitration Between States and Foreign Enterprises: The Significance of the Institute of International Law's Santiago de Compostela Resolution' (1990) 5(1) *ICSID Rev-FILJ* 54, 57, see also *ibid*, 59, about the underlying rationale of the *in favorem validitatis* principle in article 4: '[It] is grounded . . . on a premise that informs the Resolution as a whole: the institution of international commercial arbitration provides a form of dispute resolution which international practice strongly supports because of its special qualities and advantages where disputes between States, state enterprises, or state entities, on the one hand, and foreign enterprises, on the other, are in question'.

[72] See eg *Société Gatoil v National Iranian Oil Company* (1993) *Rev Arb* 281, 284: '[E]n matière d'arbitrage international, le principe de l'autonomie de la clause compromissoire est d'application générale, en tant que règle matérielle internationale consacrant la licéité de la convention d'arbitrage, hors de toute référence à un système de conflits de lois, la validité de la convention devant être contrôlée au regard des seules exigences de l'ordre public international'. See also *Comité populaire de la municipalité de Khoms El Mergeb v Dalico Contractors* (1994) 121 *J Dr Int'l* 432; and see generally Fouchard, Gaillard, Goldman (1999) 229.

[73] Article 178(2) of the Private International Law (PIL) Act, as related by Fouchard, Gaillard, Goldman (1999) 237.

This rule has the same objective as the 'substantive rule' approach applied by the French courts. It seeks to uphold the validity of the arbitration agreement in so far as it does not violate the Swiss concept of international public policy. A similar rule has apparently been more or less explicitly relied on by Swedish, English and Belgian courts in general commercial disputes between private parties.[74] Swiss law furthermore contains an express rule presuming the capacity of states to submit to arbitration irrespective of their municipal law.[75] A similar rule applicable to states has been applied by Swedish courts.[76]

This shows how international commercial arbitration is conceived as a process existing in relative independence from municipal law, drawing on a legally independent and internationally sanctioned concept of party autonomy where states are involved as parties. It would, however, be wrong to consider this an imperative rule of international law requiring recognition and enforcement in the same manner as the ICSID Convention. Although to some extent similar requirements do exist for commercial arbitral awards under the New York Convention, states are not generally and unconditionally required to enforce such awards in the same manner as under the ICSID Convention. Thus, as I shall revert to, there are escape hatches under the New York Convention that do not exist under the ICSID Convention.

The basic strength of the system thus lies in its acceptance by municipal laws, and not in any required recognition under international law. States are free to regulate international arbitration under their own municipal law as a matter of civil jurisdiction. The consequence is that states can accept or reject the operation of the arbitral process as a largely self-contained system with its own substantive standards and conditions. To the extent that other states are concerned as parties, this invokes principles of state immunity under international law. The main role of international law in this regard is to allow enforcement under a recognised exception to state immunity, to which I will return shortly. Under this perspective, there is no contradiction between saying that the source of authority rests upon a substantive concept of party autonomy, and that this is ultimately

74 Redfern and Hunter (2004) 128.

75 Article 177(2) of the Swiss PIL Act as related by Redfern and Hunter (2004) 147: 'If a party to the arbitration agreement is a state or enterprise or organisation controlled by it, it cannot rely on its own law in order to contest its capacity to be a party to an arbitration or the arbitrability of a dispute covered by the arbitration agreement'.

76 Decision of the Svea Court of Appeal in *LIAMCO v Libya* (18 June 1980), 20 ILM 893. see especially the concurring opinion of Judge Tillinger: 'It has become ever more common during recent years that states and state-owned organs act as parties to agreements of a commercial nature. If such agreements provide for arbitration, it is shocking *per se* that one of the contracting parties later refuses to participate in the arbitration or to respect a duly rendered award. When a state party is concerned, it is therefore a natural interpretation to consider that said party, in accepting the arbitration clause, committed itself not to obstruct the arbitral proceedings or their consequences, by invoking immunity'.

subject to municipal law. There is no principle of international law which allocates the regulation of this issue to a specific municipal law. Since arbitral proceedings might make contact with several municipal laws at different stages, all of which are to some extent free to impose their own terms upon them for the purpose of their effect within that system, it is meaningless to consider such proceedings definitively subject to one particular municipal law. The result of a growing awareness of autonomy and uniformity within the process itself is nevertheless that 'international principles' are increasingly gaining ground. Finding the way of least resistance, the process will tend to gravitate towards those 'havens' where it has the freest rein, invariably lending their stamp of approval to the process according to its own terms.

B. Recognition and Enforceability under Municipal Law—State Immunity and the Requirements of the New York Convention

A reasonable corollary of the 'irrevocability rule' examined above, is that the respondent state has an obligation under international law to comply with the resultant award. This is merely another facet of the obligation to stand by a submission to arbitrate once it has been validly made.[77] If effective only on the level of international law an eventual arbitral award would, however, be of little value to an aggrieved investor.[78] The commercial value of an award depends on whether it can be enforced against the respondent state under municipal law. The main advantage of investment arbitration is precisely the conception of it as a hybrid: international for the purpose of authority; municipal (or 'foreign') for the purpose of enforceability. In this section I provide a brief account of the enforceability of state contract awards under municipal law, as seen from the perspective of international law.[79] There are two aspects to this, one issue being whether a state is permitted to enforce an arbitral award against another state under its municipal law, and another being whether a state may also have an obligation to do so under international law. The former concerns whether a state may claim immunity against enforcement proceedings

[77] In terms of conventional international law the undertaking may be conceived as an acquired right which is transformed into a binding award as soon as it is rendered, see eg the decision of the ECHR in the case of *Stran Greek Refinereries and Stratis Andreadis v Greece* (1994) Series A301-B.

[78] Although it could conceivably be made subject of a claim by the investor's home state exercising diplomatic protection, and provide a more specific and solid basis for such a claim, cf eg the history around the *Lena Goldfields case* as related by Veeder (1998) 747, 786 et seq.

[79] It is impossible within the scope of this book to do credit to the full complexity of this issue, which depends on a close interaction and no clear division between principles of international law and municipal regulation. Thus, my objective is basically to account for the main issues involved.

before the courts of another state; the latter relates to the scope and extent of the 1958 New York Convention on Recognition and Enforcement of Foreign Arbitral Awards in respect of arbitral awards against a state.

(i) State Immunity

The principal importance of international law in connection with the enforceability of an arbitral award against a state is that the underlying consent to arbitration is considered a waiver of state immunity. To the extent of such waiver, another state is thus permitted to maintain jurisdiction in its courts over both the arbitral proceedings and a resultant award. It is generally recognised that this applies to supervisory jurisdiction over the arbitral proceedings, including confirmation and challenge of the award under the municipal law applicable to it.[80] The difficult issue is whether a submission to arbitration can be considered a waiver of the state's immunity from enforcement and execution.[81] This issue has seen an abundant practice of municipal courts, the nuances and varieties of which are beyond the scope of this study.[82] A distillation of municipal court practice, together with the rules promulgated in the recently adopted (but not yet in force) UN Convention on State immunity, suggests the following main rules however.[83]

First, a state may expressly waive immunity for the purpose of enforcement proceedings, either in the arbitration clause or the contract at issue, or by specific agreement.[84] It depends upon interpretation of the concrete submission whether it indeed constitutes a sufficient waiver to cover the enforcement proceedings at issue. If a provision for arbitration stipulates that an award shall be enforced pursuant to the New York convention, this must presumably be construed as an express waiver of immunity in relation to enforcement.

Secondly, it is at least arguable that even a non-specific submission to arbitration ought to be construed as a general waiver of immunity against enforcement proceedings, both (and at least) in relation to the municipal legal system governing the arbitration *and* in countries without any substantial connection to the arbitration. This is a natural inference from the normal objective of submitting to international commercial arbitration,

80 See generally and with further references, Schreuer, *State Immunity: Some Recent Developments* (Grotius Publications, Cambridge, 1988) 75 et seq; and Fox, *The Law of State Immunity* (Oxford University Press, Oxford, 2002) 269.

81 See eg Sornarajah, *The Settlement of Foreign Investment Disputes* (Kluwer, The Hague, 2000) 300; Fox (1988) 10; and Delaume (1981) 786.

82 For an extensive account see Schreuer (1988) 75 et seq.

83 UN Convention on Jurisdictional Immunity of States and their Property (the UN Convention), as adopted by the UN General Assembly 2 December 2004, UNGA Res 59/38 (2004).

84 Cf the UN Convention art 19(a).

which is to create an enforceable remedy. Where only a non-specific waiver of immunity has been given, enforcement will, however, be limited to property and assets which are not subject to any specific immunity, viz assets and property used or intended to be used for 'commercial' or 'non-governmental' purposes.[85] Execution otherwise requires an express waiver in relation to the specific property involved.

Thirdly, insofar as the proceedings are brought against a state agency or corporation with separate legal personality, all its assets and property would seem in principle subject to attachment and execution in the same manner as for private persons and companies.[86] This means that an independent state entity usually will not be able to claim that its property is used for a public purpose and thereby is subject to immunity.[87]

In conclusion, it is suggested that a submission to arbitration in most circumstances ought to be construed as a general waiver of immunity in relation to enforcement as well as supervision, but it will not extend to state property and assets subject to specific immunity against execution by reason of their public purpose.[88]

(ii) The New York Convention and State Contract Awards—Recognition and Enforcement under Municipal Law

Although the rules on state immunity permit enforcement to a limited extent as outlined above, there is no similarly general requirement for a state to place its municipal legal apparatus at the disposal of a private party seeking to enforce an award against another state. While such a requirement does not follow from general international law, it does, however, to a limited extent, follow from the 1958 New York Convention on Recognition and Enforcement of Foreign Arbitral Awards, currently binding on 140 or so participating states. The main issue is whether the New York Convention covers arbitral awards rendered against a state and for what sort of disputes.

That commercial arbitration involving states and state entities as parties generally is subject to the New York Convention is not in doubt.[89] An arbitral award against a state must in principle be recognised and enforced

[85] Cf the UN Convention art 19(c); and Fox (2002), 394 et seq.

[86] Fox (2002) 399.

[87] But there are exceptions, see eg for the situation in relation to central banks, Fox (2002) 393–4.

[88] See the UN Convention art 21 for normal categories of property considered non-commercial.

[89] See Delaume (1997) 476; see also van den Berg, *The New York Arbitration Convention of 1958: towards a uniform judicial interpretation* (Kluwer Law and Taxation Publishers, Deventer, 1981) 277 et seq; and van den Berg, 'Recent Enforcement Problems under the New York and ICSID Conventions' (1989) 5 *Arb Int'l* 2.

in the same manner as other foreign commercial arbitral awards.[90] In practice the issue nevertheless is more complex because the convention does not exhaustively regulate the conditions of enforceability. The convention's system is a main requirement of recognition and enforcement of 'foreign' arbitral awards,[91] subject to a limited number of exceptions.[92] As a general starting point recognition and enforcement are therefore also dependent on the municipal rules and policies of the *lex fori*. However, while the convention in this regard defers to the municipal law of the participating states, the exceptions must also be applied in line with the general objectives of the Convention. Thus, a national court applying the Convention cannot apply the exceptions as discretionary escape hatches from the general obligation to recognise and enforce. It is clearly assumed and inherent in the general objectives and requirements of the Convention that the exceptions have a limited scope and must be applied restrictively.

The first and most significant valid exception to enforceability is the so-called public policy exception in article V(2). This states that enforcement may be refused either if

> (a) the subject matter of the difference is not capable of settlement by arbitration under the law of that country,
>
> or (b) the recognition or enforcement of the award would be contrary to the public policy of that country.

By virtue of this a state may refuse to enforce state contract awards on the basis of pressing internal political and policy concerns. Moreover, the convention expressly yields to each country's own conception of arbitrability, which typically also is shaped by similar concerns. The nature and character of such underlying concerns are not qualified by the Convention. It is thus conceivable that a country sceptical toward foreign

[90] For particular countries, other conventions applicable to international commercial arbitration could have a bearing on the same issue. Since the New York Convention is the only convention which has been almost universally recognised, they are omitted here for the sake of brevity. However, the 1961 European Convention on International Commercial Arbitration (the Geneva Convention) deserves mention; its article II expressly assumes the obligatory nature of arbitration agreements and awards for states and state entities ('legal persons of public law').

[91] The precise criterion is set out in art I(1): 'This Convention shall apply to the recognition and enforcement of arbitral awards made in the territory of a State other than the State where the recognition and enforcement of such awards are sought, and arising out of differences between persons, whether physical or legal. It shall also apply to arbitral awards not considered as domestic awards in the State where their recognition and enforcement are sought'.

[92] Article V(1) sets out five main exceptions to the main rule of recognition and enforcement; (a) that the arbitration agreement is invalid, (b) violation of due process or notice, (c) excess of authority, (d) irregularities of composition or procedure, and (e) that the award is invalid or not binding under the *lex arbitri*. In addition the second paragraph stipulates that the main rule does not apply if, (a) the subject matter of the dispute was not capable of settlement by arbitration under the *lex fori*, or (b) it is contrary to the public policy of the *lex fori*.

investment could enact a national policy to refuse enforcement of awards rendered in investment disputes against a recalcitrant state, and that it would be at liberty to do so, at least where elements of public power where involved, for instance with regard to a state contract placing clear restrictions upon public power.

A wide discretion to refuse enforcement of ordinary commercial awards against foreign states is nevertheless hard to reconcile with the New York Convention. Thus, the mere fact of the respondent being a state or state entity would not seem to provide a valid ground upon which to refuse enforcement under the public policy exception. In actual fact, most countries may be expected to consider as arbitrable all disputes falling under a loose definition of 'commercial', and consequently may be expected to recognise and enforce all awards deemed to arise from a commercial dispute.[93]

Whether a given dispute arising under a state contract may indeed be deemed sufficiently 'commercial', and consequently arbitrable, ultimately depends on the municipal law where enforcement is sought. Most significant municipal laws will, however, consider ordinary state contract awards as plainly commercial for the purpose of recognition and arbitrability, even though elements of contracting with public power are involved.[94] A number of countries distinguish between 'domestic' and 'international' arbitration in this respect, maintaining a looser criterion of arbitrability encompassing, inter alia, state contract disputes in respect of the latter.[95]

Another significant exception is article V (1)(e), which provides that enforcement may be refused if an award has been annulled in its country of origin. The consequence of this is that state contract awards rendered by a tribunal seated in the host country and susceptible to annulment by its courts, also may be refused enforcement by the courts of other states pursuant to such annulment.[96] In other words, while it is conceivable that a state may rightfully refuse to abide by such an annulment and enforce the award in any case, the fact that such annulment is listed in the Convention as a valid justification for refusal makes it hard to deny that a state would be at liberty to do so, with one exception, namely if the annulment were to be deemed a violation of international law. In such

[93] While the criterion of arbitrability does not correlate strictly with a 'commercial' criterion in all municipal laws, 'commercial' may nevertheless serve here as a loose criterion of arbitrability encompassing the main concerns that will be recognised by most municipal laws as lying at the core of arbitrability, since the main reasons why arbitration is recognised are economic and commercial interests. See further and generally, Fouchard, Gaillard, Goldman (1999) 35 et seq.

[94] See eg Delaume, 'Recognition and Enforcement of State Contract Awards in the United States: A Restatement' (1997) 91 *AJIL* 476, and Fouchard, Gaillard, Goldman (1999) 41.

[95] Fouchard, Gaillard, Goldman (1999) 41.

[96] See eg *Himpurna v Persero* (Award, 1999), (2000) 25 *YbCA* 13, where this was the case.

case, it would seem a compelling argument that the annulment must be disregarded by virtue of its illegality, and that the award should consequently be treated as valid under the New York Convention as if it had not been annulled.

Finally, the convention article V (1)(a) assumes that recognition and enforcement may be refused if a state (or state entity) lacked capacity under its own law to enter into the arbitration agreement. This must, however, be seen in connection with the principle of international law examined above, whereby a state or state entity is prohibited from invoking its own incapacity to arbitrate. While a state may refuse to give effect to an award against another state for reasons of public policy, it would consequently seem doubtful whether a state could refuse to give effect to an award by reason of that state's incapacity to arbitrate under its own law, at least if this was not manifestly evident at the time the arbitration agreement was made.

In conclusion, while state contract awards at the outset are subject to the New York Convention, the convention does not definitively require enforcement in all circumstances. As set out above, this is to some extent subject to the national policy of the country of enforcement. Crucially, however, this is no opportunity for states to escape enforcement in their capacity as respondents to arbitral proceedings, merely to refuse enforcement of awards against other states when chosen as a forum for enforcement. This is because the applicability of the Convention does not depend on whether the respondent state is a party to the Convention, but on whether the award was made in a contracting state.[97] Subject to state immunity, the practical consequence of this is that state contract awards usually are enforceable as foreign and commercial awards under the New York Convention.

4.3 JURISDICTION AND ENFORCEMENT UNDER THE ICSID CONVENTION

At the centre of the contemporary practice of investment arbitration is ICSID (the International Centre for Settlement of Investment Disputes), which is an agency of the World Bank. It was established under the ICSID Convention in 1965, as a permanent secretariat and procedural framework for the resolution of individual investor-state disputes through arbitration.[98] As I have already alluded to and will also come back to in greater

[97] Delaume (1997) 477.

[98] Convention on the Settlement of Investment Disputes between States and Nationals of other States (Washington DC, 18 March 1965) 575 UNTS 159. Reproduced with commentary in (1965) 4 ILM 524. See also generally Broches, 'The Convention on the Settlement of Investment Disputes between States and Nationals of other States' (1972-II) 136 *Recueil des Cours* 331.

detail in the next section, the convention has increasingly become the hub of an extensive and expanding network of Bilateral Investment Treaties (BITs),[99] as well as some multilateral treaties,[100] which make separate provision for arbitration under ICSID. Combined, this provides a fragmented and complex framework of international investment law, which has engendered a rapid proliferation of investment treaty arbitration as the preferred means of settling disputes between states and foreign investors.[101] This is not intrinsic to the ICSID procedure as such, however, but represents a development originating outside ICSID. The most significant characteristic of the ICSID regime as a stand-alone system is that awards can not be challenged and set aside by municipal courts, not even on the limited grounds allowed under the New York Convention. Awards must be recognised and enforced by member states, without any form of review, as a binding judgment of their national courts. The system constitutes, in short, a near self-contained international legal regime for arbitration of investment disputes, which produces awards that are binding and enforceable under municipal law. This is what constitutes its prime attractiveness for use as a dispute settlement procedure under investment treaties. The 'original' procedural modality envisaged under the ICSID Convention is nevertheless that of international commercial arbitration, based on a mutual consent, which at the same time constitutes a waiver of access to the courts, as I have already touched upon in chapter two above. In the following I first discuss the main jurisdictional requirements under ICSID, showing how they have been interpreted to give way to what is no longer used primarily as an ordinary arbitral procedure based on mutual consent, but a mandatory claims procedure or a form of 'arbitration without privity', as it has aptly been termed.[102] I then conclude with a brief outline of the main requirements of enforcement under ICSID, showing how the procedure is ultimately dependent on enforcement under municipal law.

[99] UNCTAD counted 2495 BITs by the end of 2005, see UNCTAD, *World Investment Report 2006* 26.

[100] The most important are the North American Free Trade Agreement (NAFTA) (signed San Antonio, 17 December 1992, entered into force 1 January 1994), and the Energy Charter Treaty (Lisbon, December 1994) (1995) 34 ILM 360. Both have separate chapters on investment that allow investors individual access to arbitration under ICSID or ad hoc procedures, see NAFTA Chapter 11, section B (Arts 1115 to 1138), and the Energy Charter Treaty, art 26.

[101] This is illustrated by the caseload of ICSID, which as of November 2006 numbered 103 pending cases out of a total of 215 submitted cases, of which only about 60 had been filed before 2000; see the ICSID website, www.worldbank.org/icsid/cases/cases.htm. To this comes probably a similar number of UNCITRAL or ad hoc proceedings filed under investment treaties outside ICSID.

[102] Paulsson, 'Arbitration without Privity' (1995) 10 *ICSID Rev-FILJ* 232.

A. The ICSID Requirements of Jurisdiction—Dual Levels of Consent

The fact of ICSID arbitration being a remedy undeniably rooted in international law, coupled with the consensual model of international commercial arbitration which it imitates, is reflected in the two levels of consent required to establish jurisdiction under the Convention.[103] On the one hand the state must have acceded to ICSID to bring into effect its general system. On the other hand, the convention requires a contractual link between the state and the investor, mirroring in this respect the consensual model of international commercial arbitration. In consequence, the authority of ICSID tribunals has a dual basis, being based on the ICSID Convention itself as well as the concrete contract or mutual consent between the state and the investor. The basic jurisdictional requirements of ICSID are set out in Article 25(1) of the Convention as follows:

> The jurisdiction of the centre shall extend to any legal dispute arising directly out of an investment, between a Contracting State (or any constituent subdivision or agency of a Contracting State designated to the Centre by that State) and a national of another Contracting State, which the parties to the dispute consent in writing to submit to the Centre. When the parties have given their consent, no party may withdraw its consent unilaterally.

This provision constitutes the state's consent to jurisdiction on the level of international law. The requirement of such 'consent' is expressly reflected in the limitation of jurisdiction to disputes between a 'contracting state' and 'nationals of another contracting state'.[104] The provision further envisages three requirements. Jurisdiction can only be entertained in respect of, (i) a *legal dispute,* which (ii) arises directly out of an *investment,* and (iii) the parties have *mutually consented in writing* to submit to the centre's jurisdiction. The primary basis of jurisdiction envisaged is thus an agreement between the state and the investor covering the actual dispute, limited by the condition that it will only be effective in respect of a legal dispute arising out of an investment. The former can be seen to encompass the ordinary requirements of legal interest, actuality, and an existing 'disagreement on a point of law or fact',[105] and raises no particular issues in this context.[106] The latter, on the other hand, sets out a particular criterion

[103] Collier and Lowe, *The Settlement of Disputes in International Law* (Oxford University Press, Oxford, 2000) 61; and see also *Autopista Concesionada de Venezuela CA (Aucoven) v Republic of Venezuela* (Decision on Jurisdiction, 2001) para 94.

[104] See further Schreuer, *The ICSID Convention: a Commentary* (Cambridge University Press, Cambridge, 2001) 141 and 158 et seq.

[105] This is the classical criterion of a 'dispute' as it was set out by the PCIJ in the *Mavromattis Palestine Concessions case* PCIJ Series A No 2 (1924) 11.

[106] But see *El Paso v Argentina* (Decision on Jurisdiction, 2006) para 47 et seq. The tribunal seemingly considered the issue of 'legal nature' to depend on whether the claims in question were purely contractual or had a plausible treaty basis. This confuses the requirement of legal nature under the ICSID Convention—which, since ICSID expressly authorises tribunals to

of arbitrability specific to the ICSID Convention. Only disputes arising directly out of an investment are capable of settlement under ICSID. This reflects the specific purpose of the Convention, as stated in the preamble, to facilitate private investment in order to further economic development.[107] The essential point is that the convention sets up an extraordinary remedy completely beyond the control of municipal courts. This is justified in the first place by its specific objective to further investment, but is therefore also, in the second place, limited by it. The investment criterion is nevertheless not of much practical significance where jurisdiction is based on a mutual agreement specific to the individual dispute. As I return to below, its main significance is in respect of investment treaty arbitration under ICSID, ie, where jurisdiction is based on consent in a treaty and consequently extending to unspecified numbers and categories of disputes.

The requirement of a mutual consent in writing is at first glance quite similar to the parallel requirement applicable to international commercial arbitration under article II of the New York Convention. Unlike what pertains in ordinary international commercial arbitration, the consent requirement under ICSID is, however, completely autonomous of any municipal law. The main requirement in respect of the state's consent is that it is reflective of an intention to submit, and evidenced to that effect in writing. Significantly, it has been held that this includes no requirement of specificity.[108] This is what has opened up for the practice of investment treaty jurisdiction under ICSID. Thus, practice has conclusively established that a state may give a standing offer to submit to arbitration in respect of an unspecified number of investors,[109] for instance in its legislation,[110] or,

apply municipal law, quite obviously is unrelated to the legal basis of the claim—with the available causes of action encompassed by jurisdiction under the relevant investment treaty.

[107] Cf the ICSID Convention (1965), first preambular provision.

[108] Whereas, for instance, in the New York Convention (and most municipal laws), the requirement is that the agreement must be in respect of a 'defined legal relationship', and the 'in writing' requirement is stipulated quite narrowly to 'include an arbitral clause in a contract or an arbitration agreement, signed by the parties or contained in an exchange of letters or telegrams'. See Redfern and Hunter (2004) 134.

[109] This was envisaged already in the Report of the Executive Directors that accompanied the Convention, reproduced in 4 ILM 524, 527: 'Nor does the Convention require that the consent of both parties be expressed in a single instrument. Thus, a host State might in its investment promotion legislation offer to submit disputes arising out of certain classes of investments to the jurisdiction of the Centre, and the investor might give his consent by accepting the offer in writing'.

[110] *Southern Pacific Properties (Middle East) Ltd (SPP) v Arab Republic of (Middle East) Ltd (SPP) v Arab Republic of Egypt* (Decision on Jurisdiction, 1988) 3 ICSID Rep 131; and *Tradex Hellas SA v Republic of Albania* (Decision on Jurisdiction, 1996) 5 ICSID Rep 43. The latter case explained the mechanism by which jurisdiction was established in this way as follows (at 63): 'although consent by written agreement is the usual method of submission to ICSID jurisdiction, it can now be considered as established and not requiring further reasoning that such consent can also be effected unilaterally by a Contracting State in its national laws, the consent becoming effective at the latest if and when the foreign investor files its claim with ICSID making use of the respective national laws'.

more significantly, in a bilateral or multilateral investment treaty.[111] This does not mean that practice has abrogated the mutual consent requirement in Article 25. The construction which is applied is that the unilateral promise, either in a BIT or municipal legislation, is held to constitute an offer from the state to submit to arbitration, which is accepted by the individual investor if and when it files a claim with ICSID.[112] The mutual consent requirement is nevertheless relegated to something of a fiction by this construct, as the necessary agreement is considered to come into existence only at the moment of being acted upon by the investor. The most distinguishing feature of investment treaty arbitration is in reality that it is not consensual.[113] This is revealed by the fact that the investor has a choice of remedies, which he would not have had in respect of an arbitration based in a contract. Until a claim has been filed, the investor can choose to resort to municipal courts, whilst an arbitration clause in a contract would have prevented this. The state, on the other hand, is bound to accept the investor's choice. Once rendered, the submission to arbitration is irrevocable, which is expressly stipulated by the last sentence of Article 25(1). While this nominally applies to both parties,[114] it mainly carries significance for the state. For the investor, the main consequence of its consent is that, as in ordinary commercial arbitration, it constitutes a waiver of access to the municipal courts.[115] For the state, the more significant consequence is that it loses the ability to rescind its consent. Irrevocability ensures the consent's survival of the state's termination of the contract, even though the applicable law may be the state's own municipal law. It thus fulfills the same function as the principle of separability in ordinary commercial arbitration.

B. The Limits of Self Containment—the ICSID Requirement of Municipal Recognition and Enforceability

An ICSID award is directly binding for the parties by virtue of Article 53 of the convention. Article 27 ensures that the award for practical purposes also binds the investor's home state, at least if complied with by the respondent

[111] Practice is abundant, the earliest examples are *Asian Agricultural Products Ltd (AAPL) v Democratic Socialist Republic of Sri Lanka* (Award, 1990) 4 ICSID Rep 246; and *American Manufacturing and Trading Inc (AMT) v Republic of Zaire* (Award, 1997) 5 ICSID Rep 11.

[112] See eg *SGS Societe Generale de Surveillance SA v Republic of the Philippines* (Decision on Jurisdiction, 2004) para 31: 'In the present case, the claimant relies upon the consent to ICSID arbitration given by the Philippines in the BIT, combined with its own written consent contained in the Request for Arbitration. It is well established that the combination of these forms of consent can constitute "consent in writing" within the meaning of Article 25(1) provided that the dispute falls within the scope of the BIT'.

[113] See Paulsson (1995).

[114] Cf the last sentence: 'When the *parties* have given their consent . . .' (emphasis added)

[115] Cf the ICSID Convention Art 26.

state.[116] More significant than this, however, is the duty of all member states to recognise and enforce an award 'as if it were a final judgment of a court in that State'.[117] What particularly distinguishes ICSID arbitration from international commercial arbitration in this regard is that an ICSID award is less susceptible to judicial control.[118] The Convention system is self-contained; an award can only be challenged through the annulment procedure set out in the Convention itself. For an investor, this provides a significant advantage over international commercial arbitration. First, enforceability under the municipal law of all member states is obligatory. Secondly, where a municipal court may, under the New York Convention, itself review the validity of an award and refuse enforcement according to the exceptions in article V of the Convention, this opportunity is closed under the ICSID Convention. The ICSID Convention instead has its own challenge and annulment procedure,[119] which requires an appeal to a new tribunal constituted as an ad hoc committee with limited powers of review.[120] The objective grounds on which an award may be annulled are also more limited than under the New York Convention.[121] While a New York Convention award may be set aside for lack of arbitrability or violation of public policy under the *lex fori*, no such exception is envisaged for ICSID awards.[122] In one sense this is a corollary of the positive criterion of arbitrability provided by the Convention itself, limiting jurisdiction to investment disputes. In another, it reflects that the only substantive public policy conceivably recognised by the Convention is that manifested by applicable rules of international law. Both if a tribunal exercises jurisdiction in a non-investment dispute, and, conceivably, if it manifestly fails to apply applicable rules of international law, these constitute possible grounds of annulment under the excess of powers exception in Article 52(1)(b).

[116] ICSID Convention Art 27(1): 'No Contracting State shall give diplomatic protection, or bring an international claim, in respect of a dispute which one of its nationals and another Contracting State shall have consented to submit or shall have submitted to arbitration under this Convention, unless such other Contracting State shall have failed to abide by and comply with the award rendered in such dispute'.

[117] Cf the ICSID Convention Art 54(1), first sentence: 'Each Contracting State shall recognize an award rendered pursuant to this Convention as binding and enforce the pecuniary obligations imposed by that award within its territories as if it were a final judgment of a court in that State'.

[118] Cfr Van Houtte, 'Article 52 of the Washington Convention—A Brief Introduction' in Gaillard and Banifatemi (eds), *Annulment of ICSID Awards* (Juris Publishing, Huntington (NY), 2004), commenting (at 11): 'ICSID awards thus are liberated from the pitfalls of national legal systems in a way commercial arbitration can only dream of'.

[119] Cf the ICSID Convention Art 52.

[120] See generally Gaillard and Banifatemi (2004).

[121] See Baldwin, Kantor and Nolan, 'Limits to Enforcement of ICSID Awards' (2006) 23(1) *J Int'l Arb* 1.

[122] Nevertheless, while there is as of yet not much municipal court practice relating to enforcement of ICSID awards, the practice of French courts indicates that the possibility of challenge on the basis of (international) ordre public is not quite excluded, see further Baldwin, Kantor and Nolan (2006) 3.

While the ICSID Convention thus attempts to exclude judicial review by municipal courts, a word nevertheless ought to be said about the envisaged finality of ICSID awards. As much as the ICSID Convention constitutes a self-contained regime, the last word nevertheless necessarily remains with the municipal court confronted with a claim for recognition or enforcement. This shows the dilemma and complexity of an international remedy relying on municipal law for its strength. When that strength needs to be exerted, it ultimately still depends on the compliance of the municipal law in question. For the municipal court, the obligation to recognise and enforce will be an international obligation incorporated into its municipal law, which may be held to collide with its general procedural law, separate constitutional requirements, as well as, possibly, other international obligations. Thus, it has been suggested, as also indicated by the language of the Convention itself (cfr article 54: '. . . as if it were a final judgment of a court in that state'), that finality only means finality to the same extent as a municipal court judgment. This would not exclude the possibility of challenging an award at least in so far as grounds can be pleaded upon which it could have been re-opened according to the forum state's own procedural law.[123] One could also conceive of an award set aside as a nullity by a municipal court, although this is decidedly more problematic in view of the system contemplated by the Convention and would in most instances represent a clear violation.[124] A more practical dilemma is that represented by an award deemed to violate fundamental constitutional or international obligations. What will a court do, for instance, if it finds that an ICSID award violates fundamental human rights or principles of due process, which may also be incorporated into its municipal law on the same or a higher level than the ICSID Convention? While the ICSID Convention itself would seem to envisage that the annulment procedure is exhaustive in this respect, this may not necessarily appear decisive for a municipal court faced with a normative conflict where it would otherwise have invoked the *ordre public* reservation. It is consequently not possible to wholly exclude in practice the final power of review vested in the municipal court where enforcement of an award is sought. When that is said, the clearest obstacle to the enforceability of ICSID awards is, in the same manner as for ordinary commercial arbitration, that submission to ICSID does not exclude the normal rules of state immunity against execution.[125]

123 See Baldwin, Kantor and Nolan (2006) 8.
124 Van Houtte (2004) at n 1.
125 See the ICSID Convention art 55.

4.4 INVESTMENT TREATY JURISDICTION OVER CONTRACT CLAIMS

The above comparison between ordinary commercial arbitration and the more internationally self-contained system of the ICSID Convention, reflects a gradual movement away from ordinary reciprocally-based arbitration into a claims resolution procedure more concerned with upholding rules and principles of international law. The culmination of this development is the contemporary system of investment treaty arbitration. As mentioned, this is an arbitral mechanism based on general consent in a treaty, usually a bilateral investment treaty between the investor's home state and the host state. Usually the reference is to ICSID, but other arbitral procedures than ICSID are also frequently referred to, such as arbitration under the UNCITRAL rules or the rules of a standing institution such as the Court of Arbitration of the International Chamber of Commerce or the Arbitration Institute of the Stockholm Chamber of Commerce. In the latter cases the arbitral proceedings are conducted under the general framework of international commercial arbitration.[126] The awards will then usually be enforceable under the New York Convention in the manner discussed above, either by express reference or by implication.[127] In the former instance, the awards are enforceable in the ordinary manner under the ICSID Convention as discussed above. This mechanism presents obvious advantages for a foreign investor. It will often seem to be preferable over the ordinary contractual dispute resolution procedures that would otherwise be available, even in respect of a purely contractual claim against the state. This raises the crucial issue of precedence if contractual and investment treaty jurisdictions overlap, an issue which I revert to in section 4.5 below. Preliminary to this is, however, the question whether investment treaty jurisdiction exists in the first place over claims that are, at least initially, contractual. Two main questions arise in this context and will be discussed in the following. The first question is how a contractual claim can be squared with the concept of 'investment', which has come to play a central role as a criterion of arbitrability in investment treaty arbitration. The second question is whether and to what extent investment treaty jurisdiction exists in respect of claims which are essentially or merely contractual, in the sense of lacking any separate basis in the treaty of which the arbitration provision is a part.

[126] Thus the award will also be subject to supervision and challenge under the law of the seat of the arbitration, see eg *United Mexican States v Metalclad Corp* (Decision of the Supreme Court of British Columbia, 2 May 2001), 2001 BCSC 664; and *Czech Republic v CME Czech Republic BV* (Decision of the Svea Court of Appeals, 15 May 2003), 42 ILM 919.

[127] See eg *Republic of Ecuador v Occidental Exploration and Production Co* [2006] QB 432 (CA); and see also Douglas (2003) 226 et seq.

A. The Notion of 'Investment'

As mentioned, the main criterion of 'arbitrability' under the ICSID Convention is a limitation of jurisdiction to disputes 'arising directly out of an investment'.[128] The concept of 'investment' is normally also a crucial criterion of jurisdiction in investment treaties referring to investor-state arbitration.[129] As such it is primarily subject to definition in the relevant treaty. In principle, what is involved here is consequently a double test: an investment treaty claim brought under ICSID needs to satisfy both the requirement under ICSID and the relevant investment treaty to qualify for jurisdiction.[130] In most cases, it is nevertheless questionable whether there is any great need to distinguish the two concepts, since what is at issue is whether the notion of investment should generally be conceived to contain an inherent limitation of the scope of investment treaty jurisdiction. Whereas there is no great need to limit the category of disputes referred to ICSID by a mutual consent in respect of the individual dispute, there is clearly a need to have some criterion of admissibility with regard to investment treaty arbitration based on a general consent directed at an unspecified number of potential claimants. As remarked by Douglas, if no such inherent limitation in the notion of investment were assumed, then 'pursuant to some investment treaty definitions of an investment, a metro ticket might qualify as "claim to money or to any performance under contract, having a financial value" and thus as an investment'.[131]

By the term 'investment' one would commonly envisage a transaction involving some kind of influx of capital, knowledge or resources into the territory of a state, which in addition acquires a certain permanency of attachment to that state. While it is often treated as a criterion inherent to the ICSID Convention, the notion of investment is not further defined in the Convention itself however, supposedly because the drafters wanted to leave a margin of appreciation to the parties involved as to the appropriate definition in concrete circumstances.[132] ICSID practice in disputes where the

[128] The ICSID Convention, art 25.

[129] See generally Douglas, *The International Law of Investment Claims* (Cambridge University Press, Cambridge, 2009) 161 et seq, Rubins, 'The Notion of 'Investment' in International Investment Arbitration' in N Horn (ed), *Arbitrating Foreign Investment Disputes* (Kluwer, The Hague, 2004) 283, and Yala, 'The Notion of 'Investment' in ICSID Case Law: A Drifting Jurisdictional Requirement?' (2005) 22(2) *J Int'l Arb* 105.

[130] See eg *Salini Costruttori SpA and Italstrade SpA v Kingdom of Morocco* (Decision on Jurisdiction, 2001) (2002) 129 *J du Dr Int'l* 196, para 44; and see also Rubins (2004) 290; and Yala (2005) 107 et seq.

[131] Douglas (2009) 163.

[132] The Report of the Executive Directors explained this as follows, (1965) 4 ILM 524, para 27: 'No attempt was made to define the term 'investment' given the essential requirements of consent by the parties, and the mechanisms through which Contracting States can make known in advance, if they so desire, the classes of disputes which they would or would not consider submitting to the Centre (Article 25(4))'. And see also Broches, 'The Convention on

consent was given in respect of the individual dispute not surprisingly also supports such a liberal approach, although a certain objective minimum requirement has been assumed.[133] In *Aucoven v Venezuela* the tribunal considered the essential requirement to be that 'the criteria agreed upon by the parties are reasonable and not totally inconsistent with the purposes of the Convention'.[134] ICSID itself has indicated that an ordinary supply contract for sale of goods will not in any case satisfy the investment criterion.[135] At least in so far as the contract involves a minimum of attachment to the internal economy of the state in question, it is nevertheless hard to envisage that jurisdiction should be denied under an individual agreement referring to ICSID for the reason of lacking sufficient connection with an investment. This lenient attitude is justified precisely because jurisdiction is based in an individual contract with the investor. It provides latitude for the respective member states to resolve this individually for themselves in concrete circumstances. The liberal construction of the criterion means that the member states, when initially acceding to the Convention, effectively delegated some latitude to themselves for the future. In the broader consensual scheme of the Convention, it is furthermore not material at which level final and definitive consent is given. As long as a real consent is given in respect of the individual dispute, the broader legitimacy of the Centre's jurisdiction is thereby also established.

As already alluded to, this latter consideration does not apply when jurisdiction is based on the general and unspecific consent given in a treaty. The definition of 'investment' provided for in investment treaties may, of course, be narrower and more specific than the liberal and open-

the Settlement of Investment Disputes: Some Observations on Jurisdiction' (1966) 5 *Col J Transnat'l Law* 261, 268, who as one of the main drafters of the convention explained the prevailing concern as follows: 'During the negotiations several definitions of 'investment' were considered and rejected. It was felt in the end that a definition could be dispensed with given the essential requirement of consent by the parties. This indicates that the requirement that the dispute must have arisen out of an investment may be merged into the requirement of consent to jurisdiction. Presumably, the parties' agreement that a dispute is an 'investment dispute' will be given great weight in any determination of the Centre's jurisdiction, although it would not be controlling'. See also (obiter) *Societe Ouest Africaine des Betons Industriel (SOABI) v Senegal* (Award, 1988) 2 ICSID Rep 190, 219: '[T]he object of the General Undertaking was limited to construction of a building to be paid for by the client as work progressed, and could thus not be said to be an agreement concerning investments. Disputes arising thereunder could therefore not be investment disputes as required by Article 25 of the ICSID Convention'.

133 See *Autopista Concesionada de Venezuela CA (Aucoven) v Republic of Venezuela* (Decision on Jurisdiction, 2001) para 96, *CSOB v Slovakia* (Decision on Jurisdiction, 1999) 5 ICSID Rep 330 (para 66), and *Fedax NV v Republic of Venezuela* (Decision on Jurisdiction, 1997) 5 ICSID Rep 186 (paras 21–2).

134 *Aucoven v Venezuela* (Decision on Jurisdiction, 2001), para 97.

135 Apparently, the ICSID secretariat in one case rejected a dispute arising out of such an ordinary supply contract for sale of goods for 'manifest incompliance' with the investment criterion, see Shihata and Parra, 'The Experience of the International Centre for Settlement of Investment Disputes' (1999) 14 *ICSID Rev-FILJ* 299, 308.

ended criterion envisaged under ICSID.[136] Most BITs nevertheless provide a liberal and unspecific definition of 'investment' composed of two elements. The first element is commonly the requirement of an attachment to the territory of the host state.[137] The second element is a broad definition to include 'any kind of asset' and further exemplified by a non-exhaustive list of covered assets, encompassing everything from movable and immovable property to intellectual property rights, shares in companies, debts, contracts, concessions, licences etc.[138] This lack of specificity may suggest that some inherent meaning is intended to be implied into the term itself, presumably based on the common-sensical understanding of investment as something involving a commitment or influx of capital, in order to limit the number and category of disputes coming within the ambit of jurisdiction under the treaty. A crossing concern is nevertheless that of predictability.[139] It is clearly not a satisfactory solution to have the existence or not of arbitral jurisdiction in a given case depend on a more or less discretionary notion of investment that may be subject to differing interpretations by different tribunals. While not fully satisfactory from either perspective, arbitral practice may be seen to reflect these crossing concerns, although it may be overly optimistic to posit that arbitral practice presents an entirely consistent picture. While generally employing a liberal interpretation of the 'investment' criterion, subject to the terms of the investment treaty involved, it is at least possible to discern a tendency in practice to attach greater significance to an objective meaning of investment where jurisdiction under an investment treaty is at issue, than with respect to an individual consent based in a contract.

The main concern is to distinguish contracts conceived as investments from 'ordinary commercial transactions' that do not fall under the natural ambit of an investment treaty. In *Fedax v Venezuela*, the tribunal reasoned that an apparent objective of the investment criterion was to exclude 'ordinary commercial' transactions from the ambit of the ICSID Convention.[140] It nevertheless held that 'loans and other credit facilities'

[136] See eg the exhaustive NAFTA definition of investment in art 1139, especially letter (h) qualifying contractual rights as investment only to the extent of involving 'the commitment of capital or other resources in the territory of a Party to economic activity in such territory', and see also letter (i) excluding 'claims to money that arise solely from (i) commercial contracts for the sale of goods or services . . . and (ii) the extension of credit in connection with a commercial transaction . . .'.

[137] This may either be a part of the initial definition of 'investment', see eg Agreement between Norway and Russia on Promotion and Mutual Protection of Investments (signed Oslo, 4 October 1995, entered into force 21 May 1998) art 1, or an additional requirement specifically limiting jurisdiction to investments attached to the host state's territory, see eg The Energy Charter Treaty Art 26(1).

[138] See eg the Energy Charter Treaty Art 1(6), and see generally Dolzer and Stevens, *Bilateral Investment Treaties* (Martinus Nijhoff Publishers, The Hague, 1995) 26.

[139] See also Douglas (2009) 190.

[140] *Fedax NV v Republic of Venezuela* (Decision on Jurisdiction, 1997) 37 ILM 1378, para 28.

qualified as investment.[141] The case concerned a claim based on promissory notes issued by the respondent and later purchased by the claimant. This was considered to fall within the centre's jurisdiction, based on the broad definition of investment in the concrete investment treaty. What is then meant by an 'ordinary commercial transaction' is less obvious. It is revealing that in the context of international commercial arbitration and state immunity, national court practice and literature have sometimes gone to great lengths to qualify investment contracts as commercial transactions.[142] Thus a 'commercial' criterion is clearly not in itself decisive. As a rule, investment transactions obviously are commercial. A criterion that has been suggested is nevertheless whether the essential interest of the investor in the transaction lies in generating a profit by accumulation of value,[143] or merely by getting paid for a delivery of goods or services.[144] This would exclude mere sale and purchase transactions from the ambit of the Convention. There is also some support for such a distinction in practice. Thus, in *SOABI v Senegal*, the tribunal held that a construction contract based on progressive payment could not have been considered an investment.[145] And in one of the few reported cases so far to have denied jurisdiction for non-compliance with the investment criterion, *Joy Mining v Egypt*, the tribunal held that a contract for delivery of mining equipment was not an investment in relation to the ICSID Convention Article 25.[146] This transaction was not considered to include the expectation of a 'regularity of profit and return' considered by the tribunal as a key factor to qualify a transaction as an investment.[147]

This distinction between an accumulation of profits, or a 'regularity of profit and return', and payment of an agreed price, does not stand the test of other cases however. Several decisions have held that contracts for delivery of services at a price may qualify as investment. First, and significantly, several tribunals have found construction contracts to qualify as investment, for the purpose both of the relevant investment treaty and the ICSID Convention.[148] Secondly, in the two *SGS* cases, the

141 *ibid*, para 37.

142 See eg Schreuer (1988) 29, and see the commentary to Article 17 of the UN Convention on State Immunity (2004) in the *Report of the Ad Hoc Committee on Jurisdictional Immunities of States and their Property* (A/58/22).

143 Cf the separate opinion of Brownlie, in *CME Czech Republic BV v Czech Republic* (Final Award, 2003) para 34, characterising 'the nature of an investment as a form of expenditure or transfer of funds for the precise purpose of obtaining a return'.

144 Yala (2005) 112.

145 *SOABI v Senegal* (Award, 1988) 2 ICSID Rep 190, 219.

146 *Joy Mining Machinery Ltd v Arab Republic of Egypt* (Award, 2004) paras 48–63.

147 *Joy Mining v Egypt* (Award, 2004) para 53; see also the separate opinion of Brownlie, in *CME Czech Republic BV v Czech Republic* (Final Award, 2003) para 34.

148 See especially *Salini Costruttori v Morocco* (Decision on Jurisdiction, 2001) paras 50–58, and see also for some of the most recent cases, *Toto Costruzioni Generali SpA v Republic of Lebanon* (Decision on jurisdiction, 2009); *Noble Energy Inc and Machalapower CIA Ltd v Ecuador* (Decision on jurisdiction, 2008); *LESI SpA v Algeria* (Decision on Jurisdiction, 2006); *Jan de Nul*

contracts for import supervision services were considered to qualify as investment by both tribunals. The service delivered consisted in pre-shipment inspections conducted by the company in the exporting country, that is, outside the territory of the host state.[149]

The criteria increasingly relied on by the cases has instead been related to a requirement of 'substantial contribution' or 'commitment' to the economy of the host state. The requirement was first set out in *Salini v Morocco*, which concerned a construction contract, as a three or four-pronged criterion (dependent on whether criteria (i) and (iv) are treated as mutually distinct), requiring (i) a 'contribution' (of capital and resources), (ii) 'a certain duration of performance of the contract', (iii) 'a participation in the risks of the transaction' and (iv) a 'contribution to the economic development of the host state'.[150] Of these the 'contribution' and 'risk' elements would seem to be the central factors when measured against other cases. In *Joy Mining v Egypt* the tribunal tellingly distinguished the delivery contract in that case from the long-term construction contract in *Salini v Morocco*, primarily, it might seem, on the basis of the magnitude of the capital commitment, and the nature of the risk involved.[151] The particular risk element relied upon here may be seen in relation to the criterion relied on in the *Joy Mining* case of 'regularity of profit and return'.[152] This may be seen as connected to the rationale and justification of investment protection more generally, namely to facilitate the commitment of capital and resources to the territory of a state, and to alleviate the particular risk involved in thus placing both the invested capital and, significantly, the expectation of returns at the mercy of the government and policies of the state involved.

A number of cases nevertheless do not fit well with a strict application of these criteria. In the two partly conflicting decisions rendered in the *SGS* cases, both claims were based on alleged breach of payment for services performed essentially *outside* the territory of the respondent states. In the opinion of both tribunals this did not preclude that the claims arose out of investments 'in the territory' of these states. In order to perform the

and Dredging International v Egypt (Award, 2006); *Bayindir Insaat Turizm Ticaret ve Sanayi AS v Islamic Republic of Pakistan* (Decision on Jurisdiction, 2005); and *Consortium Groupement LESI v Algerie* (Decision on Jurisdiction, 2005).

149 *(SGS) Societe Generale de Surveillance SA v Islamic Republic of Pakistan* (Decision on Jurisdiction, 2003) para 140 (2003) 18 *ICSID Rev-FILJ* 307; *(SGS) Societe Generale de Surveillance SA v Republic of the Philippines* (Decision on Jurisdiction, 2004) para 112.

150 *Salini Costruttori v Morocco* (Decision on Jurisdiction, 2001) para 52.

151 *Joy Mining v Egypt* (Award, 2004) paras 53–4 and para 62: '*Salini v Morocco* has also occupied the attention of the parties. In that case however, a major project for the construction of a highway was involved and this indeed required not only heavy capital investment but also services and other long-term commitments'. See also *Jan de Nul and Dredging International v Egypt* (Award, 2006) para 92.

152 *Joy Mining v Egypt* (Award, 2004) para 53; see also the separate opinion of Brownlie in *CME v Czech Republic* (Final Award, 2003) para 34.

services, certain expenditures and a certain establishment had had to be made in the respective states. Both tribunals held that this was sufficient, under the circumstances, to classify the contracts as investments in their totality, although the expenditures were admitted to be relatively insignificant in comparison with the total costs of providing the services abroad.[153] The reasoning of these two tribunals suggests an alternative factor that is relevant for classification of a contract as an investment, namely the public nature of the performance or service involved. Thus, in *SGS v Pakistan* it was considered especially significant that the contract involved the performance of a government function, which thus distinguished the contract from an ordinary private law contract.[154] As to the territorial connection of the investments in question, it was emphasised in *SGS v Philippines* that although tenuous, the investment did not have a substantial connection with any other territory; thus the main territorial connection of the investment was with the territory of the Philippines.[155] Thus, the cases may be explained on the basis that there was no other territory than the Philippines and Pakistan which had a closer connection to the performance of the contracts, while at the same time the contracts had a distinct government purpose distinguishing them from other and more ordinary contracts for delivery of services.

Other cases also emphasise the openended-ness of the 'investment' criterion as a jurisdictional requirement, and suggest that the Salini criteria cannot serve as anything more than a strong indication of the characteristics normally present in an investment.[156] A recent case is the annulment committee's decision in *Malaysian Historical Salvors v Malaysia*, overturning the initial award in that case. The case concerned a salvage contract entered into by the marine salvage company Malaysian Historical Salvors with the Malaysian government, to search for and salvage cargo carried by the British vessel *Diana*, which shipwrecked and sank in Malaysian territorial waters in 1817. The contract was entered into on a 'no-salvage no-pay' basis, whereby the salvage company would if successful be entitled to receive a salvage fee of 70 per cent of the value of recovered cargo. When a dispute arose over the determination of the appropriate salvage fee, the company eventually presented a claim against the Malaysian government under the

[153] Described in *SGS v Philippines* as 'a fraction of the cost of conducting the actual inspections abroad' (Decision on Jurisdiction, 2004) para 105.

[154] *SGS v Pakistan* (Decision on Jurisdiction, 2003) para 135 and 138–40.

[155] *SGS v Philippines* (Decision on Jurisdiction, 2004) para 112: 'There was no distinct or separate investment made elsewhere than in the territory of the Philippines but a single integrated process of inspection arranged through the Manila Liaison Office, itself unquestionably an investment 'in the territory of' the Philippines'.

[156] *Malaysian Historical Salvors SDN BHD v Govt of Malaysia* (Decision on Annulment, 2009) para 56 et seq; *Biwater Gauff (Tanzania) Ltd v United Republic of Tanzania* (Award, 2008) para 307 et seq, and see also Schreuer (2001) 140. See for a crititique of each of the respective criteria Manciaux, 'The Notion of Investment: New Controversies' (2008) 9(6) *JWIT* 443.

terms of the UK-Malaysia BIT. The initial award rendered by a sole arbitrator refused jurisdiction pursuant to a 'fact-specific and holistic assessment' of whether the relevant hallmarks of an investment (as identified, inter alia, by the *Salini* case) were present, emphasising particularly how the risk assumed by the company was primarily commercial, consisting in the uncertainty of finding and salvaging the cargo, and that the contract did not present any significant contribution to the economy of the host state different from 'the benefits flowing to the place of performance of any normal service contract'.[157] This approach was effectively squashed by the annulment committee, annulling the award on the basis that the tribunal had manifestly exceeded its powers for failing to exercise jurisdiction under ICSID and the BIT. In contrast to the 'fact-specific and holistic assessment' advocated by the initial tribunal, the annulment committee emphasised the open-ended and unqualified definition of 'investment' under both the ICSID Convention and the terms of the UK-Malaysia BIT.[158] To support its conclusion that the salvage contract indeed constituted an investment for the purpose of ascertaining jurisdiction, the committee referred to the open definition of investment in the BIT as 'every kind of asset', and on this basis held as follows:

> The Contract between the Government of Malaysia and Malaysian Historical Salvors is one of a kind of asset; what is precisely at issue between the Government and the Salvor is a claim to money and to performance under a contract having financial value; the contract involves intellectual property rights; and the right granted to salvage may be treated as a business concession conferred under a contract.
>
> It follows that, by the terms of the Agreement, and for its purposes, the Contract is an investment. There is no room for another conclusion.[159]

There are strong reasons underlying such a flexible understanding of the 'investment' criterion. It would be meaningless if the notion of investment as a jurisdictional requirement should be given a more restricted ambit than the scope of rights actually protected by the investment treaty in question. This can obviously not be inferred from the investment treaty itself, and to impose such a requirement on the sole basis of the notion of investment in the ICSID Convention would, as aptly stated by the annulment committee in *Malaysian Historical Salvors v Malaysia*, create the risk of 'crippling the

[157] *Malaysian Historical Salvors v Malaysia* (Award on jurisdiction, 2007) para 144.

[158] *Malaysian Historical Salvors v Malaysia* (Decision on Annulment, 2009) para 57; see also *Biwater Gauff (Tanzania) Ltd v Tanzania* (Award, 2008) para 312: 'In the Tribunal's view, there is no basis for a rote, or overly strict, application of the five Salini criteria in every case. These criteria are not fixed or mandatory as a matter of law. They do not appear in the ICSID Convention. On the contrary, it is clear from the travaux préparatoires of the Convention that several attempts to incorporate a definition of "investment" were made, but ultimately did not succeed. In the end, the term was left intentionally undefined, with the expectation (inter alia) that a definition could be the subject of agreement as between Contracting States'.

[159] *Malaysian Historical Salvors v Malaysia* (Decision on Annulment, 2009) paras 60–61.

institution'.[160] At least where ICSID is the only arbitral institution referred to in the investment treaty, it would mean creating a fortuitous distinction between rights covered both by the notion of investment in the treaty and in the ICSID Convention, where jurisdiction would exist; and rights covered by the notion of investment in the treaty but not in ICSID, where the lack of jurisdiction under ICSID would largely undermine the effectiveness of protection under the treaty. Surely this cannot have been the meaning of the unspecific reference to 'arising directly out of an investment' in Article 25 of the ICSID Convention, and no true basis can either be found in the language, prehistory or objectives of the Convention for such an inference.[161]

The underlying rationale justifying a limitation of jurisdiction based on the 'investment' criterion is, according to this understanding, that there is a natural limit to the scope of protection under an investment treaty. While commonly subject to definition in the investment treaty as different categories of protected assets, the natural scope of such protection may also, to some extent, be considered inherent in the notion of investment in itself. To take an example, arms manufacturers receive colossal orders from foreign states for purchases of military equipment. Both before and after a contract is awarded they may have expended considerable resources in the territory of the state making the order, in clear expectation of a future return, and there may be substantial and long-term risk involved in the deal for the manufacturer, even of a political nature. Irrespective of this, Lockheed-Martin clearly does not make an 'investment' in Turkey within the terms of the US-Turkey BIT by selling F-35 fighters to that country. Purely in linguistic terms, a claim by Lockheed-Martin for payment under the F-35 sales contract could, in isolation, be seen to be covered both by the term 'claim to money or a claim to performance having economic value, and associated with an investment', or the term 'any right conferred by law or contract, including rights to search for or utilize natural resources, and rights to manufacture, use and sell products'.[162] That something more than fulfillment of the mere formal, or legal, characteristics herein provided is required, is nevertheless, in the particular example of the US-Turkey BIT, indicated by the circularity of the definition provided in the treaty itself, where 'investment' is defined to mean 'every kind of investment', including 'a claim to money or a claim to performance', which also is said to require an association with an 'investment'. Despite the linguistic confusion created by the circularity, it does at least clearly indicate that the notion of 'investment' in itself is intended to contain an inherent meaning, which cannot, according to any

[160] *Malaysian Historical Salvors v Malaysia* (Decision on Annulment, 2009) para 73.
[161] *ibid*, para 62 et seq.
[162] US-Turkey BIT (signed 3 December 1985, entered into force 18 May 1990) art 1 (c).

common-sensical understanding of the term, be deemed to cover the sale of military aircraft produced in the United States. This is even more pronounced in the 2004 US Model BIT, where 'investment' is defined as 'every asset that an investor owns or controls, directly or indirectly, that has the characteristics of an investment, including such characteristics as the commitment of capital or other resources', which is then followed by the conventional list of possible legal forms of an investment.[163]

Even where the treaty-provided definition of the term lacks the specificity of language of the US Model BIT, cogent reasons suggest that the notion of 'investment' in itself must be deemed to contain some inherent qualification of covered assets along these lines. One recent publication proposes that the notion of investment must be deemed to contain a dual requirement of respectively 'legal' and 'economic' characteristics that must be present for something to constitute an investment.[164] Whereas the former is proposed to limit the meaning of the term to rights having the characteristics of property rights or rights *in rem*,[165] the latter is proposed to require 'a commitment of resources to the economy of the host state by the claimant entailing the assumption of risk in expectation of a commercial return'.[166]

The former proposition arguably goes too far. One of its envisaged consequences is that where the claimant relies upon a contract to establish an investment 'the rights *in personam* do not generally qualify as an investment independently of the rights *in rem*'.[167] At least superficially, this would seem to exclude rights *in personam* against the state or state entities from being able to constitute protected investments as such. This cannot be correct as a general and unqualified proposition. Whether a given contractual undertaking by a state or state entity creates rights that are recognisable as investments is obviously a substantive issue. It consequently ought not to be determined prima facie one way or another at the jurisdictional stage. Moreover, it is to jump to conclusions to assume, prima facie, that this issue is necessarily dependent upon whether the rights have matured sufficiently to achieve an *in rem* quality. There is no conclusive basis in either the commonly open-ended definition of 'investment', or the objective of investment protection to support this as a general and unqualified proposition. Although it is not difficult to see that the *in rem* qualities of a right may be crucial for its protection under relevant substantive standards, this is not to say that only rights *in rem* enjoy such protection. As I will come back to in chapter five below, a main concern is that it is difficult to maintain a meaningful distinction between

163 US Model BIT (2004) art 1.
164 Douglas (2009) 163.
165 *ibid*, 170.
166 *ibid*, 189.
167 *ibid*, 202.

a right *in rem* and a right *in personam* when the state itself is involved as a party, since the crucial issue in any case is whether the state is bound by the corresponding contractual obligation it has undertaken.

What remains is thus, arguably, that an investment in some manner must involve (i) a distinct right or entitlement (though not necessarily of an *in rem* variety), which (ii) in some manner must arise out of or be directly associated with a 'commitment of resources' to the state and sharing in the attendant risk elements which this entails. The first 'legal' or 'formal' requirement stems from the definition of investment in investment treaties as categories of different rights or entitlements, having as a 'common thread' the existence of a 'proprietary or contractual' right.[168] In respect of contractual undertakings, this suggests that the existence of a valid contractual attachment with the state, or a state entity, creates a presumption to the effect that there is an investment also within the terms of the treaty, whereas the lack of such a valid contractual undertaking conversely suggests that jurisdiction is excluded. Indeed, some cases have expressly refused jurisdiction on the basis that the claims in question concerned pre-contractual expenditures, clearly assuming that if a binding commitment had come into place there would also have been an investment.[169] The second substantial requirement entails, however, that the jurisdictional issue is not exhausted simply by virtue of the fact that there is a valid contractual right or entitlement. Instead it invokes the main 'objective' elements of the *Salini* criteria as something residual, being inherent in the very term and notion of an 'investment'. As already examined above, there is support in arbitral practice for assuming some such inherent limitation in the scope of protection extended under investment treaties, most decidedly in the few cases where tribunals have in fact refused jurisdiction based on the lack of sufficient characteristics of an investment.[170] The common element of the decisions in *Joy Mining v Egypt* and *Petrobart Ltd v Kyrgyz Republic,* which both concerned essentially a contract of sale, is the lack of a lasting commitment of resources as an essential part of the contract.[171] Opposite this, however, as examined, stands a strong line of cases which in accepting jurisdiction have expressly refused to lay

[168] See eg *F-W Oil Interests, Inc v Republic of Trinidad and Tobago* (Award, 2006) para 125.

[169] See eg *F-W Oil Interests, Inc v Trinidad and Tobago* (Award, 2006) para 145; *PSEG Global et al v Republic of Turkey* (Decision on jurisdiction, 2004) para 80 et seq; *Mihaly International Corporation v Democratic Socialist Republic of Sri Lanka* (Award, 2002) para 59; *Lanco Int'l Inc v Argentine Republic* (Decision on Jurisdiction, 1998) para 15.

[170] See *Joy Mining v Egypt* (Award, 2004) paras 48–63; and *Petrobart Ltd v Kyrgyz Republic* (Award, 2005) 69 et seq; and see also the award in *Malaysian Historical Salvors v Malaysia* (Award on jurisdiction, 2007) para 42 et seq, which was however later set aside by the decision of the Annulment Committee in that case on the basis of this very issue.

[171] *Petrobart Ltd v Kyrgyz Republic* (Award, 2005) 69: 'The Arbitral Tribunal further notes that the Contract did not involve any transfer of money or property as capital in a business in the Kyrgyz Republic but was a sales contract. It concerned the sale of goods at an agreed price'.

down any strict requirement of at least a significant capital contribution, a particular risk element or a given duration, or for that matter any significant 'contribution to the economic development' of the host state.[172] Especially the requirements of duration and contribution to the economic development of the host state are difficult to find any clear basis for in the underlying rationale of investment protection.[173] However, the tendency of decided cases, as particularly reflected by the line of cases where jurisdiction has been accepted in respect of contracts not involving any significant capital commitment as such, also suggests that the objective criteria of 'contribution' and 'risk' must be given flexible meanings.

An approach taking as its starting point 'the ordinary meaning to be given to the terms of the treaty in their context and in the light of its object and purpose',[174] suggests in this respect that the notion of 'investment' cannot be viewed in separation from what it means to make an investment 'in' or 'in the territory' of the state in question, which is the term commonly used in investment treaties. Arguably it is this latter combined notion and not some principled stand-alone notion of 'investment' seen in isolation which is the real object of interpretation to determine the scope of an investment treaty. Whether it is strictly formulated in such terms or not, the presumed objective of investment treaties is always to render protection to investments that in some way can be considered 'in' or 'in the territory of' the respective contracting states.

In conceptual terms, the issue is consequently not whether a contract (or rather a right or entitlement inferred from a contract) qualifies as an investment per se, but rather whether it qualifies as an investment 'in' the state in question. This conceptually involves an element of commitment of resources and a certain territorial attachment over some time, together with the particular risk factors this entail. Arbitral decisions such as in the *SGS* cases and the *Malaysian Salvors* case nevertheless suggest that this is not a requirement to be applied strictly. Far from employing a strict requirement of 'contribution' and 'risk', the tendency of arbitral practice is rather to apply the criteria flexibly, and mainly to disqualify ordinary commercial contracts lacking any significant elements of this nature. This can be justified in light of the overriding objective of investment treaty arbitration to stimulate host state access to capital and resources by providing a remedy against public power. However, this suggests that not only the commitment of capital and resources, but also the nature of the contractual performance itself, may play a significant part in making a

[172] See particularly *Malaysian Historical Salvors v Malaysia* (Decision on Annulment, 2009) para 56; *Biwater Gauff (Tanzania) Ltd v Tanzania* (Award, 2008) para 307; *SGS v Philippines* (Decision on Jurisdiction, 2004) para 112.

[173] Douglas (2009) 198.

[174] The Vienna Convention on the Law of Treaties (signed Vienna, 23 May 1969, entered into force 27 January 1980) 1155 UNTS 331, art 31.

contractual right qualify as an investment. Where some element of delegation or restriction of public power is involved, this also brings in an element of political risk for the private party in relying on payment for its rendered performance, which is beyond the mere commercial and may be seen to take on crucial aspects of an 'investment' as conceived in a broad sense. There are also clear traces of this view in arbitral practice. Thus, one of the elements clearly distinguishing the contracts in the *SGS* cases from ordinary private and commercial contracts was the public service they concerned.[175] Conversely, in *Joy Mining v Egypt* the absence of characteristics normally associated with 'contrats de développement económique' was expressly cited as a reason for refusing jurisdiction.[176]

B. Jurisdiction in respect of Claims which are 'Essentially Contractual'

While a contract may qualify as investment in a given case, it does not necessarily follow that jurisdiction may be exercised over claims which are *essentially* contractual. It may first follow from the jurisdiction clause in the treaty in question that it extends only to certain specified causes of action. An example is the Norway-Russia BIT, which extends jurisdiction to

> [d]isputes between an investor of one Contracting Party and the other Contracting Party arising in connection with an investment in its territory and concerning the consequences of the non-implementation, or of the incorrect implementation of the obligation under this Agreement.[177]

This is similar to the arrangement envisaged by the Energy Charter Treaty,[178] while NAFTA chapter 11 similarly provides for arbitral jurisdiction only in respect of breaches of specific provisions.[179] Certain BITs, notably often those of China, go even further, and provide jurisdiction only in respect of specific issues that may arise under the BIT, typically the amount of compensation due for expropriation.[180]

The consequence of these stipulations is that jurisdiction is reserved for claims based upon the treaty itself, or even more specified types of claims. This does not preclude a claim because it arises out of a contractual relationship, but excludes claims based only on a breach of contract unless these can be framed as treaty claims.

[175] See especially *SGS v Pakistan* (Decision on Jurisdiction, 2003) para 135 and 138–40.

[176] *Joy Mining v Egypt* (Award, 2004) para 57.

[177] Norway-Russia BIT (1995) Art 8.

[178] Article 26 of the Energy Charter Treaty (Lisbon, 1994) gives the consent of each contracting party to submit to arbitral jurisdiction in respect of 'Disputes between a Contracting Party and an Investor of another Contracting Party relating to an Investment of the latter in the Area of the former, which concern an alleged breach of an obligation of the former under Part III.

[179] Articles 1116–17.

[180] See Norway-China BIT (1984) para 2 of the protocol.

A question which has attracted much attention is whether purely contractual claims can be made into treaty claims ipso facto by virtue of an 'umbrella clause'.[181] To some extent this perpetuates the controversy about internationalisation discussed in chapter three above, and the appropriate conclusion to be drawn is accordingly quite similar. Thus, even if a breach of contract should automatically also constitute a breach of treaty—which, as I come back to in chapter five, is doubtful in terms of substantive law but entirely possible as a matter of principle—the umbrella clause does not make the contract into an obligation on the level of the treaty. It is difficult to fault the analytical merit of the decision on jurisdiction in *SGS v Philippines*, where the umbrella clause was held to require strict observance of contractual undertakings, but simultaneously to entail that the existence of a breach had to depend on interpretation of the contract according to its own terms and subject to its applicable law.[182] As held by the tribunal, this also meant that jurisdiction to determine breach in the first place had to rest with the contractually-selected forum, the combined effect of which was to make the umbrella clause into 'an empty shell' for the purpose of jurisdiction.[183]

Some investment treaties, such as the US Model BIT, do not restrict jurisdiction only to treaty claims, but also cover disputes arising out of more closely defined legal relationships between states and investors, such as those concerning an 'investment authorisation' or 'investment agreements' in addition to 'alleged breach of any right conferred, created or recognised by this Treaty with respect to a covered investment'.[184] Most common, however, for a jurisdiction clause is not to provide any such specification at all, encompassing instead all 'disputes relating to an investment'. Having made an extensive survey of different investment treaties, Douglas has found this to be 'by far the most prevalent type of clause in BITs'.[185] A typical formulation is the arbitration provision in the Denmark-Croatia BIT, which extends jurisdiction to 'any dispute

[181] See for recent literature Wälde, 'The Umbrella Clause in Investment Arbitration—a Comment on Original Intentions and Recent Cases' (2005) 6(2) *JWIT* 183; Sinclair, 'The Origins of the Umbrella Clause in the International Law of Investment Protection' (2005) 20(4) *Arb Int'l* 411; Schreuer, 'Travelling the BIT Route: Of Waiting Periods, Umbrella Clauses and Forks in the Road' (2004) 5(2) *JWIT* 231; Alexandrov, 'Breaches of Contract and Breaches of Treaty: The Jurisdiction of Treaty-based Arbitration Tribunals to Decide Breach of Contract Claims in *SGS v Pakistan* and *SGS v Philippines*' (2004) 5(4) *JWIT* 555; and Gill, Gearing and Birt, 'Contractual Claims and Bilateral Investment Treaties: A Comparative Review of the SGS Cases' (2004) 21(5) *J Int'l Arb* 397.

[182] *SGS v Philippines* (Decision on Jurisdiction, 2004) paras 153–4.

[183] Gaillard, 'Investment Treaty Arbitration and Jurisdiction over Contract Claims—The SGS Cases Considered' in Weiler (ed): *International Investment Law and Arbitration: Leading Cases*, (Cameron May, London, 2005) 325, 334.

[184] See the US Model BIT (2004) Art 24(1)(a), which confines jurisdiction to claims based on the treaty, but provides a specific basis for jurisdiction in respect of breaches of 'an investment authorization' or 'an investment agreement'.

[185] Douglas (2009) 234.

concerning an investment between an investor of one Contracting Party and the other Contracting Party'.[186] Does this mean that this type of clause can be held to confer jurisdiction in respect of any contractual claim that does not have any basis in the treaty as such? As a starting point, the language of the provisions clearly suggests this, indicating that investors are given an independent right to pursue any grievances against the state concerning an investment, whatever their cause or substantial content, before an international arbitral tribunal. However, in *SGS v Pakistan* this was cast into doubt by the tribunal, which refused to exercise jurisdiction over claims considered essentially contractual and raising no issues under the substantive provisions of the BIT:

> We recognize that disputes arising from claims grounded on alleged violation of the BIT, and disputes arising from claims based wholly on supposed violations of the PSI Agreement, can both be described as 'disputes with respect to investments', the phrase used in Article 9 of the BIT. That phrase however, while descriptive of the *factual subject matter* of disputes, does not relate to the *legal basis* of the claims, or the *cause of action* asserted in the claims. In other words, from that description alone, without more, we believe that no implication necessarily arises that both BIT and purely contractual claims are intended to be covered by the Contracting Parties in Article 9.[187]

The tribunal thus presumed that the BIT would provide jurisdiction only in respect of claims based on the treaty itself.[188] In terms of theory, this invokes a strictly dualist premise in relation to division of competence. Competence to apply the treaty would be vested with the treaty tribunal, while competence to apply municipal law would rest with the domestic courts. The tribunal found support for its view in the decision of the annulment committee in the *Vivendi* case, and its distinction between treaty claims and contract claims:

> [W]hether there has been a breach of the BIT and whether there has been a breach of contract are different questions. Each of these claims will be determined by reference to its own proper or applicable law—in the case of the BIT, by international law; in the case of the Concession Contract, by the proper law of the contract, in other words, the law of Tucumán.[189]

It is relatively clear that the tribunal in *SGS v Pakistan* here took its reliance on the celebrated *Vivendi* decision a step too far. The significance drawn from the distinction between treaty claims and contract claims in the *Vivendi* annulment decision was that a contractual jurisdiction clause in the contract would not affect the competence of a BIT tribunal in respect

[186] Denmark-Croatia BIT, Art 8. See also Douglas (2009) 234 for further references.

[187] *SGS v Pakistan* (Decision on Jurisdiction, 2004) para 161.

[188] See also to this effect Douglas (2003) 256.

[189] *Compania de Aguas del Aconquija (CAA) SA and Vivendi Universal SA v Argentine Republic* (Decision on Annulment, 2002) para 96.

of claims based on the BIT.[190] The committee also assumed, in direct contrast to the finding of the tribunal in *SGS v Pakistan*, that the jurisdiction under the treaty was not confined to treaty claims.[191] The question addressed by the annulment committee was in fact not concerned with jurisdiction, but with whether the first tribunal had been right in dismissing the contractual claims on the merits, by reason of an exclusive jurisdiction clause in the contract.[192] The committee held that it had not, seemingly considering that this confused a possible objection to admissibility with a substantive basis for dismissing the claim.[193] According to the *Vivendi* annulment committee, the first tribunal should not have refrained from making its own appreciation of the contract under municipal law insofar as necessary to determine whether there had been a breach of the BIT.[194] The crucial point of the committee was thus virtually the opposite of that relied upon in *SGS v Pakistan*, namely that the tribunal should not confine itself to the role of a 'treaty organ' and agent of international law, but also had an incidental competence to apply municipal law relative to the treaty claim.

The analysis developed by the tribunal in *SGS v Pakistan* was also later rejected by the tribunal in its sibling case *SGS v Philippines*. Noting the stand taken in *SGS v Pakistan*, the latter tribunal expressly disagreed with the decision in the first case, citing a number of arguments supporting its own interpretation of the clause to encompass also 'claims of an essentially contractual character'.[195] First, it held that the language of the provision suggested a prima facie presumption to the effect that contractual as well as treaty claims were encompassed. Secondly, it also found this conclusion to be supported by 'a number of further considerations, both within the BIT itself and extrinsic to it'.[196] The tribunal pointed out that an ICSID tribunal, as well as an ad hoc tribunal established pursuant to the UNCITRAL rules, would be prima facie envisaged to have the same competence to apply municipal contract law as domestic courts. Moreover, on interpretation of the BIT, the investor-state dispute settlement provision was contrasted with the state-state dispute settlement provision, which expressly contemplated 'disputes . . . regarding the interpretation or application of the provisions of

[190] *ibid*, para 101.

[191] *ibid*, para 55: 'Article 8 does not use a narrower formulation, requiring that the investor's claim allege a breach of the BIT itself. Read literally, the requirements for arbitral jurisdiction in Article 8 do not necessitate that the Claimant allege a breach of the BIT itself; it is sufficient that the dispute relate to an investment made under the BIT'.

[192] *ibid*, para 93.

[193] *ibid*, para 102.

[194] *ibid*, para 105: '[I]t is one thing to exercise contractual jurisdiction (arguably exclusively vested in the administrative tribunals of Tucumán by virtue of the Concession Contract) and another to take into account the terms of a contract in determining whether there has been a breach of a distinct standard of international law, such as that reflected in Article 3 of the BIT'.

[195] *SGS v Philippines* (Decision on Jurisdiction, 2004) para 92.

[196] *ibid*, para 132.

the BIT'.[197] Finally, the suggested broader choice of forum for investors was held to be most consistent with the purpose of the BIT to 'promote and protect foreign investment'.[198]

Ostensibly, arbitral practice subsequent to the *SGS* cases has continued to diverge, but on a closer analysis of the cases, it may be possible to reconcile most of the subsequent cases with the analysis of the tribunal in the latter of the *SGS* cases. In *Joy Mining v Egypt*, which was decided after *SGS v Philippines*, the tribunal again seems closer to the *SGS v Pakistan* formula of jurisdiction, however. The tribunal here introduced a distinction between 'commercial aspects of a dispute and other aspects involving the existence of some form of State interference with the operation of the contract involved'.[199] The former was seemingly equiparated to the 'purely contractual' formula of the *SGS* cases, and assumed by the tribunal to fall outside the normal jurisdiction of an investment treaty tribunal:

> To the extent that a dispute might involve the same parties, object and cause of action it might be considered to be a dispute where it is virtually impossible to separate the contract issues from the treaty issues and to draw any jurisdictional conclusions from a distinction between them. A purely contractual claim, however, will normally find difficulty in passing the jurisdictional test of treaty based tribunals, which will of course require allegation of a specific violation of treaty rights as the foundation of their jurisdiction.[200]

Since the tribunal considered that the issue in question, the release of a bank guarantee, clearly concerned 'a commercial element of the contract',[201] it concluded that it did not have jurisdiction over the claim.[202]

Although not evident from the reasoning of the tribunal, a point of distinction between the latter case and the *SGS* cases may be that it concerned a claim that seems to have been based on a contract entered into between an independent state company and the foreign investor. This is more evident in *Salini v Jordan*. The tribunal was careful not to adopt any particular stance in respect of the *SGS* controversy, merely noting that

[197] *ibid*, para 132.

[198] *ibid*, para 132: '[T]he purpose of the BIT is to promote and protect foreign investment. Allowing investors a choice of forum for resolution of investment disputes of whatever character is consistent with this aim. By contrast drawing technical distinctions between causes of action arising under the BIT and those arising under the investment agreement is capable of giving rise to overlapping jurisdictions and jurisdictional uncertainty. It may be necessary to draw such distinctions in some cases, but it should be avoided to the extent possible, in the interests of the efficient resolution of investment disputes by the single chosen forum'.

[199] *Joy Mining v Egypt* (Decision on Jurisdiction, 2004) para 72.

[200] *ibid*, para 75.

[201] *ibid*, para 78.

[202] *ibid*, para 82: 'The tribunal concludes therefore that, even if for the sake of argument there was an investment in this case, the absence of Treaty-based claim, and the evidence that, on the contrary, all claims are contractual, justifies the finding that the Tribunal lacks jurisdiction'.

there were 'divergent positions' in arbitral practice, but distinguished itself from these cases on the basis that the state agency which was party to the contract had a separate legal personality under Jordanian law.[203] It could to this effect also rely on earlier cases holding that investment treaty tribunals cannot exercise jurisdiction over claims based on a contract to which the state itself is not a party.[204] Thus, in the earlier case of *Salini v Morocco*, the tribunal had held that where a state has 'organised a sector of activity through a distinct legal entity', the offer of jurisdiction extended by a state in a BIT would not prima facie extend to breaches of contract committed by that separate legal entity.[205] This suggests that breaches of contract committed by the state itself would be included. Thus, in the latter case, the tribunal held, as the natural antithesis of its argument, that jurisdiction would extend 'to any breach of contract that binds the State directly',[206] and 'breaches of contracts that would constitute, at the same time, a violation of the Bilateral Treaty by the State'.[207] In other words, jurisdiction was effectively held to require a direct basis for a claim against the state, whether in a contract entered into by the state as such, or through attribution of responsibility for a breach of the investment treaty.

A similar conclusion was reached by the tribunal in the more recent case of *Impregilo v Pakistan*. This tribunal relied on what it conceived as 'a clear distinction . . . between the responsibility of a state for the conduct of an entity that violates international law, and the responsibility of a State for the conduct of an entity that breaches a municipal law contract'.[208] On interpretation of the jurisdiction clause in the BIT, it thus held as follows:

> In the Tribunal's view, the jurisdiction offer in this BIT does not extend to breaches of a contract *to which an entity other than the State is named a party*. Indeed, had the intention been to extend each Contracting Party's jurisdiction offer in this way, the language of Article 9 would have been so crafted.[209]

Thus, both the first *Salini* tribunal and the tribunal in the later case of *Impregilo v Pakistan* effectively assumed they would have had jurisdiction over the contractual claims, if the party to the contract had been the state itself. These cases thus implicitly support the *SGS v Philippines* line of argument.

Some later cases have seemingly, following the *SGS v Pakistan* approach, rejected jurisdiction over essentially contractual claims, but arguably

[203] *Salini Costruttori SpA and Italstrade SpA v Hashemite Kingdom of Jordan* (Decision on Jurisdiction, 2004) para 100.

[204] *Salini Costruttori v Morocco* (Decision on Jurisdiction, 2001) paras 60–62; and *Consortium RFCC v Kingdom of Morocco* (Decision on Jurisdiction, 2001) paras 68–69.

[205] *Salini Costruttori v Morocco* (Decision on Jurisdiction, 2001) para 60.

[206] *ibid*, para 61.

[207] *ibid*, para 62.

[208] *Impregilo SpA v Islamic Republic of Pakistan* (Decision on Jurisdiction, 2005) para 210.

[209] *ibid*, para 214.

without providing any real justification for this conclusion.[210] On final analysis it would nevertheless seem that a general exclusion of contract claims, where no such limitation is specified by the clause itself, is not supported by the general tendency of practice. It may also seem that the main concern of the tribunal in *SGS v Pakistan* was more limited, namely to uphold a separate jurisdiction clause in the contracts, without exempting claims based on the treaty itself from BIT jurisdiction, as I come back to in the next part of this chapter.

The tendency of arbitral practice can here be said to correspond with fundamental concerns related to the ICSID system and the objective of investment arbitration as a means of investment protection more generally. The most crucial argument in favour of an extensive interpretation of open-ended jurisdictional provisions in investment treaties to cover also contractual claims, is that the general system of ICSID itself fails to provide a basis for restricting jurisdiction to claims based on treaty or international law. According to the ordinary scheme of ICSID, contractual claims are covered irrespective of whether the cause of action is based in municipal or international law; indeed, under Article 42 of the ICSID Convention the municipal law of the host state is even envisaged as the law being primarily applicable to disputes under the ambit of the Convention. Where an investment treaty makes a simple reference to ICSID without further specification, the presumption would seem to be that it incorporates the standard ICSID model into the BIT. Moreover, the same concern relating to certainty and predictability that was shown to play a crucial role in the delimitation of the 'investment' criterion is at issue also here. Where no delimitation to specific causes of action is clearly envisaged by the treaty itself, the general purpose of BITs to protect and promote investment militates strongly against a restrictive interpretation. Instead, this suggests conceiving investor-state arbitration as a separate right for investors in relation to claims against the state, being not only complementary but parallel to the substantive rights otherwise stipulated in the treaty, as a substitute for municipal court proceedings.

4.5 OVERLAPPING JURISDICTIONS—CONTRACTUAL JURISDICTION CLAUSES AND INVESTMENT TREATY JURISDICTION

Complex contracts usually include a jurisdiction or arbitration clause providing for dispute resolution through a designated court or arbitral procedure. If exclusive this imposes a contractual obligation upon each party to bring claims only before the designated court or tribunal, ie, to the

[210] *El Paso Energy International Co v Argentine Republic* (Decision on jurisdiction, 2006) para 65, and *Consortium Groupement LESI-Dipenta v Algeria* (Award, 2005) para 25 (Douglas (2009) 240).

exclusion of any other forum. An investment treaty claim may concern vindication of a contract containing such an exclusive jurisdiction clause. This creates an apparent conflict between the investment treaty procedure and the procedure envisaged by the contract itself.

Under traditional international law, such jurisdictional conflicts are avoided by virtue of the principle that municipal remedies must be exhausted before international law remedies can be invoked.[211] If applicable, this functions as a criterion of admissibility. The international tribunal will be obliged not to exercise jurisdiction until national courts have forfeited their chance to remedy the alleged breach.[212] This has the result that jurisdictional conflicts are avoided, while the international tribunal is cast as a hierarchically superior, appellate body over national courts in relation to the application of international law. In investment treaty arbitration however, the principle of exhaustion of local remedies, as a rule, does not apply. Consent to arbitration under ICSID is presumed to exclude recourse to other remedies insofar as nothing else is specified.[213] Most BITs similarly provide for arbitration as an alternative to municipal courts, and exclude any requirement of prior recourse to municipal courts. Often, BITs even include a so-called 'fork in the road' provision, whereby the choice of either arbitration or municipal courts is irrevocable once made.[214] Recourse to municipal courts may thus be an impediment to the subsequent invocation of investment treaty arbitration. As a result, investors usually may, and sometimes must, choose between investment treaty arbitration and proceedings in municipal courts. The critical issue is whether such a right of choice still exists if the investor has made a contractual promise to confine proceedings to a stipulated tribunal, typically the municipal courts of the state party to a contract. If an investor could make such a promise with final consequences, it would effectively constitute a waiver of its right under the investment treaty. Thus, this issue, as it has come up in ICSID practice, has effectively revived the old controversy over so-called 'Calvo clauses'.[215] Partly on the basis of the early twentieth century practice of mixed claims commissions pertaining to *Calvo* clauses, modern investment treaty practice has converged to rely on what has been termed a 'cause of action' analysis.[216] This

211 Douglas (2003) 240.

212 Cf the *Interhandel Case (Switzerland v United States)* [1959] ICJ Rep 6, 27; and the *Elettronica Sicula SpA (ELSI) Case (United States v Italy)* [1989] ICJ Rep 15, 42.

213 Cf the ICSID Convention Art 26: 'Consent of the parties to arbitration under this Convention shall, unless otherwise stated, be deemed consent to such arbitration to the exclusion of any other remedy. A Contracting State may require the exhaustion of local administrative or judicial remedies as a condition of its consent to arbitration under this Convention'.

214 See generally Douglas (2003) 274; and Schreuer (2004) 239 et seq.

215 See generally Summers (1933).

216 See in particular, Douglas (2003), 236 et seq.

seeks to strike a balance between, on the one hand maintaining the effectiveness of investment treaty protection, and on the other hand giving effect to the expression of party autonomy in a contractual jurisdiction clause. The crucial distinction is that between contract claims and treaty claims already introduced above.[217]

A. Contractual Claims—Precedence of the Contractually Agreed Jurisdiction

For a state entering into an investment contract, an exclusive jurisdiction clause pointing to its own courts may constitute an 'indispensable part' of the totality of the contract.[218] This is a concern where jurisdiction under an investment treaty is asserted over a claim related to the contract. If an investor could simply neglect the contractual jurisdiction clause and invoke the arbitral procedure under an investment treaty, it would violate the basic structure and balance of the contractual arrangement entered into by the parties. This consideration received early sanction in the practice of claims commissions relating to *Calvo* clauses.[219] The so-called *Woodruff* case is illustrative.[220] Based on the notion of the fundamental equilibrium and integrity of the contract,[221] Umpire Barge dismissed the claim for the reason that 'by the very agreement that is the fundamental basis of the claim, it was withdrawn from the jurisdiction of this commission'.[222]

The annulment committee in the *Vivendi* case relied on this to set out the following premise in the context of investment treaty jurisdiction: 'In a case where the essential basis of a claim brought before an international tribunal is a breach of contract, the tribunal will give effect to any valid choice of

[217] For a discussion of the more fundamental ramifications of this distinction, see section 3.4 above.

[218] Cf *North American Dredging Company of Texas v United Mexican States* (US-Mexican General Claims Commission, 1926), (1926) IV RIAA 26.

[219] See generally, and with references, Douglas (2003) 242–4.

[220] See also the *North American Dredging Company Case* (US-Mexican General Claims Commission, 1926) (1926) IV RIAA 26, 32 (para 23): '[W]here a claimant has expressly agreed in writing, attested by his signature, that in all matters pertaining to the execution, fulfilment, and interpretation of the contract he will have resort to local tribunals, remedies, authorities and then wilfully ignores them by applying in such matters to his Government, he will be held bound by his contract and the Commission will not take jurisdiction of such a claim'.

[221] *Woodruff case (United States v Venezuela)* (Mixed Claims Commission United States-Venezuela, 1903) (1903) IX RIAA 213, 222: '[T]he judge, having to deal with a claim fundamentally based on a contract, has to consider the rights and duties arising from that contract, and may not construe a contract that the parties themselves did not make, and he would be doing so if he gave a decision in this case and thus absolved from the pledged duty of first recurring for rights to the Venezuelan courts, thus giving a right which by this very same contract was renounced, and absolve claimant from a duty that he took upon himself by his own voluntary action'.

[222] *ibid*, 223.

forum clause in the contract'.[223] While in that case the statement was obiter, the same proposition was reiterated and relied on in *SGS v Philippines*. The tribunal premised its reasoning on a fundamental consideration of party autonomy, considering that contractually stipulated jurisdiction clauses ought to be respected 'unless overridden by another valid provision'.[224] The question was thus whether the exclusive jurisdiction clause in the contract was 'overridden by the BIT or the ICSID Convention'.[225] The tribunal answered this in the negative, on the basis of an interpretation of the BIT itself, noting first that 'the BIT itself was not concluded with any specific investment or contract in view'.[226] Thus, it could not be presumed that it was meant to override individual contracts 'freely negotiated between the parties'.[227] Moreover, it also found support for this in its conception of the BIT's purpose as a 'framework treaty' for investment protection:

> The second consideration derives from the character of an investment protection agreement as a framework treaty, intended by the State Parties to support and supplement, not to override or replace the actually negotiated investment arrangements made between the investor and the host State.[228]

In other words, the tribunal considered it a basic purpose of the BIT to support the contractual freedom of states and investors, thus maintaining that a treaty jurisdiction clause ought to be presumed not to override individually negotiated arrangements, and thus grant a benefit to individual investors which they could not reasonably have expected on the basis of their own separate arrangement with the state. This can also be seen on the basis of a broader principle of respect for legitimate expectations, as applied to the procedural aspects of a BIT.

The rule that an exclusive jurisdiction clause in the contract itself precludes treaty jurisdiction in respect of claims which are solely based on that contract is supported by several other cases.[229] It has not been

[223] *CAA and Vivendi v Argentina* (Decision on Annulment, 2002) para 98. See also the initial award, *Compania de Aguas del Aconquija (CAA) and Compagnie Generale des Eaux (CGE) v Argentine Republic* (Award, 2000), where the tribunal relied on this concern to dismiss the claims on the merits (para 78): '[T]he Tribunal holds that, because of the crucial connection in this case between the terms of the Concession Contract and these alleged violations of the BIT, the Argentine Republic cannot be held liable unless and until Claimants have, as Article 16.4 of the Concession Contract requires, asserted their rights in proceedings before the contentious administrative courts of Tucumán and have been denied their rights, either procedurally or substantively'.

[224] *SGS v Philippines* (Decision on Jurisdiction, 2004) para 138. The tribunal referred to Art II (1) of the Claims Settlement Declaration of 19 January 1981 establishing the Iran-US Claims tribunal. This expressly overrides exclusive jurisdiction clauses in contracts, except for those relating to the courts of Iran.

[225] *ibid*, para 139.

[226] *ibid*, para 141.

[227] *ibid*, para 141.

[228] *ibid*, para 141.

[229] See for the most recent cases, *SGS v Pakistan* (Decision on Jurisdiction, 2003) para 161; *Azurix v Argentina* (Decision on Jurisdiction, 2003) para 84; and *Joy Mining Machinery Ltd v*

seriously contested in practice,[230] although some cases may be noted for having adopted a somewhat more sceptical approach to contractual jurisdiction clauses.[231] This means that, although investment treaty jurisdiction may and will usually extend, prima facie, to contractual claims without any treaty basis, as discussed above in section 4.4, the existence of a separate jurisdiction clause in the contract will nevertheless ordinarily prevent investment treaty jurisdiction. This is related to the nature of the function undertaken by a treaty tribunal when exercising jurisdiction over claims based on a breach of contract. In this situation it functions as a substitute, on the same hierarchical level as a municipal court or contractual arbitral tribunal. A treaty tribunal does not possess any primacy of authority in relation to claims relating merely to the contract or municipal law. Thus, as held by one commentator, the tribunal 'has no independent interest in hearing a case that transcends the consent of the parties'.[232] This is, however, different where a claim to vindicate a contract can also be based in one of the substantive standards of the treaty.

B. Parallel Contract and Treaty Claims

A claim based on a breach of contract may simultaneously amount to a treaty claim. This sets the stage for two opposing considerations bearing upon an apparent conflict between jurisdiction under a BIT and contractual jurisdiction. On the one hand, allowing an exclusive jurisdiction clause in favour of municipal courts to prevent treaty jurisdiction weakens

Egypt (Award, 2004) paras 89–90; and see also, *SPP v Egypt* (Decision on Jurisdiction, 1985), 3 ICSID Reports 112, para 80 et seq; and *Klöckner v Cameroon* (Award, 1983) 114 ILR 157.

[230] In its decision in the *Vivendi* case, the annulment committee held, relying on *Lanco v Argentina*, that a consequence of the ICSID Convention article 26 was to deny the effect of an exclusive jurisdiction clause in a contract. However, since both cases concerned claims expressly considered by the tribunals to be separate treaty claims, they must probably be construed and distinguished on that basis. See *CAA and Vivendi v Argentina* (Decision on Annulment, 2002) para 78; and *Lanco v Argentina* (Decision on Jurisdiction, 1998) para 39–40. See also Douglas (2003) 249–50; and Spiermann, 'Individual Rights, State Interests and the Power to Waive ICSID Jurisdiction under Bilateral Investment Treaties' (2004) 20(2) *Arb Int'l* 179, 187–90.

[231] See *Lanco v Argentina* (Decision on Jurisdiction, 1998) para 26 (1998) 5 ICSID Rep 367; *Salini Costruttori v Morocco* (Decision on Jurisdiction, 2001) para 27; and *Consortium RFCC v Morocco* (Decision on Jurisdiction, 2001) para 31 (2006) 20(2) *ICSID Rev-FILJ* 391. In *Lanco*, it was held that a contractual jurisdiction clause could not be considered 'previously agreed', since it referred to a federal administrative tribunal not subject to 'agreement or waiver', whereas in the parallel *Salini* and *RFCC* cases, the tribunals held that a clause in the contract, referring possible disputes to the administrative courts of Morocco, was not a true expression of party autonomy since the jurisdiction was obligatory under municipal law. However, as noted somewhat dryly by the tribunal in *SGS v Philippines*, the 'mere fact that "administrative jurisdiction cannot be selected by mutual agreement" does not prevent the investor agreeing by contract not to resort to any other forum'. See *SGS v Philippines* (Decision on Jurisdiction, 2004) at fn 68.

[232] Douglas (2003) 247–8.

the effectiveness of the treaty. It would realistically constitute a waiver of the investor's substantive rights under the treaty, since these are closely bound up with the possibility of arbitration against the state. In relation to a concrete contract this may suggest two things: first that a contractual jurisdiction clause ought not to be construed as a waiver of treaty jurisdiction; and secondly that a treaty jurisdiction clause ought in any case to be construed so as to override the contractual jurisdiction clause.

Opposed to this stands, on the other hand, the concern of upholding the balance and integrity of the contract. This is related to the rule already examined, which requires that effect be given to an exclusive jurisdiction clause in a contract wherever 'the essential basis of a claim brought before an international tribunal is a breach of contract'.[233] If the treaty claim is virtually identical in content to the contractual claim, or at least inseparable from it in terms of the relevant facts invoked, the exercise of jurisdiction by a treaty tribunal would violate the parties' individual arrangement as much as if the claim were solely contractual. Since it is realistically impossible for a treaty tribunal to evaluate a contract claim passing itself off as a treaty claim, without also providing an authoritative determination of the underlying contract claim, asserting jurisdiction effectively allows the investor to escape a contractual obligation by framing its claim as a treaty claim. In arbitral practice these crossing concerns are manifested in two main principles. The first principle maintains that a contractual jurisdiction clause will not, or cannot, affect the jurisdiction of a treaty tribunal over treaty claims. The second principle balances the first and requires that in so far as the treaty claim has a breach of contract as its 'essential basis', the claim is not admissible before the contractually stipulated remedies have been exhausted.

(i) Contractual Jurisdiction Clauses, Waivers and Treaty Claims

As mentioned, a contractual jurisdiction clause may be deemed ineffectual in relation to a treaty claim, either on the basis of a restrictive interpretation of the clause itself, or because it is considered to be directly overridden by the treaty jurisdiction clause. If the latter view is upheld, it would suggest that not even an express contractual waiver of investment treaty jurisdiction could be upheld in the face of a treaty jurisdiction clause. It is, however, uncertain whether such a strict understanding of treaty jurisdiction clauses is justified. Inter alia, it disregards the important principle of freedom of contract in the investor-state relationship. If an investor is willing to submit to the express condition of waiving access to investment treaty arbitration, it may be asked why it should not be able to

[233] *CAA and Vivendi v Argentina* (Decision on Annulment, 2002) para 98, and *SGS v Philippines* (Decision on Jurisdiction, 2004) para 153.

do so. A near consistent body of case law has nevertheless held that a contractual jurisdiction clause normally will not exclude a treaty claim. It is, however, difficult to present an entirely consistent picture with regard to the underlying rationale of this.

The first case involving an apparent conflict of contract and treaty jurisdiction was *Lanco v Argentina*. The case concerned claims arising out of a port concession granted by Argentine authorities to a US company. Argentina argued that the dispute was exempt from ICSID jurisdiction by virtue of a jurisdiction clause in the concession contract, referring disputes to the Federal Contentious-Administrative Tribunals of Buenos Aires. The ICSID tribunal held that this did not exclude its own jurisdiction, however, for two main reasons. First, the clause referred to what was in effect an obligatory administrative tribunal, which was 'not subject to agreement or waiver'.[234] In other words, the clause could not be construed as a contractual choice of the municipal courts over ICSID jurisdiction. Secondly, however, the tribunal also held that the consent to ICSID in the BIT in any case had the effect of overriding individually agreed procedures, by providing investors with the option to choose between such procedures and ICSID arbitration.[235]

The decision of the annulment committee in the *Vivendi* case later provided this approach with a strong conceptual basis that has received general acceptance in practice. The concession contract underlying the dispute contained an exclusive jurisdiction clause in favour of a municipal administrative court, despite which, and following the *Lanco* decision, both the original tribunal and the annulment committee found in favour of prima facie jurisdiction under the treaty.[236] However, the initial tribunal dismissed the claims on the merits, on the basis that the contractual jurisdiction clause had not been exhausted. The reason adduced was that the treaty causes of action were inseparable from eventual breaches of contract, and therefore could not be resolved without an authoritative determination of these issues by the contractually selected jurisdiction.[237] The annulment committee fundamentally disagreed with this approach. Instead it held that the tribunal's jurisdiction over the treaty claims required it to make its own evaluation of the possible breaches of contract, irrespective of the contractual jurisdiction clause. This it justified by reference to its now acclaimed distinction between, 'claims based essentially on the contract'[238] and claims where 'the fundamental basis of the claim is a treaty laying down an independent standard by which the

[234] *Lanco International Inc v Argentine Republic* (Decision on Jurisdiction, 1998) para 26.
[235] *ibid*, para 40.
[236] *CAA and CGE v Argentina* (Award, 2000) paras 53–4; *CAA and Vivendi v Argentina* (Decision on Annulment, 2002) paras 72–80.
[237] *CAA and CGE v Argentina* (Award, 2000) paras 78–9.
[238] *CAA and Vivendi v Argentina* (Decision on Annulment, 2002) para 98.

conduct of the parties is to be judged'.[239] Considering that the claims in question were based on independent treaty standards, the committee held that a contractual jurisdiction clause could not affect the competence and duty of a treaty tribunal already seised of jurisdiction, to make its own separate determination of the contractual issues for the purpose of evaluating the treaty claim:

> [W]here 'the fundamental basis of the claim' is a treaty laying down an independent standard by which the conduct of the parties is to be judged, the existence of an exclusive jurisdiction clause in a contract between the claimant and the respondent state or one of its subdivisions cannot operate as a bar to the application of the treaty standard. At most it might be relevant—as municipal law will often be relevant—in assessing whether there has been a breach of the treaty. In the Committee's view, it is not open to an ICSID tribunal having jurisdiction under a BIT in respect of a claim based upon a substantive provision of that BIT, to dismiss the claim on the ground that it could or should have been dealt with by a national court.[240]

According to the committee, the conceptual distinction between breach of contract and breach of treaty meant that determining whether a breach of treaty had occurred, even though this might entail taking account of the terms of the contract, did not override the specifically contractual jurisdiction envisaged by the jurisdiction clause in the contract.[241] Significantly, the committee could maintain this because it took as its premise that the presumed basis of the treaty claims was both conceptually and substantially distinct from the standards set by the contract.[242] In this perspective, the committee could make the separate evaluation of the contract under the treaty standards appear as an assertion of the primacy of international law over municipal law.[243] Being confined to contractual responsibility under municipal law, the non-effect of the jurisdiction clause appeared merely as

[239] *ibid*, para 101.

[240] *ibid*, para 101.

[241] *ibid*, para 105: '[I]t is one thing to exercise contractual jurisdiction (arguably exclusively vested in the administrative tribunals of Tucumán by virtue of the concession contract) and another to take into account the terms of a contract in determining whether there has been a breach of a distinct standard of international law, such as that reflected in Art 3 of the BIT.

[242] *ibid*, para 95: 'As to the relation between breach of contract and breach of treaty in the present case, it must be stressed that Articles 3 and 5 of the BIT do not relate directly to breach of a municipal contract. Rather they set an independent standard. A state may breach a contract without breaching a treaty, and vice versa, and this is certainly true of these provisions of the BIT'.

[243] *ibid*, para 96 (referring to the principle in ILC article 3, that characterisation of an act as internationally wrongful is unaffected by the characterisation of the same act as lawful by internal law): 'In accordance with this general principle (which is undoubtedly declaratory of general international law), whether there has been a breach of the BIT and whether there has been a breach of contract are different questions. Each of these claims will be determined by reference to its own proper or applicable law—in the case of the BIT, by international law; in the case of the Concession Contract, by the proper law of the contract, in other words, the law of Tucumán'.

a consequence of the incapacity of municipal law to affect lawfulness under international law. The committee here made an analogy to *Calvo* clauses in the case law of old claims commissions.[244] Essentially it thus invoked a hierarchically superior status in relation to application of the treaty standards, even as they incorporated elements of municipal law.[245] While ostensibly confined to the merits phase and assuming the existence of jurisdiction, the momentum of the initial *Vivendi* tribunal's reasoning clearly is that jurisdiction under the treaty in respect of the contractual claims was considered waived by virtue of the contractual jurisdiction clause. As commented by Spiermann, 'one may wonder whether the [first] tribunal had not effectively, though not verbally, declined jurisdiction'.[246] Conversely, the momentum of the annulment committee's reasoning clearly was to uphold jurisdiction over treaty claims at least partly inseparable from the underlying contract claims, despite an exclusive jurisdiction clause in the contract.[247]

In later practice, the *Vivendi* annulment decision has manifested itself as a strong precedent in favour of upholding treaty jurisdiction, even in the face of an explicit contractual waiver in favour of the contractually agreed forum. Relying on its treaty/contract distinction, a massive body of case law has now cemented the presumption that a contractual forum selection clause will normally be ineffective where the claims in question invoke an independent cause of action under the relevant investment treaty.[248] The most forceful reflection of this is perhaps the decision in *Azurix v Argentina*. In this case, the Argentine government could argue, quite convincingly, that there was an express waiver of ICSID jurisdiction in the relevant contractual documents. The applicable clause in the concession contract stipulated that any dispute 'regarding the construction and execution

[244] *ibid*, para 99.

[245] It cited to this effect the ILC commentary to Art 3 of the ILC Draft Articles on Responsibility of States for Internationally Wrongful Acts (*ibid*, para 97): 'Especially in the fields of injury to aliens and their property and of human rights, the content application of internal law will often be relevant to the question of international responsibility. In every case it will be seen on analysis that either the provisions of internal law are relevant as facts in applying the applicable international standard, or else that they are actually incorporated in some form, conditionally or unconditionally, into that standard'.

[246] Spiermann (2004) 204.

[247] But see also ibid. para 76, suggesting, it seems, that ICSID jurisdiction could have been explicitly waived.

[248] See eg *Azurix Corp v Argentine Republic* (Decision on Jurisdiction, 2003) para 26; *IBM World Trade Corp v Republic of Ecuador* (Decision on Jurisdiction, 2003) para 70; *Siemens AG v Argentine Republic* (Decision on Jurisdiction, 2004) para 180; *Impregilo v Pakistan* (Decision on Jurisdiction, 2005) paras 286–7; *Bayindir v Pakistan* (Decision on Jurisdiction, 2005) para 151; *Aguas del Tunari SA v Republic of Bolivia* (Decision on Jurisdiction, 2005) para 122; *Eureko BV v Republic of Poland* (Award, 2005) para 112; *Jan de Nul v Egypt* (Decision on Jurisdiction, 2006) para 133; *National Grid plc v Argentine Republic* (Decision on Jurisdiction, 2006) para 169; *Suez Sociedad General de Aguas de Barcelona SA v Argentine Republic* (Decision on Jurisdiction, 2006) paras 43–5.

of the agreement' should be confined to 'the court for contentious-administrative matters of the city of La Plata'.[249] The clause made explicit that this meant 'waiving any other forum or jurisdiction that may correspond due to any reason'.[250] Moreover, the prehistory of the contract showed that the waiver was inserted precisely to ensure the effect in relation to treaty claims that had been denied in previous case law,[251] and this was even pointed out to the investors when the contract was concluded.[252] The ICSID tribunal nevertheless denied that the clause had any effect on its jurisdiction, relying both on the 'different cause of action from a claim under the Contract Documents' of the BIT claims before it,[253] and the fact that since Argentina was not a party to the relevant contractual documents, there was 'no waiver commitment made by the Claimant in favour of Argentina'.[254] It is reasonably clear that the tribunal here disregarded a clause obviously intended to confine jurisdiction over possible parallel contract and treaty claims to the municipal administrative court, at least as a first recourse. Moreover, it is difficult to believe that this did not also coincide with the common intention of the parties when entering into the contract in question. Despite its somewhat formalistic reference to the lack of a real contractual commitment towards the state as such, the applied rationale seemingly was the notion that a contractual waiver is ineffective in principle in respect of claims based on the BIT. This is evident from the tribunal's following comment on the analogy of practice relating to *Calvo* clauses: 'The significance of the cases for this Tribunal is that private parties could waive access to the Commissions to settle *contractual disputes* with a State with which they had contracted'[255] (emphasis added). It is difficult not also to read the antithesis into this; viz they could not have waived the right to pursue a treaty claim in this manner.[256] This also seems to have been the assumption made by the tribunal in *Salini v Jordan* when commenting on a specific provision in the BIT, seemingly deferring to individually agreed dispute settlement procedures in an investment

[249] *Azurix Corporation v Argentina* (Decision on Jurisdiction, 2003) para 26.
[250] *ibid*, para 26.
[251] *ibid*, para 78.
[252] *ibid*, para 82.
[253] *ibid*, para 76.
[254] *ibid*, para 85.
[255] *ibid*, para 85.
[256] This would seem evident also from another passage, commenting on the significance of earlier ICSID cases (*ibid*, para 79): 'The tribunals in the cases cited concluded that such forum selection clauses did not exclude their jurisdiction because the subject matter of any proceedings before the domestic courts under the contractual arrangements in question and the dispute before the ICSID tribunal was different and therefore the forum selection clauses did not apply. This reasoning applies equally the waiver of jurisdiction clauses in this case. *The claims or causes of action before this Tribunal are different in nature from any claims which ABA could bring before the courts of the city of La Plata under the Contract Documents*' (emphasis added).

contract.[257] The tribunal held that this could only extend to claims based on the contract, and would not affect claims based on substantive provisions of the treaty itself, even if those provisions should be expressly directed towards a breach of contract in the manner of an 'umbrella clause'.[258]

While these cases clearly reflect an inclination to assert treaty jurisdiction despite a near explicit 'waiver' of such jurisdiction in the underlying contract, they clearly do not represent a conclusive answer to the underlying question of principle. The hierarchical perspective drawn up by the annulment committee in the *Vivendi* case does not in itself require that an express waiver would be lacking in effect, although its strict application in cases such as *Salini v Jordan* and *Azurix v Argentina* might do so. In itself the perspective entails merely a rebuttable presumption to the effect that arbitration under the treaty should be given precedence in respect of claims based on the treaty. Underlying this is also a concern with regard to upholding the effectiveness of protection under the treaty. Allowing a waiver would realistically undermine the treaty standards underlying the claims affected by a waiver, and leave the investment in question without effective protection. At the same time there is nothing about the nature of a property or contractual right suggesting that an investor cannot knowingly enter into an agreement surrendering to some extent the right as such. It could even be seen as a natural aspect of the aim of investment treaties to create individual rights.[259] This may also be the appropriate inference to draw from the *Calvo* clause analogy relied on in several of the cases hitherto cited. The *North American Dredging Company* case illustrates this. The tribunal took as a starting point the significance of the *Calvo* Clause for Mexico, as 'an indispensable provision, not separable from the other provisions of the contract . . . subscribed to by the claimant for the purpose of securing the award of the contract'.[260] It furthermore recognised the legitimate interest of Mexico in preserving its 'sovereign right of jurisdiction within its own territory'.[261] On this basis it held that the promise from the investor to avail itself exclusively of the domestic

[257] See the Jordan-Italy BIT, Art 9.2: 'In case the investor and an entity of the Contracting Parties have stipulated an investment Agreement, the procedure foreseen in such investment Agreement shall apply'.

[258] *Salini Costruttori v Jordan* (Decision on Jurisdiction, 2004) para 96: 'Lastly, the tribunal will note that the dispute settlement procedures provided for in the Contract could only cover claims based on breaches of the Contract. Those procedures cannot cover claims based on breaches of the BIT (including breaches of those provisions of the BIT guaranteeing fulfilment of contracts signed with foreign investors). Therefore Article 9(2) does not deprive the Tribunal of such jurisdiction as it may have, to entertain treaty claims of this nature under other provisions of the BIT'.

[259] See also to this effect Spiermann (2004) 207.

[260] *North American Dredging Company Case* (US-Mexican General Claims Commission, 1926) (1926) IV RIAA 26.

[261] *ibid*, para 11.

courts had to be given effect.[262] The investor was considered only to retain its right to be treated in a fair and just manner by the municipal courts, and to apply to its home state for diplomatic protection in case of denial of justice in this respect.[263] If this rationale is similarly applied to an investment treaty, it suggests the possibility of removing claims affiliated with a specific contract from the ambit of treaty jurisdiction, short of a denial of justice.[264]

While difficult to reconcile with some cases, the possibility of a waiver has also received express support in practice. In the recent case of *Aguas del Tunari v Bolivia* (albeit obiter), the tribunal reasoned as follows:

> Assuming that parties agreed to a clear waiver of ICSID jurisdiction, the Tribunal is of the view that such a waiver would be effective. Given that it appears clear that the parties to an ICSID arbitration could jointly agree to a different mechanism for the resolution of their disputes other than that of ICSID, it would appear that an investor could also waive its rights to invoke the jurisdiction of ICSID.[265]

Furthermore, in the two more recent cases of *Occidental v Ecuador* and *TSA v Argentina*, both tribunals clearly assumed that an express waiver would have been effective, although considering in both instances that the contractual provisions could not be so construed.[266] While no case, to my knowledge, has so far held that jurisdiction over separate treaty claims has been waived by virtue of a contractual jurisdiction clause, the consensual model underlying ICSID arbitration suggests this ought to be possible if the waiver is sufficiently clear and unconditional. This requirement that a waiver needs to be explicit is also emphasised by the decisions in *Aguas del Tunari*, *Occidental* and *TSA*, and is clearly implicit in the tendency of case law to uphold treaty jurisdiction over separate treaty claims to vindicate a contract in spite of a contractual jurisdiction clause. However, if the

[262] *ibid*, para 10: 'What Mexico has asked of the North American Dredging Company of Texas as a condition of awarding it the contract which it sought is, "If all the means of enforcing your rights under this contract afforded by Mexican law, even against the Mexican Government itself are wide open to you, as they are wide open to our own citizens, will you promise not to ignore them and not to call directly upon your own Government to intervene in your behalf in connection with any controversy, small or large, but seek redress under the laws of Mexico through the authorities and tribunals furnished by Mexico for your protection?" and the claimant, by subscribing to this contract and seeking the benefits which were to accrue to him thereunder, has answered, "I promise"'.

[263] *ibid*, para 14: 'It did not take from him his undoubted right to apply to his own government for protection if his resort to the Mexican tribunals or other authorities available to him resulted in denial or delay of justice as that term is used in international law. In such a case the claimant's complaint would be not that his contract was violated but that he had been denied justice'.

[264] Compare eg *Azinian v United Mexican States* (Award, 1999) para 99.

[265] *Aguas del Tunari v Bolivia* (Decision on Jurisdiction, 2005) para 118.

[266] *Occidental Petroleum Corporation and Occidental Exploration and Production Company v Republic of Ecuador* (Decision on jurisdiction, 2008) para 62 et seq, and *TSA Spectrum de Argentina SA v Argentine Republic* (Award, 2008) para 62 (and see also the concurring opinion of Professor Abi-Saab).

consensual model retains any reality in the context of investment treaty arbitration, an explicit waiver ought to be given effect.[267] Essentially, the argument is that the ability of an investor to accept an offer of treaty jurisdiction also entails, as a complementary aspect, the ability to expressly opt out of that offer, and decline it by making a different agreement.

(ii) Exhaustion of Contractual Remedies as a Condition of Admissibility

Having established that an exclusive jurisdiction clause in a contract normally will not exclude treaty jurisdiction over separate treaty claims concerned with safeguarding the economical and commercial integrity of that contract, a different issue is whether such a treaty claim is always admissible before the contractual dispute resolution procedure has been exhausted. While it should not, as discussed earlier, easily be construed as a waiver of treaty jurisdiction, the commercial totality of the contract might suggest that a contractual jurisdiction clause should at least be exhausted before a treaty claim is made, at least in so far as the essential basis of the claim is an ordinary breach of contract. Such a requirement has indeed, eventually, received support also in arbitral practice.

On the one hand, such concerns provided the rationale of the initial award in the *Vivendi* case, where the tribunal dismissed the claims because the contractually stipulated procedure had not been exhausted.[268] At the same time, this was the essential reason for the subsequent annulment of the award.[269] An alternative and more sophisticated justification and conceptualisation of a requirement to exhaust contractually stipulated remedies was then relied on in *SGS v Philippines*. The tribunal essentially held any eventual claims under the treaty to be inadmissible for being premature and unresolved under the contractually agreed procedure.[270] The fundamental premise of the tribunal, which reconciles this approach with that of the annulment committee in the *Vivendi* case,[271] was that the claims under the treaty were virtually identical to the contract claims. The claims essentially concerned alleged non-payment for services rendered by the company, which again was related to a disagreement between the parties on the amount of payment due for the company's services. Thus, no claim liable to be determined 'independent of the contractual issues referred to the Philippine courts' could be discerned.[272]

[267] Cf Spiermann (2004), 204.

[268] *CAA and CGE v Argentina* (Award, 2000) paras 78–9.

[269] *CAA and Vivendi v Argentina* (Decision on Annulment, 2002) para 101 (as quoted above at n 292).

[270] *SGS v Philippines* (Decision on Jurisdiction, 2004) para 154.

[271] The annulment committee held that a treaty tribunal should decline to exercise jurisdiction if 'the essential basis' of the treaty claim is a breach of contract, see *CAA and Vivendi v Argentina* (Decision on Annulment, 2002) para 98.

[272] *SGS v Philippines* (Decision on Jurisdiction, 2004) para 156 et seq.

This also limits the scope of the exception, and places in some doubt whether it ought not to be reconceptualised to encompass a somewhat wider ambit of treaty claims. As I argue in the next chapter, a mere breach of contract will not usually in itself be sufficient to constitute a breach of an investment protection standard; usually some kind of 'sovereign act' or 'willful repudiation' will be required to qualify a breach of contract as expropriatory or a breach of 'legitimate expectations'. This was the justification invoked by the annulment committee in the *Vivendi* case to strike down the original award.[273] This also seems to have been conducive to the reasoning in the more recent decisions of the tribunals in *Impregilo v Pakistan*[274] and *Bayindir v Pakistan*.[275]

Accepting the reasoning in *SGS v Philippines* verbatim thus seems to leave little room for a requirement that the contractual remedies should be exhausted in so far as there is, on the facts, an arguable case of expropriation, breach of an umbrella clause, or breach of the legitimate expectation standard under a BIT. In *SGS v Philippines* the tribunal effectively reserved the admissibility requirement to claims based on the umbrella clause.[276] However, since recent practice suggests that even the umbrella clause requires something beyond a breach of contract for a claim to be well founded, the exhaustion of remedies exception faces a narrow scope of applicability, virtually to the point of negligibility.

Allowing a reasonable scope for contracts to function according to their actual terms would have suggested, in contrast, an expansion of the exception to all claims where the validity or content of the contractual obligations constitute the essential issue in dispute, irrespective of whether or not an additional element sufficient to characterise the claim as a treaty claim is present. It is, for instance, conceivable that the state undertaking in question is a direct restriction of public power in some manner, eg, through a stabilisation clause, and that this is combined with a jurisdiction clause in the contract referring possible disputes to the courts of the contracting state. A direct breach of such an undertaking would without doubt also constitute a breach of an umbrella clause, it will usually be a violation of the legitimate expection standard as encompassed in a fair and equitable treatment clause, and it may also constitute expropriation. At the same time, the state's willingness to submit to the undertaking may, and usually will, have been conditional upon the contract containing the jurisdiction clause. It is clearly problematical if this, which may have been the common intention of the parties and an essential condition of the contract, should be thwarted by the private investor being entitled to

273 *CAA and Vivendi v Argentina* (Decision on Annulment, 2002) para 95.

274 *Impregilo v Pakistan* (Decision on Jurisdiction, 2005) paras 258–62.

275 *Bayindir v Pakistan* (Decision on Jurisdiction, 2005) para 139 et seq.

276 *SGS v Philippines* (Decision on Jurisdiction, 2004) para 92, and contrast para 113 and para 156 et seq.

ignore the jurisdiction clause and instead proceed directly to investment arbitration.

The best solution to this may be to say, not as the initial *Vivendi* tribunal did that the contractual jurisdiction constituted a basis upon which to dismiss the claims on their merits, but instead that the treaty claims are inadmissible until the contractual dispute resolution procedure have been exhausted, unless the grievances clearly are of such a nature that the state itself has virtually 'stepped out of' the contract. The latter would, for instance, conceivably be the case with respect to a legislative annulment of the contract. In principle there is no impediment to considering a contractual jurisdiction clause a requirement to exhaust 'local administrative or judicial remedies' under Article 26 of the ICSID Convention, but presumably limited to the contractually stipulated remedies in case of an exclusive contractual jurisdiction clause. The consensual model that sees an ICSID jurisdiction clause in a treaty as an offer to the investor, clearly suggests that the investor's acceptance of this offer must be construed in light of the totality of its contractual engagement to the state. There is no reason to assume that an investor cannot frame its acceptance of this offer in two stages, by undertaking an initial binding commitment to exhaust designated local remedies.

5

Substantive Principles Applicable to Contract Claims—the Concept of 'Legitimate Expectations'

5.1 INTRODUCTION

AN INTERNATIONAL ARBITRAL tribunal, confronted with a dispute arising out of a complex contractual arrangement that has been relied on to make an investment, is faced with a dilemma. It may feel almost compelled to apply the contract, which typically contains clear and well-formulated rules, in authoritative writing, and often directly addressing the issues at hand. Two fundamental precepts nevertheless prevent mere reliance on and application of such a contract without further legal justification. First, a contract cannot constitute its own law; it requires, at least as a formal premise, a positive legal basis external to the contract itself, which will give effect to it as a legal obligation.[1] Secondly, there is no obvious and apparent 'international law of contracts',[2] comparable to the law of treaties. The basis of contractual validity will usually have to be found in some municipal law. It is, consequently, 'well established'[3] that 'a violation of a contract entered into by a State with an investor of another State, is not, by itself, a violation of international law'.[4]

[1] See eg the classical formulation in *Saudi Arabia v Arab American Oil Company (Aramco)* (Award, 1958) 27 ILR 117, 165: 'It is obvious that no contract can exist *in vacuo*, ie without being based on a legal system. The conclusion of a contract is not left to the unfettered discretion of the parties. It is necessarily related to some positive law which gives effect to the reciprocal and concordant manifestations of intent made by the parties. The contract cannot even be conceived without a system of law under which it is created. Human will can only create a contractual relationship if the applicable system of law has first recognised its power to do so'.

[2] As claimed in *Texaco Overseas Petroleum Co v Govt of Libya* (Award, 1977) 53 ILR 389, para 32.

[3] *SGS Societe Generale de Surveillance SA v Republic of the Philippines* (Decision on Jurisdiction, 2004) para 122.

[4] *SGS Societe Generale de Surveillance SA v Islamic Republic of Pakistan* (Decision on Jurisdiction, 2003) para 167; see also Amerasinghe, *Local Remedies in International Law* 2nd edn (Cambridge University Press, Cambridge, 2004) 107 et seq.

Distinct rules or standards of international law may, however, protect contractual interests or positions as such, and may to this effect provide potential grounds for a 'contractual' claim under international law. The following analyses how investment arbitral tribunals have interpreted three such common investment treaty standards, in addition to certain general principles of customary international law, on the basis of an underlying structural rationale of contractual liberty and commitment in relation to investment. This relates to the now common occurrence of, as it was formulated by the tribunal in *F-W Oil v Trinidad and Tobago*,

> a claim of the kind which has become familiar in recent years in multi- and bilateral ICSID disputes, whereunder the foreign investor relies on a contract between itself and the host state which constitutes at the same time the investment on which ICSID jurisdiction is founded, and also the source of the obligation, the breach of which is the subject-matter of the claim.[5]

A common thread running through this chapter is that the response of arbitral practice to this is part of an underlying concern to uphold legitimate expectations in investor-state relationships.[6] As the scrutiny below will show, this concept when applied in arbitral practice operates according to a distinct transactional modality, to constitute something of a structural premise of international investment law. More specifically, the concept of legitimate expectations has three basic and cumulative elements, which I argue both extend and confine its scope of application to: (i) specific expectations pursuant to contractual or comparably definite undertakings of a state, which (ii) have been entered into and relied on in relation to specific investments, and (iii) have subsequently been repudiated by the state in its government or political capacity.

The remainder of this chapter is structured in the manner that I analyse arbitral practice first under expropriation or takings clauses in investment treaties (section 5.2), and then in relation to so-called umbrella clauses (section 5.3), before I discuss the legitimate expectations standard as a main component of fair and equitable treatment (section 5.4). I then examine the comparable responses of arbitral practice in applying principles of customary law and the concept of internationalisation of state contracts (section 5.5). Finally, I discuss how the notion of legitimate expectations in respect of each of the standards above is commonly reflected in a standard of compensation for breach based on the contractual expectation interest (section 5.6).

[5] *F-W Oil Interests Inc v Republic of Trinidad and Tobago* (Award, 2006) para 13.

[6] See also Orrego Vicuña, 'Regulatory Authority and Legitimate Expectations: Balancing the Rights of the State and the Individual under International Law in a Global Society' (2003) 5(3) *Int'l Law Forum* 188.

5.2 CONTRACT CLAIMS AND THE 'EXPROPRIATION STANDARD'

The power to regulate and interfere with and, ultimately, to appropriate and annul private property and other entitlements or privileges that confer economic benefit, is a fundamental prerogative of states. It is, however, complemented by a fundamental principle of justice, which demands that certain rights or entitlements constituting items of private wealth (in a broad sense) should not be appropriated without economic compensation to the particular individual sustaining the loss of privilege.[7] Beyond the strict and minimum requirements of justice recognised by virtually all municipal legal systems,[8] and even conceived as an international human right, adequate protection against expropriation is a central component of any effective system of investment protection. Virtually all investment treaties contain a prohibition against direct and indirect expropriation, or comparable measures, without payment of compensation to the individual investor.[9] A typical expropriation clause is that contained in article 5 of the Norway-Russia Bilateral Investment Treaty (BIT) (1995):

> Investments made by investors of one Contracting Party in the territory of the other Contracting Party cannot be expropriated, nationalised or subjected to other measures having a similar effect (hereinafter referred to as 'expropriation') except when the expropriation is done for public interest, under due process of law, is not discriminatory and is done against prompt, adequate and effective compensation.

Other clauses do not use the more common term 'expropriation' (direct or indirect) as such, but instead require compensation for measures 'depriving' investors of their investments.[10] Such clauses in any case point to what can be denoted a common, 'deprivation', 'takings',[11] or 'expropriation' standard (which is the term I mostly use in the following) under international law.[12] In the following I show how the expropriation standard in investment treaties has been applied in arbitral practice not only to protect property rights in the strict sense, but also to uphold state contractual undertakings, based on the corresponding contractual rights of the investors being conceived as protected assets, or investments, under

[7] See for a general discussion, Harris, *Property and Justice* (Oxford University Press, Oxford, 2001) 95 et seq.

[8] *ibid*, 95.

[9] See OECD (Note by the Secretariat), *Stocktaking of Developments in Investment Agreements* (DAF/INV/WD (2005) 10) 37–8.

[10] See eg the Netherlands-Poland BIT (1992) Art 5.

[11] Higgins, 'The Taking of Property by the State: Recent Developments in International Law' (1982-III) 176 *Recueil des Cours* 259.

[12] See eg Schreuer, 'The Concept of Expropriation under the ETC and other Investment Treaties' (Paper presented at Investment Arbitration and the Energy Charter Treaty, Conference, 9–10 June 2005 in Stockholm); and Reinisch, 'Expropriation' (Paper submitted to the ILA committee on the International Law on Foreign Investment, 2005).

the treaty standard. This can be conceptualised to depend on three main elements; the first being the conceptualisation of a concrete contractual undertaking owed towards the private investor as, in principle, a protected asset in the hand of that investor; the second the characterisation of the actual act or omission constituting the breach in question as expropriatory; and the third, the existence, validity and substance of the contractual right under municipal law.

A. Qualifying the Expectation Interest

Whether contractual rights as such are protected against expropriation ultimately depends on the individual clause and the definition of protected investments, but customarily it has long been established that contractual rights are subject to protection insofar as they have economic value. To consider a contractual right protected against expropriation is neither particularly strange nor problematic when it concerns two private parties; a settled right to performance or payment may be a normal part of the creditor's wealth, and may even be assigned as such to a third party for a price. As such, contractual rights can be conceived as having *in rem* qualities that appropriately qualify for protection against expropriation.[13] When, in contrast, the right in question corresponds to the state's own contractual undertaking, it might seem counterintuitive, or at least somewhat strange, to consider it subject to expropriation in the ordinary sense. On depriving the investor of its contractual right, the state does not appropriate the objective value of an external right; it merely annuls its own obligation. Conversely, the private interest involved is not in principle defined as objective and assignable wealth, but as the expectation of contractual performance by the debtor, ie the state. Arbitral practice has nevertheless quite consistently considered rights established by state undertakings to constitute 'investments' under the expropriation standard. This is suggestive of an underlying contractual logic in the application of the expropriation standard to state undertakings. The rationale that emerges from scrutiny of practice is not a concern to protect contractual rights as objective, commercially transferable assets, but to advance reliance on contractual expectations subject to a 'reliance' (instead of an *in rem*) criterion as the defining marker of protected rights.

(i) The Notion of Investment and the Reliance Criterion

The concept of expropriation is usually associated with the notion of property, which one may assume originated as exclusive rights over tangible

[13] See eg the *Norwegian Shipowners' Claims (Norway v USA)* (1922) 1 RIAA 309.

things with use value such as land and chattels.[14] This idea of property then naturally also attached itself to the corresponding concept of protection of private wealth against the state, since private wealth was usually sunk into tangible assets and land. With the rise of modern society, the increase of trade and the rise of the bourgeoisie, and the maturing realisation that private wealth was not any longer primarily constituted by land and things but by capital, this had to change. The related notion nevertheless emerged that the primary quality of entitlements engaging the protective principle is their *in rem* quality as comparable to property rights.[15] This is reflected in the relevant provisions of municipal constitutions, which usually extend to private property,[16] or to 'tangible and intangible' property.[17] Similarly, Article 1 of the First Protocol to the European Convention on Human Rights (ECHR) grants a right of protection to 'possessions'. Modern investment treaties usually employ a wider concept of protected rights however, commonly qualified by the term 'investment', which again usually is defined as 'any kind of asset' and exemplified with an extensive, but not necessarily exhaustive list of common assets with economic value. There is little doubt that contractual rights, as a generic category, may qualify as 'investment' within this scheme.[18]

[14] Harris (2001) 42.

[15] The traditional distinction between rights *in rem* (rights in things) and rights *in personam* (rights against persons) has fallen into some disrepute in the Nordic countries, especially after the acerbic critique by Alf Ross and the Nordic realists, see especially Ross, *Om Ret og Retfærdighet* (Nyt Nordisk Forlag, København, 1966) 228 et seq (available in English as *On Law and Justice* (last edn 1974)). For my purpose the distinction is quite useful. It depicts the difference of interests protected, comparing an appropriation of a contractual right to obtain its economic value (where the relevant interest is related to the *in rem* quality of the right), with an annulment or repudiation to escape its onerous effects (where the relevant interest is related to the *in personam* quality of the right).

[16] Cf eg the Fifth amendment to the US Constitution:

[17] Cf eg § 105 of the Norwegian Constitution.

[18] Usually this is even specified in the treaty definition of investment. The Energy Charter Treaty (Lisbon, December 1994) (1995) 34 ILM 360 (which here also is quite representative of most BITs), provides the following (partly circular) definition of investment in relation to contracts in art 1(6): 'Investment means every kind of asset . . . and includes; . . . (c) claims to money and claims to performance pursuant to a contract having an economic value and associated with an investment . . . (f) any right conferred by law or contract or by virtue of any licenses and permits granted pursuant to law to undertake any Economic Activity in the Energy Sector'. The NAFTA's definition of investment is somewhat narrower, specifically confined in relation to contracts as follows in art 1139: 'Investment means . . . (h) interests arising from the commitment of capital or other resources in the territory of a Party to economic activity in such territory, such as under (i) contracts involving the presence of an investor's property in the territory of the Party, including turnkey or construction contracts, or concessions, or (ii) contracts where remuneration depends substantially on the production, revenues or profits of an enterprise; but investment does not mean, (i) claims to money that arise solely from commercial contracts for the sale of goods or services by a national or enterprise in the territory of a Party to an enterprise in the territory of another Party, or (ii) the extension of credit in connection with a commercial transaction, such as trade financing, other than a loan covered by subparagraph (d)'. North American Free Trade Agreement (NAFTA) (signed San Antonio, 17 December 1992, entered into force 1 January 1994).

This does not necessarily mean that all contractual rights engage the protective principle under the expropriation standard.[19] It could, conceivably, come with an *in rem* qualification, which would, presumably, not qualify all contractual rights for protection, but only those possessed of a kind of object, or asset quality, comparable to property. It may be assumed in this regard that the defining feature of a property right is that it possesses one or both of two essential characteristics: it provides an exclusive use or privilege over something which is protected against others by trespassory rules; and/or it represents a value which may be assigned to others for a corresponding sum of money (and, of course, in the conventional case, both).[20] A defined and established debt in money would clearly be different and more acceptable according to such characteristics, than for instance the bundle of rights and obligations under a long-term co-operation agreement such as an investment contract. In the latter, future performance is always implicitly conditional on a certain continuance of circumstances, and rights and obligations are not yet resolved and actualised to the same extent as an established debt. Moreover, it may be presumed that an investment contract with typical administrative and public law aspects will not be freely assignable. In the ECHR context, such considerations have been relied on. In *Stran Greek Refinereries and Stratis Andreadis v Greece*, a contractual claim for damages, established pursuant to an arbitral award, was considered a possession within the meaning of the ECHR, First Protocol article 1. The mere contractual quality of the claim was not considered decisive, however. The crucial criterion set out by the court was whether there was 'a debt . . . that was sufficiently established to be enforceable'.[21]

Investment treaty jurisprudence, in contrast, has displayed a conspicuous lack of concern for any potential *in rem* qualification of contractual rights when deriving from state undertakings. This may be seen as partly related to the both focused and extensive language of investment treaties, to include any kind of assets with an economic value, including, in principle, an unqualified category of contractual rights. The proposition clearly cemented in practice is that contractual rights as such are protected. In the decision on jurisdiction in *Bayindir v Pakistan* the tribunal simply held that '[i]t is not disputed that expropriation is not limited to *in rem* rights and may extend to contractual rights'.[22] In *Wena Hotels v Egypt*, the tribunal expressed the same proposition in more explicit terms:

[19] See eg the US and Canadian Model BITs, which explicitly confines the standard to measures, which 'interferes with a tangible or intangible property right or property interest in an investment' (US Model BIT (2004), Annex B, para 2). It is nevertheless not altogether obvious that this *will* be interpreted more strictly by investment tribunals than how the expropriation standard generally is interpreted, as examined in the following.

[20] See generally Harris (2001).

[21] *Stran Greek Refinereries and Stratis Andreadis v Greece* (1994) Series A301-B, para 59.

[22] *Bayindir Insaat Turizm Ticaret ve Sanayi AS v Islamic Republic of Pakistan* (Decision on Jurisdiction, 2005) para 255.

> It is also well established that an expropriation is not limited to tangible property rights. As the panel in *SPP v. Egypt* explained, 'there is considerable authority for the proposition that Contract rights are entitled to the protection of international law and that the taking of such rights involved an obligation to make compensation therefore'.[23]

The *Wena Hotels* tribunal here implicitly referred to a proposition of general customary law, represented by its reference to another ICSID case, that of *SPP v Egypt*. Faced with the same issue under general international law, and the contention of the respondent state that expropriation only applied to rights *in rem*, the tribunal dismissed this and held, immediately following what was cited by the Wena Hotels tribunal, that it did not:

> Nor can the tribunal accept the argument that the term 'expropriation' applies only to *jus in rem*. The Respondent's cancellation of the project had the effect of taking certain important rights and interest of the Claimants. What was expropriated was not the land nor the right of usufruct, but the rights that SPP(ME), as a shareholder of ETDC, derived from EGOTH's right of usufruct, which had been 'irrevocably' transferred to EDTC by the State. Clearly those rights were of a contractual rather than *in rem* nature.[24]

The 'considerable authority' relied on by the two Egyptian hotels cases was, on closer inspection, less than conclusive. The first tribunal primarily relied on two cases from the Iran-US claims tribunal, which had extended protection to contractual rights as particular instances of intangible property.[25] Significantly, however, the *ratio* of these cases was definitively not that all contractual rights are protected against expropriation, but that contractual rights may constitute property in this sense. The reasoning of the first case, *Amoco International Finance Corp v Iran* illustrates this. Dismissing the contention of Iran that the contractual rights in question could not be conceived as property, the tribunal held that property also would encompass intangible rights, extending as such to 'any right which can be the object of a commercial transaction, ie, freely sold and bought, and thus has a monetary value'.[26] What was emphasised was thus the objective value of the rights in question, or in other words one of the essential characteristics of rights *in rem*; to constitute items of objective wealth.[27]

The appropriate analysis would seem to be that investment treaty jurisprudence in contrast has introduced a different qualifying criterion, specific to contractual undertakings with states or state entities, namely

[23] *Wena Hotels Ltd v Arab Republic of Egypt* (Award, 2000) para 98.

[24] *Southern Pacific Properties (Middle East) Ltd (SPP) v Arab Republic of Egypt* (Award, 1992) para 164.

[25] See *Amoco Int'l Finance Corp v Islamic Republic of Iran* (1987) 15 Iran-US CT Rep 189, para 108; and *Phillips Petroleum Co v Islamic Republic of Iran* (1989) 21 Iran-US CT Rep 79, para 105.

[26] *Amoco Int'l Finance Corp v Iran* (1987) 15 Iran-US CT Rep 189, para 108.

[27] Harris (2001) 42.

whether the contract has been relied on to make an investment.[28] A case aptly illustrating this is *RFCC v Morocco*. Based on the broad definition of 'investment' in the relevant investment treaty, and using instead a distinctly teleological argument, the tribunal implicitly dismissed the relevance of any *in rem* qualification of contractual rights, and suggested instead that what was material was whether the contract was used 'to realise' a factual investment:

> Le Tribunal reprend la définition d'investissement donnée par le Traité et considère que des droits issus d'un contrat peuvent être l'objet de mesure d'expropriation, à partir du moment où ledit contrat a été qualifié d'investissement par le Traité lui-même . . . [L]es traités modernes de protection des investissements ont la particularité d'adopter une définition large du terme investissement afin de permettre une application de leurs dispositions face à la diversité des opérations, montages financiers et contrats que les agents économiques sont à même d'utiliser dans la perspective de réaliser un investissement. Ce qui permet de penser, comme la majorité des commentateurs, que tout type d'actif peut être a priori l'objet d'une expropriation et donc protégé par les dispositions du traité.[29]

This association of 'investment', as the criterion of protected assets, with the objective of investment treaties to further investment activities, suggests an implicit and de facto qualification of protected contractual rights by virtue of the jurisdictional requirements discussed above in section 4.4. Taking the full consequence of the jurisdictional requirements naturally limits the scope of the expropriation standard—as a part procedural and part substantive cause of action—to contractual rights which eg (i) are relied on to contribute capital and resources, (ii) relate to a certain duration of contractual performance and (iii) entail a participation in the risks of the transaction.[30] At the same time, it cannot necessarily be assumed that these criteria apply similarly to the merits phase as in the context of jurisdiction. With respect to the jurisdiction phase there is a clear rationale for applying the 'investment' criterion as a flexible and open-ended requirement, the real underlying concern being whether a prima facie basis for a claim that may succeed on the merits exists.

In our context, this in reality brings us to what is the crucial turn where the state is the contracting party. By not making a distinction between contracts concluded by the state (or state entities acting in a government capacity) and ordinary commercial contracts between private entities, the expropriation standard evolves into a standard protecting, essentially,

[28] See also, at least implicitly, to this effect, Douglas, 'The Hybrid Foundations of Investment Treaty Arbitration' (2003) 74 *BYIL* 151, 197 fn 219, writing that 'contractual rights in this context should be interpreted narrowly as those contracts that regulate the investor's right to property in the host state'.

[29] *Consortium RFCC v Kingdom of Morocco* (Award, 2003) paras 60–62.

[30] *Salini Costruttori SpA v Kingdom of Morocco* (Decision on Jurisdiction, 2001) para 52.

reliance on state contractual undertakings to make capital investments subject to state power.[31] Thus, the notion that some contractual rights may constitute intangible property—engaging the protective principle as items of wealth comparable to property—has evolved into a distinct principle of investment protection, based on 'a broad concept of economic rights that are necessary for the investor to pursue its business successfully'.[32] A good reflection of this is the case of *CME v Czech Republic*.[33] The case concerned a media enterprise established in the Czech Republic pursuant to a complex contractual arrangement, involving both a local licence-holder, and the Czech media authority acting behind the scenes. The objective of the contract was to ensure to the foreign investor-company, the right to operate a TV station pursuant to a TV broadcasting licence initially granted to the local company in accordance with Czech policies. The tribunal held that subsequent state measures, by which the investor, inter alia, was forced to give up its original contractual position and lost the licence, also destroyed the substantial value of the investor's TV enterprise, in a manner tantamount to expropriation.[34] However, the rationale of the decision was clearly not a conception of a general right of TV enterprises to continue in production in accordance with established licence conditions, but that the investor in this particular instance was considered to have a legitimate expectation to continue broadcasting operations in accordance with the licence arrangement.[35] Underlying this was the tribunal's apparent perception that the investor, through the company, had a contractually ensured right which had been set up in co-operation with the Media Council,[36] and which effectively was violated when the Council caused the licence to be retracted from the company's use.[37] Thus, essentially the applied rationale in the case was that the contractual interest in the licence was protected against deprivation because the investor had a legitimate expectation that it had relied on, which had been effectively induced by the state through its own conduct.

(ii) A Concept Evolved—Protecting the Expectation Interest

When this notion of legitimate expectations is used to set the standard for protected rights pursuant to state contractual undertakings as well as concessions and licences with a contractual or quasi-contractual nature, it

[31] See eg *SGS v Philippines* (Decision on Jurisdiction, 2004) para 99 et seq and para 161; and especially *SGS v Pakistan* (Decision on Jurisdiction, 2003) para 135, placing less weight on the territorial element, and more on an emphasis of the element of public power involved.

[32] Schreuer (2005) para 64.

[33] *CME Czech Republic BV v Czech Republic* (Partial Award, 2001).

[34] *ibid*, para 591.

[35] *ibid*, esp para 446 et seq.

[36] *ibid*, para 428 et seq.

[37] *ibid*, paras 519–20.

is quite apparent that the expropriation standard really turns into a protection of the investor's expectation interest. It thus has evolved from a concept initially and traditionally thought to apply to 'reified' assets for the reason of their *in rem* qualities, to simple contractual rights *in personam* where the state is a contracting party.

One case illustrating this is *Waste Management v Mexico.* The question was whether 'persistent refusal or inability' to pay sums due under a concession contract, clearly as such amounting to a breach of contract, also could be held to constitute an expropriation of the contractual rights to such payment.[38] The tribunal did not consider that the breaches of contract in question could be equiparated to expropriation. At first sight, it might seem that this was based on a more nuanced consideration of the extent to which mere contractual rights would be protected. Inter alia the tribunal stated (paraphrasing the *Shufeldt claim*[39]) that 'simply to assert that "property rights are created under and by virtue of a contract" is not sufficient'.[40] However, on a closer inspection it appears that this qualification was directed at the nature of the breach, not against the putative protection of the contractual rights as such. This appears from the reasoning of the tribunal, which is based on the clear assumption that *had* there been an effective repudiation of the contract by the state pursuant to state prerogatives, there would also have been a compensable expropriation, requiring, presumably, compensation of the value of the contract, on the basis of what would be the appropriate amount of damages due under it.[41] Thus, a not so profitable contract with an unreliable state entity would have been transformed into a strict liability for the state, based on the expectation interest under the contract.

A second relevant case is *Eureko v Poland,* where this proposition was made explicit and relied on. The question was whether non-fulfillment by Poland of contractual undertakings under a share-purchase privatisation arrangement constituted 'a measure depriving Eureko of its investment'[42] within the terms of the relevant BIT. As to whether the contractual rights were protected against 'deprivation', the main consideration relied on by the tribunal was that the undertakings, by virtue of express contractual provisions, had 'crystallized and become a firm commitment of the State Treasury'.[43] According to the tribunal this meant that 'the Republic of Poland contracted obligations and Eureko acquired rights derived from its

[38] *Waste Management Inc v United Mexican States* (Award, 2004) para 141 et seq.

[39] *Shufeldt claim (USA v Guatemala)* (1930) II RIAA 1079.

[40] *ibid,* para 174.

[41] This is revealed particularly in the distinction made by the tribunal, between the continued effective existence of a right, even in case of breach, and effective repudiation of that same right, where only the latter were conceived expropriatory, *ibid,* para 175.

[42] *Eureko BV v Republic of Poland* (Partial Award, 2005) para 238.

[43] *ibid,* para 152.

shareholding . . . which were entitled to protection under the treaty'.[44] The actual investment in this case was a minority shareholder position acquired by the investor through the initial share purchase agreement. The essential reasoning of the tribunal was, however, that not only was this investment protected against deprivation, but also the contractual interest to acquire a further and controlling shareholder position created by the contractual undertaking entered into in connection with the purchase.[45] In other words, while the contract might have qualified as an investment because it was also relied on to purchase the minority shareholding, this did not limit the extent of extended protection. Thus, the protective rule was turned into a protection of the investor's expectation interest under the contract.

This is not a singular example, although it may be the most explicit to this effect. The same basic ratio is, however, implicit in several cases where it has been held that ordinary regulatory measures, which normally are legitimate, nevertheless may be considered (indirectly) expropriatory if individual commitments or other binding representations of the government are breached.[46] In respect of such regulation, the investor continues in possession of his property. Although some or even all of its value may be lost, this will usually not in itself constitute an indirect expropriation, if the regulation is within the state's ordinary 'police powers'. The tendency is nevertheless for the regulation to be considered tantamount to expropriation if it violates a distinct and prior commitment of the state not to regulate.[47] In case of a contractual commitment to this effect, what is appropriated is really a conceived contractual right to be exempt from regulatory change. Insofar as compensation can be claimed for deprivation of value caused by the regulation, the investor in reality receives compensation for its loss of expectation pursuant to a contractual or comparable right. In this regard, one must, however, also distinguish between situations where the commitment itself is capable of constituting a protected investment, and where the protected investment is, for example, shares in a company that has been adversely affected by a breach of commitment. In the latter instance, only the ownership interest is directly protected against expropriation, and the breach of commitment is not itself directly touched by the treaty standard.[48]

[44] *ibid*, para 157.

[45] *ibid*, paras 240–42.

[46] I come back to these cases in further detail in section 6.3 below.

[47] See especially *Methanex Corp v USA* (Award, 2005), Part IV–Chapter D, para 7: '[A]s a matter of general international law, a non-discriminatory regulation for a public purpose, which is enacted in accordance with due process and, which affects, inter alios, a foreign investor or investment is not deemed expropriatory and compensable unless specific commitments had been given by the regulating government to the then putative foreign investor contemplating investment that the government would refrain from such regulation'.

[48] See eg *National Grid Plc v Argentine Republic* (Award, 2008) paras 144–55, with further references.

B. The Sovereign Act Requirement

While the above posits that contractual rights pursuant to state contractual undertakings that have been relied on to make an investment in principle are encompassed by the expropriation standard, it does not follow that any breach of contract engages the standard.[49] The fundamental point is that any private person may breach a contract, while expropriation is a government prerogative. It follows that not all breaches of contract can qualify as expropriation.

The requirement of a sovereign act has long been considered an established principle of customary law. According to one commentator, the leading guideline that appears from case law is 'whether a state has acted in its sovereign capacity, exercising its governmental or public power or authority'.[50] An illustrative case is the *Jalapa Railroad* case, where annulment of a specific and vital clause in a contract was considered confiscatory. The tribunal held that the issue for determination was 'whether the breach of contract . . . was an arbitrary one involving no international responsibility or whether [it] was effected arbitrarily by means of a governmental power illegal under international law'.[51] In this case the breach was clearly confiscatory, since it was effected by legislative annulment. In the words of the tribunal, the government had therefore 'stepped out of the role of contracting party and sought to escape vital obligations under its contract by exercising its superior governmental power'.[52]

In recent investment treaty jurisprudence, this relatively strict requirement has evolved into a looser and more functional criterion, requiring essentially some kind of effective reliance by the state on its public capacity to repudiate the contract.[53] The underlying rationale would seem to be a more teleological emphasis on the purpose of the expropriation standard in an investment treaty context, as a more general remedy against the *political risk* element in investor-state relationships.

The general perception is that activity which an ordinary contractual party could adopt will not be expropriatory. It was stated in the following terms in *Waste Management v Mexico*:

> [S]imply to assert that 'property rights are created under and by virtue of a contract' is not sufficient. The mere non-performance of a contractual obligation

[49] See generally Schreuer (2005) para 65 et seq.

[50] Reinisch (2005) 12.

[51] *Jalapa Railroad and Power Co v Mexico (US v Mexico)* (American Mexican Claims Commision, 1948) (1976) 8 *Whiteman Digest of International Law* 908, as quoted by Reinisch (2005) 12.

[52] *ibid.*

[53] See eg *CME Czech Republic BV v Czech Republic* (Partial Award, 2001); *Consortium RFCC v Morocco* (Award, 2003); *Generation Ukraine Inc v Ukraine* (Award, 2003); *Waste Management Inc v Mexico* (Award, 2004); *SGS Société Générale de Surveillance SA v Republic of the Philippines* (Decision on Jurisdiction, 2004); *Eureko v Poland* (Award, 2005); *EnCana Corp v Ecuador* (Award, 2006); *Azurix Corp v Argentina* (Award, 2006).

> is not to be equated with a taking of property, nor (unless accompanied by other elements) is it tantamount to expropriation. Any private party can fail to perform its contracts, whereas nationalisation and expropriation are inherently governmental acts . . .[54]

While non-performance by the state could deprive the other party of the substance of its benefits under the contract, the tribunal thus held that this, in itself, is not sufficient for it to constitute expropriation. This had to do with the specific rationale of the expropriation standard in the context of an investment treaty. It is not to facilitate enforcement of government undertakings as such, but to ensure their function as effective guarantees for an investor. The tribunal explained it as follows:

> [T]he normal response by an investor faced with a breach of contract by its government counter party (the breach not taking the form of an exercise of governmental prerogative, such as a legislative decree) is to sue in the appropriate court to remedy the breach. *It is only where such access is legally or practically foreclosed that the breach could amount to an definitive denial of the right (i.e. the effective taking of the chose in action)* . . .[55] (emphasis added)

The case concerned non-payment by the state entity for services rendered by the investor. This could not be considered expropriatory, according to the tribunal, since, decisively, 'the Claimant did not loose its contractual rights, which it was free to pursue before the contractually chosen forum'.[56] Thus, the point made by the tribunal was that mere non-payment of debts could not in itself be held to constitute expropriation if the right to payment continued to exist and could be invoked in proper fora.[57] Contrastingly, in *RFCC v Morocco*, the question did not concern non-performance with contractual obligations, but allegedly wrongful and abusive exercise by the state entity of certain contractual prerogatives.[58] But the same basic principle was applied. The tribunal held that a distinction had to be made between the state as public authority, and ordinary contracting party.[59] In

[54] *Waste Management v Mexico* (Award, 2004) para 174.

[55] *ibid*, para 174.

[56] *ibid*, para 175.

[57] See also to this effect also *SGS v Philippines* (2004) para 161: 'In the Tribunal's view, on the material presented by the Claimant no case of expropriation has been raised. Whatever debt the Philippines may owe to SGS still exists; whatever right to interest for late payment SGS had it still has. There has been no law or decree enacted by the Philippines attempting to expropriate or annul the debt, nor any action tantamount to an expropriation . . . A mere refusal to pay a debt is not an expropriation of property, at least where remedies exist in respect of such a refusal. *A fortiori* a refusal to pay is not an expropriation where there is an unresolved dispute as to the amount payable'.

[58] *Consortium RFCC v Morocco* (Award, 2003) para 81 et seq. The specific claim was that the state entity wrongfully had invoked the right to claim penalty for late performance, and failed to release the contractual guarantees of the investor for its performance.

[59] *ibid*, para 65: 'Pour qu'il y ait droit à compensation il faut que la personne de l'exproprié prouve qu'il a été l'objet de mesures prises par l'Etat agissant non comme cocontractant mais comme autorité publique'.

contrast to the tribunal in *Waste Management*, the tribunal here was not confronted with mere non-performance of a contractual obligation, but with possibly abusive exercise of rights envisaged by the contract. It nevertheless held that this could not at the outset be considered expropriatory, since the requisite act would have had to be a measure taken 'by virtue of prerogatives of public power', and not merely be of the kind envisaged within the contractual framework as a contractual prerogative.[60]

Other cases nevertheless suggest that this latter statement cannot be taken as a literal requirement, in the sense that active exercise of government power is necessarily material for there to be conduct comparable to expropriation. Thus, in *CME v Czech Republic*, the tribunal held that 'it makes no difference whether the deprivation was caused by actions or inactions'.[61] It accordingly considered that the Czech Media Council's informal 'actions and inactions', which were held to have lead to a destruction of the legal basis of the investment, constituted sufficient expropriatory deprivation.[62] Moreover, in the more recent case of *Eureko v Poland*, the tribunal expressly contemplated that 'a failure to act' could constitute expropriation,[63] and went so far as to consider what appeared as a mere non-performance of a contractual obligation as an expropriatory deprivation. The Polish government had refused to carry through a clear undertaking to conduct a public offering of shares, pursuant to a share-purchase privatisation agreement. As the agreement was neither annulled nor formally repudiated, it could have been held to remain in force as a binding instrument under Polish law. Such considerations did not impress the tribunal, which held that the failure to comply with the contractual obligations constituted a 'frustration' of the investor's investment and legitimate expectations,[64] which amounted to expropriatory deprivation.[65] It is more difficult to rationalise such non-performance by omission under a sovereign act requirement. When does the state act in its government capacity by not doing something it has pledged in a contract to do? An important aspect of the *Eureko* case seems to have been that the failure to further implement the privatisation was motivated by a political decision, but it is nevertheless difficult to escape the feeling that this involved stretching considerably the natural meaning of the term 'deprivation'. In an attempt to rationalise this, it may nevertheless be argued that it receives

[60] *ibid*, para 69. The tribunal held that the measure 'avoir été prise en vertu de prérogatives de puissance publique et non dans le cadre de l'exercice d'un droit prévu par un contrat'. See also *Biwater Gauff (Tanzania) Ltd v United Republic of Tanzania* (Award, 2008) paras 457–60.

[61] *CME Czech Republic BV v Czech Republic* (Partial Award, 2001) para 605.

[62] See eg *ibid*, para 575.

[63] *Eureko v Poland* (Award, 2005) para 186: 'It is obvious that the rights of an investor can be violated as much by the failure of a Contracting State to act as by its actions'.

[64] *ibid*, para 226: 'The clear decision by the RoP to refuse to abide by and respect its legal obligations under [the agreement] frustrated the investment of Eureko in [the company] and its expectations in concluding the [agreement]'.

[65] *ibid*, paras 240–42.

some justification, based on an appreciation of the risk element materialised in the breach; in other words whether the breach is a materialisation of a commercial or a political risk.

A significant aspect of this is whether the right as such is left untouched and effectively enforceable. This is well illustrated by *Waste Management v Mexico*. The tribunal held that what was decisive was whether there had been 'an effective repudiation of the right, unredressed by any remedies available to the claimant, which has the effect of preventing its exercise entirely or to a substantial extent'.[66] In that case it was held that the test had not been passed, since there had been no 'final refusal to pay', exemplified by the tribunal as 'effective obstruction and denial of legal remedies'. Similarly, in *SGS v Philippines*, the tribunal held that there was no plausible case for an expropriation having occurred, since in its view 'a mere refusal to pay a debt is not an expropriation of property, at least where remedies exist in respect of such a refusal'.[67] These cases thus suggest as a decisive criterion, in the face of a mere failure to perform, whether municipal remedies still exist and are available. Thus, the failure to exhaust such remedies may preclude an expropriation claim, without being considered a condition of admissibility as such.[68]

Short of actual exercise of government power, the tendency of case law indicates a criterion of effective repudiation as the essential requirement of expropriation. In *EnCana v Ecuador*, this was further conceptualised to include three different and alternative indicia: (i) willfulness of breach; (ii) a lack of available (and effective) court procedures; or (iii) failure to comply with or repudiation of court decisions in favour of the claimant:

> Like private parties, governments do not repudiate obligations merely by contesting their existence. An executive agency does not expropriate the value represented by a statutory obligation to make a payment or refund by mere refusal to pay, provided at least that (a) the refusal is not merely willful, (b) the courts are open to the aggrieved party, (c) the courts' decisions are not themselves overridden or repudiated by the State.[69]

The case concerned certain alleged claims for VAT refunds under a number of oil and gas investment contracts. Since the type of claims in question had regularly been subject to effective court proceedings in the host state, and there was no suggestion that the denial of refunds was based on bad faith, the expropriation claims were denied.[70]

[66] *Waste Management v Mexico* (Award, 2004) para 175.

[67] *SGS v Philippines* (Decision on Jurisdiction, 2004) para 161.

[68] *Generation Ukraine v Ukraine* (Award, 2003) para 20.30. '[A]n international tribunal may deem that the failure to seek redress from national authorities disqualifies the international claim, not because there is a requirement of *exhaustion* of local remedies but because the very reality of conduct tantamount to expropriation is doubtful in the absence of a *reasonable*—not necessarily exhaustive—effort by the investor to obtain correction'.

[69] *EnCana Corp v Republic of Ecuador* (Award, 2006) para 194.

[70] *ibid*, paras 196–7.

A less strict view seems again to be manifested in *Eureko v Poland*. As mentioned above, the claim was based on simple non-performance of a share privatisation contract, and it was still awaiting resolution in the Polish court system,[71] pursuant to an exclusive jurisdiction clause in the contract.[72] This did not preclude the finding of the tribunal that an expropriation had occurred. At first glance the decision is thus difficult to reconcile with a distinction between non-performance and effective repudiation. Nothing in the case suggests that the right had been formally and effectively repudiated by the decision of the government not to follow through with the privatisation, or that it could not have been pursued before the ordinary courts.[73] It is nevertheless possible to distinguish this case on the basis of a separate element present in the reasoning of the tribunal, as already alluded to, namely the distinct risk factor materialised by the breach. This is revealed, as mentioned, by the considerable effort exerted by the tribunal to establish the breach as a deliberate political decision made by the competent Polish minister, with the approval and backing of the government (Council of Ministers).[74] Thus, a decisive element in the tribunal's reasoning may have been the apparent materialisation of a political risk factor in the government's decision to relinquish further implementation of the privatisation scheme. The rationale may have been that where an investor is made to suffer deprivation of its contractual benefits by a politically motivated and deliberate breach of contract, this is substantially comparable to a decision to expropriate that right.[75] Irrespective of this, it is nevertheless difficult to escape the compelling concern that the tribunal here went far to undermine the integrity of the contractual relationship itself, by not awaiting resolution of the issues according to the stipulated procedure of the contract.[76]

C. The Expectation Interest Defined—Renvoi to Municipal Law

Rights pursuant to contractual undertakings are covered by the expropriation standard through their qualification as 'assets' under the requisite definition of 'investment' in the relevant investment treaty. While the 'investment' requirement to this effect is autonomous, a sort of *renvoi* to the municipal law of the state party (or, extraordinarily, some other muni-

[71] *Eureko v Poland* (Award, 2005), see the dissenting opinion of Rajski, para 3.
[72] *Eureko v Poland* (Award, 2005) para 92 et seq.
[73] See especially to this effect the dissenting opinion of Rajski, eg paras 3–4.
[74] *Eureko v Poland*, (Award, 2005) para 207 et seq.
[75] Cfr *Encana v Ecuador* (Award, 2006) para 194, as cited above.
[76] Compare especially *SGS v Philippines* (Decision on Jurisdiction, 2004) paras 161–4; and see also generally the dissenting opinion of Rajski attached to the main *Eureko* award. See also Douglas, 'Nothing if not Critical for Investment Treaty Arbitration: Occidental, Eureko and Methanex' (2006) 22(1) *Arb Int'l* 27, 38 et seq.

cipal law) is implicit in the very definition of 'investment' as different varieties of property rights and interests qualifying as assets.[77] International law does not have a developed conception of property rights that may determine when a property right has been acquired, come into existence, been validly transferred, ceased to exist or otherwise been affected by private dispositions for different reasons.[78] The same must in principle be true where the right in question is contractual. In this respect it is, however, complicated by the wide measure of party autonomy ordinarily recognised in contract choice of law in the context of arbitration. Inter alia, this suggests that a contract claim may have to be determined in accordance with some a-national contract law or practice (*lex mercatoria*) if this is stipulated in the contract, rather than on the basis of a concrete municipal law. In any case it means that the applicable law may be a municipal law other than that of the host state.[79] How this might relate to possible mandatory rules of the host state, explicitly stipulated to override a contractual choice of law is less clear.[80] At least insofar as such mandatory rules are stipulated to govern performance within the host state's own territory, and application would not be violatory of the expropriation standard itself, general principles of conflict of laws, and the necessary deference to the host state's territorial jurisdiction, might require an arbitral tribunal to apply such rules irrespective of a contractual choice of law to the contrary.[81]

[77] Thus, where 'investment' is stipulated to encompass 'tangible and intangible, and movable and immovable, property, and any property rights such as leases, mortgages, liens and pledges', or 'shares, stock or other forms of equity participation in a company or business enterprise' (see the Energy Charter Treaty art 1(7)), this involves a reference to the municipal law under which those rights have come into existence; usually that of the host state, or, exceptionally, any other municipal law which might be identified as the applicable law by appropriate conflict of laws rules (which again usually will be those of the host state, cf art 42 of the ICSID convention.)

[78] See generally Douglas (2003) 151, 197 et seq.

[79] See especially *Maritime International Nominees Establishment (MINE) v Government of Guinea* (Decision on Annulment, 22 December 1989) 5 *ICSID Rev-FILJ* (1990) 95, 112, where the tribunal applied a 'frozen' choice of law, in accordance with a choice of law clause to that effect. Article 42 of the ICSID Convention is generally recognized to allow the parties a free choice of law (at least in so far as mere contractual responsibility is concerned), including the ability to 'completely internationalize the contract by referring exclusively to international law, to general principles of law or to a set of usages customarily governing like transactions'. See Schreuer, *The ICSID Convention: A Commentary* (Cambridge, 2001) 565. And see also Broches, 'The Convention on the Settlement of Investment Disputes between States and Nationals of Other States' (1972-II) 136 *Recueil des Cours* 371, 389: 'The provision . . . firmly confers on the parties unlimited autonomy as to the applicable law, and makes their choice binding on the tribunal. The parties are free to agree on rules of law defined as they choose and whether national or international, or a combination of both'.

[80] See generally Cordero Moss, *International Commercial Arbitration—Party Autonomy and Mandatory Rules* (Tano Aschehoug, Oslo, 1999), especially 325 et seq.

[81] See eg the old English cases of *Ralli Bros v Compañia Naviera Sota Y Aznar* [1920] 2 KB 287; and *Regazzoni v KC Sethia* [1958] AC 301.

With this possible modification, several cases confirm as a general proposition that contracts must be interpreted by reference to a municipal law, typically that of the host state, for the purpose of the viability of an expropriation claim. In *Azinian et al v Mexico* this proved fatal to the claimant's expropriation claim under NAFTA. The question was whether the cancellation of a concession contract by relevant Mexican authorities was a wrongful expropriation of the claimant's contractual rights. The essential basis of the cancellation was that the contract was invalid under Mexican law due to substantial misrepresentation by the claimants, something which had been tested and confirmed by the competent Mexican courts in accordance with the jurisdictional provisions in the contract. This meant that according to Mexican law there was no valid contractual claim, and had never been. The tribunal essentially held that it was bound by the Mexican courts' appreciation of the validity of the contract; hence there was, in the words of the tribunal, 'by definition no contract to be expropriated'.[82] Similarly, in *Encana v Ecuador*, the tribunal had to determine whether the right to VAT refunds was protected against retroactive legislation as a kind of expropriation. The tribunal did not exclude that such a right could be protected against expropriation, irrespective of whether it was based on a contract or simply created as an effective vested right under the public law of the state concerned.[83] However, while the effect of retroactivity and the protection of the vested right as such clearly would have to be based on the treaty, the tribunal held that the existence and content of the right would depend on municipal law, as 'the applicable law' of the right:

> [F]or there to have been an expropriation of an investment or return (in a situation involving legal rights or claims as distinct from the seizure of physical assets) the rights affected must exist under the law which creates them, in this case, the law of Ecuador.[84]

As a general proposition, the applicability of municipal law to determine the initial validity and content of a contractual right that is made the subject of an expropriation claim is thus well established.[85] The nature of a contractual right, and the manner in which the expropriation standard has been interpreted according to a more extended rationale of protecting legitimate expectations, may nevertheless suggest a more progressive and autonomous concept of rights in certain situations, even beyond cases of a de-nationalised choice of law as discussed above.

Certain cases suggest, more or less justifiably one might add from a more sceptical viewpoint, that this extended rationale may surface in the interpretation of contractual rights as a presumption in favour of validity. Thus,

[82] *Azinian et al v United Mexican States* (Award, 1999) para 100.
[83] *EnCana v Ecuador* (Award, 2006) para 183.
[84] *ibid* para 184.
[85] See also to this effect the recent award in *Bayindir v Pakistan* (Award, 2009) para 456 et seq.

in *Eureko v Poland* the tribunal simply assumed, without any certified basis in municipal law, that the clear and definite contractual undertakings created contractual rights protected against expropriation.[86] Similarly, in *CME v Czech Republic* the tribunal could not certify the existence of any valid contractual undertaking by the state or the Media Council under Czech law, and instead relied on a seemingly autonomous concept of legitimate expectations, to find an apparent vested right of the investor to retain its original contractual position.[87] This may, inter alia, suggest that an investment treaty tribunal is less likely to be concerned with implicit limitations of a government entity's capacity to commit to or remain bound by contractual undertakings restricting its powers, at least if such capacity is not rebutted by a clear and distinct rule of municipal law.

5.3 UMBRELLA CLAUSES—ELEVATING CONTRACT CLAIMS INTO TREATY CLAIMS

The umbrella clause was incepted in the first BITs in the 1960s, but has only recently come to the front of legal practice.[88] Although there may be variances in language, the crucial aspect of an umbrella clause is a requirement to respect undertakings and commitments made in connection with a specific investment. The term commonly denotes a provision expressly requiring observance of 'undertakings', 'commitments' or 'obligations' of a state 'entered into' in respect of an 'investment'.[89] While usually not expressly confined to contractual obligations, this is where the clause, not unnaturally, has found its main relevance (as also suggested by the common term 'entered into'). The interpretation of this clause in practice has, however, been played out against the backdrop of a conflict of views on the scope and effect of international law generally, and the umbrella clause specifically, upon contractual undertakings. One major strand of opinion, reminiscent of the classical internationalisation theory discussed in chapter three, has generally found in the umbrella clause the coveted link between international law and contractual undertakings. The clause is seen to 'pierce the dualistic veil' and draw the contract out of

[86] *Eureko v Poland* (Award, 2005).

[87] *CME v Czech Republic* (Partial Award, 2001).

[88] The first case, reportedly, to have touched on the issue of umbrella clauses, though superficially, was *Fedax NV v Republic of Venezuela* (Award, 1998) para 29. Embracing the latter approach, the tribunal held that the clause placed the state under 'the obligation to honour precisely the terms and conditions governing such investment'.

[89] A prominent example is provided by art 10(1) of the Energy Charter treaty, which *in fine* states as follows: 'Each Contracting Party shall observe any obligations it has entered into with an Investor or an Investment of an Investor of any other Contracting Party'. Many BITs, especially those entered into by European countries, contain similar provisions, see eg for some random examples; Denmark-Chile BIT (1993) art 3(1), Germany-Mexico BIT (1998) art 8, France-Bangladesh BIT (1985) art 10, and the Switzerland-Philippines BIT (1997) art X.

the confines of municipal law, effectively transforming it into an obligation under international law.[90] This notion has been countered by a more sceptical view—based on the concern that a general elevation of contract claims into treaty claims means elevating ordinary contractual responsibility into state responsibility under international law—which again is held to oppose the basic function of investment law as a remedy against state power.[91] In the following, I show how arbitral practice, though not always with full consistency, has developed on the basis of the umbrella clause a distinct requirement, which nevertheless is not structurally different from other investment protection standards. The prevailing tendencies in practice may be seen to converge out of an underlying concern to protect reasonable expectations that have been induced by distinct commitments from the state and relied on to make an investment against government power, while at the same time limiting the scope of the clause to the normal ambit of protection of investment law. As I go further into in the following, this is, however, not an altogether consistent tendency devoid of controversies.

A. A 'Sanctity of Contract' Standard—an Initial Controversy

The wording of a standard umbrella clause would seem to indicate that it imposes an essential requirement of respect for contractual and similar commitments. This notwithstanding, one of the first controversies arising

[90] See eg Weil, 'Problèmes relatifs aux contrats passes entre un état et un particulier' (1969-III) 128 *Recueil des Cours* 94, 130: 'L'intervention du traité de couverture transforme les obligations contractuelles en obligations internationals et assure ainsi comme on l'a dit, 'l'intangibilité du contrat sous peine de violer le traité;' toute inexécution du contrat, seraitelle meme régulière au regard de droit interne de l'Etat contractant, engage dès lors la responsabilité internationale de ce dernier envers l'Etat national du cocontractant'. And see also Seidl-Hohenveldern, 'The Abs-Shawcroft draft convention to protect private foreign investment: Comments on the Round Table' (1961) 10 *Journal of Public Law* 100, 104, commenting on the alleged impossibility of assimilating contracts to treaties: 'the very aim of Article II of the Abs-Shawcroft draft is *to change this* and to bring concession contracts under its umbrella of protection'. This latter quote may be the origin of the term 'umbrella' clause, while the origin of the clause itself seems to have been an opinion from Sir Elihu Lauterpacht to the Anglo-Iranian Oil Company, giving advice to protect its contractual engagement in Iran by incorporating it 'in a treaty between Iran and the United Kingdom in such a way that a breach of the contract or settlement shall be *ipso facto* deemed to be a breach of the treaty'. See Sinclair, 'The Origins of the Umbrella Clause in the International Law of Investment Protection' (2005) 20(4) *Arb Int'l* 411, 414. See also Orrego Vicuña, 'Of Contracts and Treaties in the Global Market' (2004) 8 *Max Planck Yearbook of United Nations Law* 341, 352–3.

[91] See especially Wälde, 'The Umbrella Clause in Investment Arbitration—a Comment on Original Intentions and Recent Cases' (2005) 6(2) *JWIT* 183, 193 and 203–9. And see also for a more sceptical view, Sornarajah, *The International Law on Foreign Investment* 2nd edn (Cambridge University Press, Cambridge, 2004) 433: 'It is difficult to see how a clause, hitherto regarded as insignificant, can have the effect of enhancing the obligations contained in contractual documents . . . [I]f such an extensive meaning was to be given to the clause, it would render the carefully negotiated provisions of the investment treaties nugatory'.

in respect of the interpretation of the clause was precisely whether it did indeed protect contractual expectations as such to 'transform contract claims into treaty claims'. As I discuss further in the following, the outcome of this controversy is that the umbrella clause does indeed apply to contractual undertakings as such, provided however that a certain commitment, contractual or comparable, has been undertaken or 'entered into' in relation to a specific investment. Considered as a manifestation of the general legitimate expectations standard, this may be seen to invoke the same, or at least a similar requirement as that already discussed in relation to expropriation.

The initial conflict of views upon the interpretation and significance that should be given to the umbrella clause first came to the front in the two *SGS* cases.[92] While concerning virtually identical issues and facts, the two cases adopted diametrically opposite views on the interpretation of two relatively identical umbrella clauses[93] contained in BITs entered into by Switzerland with, respectively, Pakistan[94] and the Philippines.[95] As already discussed at some length in chapter four, both cases concerned investment treaty jurisdiction over essentially contractual claims. The first case out was *SGS v Pakistan*, where the tribunal denied any such transformative effect to the umbrella clause, considering essentially that the clause did not apply to contractual undertakings as a strict imperative at all. Perhaps the most significant rationale of the decision was the unstated premise on which this was based, namely that it would 'elevate' any breach of contract into a breach of the treaty.[96] The tribunal then compared this to the 'widely accepted principle' that 'under general international law, a violation of a contract entered into by a State with an investor of another State, is not, by itself, a violation of international law'.[97] It seems that this was held by the tribunal to entail a strong presumption against

[92] For literature on the two cases, see eg; Alexandrov, 'Breaches of Contract and Breaches of Treaty: The Jurisdiction of Treaty-based Arbitration Tribunals to Decide Breach of Contract Claims in SGS v Pakistan and SGS v Philippines' (2004) 5(4) *JWIT* 555; and Gill, Gearing and Birt, 'Contractual Claims and Bilateral Investment Treaties: A Comparative Review of the SGS Cases' (2004) 21(5) *J Int'l Arb* 397.

[93] The suggestion that the conflict of perspectives might be resolved by reference to the different language of the clauses is not very convincing; at least it is difficult to see that the linguistic difference between 'shall constantly guarantee the observance of' and 'shall observe' has any clear substantive connotations. See also implicitly to this effect *SGS v Pakistan* (Decision on Jurisdiction, 2003) para 177. But contrast nevertheless *Noble Ventures Inc v Romania* (Award, 2005) para 58, and to some extent also *SGS v Philippines* (Decision on Jurisdiction, 2004) para 119.

[94] Article 11 of the Swiss-Pakistan BIT states: 'Either Contracting Party shall constantly guarantee the observance of the commitments it has entered into with respect to the investments of the investors of the other Contracting Party'.

[95] Article X (2) of the Swiss-Philippines BIT states: 'Each Contracting Party shall observe any obligation it has assumed with regard to specific investments in its territory by investors of the other Contracting Party'.

[96] *SGS v Pakistan* (Decision on Jurisdiction, 2003) para 163.

[97] *ibid*, para 167.

giving any such similar effect to the umbrella clause, from which it inferred that an umbrella clause could not be held to apply to contractual undertakings at all. The reason seems to have been that this, in the tribunal's opinion, would necessarily have had the consequence of making any breach of contract, and virtually any other obligation under municipal law, into a breach of the treaty:

> The consequences of accepting the Claimant's reading of Article 11 of the BIT should be spelled out in some detail. Firstly, Article 11 would amount to incorporating by reference an unlimited number of State contracts, as well as other municipal law instruments setting out State commitments including unilateral commitments to an investor of the other Contracting Party. Any violation of those contracts and other instruments would be treated as a breach of the BIT.[98]

From this, the tribunal drew two possible, and in its view, particularly unfortunate consequences. First, it held that the understanding would make other provisions of the treaty 'substantially superfluous'[99] and, secondly, that it would 'nullify any freely negotiated dispute settlement clause in a state contract'.[100] These dramatic prospects lead the tribunal to maintain that the clause lacked a sufficient degree of 'clarity and specificity', thus failing to provide sufficiently 'clear and convincing evidence' on which to establish that this had indeed been the intention of the parties.[101]

This ruling was then immediately and directly contradicted by the tribunal in the subsequent case of *SGS v Philippines*. Without even making any considerable effort to distinguish the cases (though this would not in any case have been readily plausible), the latter tribunal openly disagreed with the former case on certain fundamental issues. As a starting point, the tribunal rejected the 'all or nothing' approach relied on as a main assumption in *SGS v Pakistan*. Although it accepted the soundness of the principle that a breach of contract will not generally involve international law, it disagreed with the former tribunal on the proposition that this necessarily involved any presumption against the possibility of a specific international obligation to respect contracts and other specific undertakings.[102] On the one hand, it held that the far-reaching and calamitous effects predicted in *SGS v Pakistan* were exaggerated, for the main reason that the umbrella clause according to its wording did not apply to all contracts but only to specific and direct undertakings assumed by a state in respect of specific investment projects.[103] On the other hand, it rejected the apparent

[98] *ibid*, para 168.

[99] *ibid*, para 168: 'There would be no real need to demonstrate a violation of those substantive treaty standards if a simple breach of contract, or of municipal statute or regulation, by itself, would suffice to constitute a treaty violation on the part of a Contracting Party and engage the international responsibility of the Party'.

[100] *ibid*, para 168.

[101] *ibid*, para 171.

[102] *SGS v Philippines* (Decision on Jurisdiction, 2004) para 122.

[103] *ibid*, para 121.

assumption of the *SGS v Pakistan* tribunal that giving effect to the umbrella clause meant a 'full scale internationalization of domestic contracts'.[104] In its view, giving effect to the umbrella clause did not mean supplanting municipal law as the applicable law of the undertaking, it would merely ensure its effective application to the contract at hand.[105] This allowed the tribunal to adopt a more distinctly teleological approach.[106] The first tribunal had feared that the broad scope it envisaged for the clause would make superfluous all other substantive treatment standards in the treaty. The latter tribunal, in contrast, held that the consequent restrictive interpretation of the clause failed to provide the clause with any significant purpose at all.[107] Instead it held that the object and purpose of the BIT was 'entirely consistent' with an interpretation of the clause so as to 'incorporate' and bring 'commitments made by the State towards specific investments . . . within the framework of the BIT'.[108] It thus advanced an interpretation of the clause consistent with a 'conceivable function' as an effective assurance of predictability and legal certainty ('the rule of law') in respect of specific commitments undertaken by the state:

> It is a conceivable function of a provision such as Article X (2) of the Swiss-Philippines BIT to provide assurances to foreign investors with regard to the performance of obligations assumed by the host State under its own law with regard to specific investments—in effect, to help secure the rule of law in relation to investment protection. In the Tribunal's view this is the proper interpretation of Article X (2).[109]

Although several cases have adopted a more sceptical view of the scope of applicability of the umbrella clause than what is, at least evidently, apparent in the second *SGS* case, no later case can be held to have refuted the basic conception of it as a basic requirement of respect for contractual commitments entered into in connection with, and relied on to make, an investment.[110] A number of subsequent cases have expressly confirmed

[104] *ibid*, para 126.
[105] *ibid*, para 126.
[106] *ibid*, para 116.
[107] *ibid*, para 125.
[108] *ibid*, para 117
[109] *ibid*, para 126.
[110] See eg, after a fierce criticism of the second SGS case, and apparent agreement with the first, the then concluding statement of the tribunal in *El Paso Energy International Co v Argentine Republic* (Decision on Jurisdiction, 2006) para 84: '[T]here is no doubt that if the State interferes with contractual rights by a unilateral act, whether these rights stem from a contract entered into by a foreign investor with a private party, a State autonomous entity or the State itself, in such a way that the State's action can be analysed as a violation of the standards of protection embodied in a BIT, the treaty-based arbitration tribunal has jurisdiction over all the claims of the foreign investor, including the claims arising from a violation of its contractual rights. Moreover, Article II [the umbrella clause], read in conjunction with Article VII(1), also considers as treaty claims the breaches of an investment agreement between Argentina and a national or company of the United States'.

this in finding the relevant umbrella clause to have been breached by virtue of non-compliance with contractual undertakings.[111] In *Eureko v Poland*, the tribunal held that the state's failure to carry through the final stages of a privatisation process constituted a clear breach of contractual undertakings made by the state. According to the tribunal the state was therefore also '*prima facie* in violation of Article 3.5 of the treaty'.[112] In another case, *CMS Gas v Argentina*, the question before the tribunal was whether regulatory measures that effectively altered the contractual regime established in respect of a gas transmission scheme, also constituted a breach of the umbrella clause in the treaty. The contractual regime especially contained two stabilisation clauses, by which the state had undertaken not to interfere with the tariff system established by the contract, and not to alter the basic rules governing the gas transportation licence. The tribunal held that breaches of these stabilisation clauses ipso facto also constituted a breach of the umbrella clause in the treaty.[113]

Based on case law subsequent to the two *SGS* cases, the appropriate interpretation of the umbrella clause would consequently seem to be that it imposes a more or less strict obligation to respect contractual, or similar, commitments entered into directly by the state with regard to a specific investment.[114] The scope of the umbrella clause is essentially limited by the latter requirement that the commitment must have been entered into 'in connection with' or 'with regard' to an investment. In *El Paso v Argentina*, this was held to entail that the clause only applied to commitments undertaken by virtue of a so called 'investment agreement', although it is difficult to see that there is any basis in the standard language of the clause for giving it such a narrow scope. In *Continental Casualty v Argentina*, it was, in contrast, held to entail simply that the commitment had to 'concern one or more investments and, moreover, must address them with some degree of specificity'.[115] In *Duke Energy v Ecuador*, the same requirement was

[111] See eg *Fedax v Venezuela* (Award, 1998) para 29, *Eureko v Poland* (Award, 2005); *CMS Gas Transmission Co v Argentine Republic* (Award, 2005) para 302, and see also *Noble Ventures v Romania* (Award, 2005) para 46 et seq, which however must be regarded as a somewhat abstract obiter dictum.

[112] *Eureko BV v Poland* (Partial Award, 2005) para 244.

[113] *CMS Gas v Argentina* (Award, 2005), para 303.

[114] See eg to this effect *EDF (Services) Ltd v Romania* (Award, 2009) para 316, commenting on the interpretation of the umbrella clause in that case: 'This provision, when applied to the present case, clearly refers to obligations entered into by Romania with regard to Claimant's investment. There is no evidence of the assumption by Respondent of direct obligations toward Claimant, whether by contract or otherwise'. And see also *LG&E v Argentina* (Award, 2006) para 170.

[115] *Continental Casualty Co v Argentine Republic* (Award, 2008) para 297, and see also *CMS Gas v Argentina* (Annulment Decision, 2007) para 95(a): 'In speaking of "any obligations it may have entered into with regard to investments", it seems clear that Article II(2)(c) is concerned with consensual obligations arising independently of the BIT itself (ie under the law of the host State or possibly under international law). Further, they must be specific obligations concerning the investment. They do not cover general requirements imposed by the law of the host State'.

considered to denote 'a link, a relation between the obligation and the investment that also seems broad in effect'.[116] Furthermore, in these latter cases, the clause has been considered not in principle to be limited to contractual obligations but, as first held by the annulment committee in *CMS Gas v Argentina*, to be concerned more generally with 'consensual obligations arising independently of the BIT itself'.[117] The latter, more open-ended interpretation would seem more in line with both the standard language of the clause, and with a more naturally envisaged purpose of offering protection to specific expectations legitimately relied on by an investor to make an investment. There is nevertheless little doubt that in practice the essential scope of application for the clause is contractual commitments, though not necessarily limited to 'investment agreements' in a strict sense, and that it could therefore as well have been termed a 'sanctity of contracts' clause.

B. Introducing a 'Public and Commercial' Distinction—A Second Controversy

The conception of the umbrella clause as a more or less strict 'sanctity of contract' standard does not necessarily suggest that any breach of contract automatically constitutes a breach of treaty, or as such, a 'wrongful act' under international law. The underlying notion of investment treaty arbitration as a remedy to equalise structural inequality and eliminate political risk could instead suggest an inherent limitation to acts constituting in some manner a direct or indirect use of state power or privilege, ie acts where the state steps out of its role as a mere contracting party. Responding to such concerns, a number of cases have relied on a distinction between public and commercial acts of a state, delimiting the scope of application of umbrella clauses to the former.[118] No basis for such a distinction can, however, be found in the standard language of the clause, which merely requires the state to 'observe' or to 'respect' the covered obligations. Several other cases, including the seminal decision in *SGS v Philippines* that has already been discussed, have consequently not seen any need to limit the scope of the clause in this manner. This has created case law that is, at least to some extent, mutually contradictory and difficult to reconcile.

A first significant case is *Joy Mining v Egypt*, one of the first cases to address the *SGS* controversy after *SGS v Philippines*. The case concerned a

[116] *Duke Energy Electroquil Partners and Electroquil SA v Republic of Ecuador* (Award, 2008) para 324.

[117] *Continental Casualty v Argentina* (Award, 2008) para 300, citing the CMS Annulment Decision para 95(a), as quoted in the note directly above.

[118] See also Wälde (2005) 183.

UK supplier of mining equipment, which claimed under the ICSID Convention for the release of guarantees it had provided to a state agency under a contract for sale and installation of such equipment. The tribunal denied jurisdiction over the claim, considering it a purely commercial and contractual claim, which was not protected by the BIT.[119] While the BIT contained an umbrella clause almost similar to that in *SGS v Philippines*,[120] this did not impress the tribunal. In order to dismiss the claim, it introduced and relied on a distinction between commercial aspects of a dispute and other aspects involving public authority: '[A] basic general distinction can be made between commercial aspects of a dispute and other aspects involving the existence of some form of State interference with the operation of the contract involved'.[121] As the claim at issue before the tribunal was based on simple failure to perform an alleged contractual obligation to release bank guarantees, provided by the seller and to be released by the state after its performance, no regulatory or other interference by the state in its capacity as such was involved. According to the tribunal, this meant that the umbrella clause was not applicable as a cause of action:

> In this context, it could not be held that an umbrella clause inserted in the Treaty, and not very prominently, could have the effect of transforming all contract disputes into investment disputes under the Treaty, unless of course there could be a clear violation of the Treaty rights and obligations *or a violation of contract rights of such a magnitude as to trigger the Treaty protection, which is not the case*. The connection between the Contract and the Treaty is the missing link that prevents any such effect.[122] (emphasis added)

A largely similar understanding was confirmed by the tribunal in *CMS Gas v Argentina*. Although not a material aspect of its actual decision, the tribunal assumed that the clause would not have been applicable had the claims been purely contractual and commercial. It thus assumed a public/commercial distinction related to the nature of the breach, in the same manner as the *Joy Mining* tribunal:

> [T]he Tribunal believes the Respondent is correct in arguing that not all contract breaches result in breaches of the Treaty. The standard of protection of the treaty will be engaged only when there is a specific breach of treaty rights and obligations or a violation of contract rights protected under the treaty. Purely commercial aspects of a contract might not be protected by the treaty in some

[119] *Joy Mining Machinery Limited v Arab Republic of Egypt* (Award on Jurisdiction, 2004) paras 78–82.

[120] Cf the UK-Egypt BIT (1975) Art 2(2), the relevant parts of which read: 'Each Contracting Party shall observe any obligation it may have entered into with regard to investments of nationals or companies of the other Contracting Party'.

[121] *Joy Mining Machinery Limited v Egypt* (Award on Jurisdiction, 2004) para 72.

[122] *ibid*, para 81.

> situations, but the protection is likely to be available when there is significant interference by governments or public agencies with the rights of the investor.[123]

The tribunal clarified this by reference to a distinction between 'commercial disputes arising from a contract' and 'disputes arising from the breach of treaty standards and their respective causes of action'.[124] In this case, the alleged breach of contract was, however, a regulatory interference with the contractual arrangement. Although the contract was of a commercial nature—related to gas transportation and transmission—the issue as such could clearly not be described as merely commercial, as it was 'related to government decisions that have resulted in the interferences and breaches noted'.[125] Thus the distinction did not in this case prevent application of the clause. In fact, the case may be taken as a prime example of the kind of measures prima facie invoking the umbrella clause according to the public/commercial distinction (although it is more questionable whether the *obligations* in question could properly be deemed covered by the clause, see the subsequent Annulment Decision where the initial award was set aside).

A somewhat different rationale, though driven by similar concerns, is displayed by the decision in *El Paso v Argentina*. While the decision does not identify the claims involved, making it rather difficult to discern what it actually decides, the tribunal clearly rejected what it saw as the 'elevation' or 'internationalisation' approach of *SGS v Philippines*, which would automatically make any contract claim into a breach of the umbrella clause.[126] Instead, the tribunal introduced a fundamental distinction between 'the State as a merchant' and 'the State as a sovereign'[127] to suggest essentially that only commitments 'contractually agreed by the state as a sovereign' would be covered by the umbrella clause.[128] Significantly, it based this on an essentially teleological consideration of the limited rationale of investment arbitration, reasoning in this respect that 'it is essentially from the State as a sovereign that the foreign investors have to be protected through the availability of international arbitration'.[129]

While the underlying rationale invoked by the *El Paso* tribunal clearly recalls the public/commercial distinction of prior cases, it is surprising how the tribunal conceived the application of the distinction, seemingly applying it to delimit the umbrella clause according to the nature of the *undertaking* instead of the nature of the *violation or infringement* involved. The tribunal essentially suggested that the umbrella clause would make

123 *CMS Gas v Argentina* (Award, 2005) para 299.
124 *ibid*, para 300.
125 *ibid*, para 301.
126 *El Paso v Argentina* (Decision on Jurisdiction, 2006) para 77.
127 *ibid*, para 79.
128 *ibid*, para 81.
129 *ibid*, para 80.

any breach of a contractual undertaking entered into by the state in its sovereign capacity into a breach of treaty.[130] But since the tribunal then apparently equiparated such undertakings quite generally to investment agreements,[131] it may seem that its conclusion in reality undermined the restrictive interpretation it so ardently advocated elsewhere in the argument.[132] In reality the tribunal seems to have confused the umbrella clause as a basis of jurisdiction, with its material scope as a substantive standard of investment protection. This is suggested by its reliance on the jurisdiction clause in the BIT, and its provision of jurisdiction in respect of 'an investment agreement',[133] to delimit the scope of the umbrella clause.[134] As this clearly does not mean that any breach of an investment agreement necessarily has to be a breach of the BIT, the reasoning of the tribunal comes to appear somewhat inconsistent. Why should this entirely jurisdictional provision be the crucial factor for limiting the scope of the umbrella clause? It may of course be that the tribunal misunderstood *SGS v Philippines*, and really agreed with this decision that the umbrella clause should apply to any breach of contractual undertakings made in connection with an investment.[135] But this does not seem likely in view of the strong arguments advanced in favour of a restrictive interpretation of the clause. Moreover, in emphasising the limitation to undertakings entered into by the state in its sovereign capacity, the tribunal in reality may have had in mind undertakings restricting public power, as is also suggested by its reference in this regard to stabilisation clauses.[136] Since a breach would then necessarily have to manifest itself as an exercise of power, being the subject of the undertaking in the first place, this may with some goodwill be seen as a somewhat convoluted reasoning by which to reach a public/commercial distinction relative to the act constituting a potential breach. This nevertheless does not explain why use of government power to escape undertakings of a clearly commercial nature relating to an investment would be more legitimate (one would rather consider that it

[130] *ibid*, paras 81 and 84–5.

[131] The tribunal here relied on the jurisdiction explicitly envisaged by the treaty over investment agreements, see paras 84–6.

[132] See eg para 85: '[T]he tribunal, endorsing the interpretation first given to the so-called 'umbrella clause' in the Decision *SGS v Pakistan*, confirms . . . that it has jurisdiction over treaty claims and cannot entertain purely contractual claims, which do not amount to a violation of the standards of protection of the BIT. It adds that, in view of Art VII(1) of the US-Argentina BIT, a violation of an investment agreement entered into by the state as a sovereign and a national or company of the United States is deemed to be also a violation of the Treaty and can thus give rise to a treaty claim'.

[133] US-Argentina BIT (1991) Art VII, para 1.

[134] *El Paso v Argentina* (Decision on Jurisdiction, 2006), see especially para 85 (as quoted above).

[135] Although, as held above, nor does *SGS v Philippines* provide a strong ratio to this effect, as the main concern of the tribunal was to uphold the inviolability of contractual undertakings, and it considered the contractual claims de facto inadmissible.

[136] *El Paso v Argentina* (Decision on Jurisdiction, 2006) para 81.

would usually be less legitimate)—for instance the obligation to pay for construction of a highway, which generally has been held to constitute 'investment'—under BITs and the general ICSID requirement. Although somewhat speculative, and unsupported by its stated reasons, the tribunal in making the distinction between the state as a sovereign and the state as a merchant, should conceivably be read as reserving the application of the umbrella clause quite generally to breaches of contract pursuant to, or relying on, government authority. At least the underlying rationale it referred to (ie the distinction between the state as a sovereign and the state as a merchant) and ostensibly relied on, suggests this.

While the cases cited so far may suggest a strict public/commercial distinction, limiting umbrella clauses to government decisions in breach of prior contractual undertakings, such a restrictive understanding is not supported by other cases. The previously cited *SGS v Philippines* decision simply held that the content of the umbrella clause was to '[make] it a breach of the BIT for the host state to fail to observe binding commitments, including contractual commitments, which it has assumed with regard to specific investments'.[137] More recent cases similarly contradict the limited understanding of the clause proposed by the above distinction. In *Noble Ventures v Romania*, the tribunal stated on the basis of its interpretation of the umbrella clause that it would '[consider] the Claimant's claims of breach of contract on the basis that any such breach constitutes a breach of the BIT'.[138] In other words, while recognising its own stand as being obiter, the tribunal adopted a straightforward 'elevation' perspective, considering the umbrella clause 'to equate contractual obligations governed by municipal law to international treaty obligations as established in the BIT'.[139] Moreover, in *Eureko v Poland*, the tribunal also clearly relied on a similar understanding of the clause in reaching its decision. Not least the tribunal's distinguishing of the scope and meaning of the umbrella clause from that of both the deprivation clause and the fair and equitable treatment clause, suggests that it perceived the umbrella clause to be invoked simply by virtue of the breaches of contract.[140]

While opposing a strict public/commercial distinction, the actual decisions in the latter cases do not, however, necessarily entail that any breach of contract is necessarily also a breach of treaty. The actual decision in the

[137] *SGS v Philippines* (Decision on Jurisdiction, 2004) para 128.

[138] *Noble Ventures v Romania* (Award, 2005) para 62.

[139] *ibid*, para 61.

[140] *Eureko v Poland* (Partial Award, 2005) para 250: 'The immediate, operative effects of Art 3.5 are two. The first is that Eureko's contractual arrangements with the Government of Poland are subject to the jurisdiction of the tribunal . . . The second is that breaches by Poland of its obligations under the SPA and its first addendum, as read together, that are not breaches of Arts 3.1 and 5 of the treaty nevertheless may be breaches of Art 3.5 of the Treaty, since they transgress Poland's treaty commitment to "observe any obligations it may have entered into" with regard to Eureko's investments'.

Eureko case was that the actual breaches of contract, violating the umbrella clause, also constituted violations of the deprivation standard and the fair and equitable treatment standard of the treaty. A central aspect of the case was that the breaches in question were deliberate breaches of contract based on political decisions (though not government decisions in a formal sense) at the highest level of government. Thus, the case does not conclusively decide that any breach of contract would have been a breach of treaty. In *Duke Energy v Ecuador*, while the tribunal considered the weight of case law not to require any act of 'sovereign interference', it still considered this an open question which it did not need to resolve, since the acts complained of in that case were clearly of an executive nature.[141] Apart from the *Joy Mining* case and the first *SGS* case, which both rejected the application of the umbrella clause as a potential cause of action, the only case which has in fact concerned an ordinary commercial contract claim is *SGS v Philippines*. It may be telling that while applying different reasons, all cases, including the latter, reached substantially similar conclusions, and refused to exercise jurisdiction over the claims. While the latter case insisted on the applicability of the umbrella clause, it nevertheless considered the claim inadmissible and immature for not having been sufficiently settled in accordance with its applicable law and envisaged contractual procedure. This may be interpreted as based not only on a jurisdictional concern, but as an implicit realisation that the umbrella clause was not violated insofar as the remedies contemplated by the contract itself could still be exhausted. In other words, while there might have been a breach of contract, the contractual arrangement as such had not been repudiated by the state. The state had not stepped out of its role as an ordinary contracting party. Understood in this manner, the umbrella clause is interpreted so as to respond to the specific risk involved in contracting with a state. This is not the risk of breach of contract as such, which is always a risk in a contractual relationship and presents no difference from the situation in a contract between private parties. The specific risk of contracting with a state is that the state, by relying on its position as a state, breaches the contract without respecting, or even incurring, the normal consequences of breach. This would suggest that a breach of contract is only transformed into a violation of the 'sanctity of contract standard' where it involves a manifest breach or repudiation of the contract, such as an infringement of the contract by legislative decree, disregarding a claim after it has been established by relevant judicial fora, or a clear and deliberate violation reflecting a deliberate decision or policy to disregard the contract, ie that the state, so to speak, steps out of its role as an ordinary contracting party.

[141] *Duke Energy v Ecuador* (Award, 2008) paras 320–22.

C. The Applicable Law

An aspect of the interpretation of the umbrella clause suggested here, is that it should not, as some have argued, be conceived as a means to internationalise the undertakings in question and elevate them to the status of international obligations per se.[142] As a more consistent application of the umbrella clause has increasingly become cemented in practice, it also has become more obviously apparent that it does not mean the undertakings in question become subject to international law. As held by the annulment committee in the *CMS Gas* case, '[t]he effect of the umbrella clause is not to transform the obligation which is relied on into something else; the content of the obligation is unaffected, as is its proper law'.[143] The applicability of municipal law as a matter of principle was conceptualised in the *SGS v Philippines* case, where it was a central element in the reasoning of the tribunal. In response to the concerns of the first *SGS* case about the supposed internationalisation of undertakings pursuant to the clause, the second *SGS* tribunal made an effort to set out what the umbrella clause would *not* do:

> [T]he *SGS v. Pakistan* tribunal appears to have thought that the broad interpretation which it rejected would involve a full-scale internationalisation of domestic contracts—in effect, that it would convert investment contracts into treaties by means of what the tribunal termed 'instant transubstantiation'. But this is not what Article X (2) of the Swiss-Philippines Treaty says. It does not convert non-binding domestic blandishments into binding international obligations. It does not convert questions of contract law into questions of treaty law. In particular it does not change the proper law of the CISS agreement from the law of the Philippines to international law. Article X (2) of the Swiss-Philippines BIT addresses not the scope of the commitments entered into with regard to specific investments but the performance of these obligations once they are ascertained.[144]

As discussed above, the tribunal effectively held that it could not exercise jurisdiction over the claim since it had not matured into a cognisable claim. The primary applicability of municipal law to the claim appears to have been a central rationale of this decision. This suggests the validity and content of contractual undertakings recognised by the umbrella clause will usually have to be determined in accordance with a municipal law identified by ordinary conflict of laws methodology[145]—for most

[142] See eg Orrego Vicuña, 'Of Contracts and Treaties in the Global Market' (2004) 8 *Max Planck Yearbook of United Nations Law* 341, 352–3; and see also *Noble Ventures v Romania* (Award, 2005) paras 53–4; and *SGS v Pakistan* (Decision on Jurisdiction, 2003) para 172, referring to a purported mechanism of 'instant transubstantiation'.

[143] *CMS v Argentina* (Annulment decision, 2007) para 95(c).

[144] *SGS v Philippines* (Decision on Jurisdiction, 2004) para 126.

[145] See also to this effect *CMS Gas v Argentina* (Award, 2005) para 221 et seq; *MTD Equity Sdn Bhd and MTD Chile SA v Republic of Chile* (Award, 2004) para 187; but contrast *Eureko v Poland* (Award, 2005), and see especially the dissenting opinion of Rajski, para 5.

purposes the municipal law identified by the contract itself—or, absent any such choice, by the conflict of laws rules of the host state.[146] Such application of municipal law is nevertheless not something required by the nature of things; it is required and conditioned by the international standard encapsulated in the umbrella clause itself, which is clearly an autonomous standard. This has two underlying and conditioning aspects which both justify and, extraordinarily, may limit the applicability of municipal law.

First, the fact that a given undertaking addressed by the umbrella clause cannot be interpreted simply as an internationalised contract, or a *contrat sans loi*, but must be seen as a contract concluded within the context of a certain municipal law, is clearly not a consequence of a restrictive interpretation of the umbrella clause. It is a direct consequence of its rationale. The purpose of the umbrella clause is to protect legitimate contractual expectations, and most contracts explicitly or by implication contemplate the application of a municipal law. The legitimate expectation of the parties pursuant to the contract is thus naturally manifested by the contract as conceived by its applicable law. Secondly, even if the undertaking has not been concluded with a municipal law in mind—which would seem unlikely for the reason of the required connection to a specific investment in the territory of the host state—public international law nevertheless does not contain precise rules regulating the fundamental aspects of conclusion, validity, interpretation and performance of complex, commercial contracts. This suggests that reference to a municipal law in any case is necessary to consider the contract a basis of legally sanctioned expectations conceivably protected by an umbrella clause.

That said, its underlying rationale could also indicate that a clear basis of validity in municipal law will not necessarily always be decisive. Since the umbrella clause clearly is not intended to promote the applicable municipal law's conception of the state's contractual responsibility, but to protect the investor's legitimate contractual expectations, it is conceivable that it may be held to override the state's own municipal law if the investor had good reasons not to rely on it. Thus, in relation to contracts restricting public power, which may lead a precarious existence under municipal administrative law, it is conceivable that an umbrella clause, extraordinarily, may be held to entail a presumption of validity, rebuttable only by a clear rule of municipal law.[147] It has been suggested in another context

[146] Cf art 42 of the ICSID convention.

[147] The reasoning of the tribunal in *Eureko v Poland* may conceivably be read in that light, as the tribunal made no discernible effort to establish the legal status of the undertakings under Polish law, see also the strong dissenting opinion of Rajski on this point, cfr. *Eureko v Poland* (Award, 2005), dissenting opinion, at para 5: 'It is to be noted that in the long reasons to its decision, the Tribunal has not once referred to any relevant provisions of Polish civil law when interpreting the contracts concluded by the Parties. This approach makes the impression that the tribunal treats them as contracts "*sans loi*"—which facilitates their free interpretation'.

that this could be seen in light of an analogy with article 46 of the Vienna Convention on the law of treaties.[148]

D. Application of the Umbrella Clause as an Instance of Teleology

The umbrella clause, as applied in investment treaty jurisprudence, has come to encompass a strict obligation for states not to interfere with contractual positions duly established under municipal law. While this may appear to be the result of a straightforward reading of the clause,[149] it may to an even greater extent be considered an instance of the particular teleology underlying international investment law.[150] This can be conceptualised as a conception of purpose based on a transaction perspective which regards every investor-state relationship essentially as a transaction between the investor and the state. As such it involves considerations of reciprocity, trust and reliance as in every other contractual relationship. The strict application of the umbrella clause evidenced by the prevailing tendency of case law takes the consequence of this underlying perspective, by confirming the validity of a strict contractual perspective also in terms of international law. Superficially, the teleology underlying this may admittedly not always be as evident in the applied reasoning of the cases themselves.[151] To discover its effect beneath the tribunals' apparent straightforward reading of language, we may, however, compare it to another tradition of interpretative practice, situated in a different value context, namely municipal constitutional law. There is no better example than the interpretation of the contracts clause in the US Constitution, the material parts of which read as follows:

> No state shall . . . pass any . . . law impairing the Obligation of Contracts.[152]

[148] Castberg, 'International Law in our Time' (1973-I) 138 *Recueil des Cours* 1, 6: 'Article 46, item 1, of the [Vienna] Convention prescribes definite limits for the right of a State to invalidate its consent to a treaty, this consent being said to have no basis in internal law. This rule must also apply if a State wishes to allege rules of limitation of competence in internal law against a foreign enterprise in order to achieve that an agreement shall be regarded as not binding'.

[149] Se to this effect eg *SGS v Philippines* (Decision on Jurisdiction, 2004) para 115; *Eureko v Poland* (Award, 2005) para 264; and *Noble Ventures v Romania* (Award, 2005) para 51.

[150] But see also *Salini Costruttori SpA v Hashemite Kingdom of Jordan* (Decision on Jurisdiction, 2004) para 120 et seq., where the tribunal refused to consider the following clause an umbrella clause (Art 2(4) of the Italy-Jordan BIT (1996)), noting in particular the differences of language as compared to the SGS cases: 'Each Contracting Party shall create and maintain in its territory a legal framework apt to guarantee to investors the continuity of legal treatment, including compliance, in good faith, of all undertakings assumed with regard to each specific investor'.

[151] But see also *SGS v Philippines* (Decision on Jurisdiction, 2004) para 116; and *Noble Ventures v Romania* (Award, 2005) paras 51–2.

[152] US Constitution, Article I, section 10.

In terms of language, and inserted into a bilateral investment treaty, this could conceivably have passed off as a straightforward umbrella clause. Under US constitutional law it has, however, been subject to a completely different interpretation, being conceived as a protection against substantial impairment of contractual obligations, subject to the lead principle that legislative interference is allowed when 'reasonable and necessary to serve an important public purpose'.[153]

These divergent interpretations can be seen as a consequence of different structural perspectives at work. Municipal constitutional law espouses a perspective mainly concerned to justify and delimit internal state powers in relation to the same individual citizens from which these powers are derived. This stands in some contrast to the external transaction perspective of international investment law.

5.4 PROTECTION OF LEGITIMATE EXPECTATIONS UNDER THE FAIR AND EQUITABLE TREATMENT STANDARD

The third generic standard of investment treaties which may require the state not to violate contractual undertakings is the 'fair and equitable treatment' standard.[154] The requirement of 'fair and equitable treatment' was first included in investment treaties as an incorporation of the international minimum standard.[155] But it has subsequently developed into a

[153] *United States Trust Co v New Jersey* 431 US 1 (1977) 25, and see especially 21: 'Although the Contract Clause appears literally to proscribe "any" impairment, this Court observed in Blaisdell that "the prohibition is not an absolute one and is not to be read with literal exactness like a mathematical formula". Thus, a finding that there has been a technical impairment is merely a preliminary step in resolving the more difficult question whether that impairment is permitted under the Constitution. In the instant case, as in Blaisdell, we must attempt to reconcile the strictures of the Contract Clause with the "essential attributes of sovereign power", necessarily reserved by the States to safeguard the welfare of their citizens'.

[154] For general accounts of the fair and equitable treatment standard in investment law, see eg Vascianne, 'The Fair and Equitable Treatment Standard in International Investment Law and Practice' (1999) 70 *BYIL* 99; Choudhury, 'Evolution or Devolution? Defining Fair and Equitable Treatment in International Investment Law' (2005) 6(2) *JWIT* 297; Schreuer, 'Fair and Equitable Treatment in Arbitral Practice' (2005) 6(3) *JWIT* 357.

[155] As a substantive standard of treatment, the principle seems first to have been incorporated into art I of the Abs-Shawcross Draft Convention on Investment Abroad, which was a private initiative by European business interests and lawyers, headed by the German bank mogul Herman Abs and the former English Attorney General Lord Shawcross, see eg Round Table on the Proposed Convention to Protect Private Foreign Investment, (1960) 9 *Journal of Public Law* 115 et seq. (Before this the Havana Charter for an International Trade Organization included provisions for the organization to make recommendations of measures 'to assure just and equitable treatment' of foreign enterprises, capital, skills, art and technology.) The Abs-Shawcroft proposal was adopted in art 1 of the OECD's 1967 Draft Convention on the Protection of Foreign Property, which has served as the model of later BITs. The accompanying commentary assumed that the principle articulated 'the standard set by international law for the treatment due by each state with regard to the property of foreign nationals' and that 'the standard required conforms in effect to 'the minimum standard' which forms part of customary international law'. See further the *OECD Draft*

relatively autonomous concept, refined and shaped by an increasing body of investment treaty jurisprudence into a useful tool for ensuring a minimum level of good government beneficial to foreign investment.[156] In the following I show how this standard has been held to encompass a minimum requirement of respect for legitimate expectations, whereby state undertakings reasonably relied on to make an investment cannot subsequently be revoked by the state.[157] To this effect, the interpretation of the standard recalls the rationale also underlying the subsumption of contractual undertakings under expropriation clauses and umbrella clauses. But being less encumbered by the specified rules encapsulating the legitimate expectation standard, the fair and equitable treatment standard is conceivably shaped more directly by its underlying teleology, to display the concept of legitimate expectations as a more flexible and fairness-based minimum requirement of legal certainty in the context of investment.

A. A Progressive Minimum Standard—The Concept of Legitimate Expectations

The traditional formulation of the minimum standard under customary law is that provided under the famous '*Neer* Formula', articulated by the US-Mexican Claims Commission in the 1926 *Neer claim*:

> [T]he treatment of an alien, in order to constitute an international delinquency should amount to an outrage, to bad faith, to wilful neglect of duty, or to an insufficiency of governmental action so far short of international standards that every reasonable and impartial man would readily recognise its insufficiency.[158]

In practical terms, the case concerned the killing of a US citizen in Mexico by a group of bandits. The tribunal commented on the facts that the relevant authorities 'might have acted in a more vigorous and effective way than they did',[159] but did not consider this sufficient for a finding of violation, deeming it beyond its competence to determine whether 'another course of procedure . . . might have been more effective'.[160] Essentially it would seem the tribunal set the criterion of violation at

Convention on the Protection of Foreign Property (Text with Notes and Comments) (1968) 7 ILM 118, 120.

[156] See eg *Saluka Investments BV v Czech Republic* (Award, 2006) para 301.

[157] See for an in-depth discussion of the concept of legitimate expectations in this context the separate opinion of the late Professor Wälde in *International Thunderbird Gaming Corp v Mexico* (Award, 2006), separate opinion para 21 et seq.

[158] *LFH Neer and Pauline Neer (USA) v United Mexican States* (US-Mexican General Claims Commission, 1926) (1926) IV RIAA 60.

[159] *ibid*, 61.

[160] *ibid*, 62.

something comparable to malign and deliberate negligence. In the later *ELSI* case, the International Court of Justice furthermore interpreted the prohibition against 'arbitrary or discriminatory measures' in the Italy-US FCN treaty[161] in a manner which at least implicitly referred to the international minimum standard. In the more modern context of that case, the court held that the requisite standard translated into a notion of arbitrariness, as 'not so much something opposed to *a* rule of law, as something opposed to *the* rule of law'.[162] Nonetheless, this did not impose a particularly strict rule of law standard according to the court. The decisive criterion, it held, was whether there was 'a wilful disregard of due process of law, an act which shocks, or at least surprises, a sense of judicial propriety'.[163]

These relatively moderate claims on the propriety of government conduct stand in considerable contrast to contemporary formulations of the fair and equitable treatment standard by investment treaty tribunals.[164] This is first illustrated by the interpretation of the NAFTA standard of 'fair and equitable' treatment, which has expressly been equiparated to the minimum standard through a subsequent authoritative 'note of interpretation' issued by the NAFTA parties.[165] This has nevertheless not hindered a clearly developing conception of the standard as applied in the context of foreign investment,[166] as best illustrated by the decision in *Mondev v USA*. The tribunal accepted the equiparation to the minimum standard, but nevertheless expressly rejected that this confined it to the *Neer* formula: 'To the modern eye, what is unfair or inequitable need not equate with the outrag-

161 Treaty of Friendship, Commerce and Navigation (US-Italy) (2 February 1948) 63 Stat 2255.

162 *Case concerning Elettronica Sicula SpA (ELSI) (USA v Italy)* [1989] ICJ Rep 15, para 128.

163 *Ibid*.

164 This potentially broad and progressive role of the 'fair and equitable' standard was predicted by Mann, who roundly dismissed the notion that it had any relation at all to the minimum standard under international law: '[N]othing is gained by introducing the conception of a minimum standard and, more than this, it is positively misleading to introduce it. The terms 'fair and equitable treatment' envisage conduct which goes far beyond the minimum standard and afford protection to a greater extent and according to a much more objective standard than any previously employed form of words'. See Mann, 'British Treaties for the Promotion and Protection of Investments' (1982) 52 *BYIL* 241, 244.

165 Early examples of NAFTA jurisprudence went far to stipulate a progressive and autonomous standard, see especially *Pope & Talbot v Canada* (Award, 2001) para 111; and especially *Metalclad Corp v United Mexican States* (Award, 2000) para 74 et seq. The latter tribunal considered the standard to include a general requirement of transparency, but this part of the award was later annulled by the Supreme Court of British Columbia for exceeding the arbitral tribunal's competence in misstating the applicable law, see *United Mexican States v Metalclad Corp* (2001) 5 ICSID Rep 236. These progressive tendencies were sought quelled by a subsequent note of interpretation issued by the NAFTA Free Trade Commission under NAFTA art 1131(2), which expressly equiparated the 'fair and equitable treatment' standard in NAFTA art 1105 to the international minimum standard. The note is reproduced and discussed in *Mondev Int'l Ltd v USA* (Award, 2002) para 100 et seq.

166 See eg *International Thunderbird v Mexico* (Award, 2006), separate opinion of Wälde, paras 3–5.

eous or the egregious. In particular, a state may treat foreign investment unfairly and inequitably without necessarily acting in bad faith'.[167] The tribunal then relied on the *ELSI* criterion requiring a 'shock or surprise' to 'judicial propriety', but supplanting it to the more exacting context of NAFTA and investment treaty law; this was held to translate into a basic requirement against 'clearly improper and discreditable treatment':

> The test is not whether a particular result is surprising, but whether the shock or surprise occasioned to an impartial tribunal leads, on reflection, to justified concerns as to the judicial propriety of the outcome . . . the question is whether, at an international level and having regard to generally accepted standards of the administration of justice, a tribunal can conclude in the light of all the available facts that the impugned decision was clearly improper and discreditable.[168]

This has also been relied on by several later NAFTA tribunals.[169] It was further elaborated by the tribunal in *Waste Management v Mexico*, where the tribunal synthesised the apposite minimum standard in the context of NAFTA as follows:

> Taken together, the *S.D. Myers, Mondev, ADF* and *Loewen* cases suggest that the minimum standard of fair and equitable treatment is infringed by conduct attributable to the State and harmful to the claimant if the conduct is arbitrary, grossly unfair, unjust or idiosyncratic, is discriminatory and exposes the claimant to sectional or racial prejudice, or involves a lack of due process leading to an outcome which offends judicial propriety—as might be the case with a manifest failure of natural justice in judicial proceedings or a complete lack of transparency and candor in an administrative process. *In applying this standard it is relevant that the treatment is in breach of representations made by the host State which were reasonably relied on by the claimant.*[170] (emphasis added)

In referring to 'breach of representations made by the host state', the tribunal here introduced the concept of respect for legitimate expectations as a part of the minimum standard,[171] a proposition which has subsequently been confirmed and cemented by later practice.[172] In *International Thunderbird v Mexico*, the tribunal regarded it an established principle, by

[167] *Mondev v USA* (Award, 2002) para 116.
[168] *ibid*, para 127.
[169] See eg *ADF Group Inc v USA* (Award, 2003) para 180 et seq.; and *Loewen Group Inc v USA* (Award, 2003) paras 133–134.
[170] *Waste Management v Mexico* (Award, 2004) para 98.
[171] But see also the (apparent) obiter in *Mondev v USA* (Award, 2002) para 134, at least implicitly suggesting a similar application, particularly in relation to investment contracts moreover: 'Indeed a governmental prerogative to violate investment contracts would appear to be inconsistent with the principles embodied in Article 1105 and with contemporary standards of national and international law concerning governmental liability for contractual performance'.
[172] See eg *GAMI Investments Inc v United Mexican States* (Award, 2004), esp paras 90–91; *Methanex Corp v USA* (Final Award, 2005), Part IV Chapter C, para 12; and *International Thunderbird v Mexico* (Award, 2006) para 147.

virtue of the 'good faith principle of international customary law' and recent 'investment case law'.[173]

Beyond the NAFTA context, where the formal constraints of the FTC note of interpretation naturally do not apply, tribunals (and writers[174]) seemingly have felt even less restrained by any suggested connection to the minimum standard.[175] The decision in *Tecmed v Mexico* is illustrative. The tribunal considered that while the standard had to be interpreted 'as an expression and part of the bona fide principle recognised in international law',[176] this did not deprive the fair and equitable treatment clause of its own autonomous meaning.[177] Instead, the provision had to be interpreted and applied on the basis of the basic purpose of the treaty 'to strengthen and increase the security and trust of foreign investors'.[178] The tribunal then sketched out in some detail what this entailed, specifically setting out a principle of respect for the 'basic expectations' relied on to make an investment:

> The Arbitral Tribunal considers that this provision of the Agreement, in light of the good faith principle established by international law, requires the Contracting Parties to provide to international investments *treatment that does not affect the basic expectations that were taken into account by the foreign investor to make the investment* . . . The foreign investor also expects the host State to act consistently, i.e. without arbitrarily revoking any preexisting decisions or permits issued by the State that were relied upon by the investor to assume its commitments as well as to plan and launch its commercial and business activities.[179] (emphasis added)

This displays an underlying teleological rationale concerned to promote investment, something also employed by other tribunals to win the concept of legitimate expectations general acclaim. Thus, in *MTD v Chile*, the tribunal held that the standard required 'treatment in an even-handed and just manner, conducive to fostering the promotion of foreign investment'.[180] In *Saluka Investments v Czech Republic*, the tribunal held that the standard should be understood to require 'treatment, which if not proactively stimulating the inflow of foreign investment, does at least not deter foreign capital by providing disincentives to foreign investors'.[181] Significantly,

[173] *International Thunderbird v Mexico* (Award, 2006) para 147.

[174] See eg Schreuer, 'Fair and Equitable Treatment in Arbitral Practice' (2005) 6(3) *JWIT* 357, 363–4.

[175] See eg *Saluka Investments v Czech Republic* (Award, 2006) para 285 et seq; *MTD v Chile* (Award, 2004) paras 111–12; *Tecnicas Medioambientales (Tecmed) SA v United Mexican States* (Award, 2003) esp para 155.

[176] *Tecmed v Mexico* (Award, 2003) para 153.

[177] *ibid*, para 155.

[178] *ibid*, para 156.

[179] *ibid*, para 154.

[180] *MTD v Chile* (Award, 2004) para 113.

[181] *Saluka Investments v Czech Republic* (Award, 2006) para 301.

both tribunals expressly espoused the *Tecmed* conception of legitimate expectations as, in the words of the latter case, 'the dominant element of [the] standard'.[182] The initial tribunal in *CMS Gas v Argentina* developed this even further, both equating the standard to the minimum standard under international law and giving it a teleological interpretation:

> [O]ne principal objective of the protection envisaged is that fair and equitable treatment is desirable 'to maintain a stable framework for investments and maximum use of economic resources'. There can be no doubt, therefore, that a stable legal and business environment is an essential element of fair and equitable treatment.[183]

Relying inter alia on the *Tecmed* case, it then set forth a conception of the legitimate expectation standard as an objective standard, unrelated to any requirement of bad faith.[184] Somewhat astonishingly, the tribunal then considered this conception of the fair and equitable treatment standard to be 'not different from the international law minimum standard and its evolution under customary law'.[185]

Whether it is possible to identify one such common and converging legitimate expectation standard under both treaties and customary law remains an open question, as does the exact content of the principle. The minimum standard as such (whether that of customary law or an autonomous fair and equitable treatment requirement) is bound to be flexible, ultimately depending on the specific circumstances of each case.[186] What the above scrutiny of the cases shows, however, is the evolution, in an investment treaty context, of a conceived minimum standard of legal certainty and the rule of law into a more objective standard, which is not necessarily in principle dependent on the egregious or outrageous, bad faith or willful neglect of duty, but requires instead a basic level of regard for reasonable expectations induced by the government's own promises or prior conduct.[187] Underlying this, as will be further discussed in the next section, is a common rationale based in something comparable to a contractual logic, which again is clearly related to the basic transaction perspective underlying investment arbitration.

[182] *ibid*, para 302.
[183] *CMS Gas v Argentina* (Award, 2005) para 274.
[184] *ibid*, para 280.
[185] *ibid*, para 284.
[186] See eg *Mondev v USA* (Award, 2002) para 118.
[187] See also for some of the more recent cases eg *EDF v Romania* (Award, 2009) para 216; *Bayindir v Pakistan* (Award, 2009) para 179; and *Duke Energy v Ecuador* (Award, 2008) paras 339–40.

B. Contractual Rights and the Legitimate Expectations Standard

The application of this standard to rights and expectations pursuant to state undertakings raises two crucial and interrelated issues: first, what sort of conduct it requires for a breach to have occurred; and secondly, when a contractual undertaking *is* creative of a protected legitimate expectation. In contrast to the other two standards addressed above, the 'fair and equitable treatment' standard may be held to start out from what I denote an 'abuse of power' criterion. I argue in the following that this nevertheless has come largely to be defined through a criterion of 'reasonable reliance', which functions according to the same underlying structural parameters as operate in respect of expropriation and umbrella clauses. A particular objective of the following is to show how this underlying structural perspective shapes the application of the standard in relation to representations and promises which are not formally contractual. This is reflected in the fact that although a formal contract is not necessarily required for an expectation to be legitimate, the application of the reasonable reliance standard to state representations is dependent on indicia of an understanding between the state and the investor, either formally conceptualised as an agreement or implicitly conceived as one.

(i) The Abuse of Power Criterion

As shown above, the fair and equitable treatment standard has been seen as a specific application of the 'international minimum standard' in the context of foreign investment. This has consequences for its normative structure. Somewhat schematically, the minimum standard under international law has two concrete aspects or modalities, one negative and one positive. Requiring on the one hand a minimum level of use of power (in a broad sense) to protect foreigners,[188] it prohibits on the other hand arbitrary use or abuse of power (similarly in a broad sense).[189] It is relatively clear that the 'fair and equitable treatment' standard encompasses primarily the latter of these aspects.[190] It constitutes, in other words, an abuse of power standard which is intended to place restraints on the use of public power.

Applied to breach of contract, this clearly entails a different structural perspective from that provided by the other two standards addressed above. In contrast to expropriation and umbrella clauses, the 'fair and

[188] Cf eg *the Neer claim* (US-Mexican General Claims Commission, 1926) IV RIAA 60.

[189] *The ELSI Case (USA v Italy)* [1989] ICJ Rep 15, para 128.

[190] Conversely, it may be held that the former aspect is mainly encompassed by the requirement of 'full protection and security', which usually accompanies the requirement of 'fair and equitable treatment'.

equitable' standard is not directed at protecting contractual rights or requiring observance of state undertakings as such. Its concern is to prevent abuse or arbitrary use of power. Whether a breach of contract is a breach of the standard thus prima facie depends not on the nature of the right or undertaking affected, but on whether the breach of contract constitutes an abuse of power. This could in principle have suggested a stricter focus on whether abuse of public power as such is involved in relation to a distinct breach of contract claim. While there are indicia of this, the decisive element seems nevertheless to be a somewhat looser evaluation of whether the state unjustifiably has relied on its structurally superior position to disregard an otherwise legitimate expectation of the investor.

In the case of *RFCC v Morocco* the tribunal ostensibly relied on a relatively limited application of the standard to construe abuse of government authority in a narrow sense. The tribunal refused to consider that a state company's 'ordinary' non-performance of a road construction contract invoked the fair and equitable treatment standard, since, significantly, no distinct state prerogatives had been relied on to breach the contract.[191] What was material, according to the tribunal, was whether the breaches of contract constituted behaviour going beyond measures that an ordinary contracting party might have adopted.[192] Similarly, in both *Duke Energy v Ecador* and *Bayindir v Pakistan*, the tribunals held that in order for the fair and equitable treatment standard to be applicable 'the Claimants must establish a breach different in nature from a simple contract violation, in other words one which the State commits in the exercise of its sovereign power'.[193]

It is nevertheless reasonably clear that the standard has a scope beyond actual exercise of public authority such as it has been applied in a number of other cases. In *Waste Management v Mexico*, the tribunal held that even 'persistent non-payment of debts' was 'not to be equated with a violation . . . provided that it does not amount to an outright and unjustified

[191] *Consortium RFCC v Morocco* (Award, 2003) para 51: 'L'Etat, ou son émanation, peuvent s'être comportés comme des cocontractants ordinaires, ayant une divergence d'approche, en fait ou en droit, avec l'investisseur. Pour que la violation alléguée du contrat constitue un traitement injuste ou inéquitable au sens de l'Accord bilatéral, il faut qu'elle résulte d'un comportement exorbitant de celui qu'un contractant ordinaire pourrait adopter. Seul l'Etat, en tant que puissance publique, et non comme contractant, a assumé des obligations au titre de l'Accord bilatéral. L'interprétation retenue par le présent Tribunal est donc celle d'un obligation de traitement juste et équitable qui, tout en garantissant les droit élémentaires de l'investisseur, ne s'y limite pas et s'applique uniquement dans la mesure où l'Etat d'accueil a fait usage de ses prérogatives de puissance publique'.

[192] *Ibid*: '[I]l faut qu'elle résulte d'un comportement exorbitant de celui qu'un contractant ordinaire pourrait adopter'. See also, adopting almost verbatim the reasoning of the former case, *Salini Costruttori v Jordan* (Decision on Jurisdiction, 2004) para 155; and see also generally and implicitly to this effect, *Joy Mining v Egypt* (Award on Jurisdiction, 2004) para 72.

[193] *Bayindir v Pakistan* (Award, 2009) para 180. The formulation in *Duke Energy* is almost identical, see *Duke Energy v Ecuador* (Award, 2009) para 345.

repudiation of the transaction and provided that some remedy is open to the creditor to address the problem'. In other words, effective and unjustified repudiation of a debt might constitute a violation of the fair and equitable treatment standard. Moreover, in *Eureko v Poland*, the tribunal held that the breaches of the state's contractual obligations also constituted breaches of the fair and equitable standard, even though no exercise of public power as such was involved. The reasons of the tribunal instead would appear to be the deliberate character of the breach,[194] and its basis in clear political reasons lacking a specific legal justification.[195] This shows that the abuse of power criterion does not strictly limit the standard to state power, but has been interpreted more loosely and in conformity with a broader political risk assessment, largely in the same manner as the other two standards addressed above. Moreover, an aspect of this is that the 'abuse' element is primarily conceptualised through a strict requirement not to disrespect expectations reasonably relied on by the investor, as further discussed in the next section.

(ii) The Reasonable Reliance Criterion

While the above shows that the fair and equitable treatment standard may be invoked by a breach of contract—even one which does not constitute a clear abuse of government power in a strict sense—it is equally clear that the standard is not invoked by contractual expectations merely because contractual. The crucial criterion is whether the expectation has been reasonably relied on to make an investment.[196] In such case, the effective repudiation or wilful neglect of such expectations will typically constitute a breach of the fair and equitable treatment standard because the investor had legitimate reasons to expect otherwise. As it has been conceived in practice, this may nevertheless be held to depend on an essentially contractual perspective. In order to show reasonable cause, the investor needs to show that his reliance was based on something comparable to an effective understanding with the state. This has certain more specific aspects.

[194] *Eureko v Poland* (Award, 2005) para 232: 'Eureko's investment, its contractual rights to an IPO, which would have led it to acquire majority control of PZU, have been, in the opinion of the Tribunal, unfairly and inequitably treated by the Council of Ministers and Minister of the State Treasury. Those organs of the RoP, consciously and overtly, breached the basic expectations of Eureko that are at the basis of its investment in PZU'.

[195] *ibid*, para 233: 'The tribunal has found that the RoP, by the conduct of organs of the State acted not for cause but for purely arbitrary reasons linked to the interplay of Polish politics and nationalistic reasons of a discriminatory character'.

[196] See eg *International Thunderbird v Mexico* (Award, 2006) para 147: '[T]he concept of 'legitimate expectations' relates, within the context of the NAFTA framework, to a situation where a Contracting Party's conduct creates reasonable and justifiable expectations on the part of an investor (or investment) to act in reliance on said conduct, such that a failure by the NAFTA party to honour those expectations could cause the investor (investment) to suffer damages'.

First, the few cases which have in fact found a violation of the standard on the basis of breach of state undertakings clearly illustrate that a bare contractual expectation is not sufficient to invoke the standard. Thus, in *CMS Gas v Argentina*, a subsequent law that repudiated a contractually agreed tariff formula for gas transmission was also deemed to be in breach of the fair and equitable treatment requirement. The tribunal stated as the decisive reason for this that '[t]he measures that are complained of did in fact entirely transform and alter the legal and business environment under which the investment was decided and made'.[197] In *CME v Czech Republic* the tribunal similarly held that '[t]he Media Council breached its obligation of fair and equitable treatment by evisceration of the arrangements in reliance upon [which] the foreign investor was induced to invest'.[198] And in *Eureko v Poland*, the tribunal based its decision that the fair and equitable treatment standard had been breached on the consideration that the government had 'consciously and overtly, breached the basic expectations of Eureko that are at the basis of its investment in PZU'.[199] All these cases thus based their decision on the fact that the undertakings in question had in fact been relied on by the investor in question.

Secondly, however, the cases also show that mere reliance without more is not sufficient; the investor's reliance must be reasonable in order to be legitimate. To this effect the prevailing tendency is that it needs to be based on something comparable to a contractual undertaking from the state. Thus, in both *Eureko v Poland* and *CMS Gas v Argentina* the finding of the tribunals that a legitimate expectation had been breached was clearly based on the contractually binding character of the respective undertakings of the two states.[200] Moreover, in *Tecmed v Mexico*, the tribunal noted the lack of a formal and signed agreement, but then held that 'the evidence submitted leads to the conclusion that there was such an agreement',[201] allowing the tribunal to conclude that the claimant had 'reasonably trusted' that its permit would remain in force.[202] In *CME v Czech Republic*, in contrast, there was no contract or comparably binding undertaking or representation made by the state to the foreign investor. Indeed, in *Lauder v Czech Republic* (based on the same factual case but brought by the owner of CME before a different arbitral tribunal and pursuant to another BIT) this was cited as a decisive consideration for *dismissing* the fair and equitable treatment claim in that case.[203] The different result reached in the *CME* case should, however, be seen mainly

[197] *CMS Gas v Argentina* (Award, 2005) para 275.

[198] *CME v Czech Republic* (Partial Award, 2001) para 611.

[199] *Eureko v Poland* (Award, 2005) para 232.

[200] *ibid*, especially para 232, and paras 151–60; and *CMS Gas v Argentina* (Award, 2005) para 275, and para 212 et seq.

[201] *Tecmed v Mexico* (Award, 2003) para 160.

[202] *ibid*, para 160.

[203] *Lauder v Czech Republic* (Award, 2001) para 297 et seq.

as a different rationalisation of the relevant facts, and not necessarily as a disagreement on the law underlying the dispute. As a closer reading of the case shows, the tribunal based its reasoning on a contextual reading of the relevant licence-arrangement, whereby an actual understanding between the government and the foreign investor was inferred on the basis of the factual situation. The facts, as set out by the tribunal, concerned a contractual arrangement set up by the foreign investor company with a locally owned company to ensure the benefit of the licence granted to the latter. As strongly emphasised by the tribunal however, this was done in clear co-operation with the Czech government in order to evade the requirement of Czech law that only locally owned companies could be granted a broadcasting licence.[204] The reasoning of the tribunal seems to have been that the contractual arrangement was set up in direct co-operation with the government, as an alternative to a licence agreement between the foreign investor and the government, which would have been the normal procedure. Thus, the case can plausibly be read in the light that there was indeed, in the opinion of the tribunal, a repudiation of an implicit understanding, comparable to a contract, between the state and the foreign investor, on which the investor was induced to rely when making the investment.[205]

As telling, and supporting the same proposition, are certain cases where the fair and equitable treatment standard was found not to have been breached, for the reason that the state did not substantially commit itself. This was the case in the *Lauder* case, as referred to above. The tribunal here interpreted the underlying licence arrangement differently from the *CME* tribunal, holding that it did not constitute a 'specific undertaking' by the state, which again was the decisive reason for dismissing the claim.[206] Moreover, in *MTD v Chile*, the tribunal held that the government had breached the fair and equitable treatment standard by authorising an investment on conditions which contradicted its internal policy and therefore failed to achieve the necessary subsequent permits and approvals. However, it also held that the failure to accord those permits and approvals

[204] *CME v Czech Republic* (Partial Award, 2001) para 428 et seq.

[205] See eg *ibid*, paras 529–30: 'The Media Council jointly with CEDC developed the investment scheme by creating the 1993 split structure which was thereafter also used by other broadcasters. CME and its predecessor as foreign investor could reasonably rely on this structure which was developed in close conjunction with and approved by the Media Council . . . The Media Council was obligated to defend and secure this structure, after having attracted foreign investment on the basis of it. This placed the obligation on the Media Council not to interfere with the legal foundation of the Claimant's predecessor's investment'.

[206] *Lauder v Czech Republic* (Award, 2001) paras 297–8: 'There cannot be any inconsistent conduct in a regulatory body taking the necessary actions to enforce the law, absent any specific undertakings that it will refrain from doing so. No such undertaking was given by the Media Council or any other organ of the Czech Republic . . . The prior approval by the Media Council of the MOA, in the context of the License being granted to CET 21, contained no commitment to allow CET 21 and CNTS to violate the Media Law'.

could not be considered in itself to constitute a breach of any legitimate expectations, since the state had not, by the relevant investment contracts, become contractually bound to grant the necessary permits and approvals.[207] It is, similarly, entirely plausible to read the majority opinion in *Thunderbird v Mexico* in the light that no real and effective understanding between the investor and the relevant state entity had been reached with regard to the admission and operation of the gaming machines in Mexico. The case concerned a US company that had set up a business for the operation of 'gaming facilities' in Mexico, which was later closed down by the relevant Mexican authorities. The question was whether the company had had legitimate reason to trust a letter solicited from the government, in which it was pledged that gaming machines of the kind described by the company would *not* be in contravention of Mexican policies and regulations. The majority of the tribunal held that this was not sufficient to create a legitimate expectation, since the claimants had misrepresented the exact nature and characteristics of the machines in their initial contact with the relevant authority.[208] In other words, there was nothing comparable to an understanding between the government and the investor.

The above scrutiny of certain significant cases displays how the legitimate expectation standard has been applied according to a distinctly transactional or contractual modality. By this I mean that the relationship between the investor and the state has been conceptualised in terms of a contractual perspective, irrespective of whether formally based in a contract or not.[209] This is particularly evident in the qualification of reliance as reasonable or legitimate, according to a number of distinctly contractual factors, including: whether there has in fact been 'a meeting of minds';[210] whether reliance was based on a clear and definitive representation of the state to be bound, which could not reasonably be misunderstood or interpreted otherwise;[211] or whether the relevant state organ induced reliance by conducting itself in a way clearly implying a tacit understanding between itself and the investor.[212] All these could also have been seen as indicia of a contract or quasi-contract. In this perspective, a formally binding contract setting out in explicit terms what the parties are entitled to expect merely expresses the most determinate and certain criterion of what may reasonably be relied on.[213]

207 *MTD v Chile* (Award, 2004) para 188.

208 *International Thunderbird v Mexico* (Award, 2006) para 149 et seq.

209 But contrast nevertheless, for a seemingly less strict perspective *Occidental Exploration and Production Co v Republic of Ecuador* (Award, 2004) para 191.

210 *International Thunderbird v Mexico* (Award, 2006) para 149 et seq.

211 *MTD v Chile* (Award, 2004) para 188; and *Lauder v Czech Republic* (Award, 2001) paras 297–9.

212 *CME v Czech Republic* (Partial Award, 2001) para 428 et seq and especially paras 529–30.

213 See eg to this effect *Bayindir v Pakistan* (Award, 2009) para 197.

C. Legitimate Expectations and Municipal Law

An aspect of the legitimate expectation criterion encompassed in the fair and equitable treatment standard is that—unlike the expropriation standard, and to a lesser extent, the 'umbrella' standard—it is not linked at the outset to any municipal law conception of rights. Whether a legitimate expectation under the fair and equitable treatment standard has materialised is in principle independent of whether it has been able to crystallise into a right under municipal law. According to the surface structure of the relevant standard itself, it depends simply on whether the investor, having suffered a breach of its expectations, has been treated unfairly and inequitably. Several cases have emphasised this autonomy of the legitimate expectations standard, as connected directly to a conceived treaty purpose of promoting and facilitating investment.[214] There are two fundamental aspects to this. First, it means a contractual right recognised by municipal law is not necessarily protected if it does not meet the treaty requirement of a legitimate expectation. Secondly, it means expectations pursuant to contractual undertakings not recognised by municipal law as contractual rights, but which do meet the standard, may nevertheless be protected.

As regards the latter proposition, it is clearly implicit in a number of cases.[215] It has also received positive confirmation in at least one case. Thus, in *CME v Czech Republic*, the tribunal expressly held that the investor had a protected position, irrespective of its formal rights under Czech law against the government. The respondent state claimed that there was no vested right, since the original investment arrangement 'would not have been enforced by a court as the Media Law prohibited the transfer of the License'.[216] In response to this, the tribunal held that the position under Czech law was not crucial:

> This contention is unsustainable . . . Whether a Czech National Court would support and defend this structure is not dispositive. *The Media Council was obligated to defend and secure this structure, after having attracted foreign investment on the basis of it*.[217] (emphasis added).

Thus, instead of inquiring into whether the investor had a protected right by virtue of the applicable municipal law, the tribunal held that its

[214] See eg *Tecmed v Mexico* (Award, 2003) para 156; *MTD v Chile* (Award, 2004) para 113; *CMS Gas v Argentina* (Award, 2005) para 274; *Saluka Investments v Czech Republic* (Award, 2006) para 301.

[215] See especially *Tecmed v Mexico* (Award, 2003) para 155, and para 160 et seq; and *International Thunderbird v Mexico* (Award, 2006) para 149 et seq; but contrast *Lauder v Czech Republic* (Award, 2001) paras 297–8.

[216] *CME v Czech Republic* (Partial Award, 2001) para 528.

[217] *ibid*, paras 529–30.

position was protected directly by virtue of its reasonable reliance on the arrangement set up in co-operation with the state.

If, however, the basis of the expectation *is* an alleged contractual understanding with the state, the legitimate expectation standard may nevertheless, and usually would, require by its own account that the applicable municipal law is given effect. Clearly, an expectation based on a formalised contract cannot plausibly be sustained independently of the validity and fate of the contract under its applicable law. Most of the cases where a formal contract has been at the base of the relationship confirm this.[218] However, the autonomous rationale of the legitimate expectation standard entails that this is merely a starting point. Being primarily concerned with predictability and certainty, this may override implicit policies ingrained in municipal law, which are not made formally explicit in the law at the time of contracting. In other words, it may apply to the interpretation of municipal law as a presumption of validity.[219] What is perhaps most significant about the autonomy of the legitimate expectation standard in this connection is that it also has influenced the interpretation and application of expropriation and umbrella clause standard, which at the outset are concerned with protecting rights and undertakings under municipal law. This demonstrates how an autonomous legitimate expectation standard comes to substitute its own teleology for policies and concerns prevalent in municipal law, which is thereby to some extent deprived of its idiosyncratic nature as a living law when applied in investment arbitration.

5.5 CUSTOMARY INTERNATIONAL LAW— THE INTERNATIONALISED CONTRACT AND PROTECTION OF ACQUIRED RIGHTS

In this section we move from arbitral tribunals interpreting treaty standards to arbitral tribunals evoking customary law (or general principles of international law) in response to claims based on state contracts. I analyse the phenomenon of internationalised contracts and the more conventional

[218] See eg *EDF v Romania* (Award, 2009) para 240 et seq; *CMS Gas v Argentina* (Award, 2005) para 212 et seq; and *MTD v Chile* (Award, 2004) para 187; but contrast *Eureko v Poland* (Award, 2005) as discussed above.

[219] The *CMS* case may provide an illustration of this. In its discussion of Argentine law, the initial tribunal may have applied the formal provisions of that law, but at the same time it clearly did not rely to any significant effect on Argentine case law or policies which an Argentine court might have used. Thus, the tribunal found that the extreme economic crisis in the country did not constitute a relevant change of circumstances for continued performance of the contract. Although it remains a speculation, it would not have been surprising if Argentine courts had come to a different conclusion. See *CMS Gas v Argentina* (Award, 2005) para 212 et seq.

approach based on a notion of acquired rights, as two interrelated tendencies that display affinities with the underlying structure and rationale of investment treaty standards that have been revealed above. The customary international law relating to foreign investments used to be one of the main areas of contention in international law,[220] and perhaps no part of it more so than the subject of states' responsibility for their contractual undertakings.[221] The controversy surrounding it has sometimes seemed most like a conflict of faiths. It is quite noteworthy then, that these long-raging controversies are hardly present in arbitral practice on the subject. In the following I will show how, instead, a relatively consistent practice of arbitral tribunals has protected expectations under contractual undertakings by invoking what has been deemed established and self-evident principles of customary international law. The particular objective of this section is to analyse further the reasons and justifications for these principles such as they have been applied in arbitral practice. It is suggested that most of the relevant decisions—theoretical and conceptual differences aside—display a remarkably common undercurrent of prevailing concerns. In most respects, as we shall see, these find their counterparts in the treaty standards already addressed. This may reflect a common set of values innate to the function and objective of the arbitral process as a means of investment protection.

A. Internationalisation and the Sanctity of Contract Standard

As mentioned, it is often said to be a general rule that breach of contract is not in itself a wrongful act, and that something more is required for a breach of international law to occur.[222] The crucial proposition assumed is that no rule of customary or general international law requires the observance of mere contractual undertakings as such. In contrast to this stands, however, a fair number of cases which rely on what they claim is an undoubted principle of customary international law, namely *pacta sunt servanda*, and the consequent ability of sovereign states to make binding commitments to whomsoever they want. These cases do not suggest that all contracts concluded by a state with foreigners are subject to this

[220] See eg Sornarajah (2004) 22 et seq; and Lowenfeld, *International Economic Law* (Oxford, 2002) 391 et seq.

[221] See for useful accounts of conflicting opinions in the literature, eg Maniruzzaman, 'State Contracts in Contemporary International Law: Monist versus Dualist Controversies' (2001) 12 *EJIL* 309; Lillich, 'The law Governing Disputes under Economic Development Agreements: Reexamining the Concept of internationalization' in Lillich and Brower (eds), *International Arbitration; towards judicialization and uniformity* (Transnational, Irvington (NY), 1994) 61, 92 et seq; and Paasivirta, 'Internationalization and Stabilization of Contracts versus State Sovereignty' (1989) 60 *BYIL* 315, 316 et seq.

[222] See eg *SGS v Philippines* (Decision on Jurisdiction, 2004) para 122; *SGS v Pakistan* (Decision on Jurisdiction, 2003) para 167; and *Noble Ventures v Romania* (Award, 2005) para 53.

principle. The idea is that it only applies to certain contracts that have been made directly subject to the international legal order. This is the concept of 'internationalisation', which I have already discussed and criticised as a conceptual construct in chapter three. In the following I discuss the basic rationale of these cases, and claim that it is based on an underlying structural concept of commitment based on reliance, which recalls the underlying rationale of protection of legitimate expectations discussed above in relation to the relevant treaty standards.

(i) Internationalisation as the Basis of Contractual Commitment

The crux of the cases applying the 'sanctity of contract standard' is that it is purportedly made applicable by the direct submission of the contract to international law. The famous case of *Texaco v Libya* is the prime example of this,[223] but several other cases reveal a close similarity of approach.[224] Its continued relevance is attested to by the recent *Himpurna* and *Patuha* cases, which will be discussed further below.[225] These cases and the theory they propound have been described and discussed in detail elsewhere.[226] What I am concerned with here is not so much the theory and postulates made in the cases about applicable principles as such, but with the arguably common *rationale* on which the cases were based. For this we shall take the *Texaco* case as our starting point and prime example.

The substantive issue in the case was whether the Libyan government's cancellation of a number of concession contracts was a breach of international law. The main part of the 'substantive' argument was nevertheless devoted to the question of the applicable law. The reason for this is explained early in the award as follows:

[223] *Texaco v Libya* (Award (Merits), 1977) 53 ILR (1979) 389.

[224] *Lena Goldfields v Soviet Union, The Times* (London), 3 September 1930, reprinted in Nussbaum, 'The Arbitration between the Lena Goldfields Ltd. and the Soviet Government' (1950–51) 36 *Cornell Law Quarterly* 31; *Sapphire International Petroleums Ltd v National Iranian Oil Company (NIOC)* (Award, 1963) 35 ILR 136; *Saudi Arabia v Aramco* (Award, 1958) 27 ILR 117; *BP Exploration Co (Libya) Ltd v Govt of Libya* (Award, 1973) 53 ILR (1979) 297; *Libyan American Oil Co (LIAMCO) v Govt of Libya* (Award, 1977) 62 ILR (1982) 141; *Revere Copper and Brass Inc v Overseas Private Investment Corp (OPIC)* (Award, 1978) 56 ILR 258; *AGIP SpA v Congo* (Award, 1979) 21 ILM (1982) 726; *SARL Benvenuti & Bonfant v Congo* (Award, 1980), (1981) 20 ILM 878; *Elf Aquitaine Iran v National Iranian Oil Company (NIOC)* (Award, 1982), (1986) 11 *YbCA* 97; *American Independent Oil Co (AMINOIL) v State of Kuwait* (Final Award, 1982) 21 ILM 976; *Deutsche Schachtbau- und Tiefbohrgesellschaft mbH v R'as Al Khaimah (United Arab Emirates) and The R'as Al Khaimah Oil Company (Rakoil)* (ICC case No 3572, 1982); and see also *Petroleum Development Ltd v Sheikh of Abu Dhabi* (1951) 18 ILR 144; *Petroleum Development (Qatar) Ltd v Ruler of Qatar* (1951) 18 ILR 161; *Ruler of Qatar v International Marine Oil Company Ltd* (1953) 20 ILR 534.

[225] *Himpurna California Energy Ltd (Bermuda) v PT (Persero) Perusahaan Listruik Negara (Indonesia)* (Award, 1999), (2000) 25 *YbCA* 13; and *Patuha Power Ltd v PT (Persero) Perusahaan Listruik Negara (Indonesia)* (Award, 1999) (1999) 14(12) *Mealey's Int'l Arb Rep*. Since these cases are virtually identical I refer only to the *Himpurna case* in the following.

[226] See eg for one of the most recent contributions, Lillich (1994).

> [T]he juridical value and consequently, the binding nature of the Deeds of Concession in dispute can only be judged on the basis of the law which is applicable to them because it is obvious that, if—assuming arguendo—these contracts were governed by Libyan law, the result would have been that their binding nature could be affected *a priori* by legislative or regulatory measures taken within the Libyan national legal order.[227]

In other words, since the concessions had in fact been annulled by a formally valid government act,[228] their continued validity could only depend on a rule external to that law. This rule the arbitrator found without difficulty in international law. As the contract had been entered into by direct submission to international law, it was also subject to the most fundamental principle of international law; *pacta sunt servanda*—a state must abide by its undertakings.[229] This is not the crux of the decision's substantive argument, however. The crucial part is instead how it justified that international law was directly applicable in the first place; in other words, how the 'internationalisation' of the contract was explained. This it did essentially by introducing certain criteria held to be conducive to 'internationalisation'.[230] Three distinct criteria were singled out by the arbitrator: one, the express submission of the contract to 'the general principles of law' instead of the host state's law;[231] two, the reference in the contract to arbitration instead of the host state's courts;[232] and three, and perhaps most significantly, a specific objective relating to the economic development of the host state.[233] These factors provided the objective characteristics of the contract that justified treating it as a substantive commitment under international law.[234] In other words, this was not considered an ordinary consequence of a state committing itself by contract. Only certain commitments were conceived to have the characteristics invoking international law in a real sense.[235]

227 *Texaco v Libya* (Award (Merits), 1977) paras 22.

228 *ibid*, para 75.

229 *ibid*, para 51: 'No international jurisdiction has ever had the least doubt as to the existence, in international law, of the rule *pacta sunt servanda*: it has been affirmed vigorously both in *the Aramco* award in 1958 and in the *Sapphire* award in 1963. On [sic] can read, indeed, in the *Sapphire award*, that 'it is a fundamental principle of law, which is constantly being proclaimed by international Courts, that contractual undertakings must be respected. The rule "pacta sunt servanda" is the basis of every contractual relationship'. This tribunal cannot but reaffirm this in its turn by stating that the maxim *pacta sunt servanda* should be viewed as a fundamental principle of international law'.

230 *ibid*, para 40 et seq.

231 *ibid*, paras 41–2.

232 *ibid*, para 44.

233 *ibid*, para 45.

234 Weil, 'Droit international et contrats d'Etat' in *Mélanges offerts à Paul Reuter* (Paris, 1981) 549, esp, 572 et seq.

235 *Texaco v Libya* (Award (Merits), 1977) para 43, and see also for further discussion, Weil (1981), eg 562, and 572 et seq.

The clues to the substantive rationale are provided by the further justification of these criteria. The first concern relied on was the 'need for the private party to be protected against unilateral and abrupt modifications of the legislation in the contracting state'.[236] This was further connected with the third criterion, namely that the contract in question was one of 'a new category of agreements between States and private persons: economic development agreements'.[237] The distinct characteristic of such agreements, according to the arbitrator, was that they were conducive to economic development in the host state, and that they required huge investments of capital, resources and technology as well as close co-operation between the state and the investor for a long period of time.[238] This concept of 'economic development agreement'[239] has more or less aptly been criticised by commentators for not providing a sufficiently clear criterion of internationalisation.[240] That need not concern us here, because it is in any case the crucial clue to the underlying concerns at work in the case. This was explained by the arbitrator as follows:

> [B]ecause of the purpose of the cooperation in which the contracting party must participate with the State and the magnitude of the investments to which it agreed, the contractual nature of this type of agreement is reinforced: the emphasis on the contractual nature of the legal relation between the host State and the investor is intended to bring about an equilibrium between the goal of the general interest sought by such relation and the profitability which is necessary for the pursuit of the task entrusted to the private enterprise. The effect is also to ensure to the private contracting party a certain stability which is justified by the considerable investments which it makes in the country concerned.[241]

Thus, the whole internationalisation construct was in reality only another way of saying that the underlying interests required that sufficient trust could be placed in the undertaking of the state, in order that the investor might feel confident to make the necessary commitment of capital and resources to its territory.

This was clearly also one of the concerns inducing the other, and earlier, pioneer case in this field, the *Sapphire* case, to adopt a similar construction. While also shrouded in the guise of a discussion of the applicable law, this reasoning has nothing to do with the 'jurisdiction selecting' formulas normally employed in the conflict of laws science:

236 *Texaco v Libya* (Award (Merits), 1977) para 42.
237 *ibid*, para 45.
238 *ibid*, para 45.
239 The concept seems to have been termed first by McNair, 'The General Principles of Law Recognized by Civilized Nations' (1957) 33 *BYIL* 1, see also Hyde, 'Economic Development Agreements' (1962-I) 105 *Recueil des Cours* 266.
240 See eg Paasivirta, *Participation of States in International Contracts* (Lakimiesliiton Kustannus, Helsinki, 1990) 93; and Leben, 'La Théorie du Contrat d'État et l'Évolution du Droit International des Investissements' (2003-II) 302 *Recueil des Cours* 197, 247.
241 *Texaco v Libya* (Award (Merits), 1977) para 45.

> Under the present agreement, the foreign company was bringing financial and technical assistance to Iran, which involved it in investments, responsibilities, and considerable risks. It therefore seems natural that they should be protected against any legislative changes which might alter the character of the contract, and that they should be assured of some legal security. This could not be guaranteed to them by the outright application of Iranian law, which it is within the power of the Iranian State to change.[242]

Thus, the main motive for applying the general principles of law was that this, in the mind of the arbitrator, best ensured that the investor could rely on the contract as the fundamental legal basis of its investment.[243] While it might appear that this side-stepped the substantive question—whether a state is bound by its commitments—it did so only as a matter of form and by this supplied the crucial argument in favour of an affirmative answer to that question. As in the *Texaco* case, to say that the contract was governed by the general principles of law was really to say that the contract was binding: thus, to justify this was really to justify that the state was bound by its commitment.

In the later case of *Revere Copper v OPIC*, the similar substantive rationale for applying international law is put in plain language.[244] The contract at issue contained neither a choice of law clause nor an international arbitration clause.[245] It was, however, a classical investment contract, concluded with the government of Jamaica and concerning a bauxite-mining and aluminium production project to be operated by the company in Jamaica. Inter alia, the contract contained commitments by the state to impose no further taxes and royalties. Subsequently, a new Bauxite Levy was imposed on the operations of the company, pursuant to a new government policy designed to secure a greater part of the income from the bauxite and aluminium industry for government purposes. This violation of the tax freeze in the contract had been justified by the Jamaican government and municipal courts on the basis of parliamentary supremacy and state sovereignty, under the so called '*Amphitrite* principle' in common law.[246] To this the tribunal reasoned, however, that the very characteristics of the contract, as an international and long-term economic development contract, invoked the principles of international law relating to such contracts:

242 *Sapphire v NIOC* (Award, 1963), 35 ILR 136, 171.

243 See also *ibid*, 175: 'Such a solution seems particularly suitable for giving the guarantees of protection which are indispensable for foreign companies, since these companies undergo very considerable risks in bringing financial and technical aid to countries in the process of development'.

244 *Revere Copper v OPIC* (Award, 1978) 56 ILR 258.

245 *ibid*, 274.

246 This is normally held to constitute a presumption to the effect that the executive cannot restrict its statutory powers by contract, see *Rederiaktiebolaget Amphitrite v The King* [1921] 3 KB 500 (Court).

> Under international law the commitments made in favour of foreign nationals are binding notwithstanding the power of Parliament and other governmental organs under the domestic Constitution to override or nullify such commitments. Any other position would mean in this case that Jamaica could not in the exercise of its sovereign powers obtain foreign private capital to develop its resources or attract foreign industries.[247]

The company's actual reliance on the promises of the state, both in making its investment and in planning the financing of the operations, was heavily emphasised as a decisive factor in the internationalisation of the contract.[248] Thus, in substance, and according to its expressed rationale, the tribunal assumed the existence of an international legal rule, requiring essentially that state undertakings intended to be relied on by an investor to commit capital and resources to the state are observed. This is something quite different from saying that contractual undertakings as such are binding on a state under international law. In fact it closely resembles, and is hardly distinguishable from, the more limited rationale of protecting contractual rights and legitimate expectations pursuant to reliance on state undertakings made in relation to specific investments, such as manifested in the application of contemporary investment treaty standards by practice.

(ii) Reliance and Commitment of Resources

To consider reliance and reasonable trust as the decisive rationale of the internationalisation formula, as suggested above, provides a conceptualisation of its main criteria of application which is radically different from the doctrine's own conceptual basis and pretensions. The conceptual surface of the doctrine focuses on the submission of the contract to international law, perceiving its legal force as a corollary of the external autonomy of state sovereignty (ie the capacity of the state to commit) under international law.[249] If internationalisation is really considered as a substantive argument concerned with the protection of reliance and trust, this is reduced to a fiction. The reason why the state is bound is not some metaphysical quality of its sovereign will—finally allowed to make its force felt after submission of the contract to the friendly climate of international law—but a functional concern relating to the state's need to

[247] *Revere Copper v OPIC* (Award, 1978) 56 ILR 258, 284, see also especially 272 and 276–7.
[248] *ibid*, 276–9.
[249] See eg *Texaco v Libya* (Award (Merits), 1977) paras 66–7, *Revere Copper v OPIC* (Award, 1978) 56 ILR 258, 282–4; *Saudi Arabia v Aramco* (Award, 1958) 27 ILR 117, 168. See also for an elegant conceptualization of this in terms of theory, Leben, 'Quelques Reflexions Theoriques a propos des Contrats d'Etat' in *Souveraineté étatique et marchés internationaux à la fin du 20ème siècle; Melanges en l'honneur de Philippe Kahn* (Litec, Paris, 2000) 119.

'tie itself to the mast' in order to attract capital and resources.[250] This recalls what may be deemed the rationale of investment treaties more generally, namely the particular risk element involved in placing capital, resources and, significantly, the expectation of returns on the initial investment, at the mercy of changing government policies.

On the facts, this may at least seem a possible rationalisation of the internationalisation cases, as they all concerned contracts actually relied on to make an investment. If it is the real decisive factor, it should, however, also signify that a contract might only provide a substantive basis for claims against the state insofar as it has actually been relied on to make an investment. Several cases do in fact also suggest this. In *AMINOIL v Kuwait* one of the questions facing the tribunal was the amount of compensation due for the (lawful) cancellation of the concession contract. As the requisite criterion on which to decide this, the tribunal introduced the concept of legitimate expectations, and applied it to the investor's reasonable expectation of profit based on the contract.[251] Significantly, it held that the determination of the reasonable profit expectation had to take account of the actualised risk involved by the capital investment. When the concession was terminated this also made the future risk element vanish, reducing, in the minds of the tribunal, the reasonable profit margin.[252] Admittedly, however, such reasoning might arguably to some extent be rationalised under normal contractual principles, as subtraction of saved costs (in other words, considering risk as a cost).

More illustrative, on the facts at least, is the more recent case of *Himpurna v Persero (Indonesia)*. In several respects this case can be said to replicate the internationalisation formulae, though not quite in explicit terms. Specifically, it held that a presidential decree suspending the contracts in question could not affect the state's legal responsibility, as this was expressly prohibited by various terms of the contract itself, although the contract was governed at the outset by Indonesian law.[253] The case

[250] This might thus be seen as a response of arbitral practice to what Guzman calls the 'dynamic inconsistency problem', or 'wanting to tie oneself to the mast, but being unable to do so'. (The apposite response from a functional perspective is then of course that states should be able to do so). See Guzman, 'Why LDCs Sign Treaties That Hurt Them: Explaining the Popularity of Bilateral Investment Treaties' (1997–98) 38 *Va J Int'l Law* 639, 658 et seq.

[251] *AMINOIL v Kuwait* (Award, 1982) para 148 et seq.

[252] *ibid*, para 163: 'Assuming that a normal level of profits has been determined having regard to the total capital invested, it would be ordinary business practice in the case of a concession intended to last, to add a reasonable profit margin that would preserve incentives, and allow for risks whether commercial or technological. But this necessity disappears when it is a question of deciding on the amount of compensation due for a concession that has already been terminated—for in that event the risk (for the concessionaire) has *ex hypothesi* vanished'.

[253] *Himpurna v Persero* (Award, 1999), (2000) 25 *YbCA* 13, para 41. In relation to its discussion of the applicable law, the tribunal held that this was basically applicable only *subject* to the contract (instead of vice versa), pursuant to a prevalent concept of party autonomy in international arbitration, thus immunising the contract against subsequent legislative change

concerned a complex contractual arrangement (based on a so-called 'independent power project' contract model[254]) relating to the development of a geothermal power facility in Indonesia. The crux of the arrangement was an energy sales contract between the American-owned project company *Himpurna California Energy*, and the Indonesian state-owned electricity company *Persero*, committing the latter to buying a set amount of electricity at a fixed price set in US dollars, and for a pre-determined period of 30 years, at which time the power plant would become the property of the Indonesian state.[255] Moreover, the contract entitled the investor to invest and develop a certain fixed maximum capacity of electricity production volume, with guaranteed sales for the entire period on these terms. The contract was suspended pursuant to the severe impact on Indonesia of the 1997–99 East Asian crisis. The company then terminated the contract for breach of contract, and sued for recovery of the investment (*damnum emergens*) and lost profits (*lucrum cessans*). In principle this was accepted by the tribunal, but with one important modification; it would not grant recovery of lost profits for investments not actually made.[256] This is difficult to explain under ordinary principles of contract law, given that the investor had a valid contractual right to make further investment on the agreed terms. The tribunal relied principally on the doctrine of abuse of rights, essentially because it considered it singularly unfair that the claimant should be able to make an 'astonishing bargain', from a contractual right to develop and sell electricity that had no comparable use- or sales-value for the respondent in the circumstances that had developed:

> Even if such a right may be said to derive from explicit contractual terms, the Arbitral tribunal cannot fail to be struck by the fact that the claimant is seeking to turn [the contract] into an astonishing bargain in circumstances when performance of the Contract would be ruinous to the respondent.[257]

not envisaged by the contract itself. Citing in particular the classical *Lena Goldfields case*, it reasoned as follows: 'The concept of party autonomy is central to international arbitration. There is nothing unusual or improper about a contractual stipulation to the effect that a certain law shall apply only to the extent that it is consistent with the terms of the contract. To the contrary, it is a frequently recurring feature in contracts involving States and foreign investors, and has for a long time unfailingly been upheld in arbitral awards'.

254 See generally Inadomi, 'Independent Power Projects in Developing Countries—Legal Investment Protection and Consequences for Development' (Phd Thesis, University of Oslo, 2005, unpublished).

255 This meant inter alia shifting all commercial risk connected to available demand and currency fluctuations to the state for the entire duration of the contract, the basic objective being to ensure the project a guaranteed income in order to secure financing. Thus, in reality the transaction was a sort of hire-purchase arrangement, a means for the state to acquire a power plant by paying in instalments over 30 years, see Inadomi (2005) 42.

256 *Himpurna v Persero* (Award, 1999) para 315 et seq.

257 *ibid*, para 318.

The extreme circumstances, and the evident fairness of this reasoning, cannot hide the fact that it virtually invalidated the contractual right in question by dismantling the available remedy—the right of the claimant to claim his net-expectation interest.

A narrowly contractual perspective might instead have afforded the respondent a right to cancel.[258] This might have extended a right not to accept further performance, but accompanied by a corresponding duty to compensate lost profits, though subject to saved costs and the claimant's obligation to mitigate loss by exploiting alternative opportunities.[259] In this perspective the crux of the tribunal's reasoning might instead be that the claimant had no effective contractual right to net-expectation interest that could withstand cancellation in respect of investments not made. It is of course possible, and even likely, that this was based, quite concretely, on the extreme unfairness of profit being made on what had turned out to be an extremely unfortunate bargain for the state. Nevertheless, the normal avenue would then have been to hold the specific right in question to be frustrated by changed circumstances. This line of argument was expressly rejected by the tribunal.[260] Another explanation therefore seems more likely, suggesting rather that the tribunal intuitively accepted the limited rationale and justification of the perceived rule under which it upheld the contract in the first place.

This is supported by its reasoning elsewhere. First, rejecting the respondent's claim that the Indonesian officials had not had competence to enter into the contract under Indonesian law, the tribunal held that, irrespective of Indonesian law, the very characteristics of such contracts and the international arbitral process itself, as significant means to attract foreign investment, also invoked a presumption in favour of the validity of the contract. This it expressed as follows:

> [A]n over-readiness by international arbitrators to accept illegality defences may harm an international mechanism which benefits numerous countries that rely on access to international funding, technology and trade . . . [Nothing] should be taken to mean that PLN's illegality or invalidity defences have not been considered. The point is simply that there is a presumption in favour of the validity of contracts; that this presumption is healthy; that it is strengthened when contracts have provided the basis upon which many persons have acted over time . . .[261]

[258] See also Inadomi (2005) 338. This would of course depend on whether a basis for this could be inferred from the contract or from the applicable Indonesian law. In general it would seem such a right is often recognized in relation to manufacturing and fabrication contracts. See eg (in relation to Norwegian law) Hagstrøm, *Obligasjonsrett* (Universitetsforlaget, Oslo, 2003) 234 et seq.

[259] *ibid*, 236.

[260] *Himpurna v Persero* (Award, 1999) para 188 et seq.

[261] *ibid*, paras 114–16.

Secondly, as argued above, the tribunal's reasoning is impossible to rationalise under any other perspective than one supposing an autonomous concept of party autonomy.[262] This it applied both as a bar to subsequent invalidation of the contract and, in this context, as a presumption of its initial validity. The citation can be considered to bring out the specific justification and rationale of this, as it was perceived by the tribunal, by connecting it to the international function of contracts and the arbitral process in protecting investments.

In this perspective, the limitation of expectation damages (*lucrum cessans*) to investments already made is merely a natural consequence of the inner limitation of the applied rule; its essential rationale being to ensure reliability where capital and resources are committed on the strength of state undertakings. It is submitted that this is what is principally illustrated by the *Himpurna* award. The contract was repudiated by a formal decision of the state, but upheld by the arbitral tribunal insofar as it had been relied on to invest capital and resources. The implicit limitation of the rationale of contractual commitment here almost forced itself on the tribunal by the extremity of the circumstances. Thus chastened by the circumstances to its elemental core, the more compelling rationale applied could arguably have been conceptualised in different terms: only when an investment is actually committed on the trust of an undertaking can it be said that it is definitively constitutive of a legitimate expectation immune to subsequent government cancellation.

B. The 'Traditional' Approach—Acquired Rights

If accepted as a substantive argument based on reliance, the internationalisation approach becomes almost analogous to a more traditional concept of international law, which is the concept of 'acquired rights'. This is a basic rule of international law, inter alia, underlying a general prohibition against uncompensated confiscation of tangible and intangible property.[263] There is a massive body of precedent to support the general proposition that contracts may, and usually will, constitute acquired rights.[264]

[262] *ibid*, paras 41–2.

[263] In international law this concept lies at the root of such diverse issues as the prohibition of uncompensated confiscation of property, the rule that individual rights are not affected by a change of government (state succession), and the general requirement against the arbitrary and abusive retroactivity of laws. See for a classical account, Kaeckenbeeck, 'La Protection Internationale des Droits Acquis' (1937-I) 59 *Recueil des Cours* 317; and see also Lalive, 'The Doctrine of Acquired Rights' in *Rights and Duties of Private Investors Abroad* (Matthew Bender, Albany (NY), 1965).

[264] See eg *Certain German Interests in Polish Upper Silesia Case*, PCIJ Series A No 7, 42; *Norwegian Shipowners Claims* (1922) I RIAA 307; *Amoco Int'l Finance Corp v Iran* (Award, 1987) 15 Iran-US CT Rep 189, para 108; and *Phillips Petroleum Co v Iran* (1989) 21 Iran-US CT Rep 79, para 105; and *SPP v Egypt* (Award, 1992) para 164.

At the same time, it is generally recognised that contracts principally exist in and by virtue of municipal law,[265] and are not as such immutable against legislative change or limitation. In the following I discuss how this concept of customary law in application to investment has invoked concerns largely analogous to those reflected by the internationalisation cases, displaying a largely similar structure of commitment.

I start with the classical case conceptualising this approach, namely *Saudi Arabia v Aramco*. This case is often seen as exemplifying a strict sanctity of contracts approach to the concept of acquired rights. The case may, however, also be read as reflecting a more nuanced and limited rationale, confining its application to contractual interests based on actual commitment of resources pursuant to state undertakings. The *Aramco* tribunal initially rejected the argument that the contract was internationalised and therefore directly subject to international law, relying to this effect on the classical dictum of the Permanent Court of International Justice in the *Serbian Loans case*.[266] Instead it held that at the outset the law of Saudi Arabia applied, but that this had to be applied so that it coincided with 'the economic milieu' of the contract.[267] Specifically, this meant, according to the tribunal, that the fundamental law of the parties was the concession contract itself:

> The Concession Agreement is thus the fundamental law of the Parties, and the Arbitration Tribunal is bound to recognize its particular importance owing to the fact that it fills a gap in the legal system of Saudi Arabia with regard to the oil industry.[268]

The tribunal then, admittedly, conceptualised its argument more formally, by introducing the concept of acquired rights as a consequence of the state's sovereign will:

> The tribunal holds that the Concession has the nature of a constitution which has the effect of conferring acquired rights on the Contracting Parties. By reason of its very sovereignty within its territorial domain, the State possesses the legal power to grant rights which it forbids itself to withdraw before the end of the Concession . . . Nothing can prevent a State, in the exercise of its sovereignty, from binding itself irrevocably by the provisions of a concession and from granting to the concessionaire irretractable rights. Such rights have the character of acquired rights.[269]

Superficially, this argument invokes the sanctity of contract argument. The state has willed the existence of irretractable rights, and by virtue of its

[265] See eg *Serbian Loans case*, PCIJ Series A No 20; *Panevezys-Saldutiskis Railway case (Estonia v Lithuania)*, PCIJ Series A/B No 76 (1939) 18.
[266] *Saudi Arabia v Aramco* (Award, 1958) 165.
[267] *ibid*, 167.
[268] *ibid*, 168.
[269] *ibid*, 168.

very sovereignty these are therefore granted. Other considerations nevertheless suggest that it is difficult to make sense of this reference to sovereignty if not as a merely formal argument comparable to the internationalisation approach described above. Thus, if not all contracts and promises made by the state should be considered 'irretractable' as acquired rights, the question is what substantive criterion may decide when a right *is* to this effect 'acquired'. As quoted, the main substantive reason adduced by the *Aramco* tribunal was that the concession filled a lacuna in the law of Saudi Arabia, which until then had no positive law in force relating to the oil industry.[270] A main argument was that the concession, because of this, had come to play a particularly important role for the regulation of the relationship between the parties. The key to the case is therefore arguably, the particular character of the concession as a commitment meant to be relied on by the company both to commit and to continually entrust its operations to that country. This was the 'particular importance' of the contract, as referred to by the tribunal.[271] In this light, it is possible to read the *Aramco* case so that it was not the 'naked' contractual character of the concession as such, nor in itself the sovereign status of the promisor state, which ensured that the concession had to be treated as an 'acquired right' under international law. Instead, what justified this was its particular importance in the context of a complex investment-operation in an otherwise undeveloped and insecure legal environment. This is also where the reference to sovereignty finds its substantive rationale, as a manifestation of the state's particular need to commit.[272]

Certain other cases often invoked in favour of a strict sanctity of contracts approach may, at least, support a similar inference. In the *Shufeldt case (USA v Guatemala)*, the tribunal was confronted with the issue of whether a contract, regulating and granting concession to an operation to extract chicle from public lands of Guatemala, constituted a protected property right, or in analogous terms, an 'acquired right':

> Having found that the contract was a valid contract and that there was no breach thereof by Shufeldt, the question arises did Shufeldt acquire any rights of property under the contract. There cannot be any doubt that property rights are created under and by virtue of a contract . . .[273]

Did this mean that any contractual undertaking might have been enforced against the state as an 'acquired' property right, even if it had not been relied on, being, to that extent, a naked promise? At least it is clear that the contract in question was not merely a naked promise. It had been relied on by the claimant to invest resources and run its operation for a significant

270 *ibid.*
271 *ibid.*
272 Guzman (1998) 658.
273 *Shufeldt claim (USA v Guatemala)* (Award, 1930) II RIAA 1079, 1097.

period of time. Prior to the above quote this was emphasised by the tribunal as follows:

> During all these six years Shufeldt had been carrying out his contract, expending money on it and paying what the contract called for to the Government. Relying on the good faith of the Government he expended large sums in providing the necessary appliances, roads etc. for facilitating and expediting the extraction and export of chicle in the hope of recouping his expenditure by the time the contract expired. During these six years the Government . . . recognized and treated the contract as a legal contract . . .[274]

A similar factual situation was that presented in the *Lena Goldfields case* where the tribunal also held that the contract in question had been breached by the government's action. The tribunal nevertheless chose to not rely on a contractual 'right of action for damages', but instead based the claim on the principle of 'unjust enrichment':

> [T]he conduct of the Government was a breach of the contract going to the root of it. In consequence Lena is entitled to be relieved from the burden of further obligations thereunder and to be compensated in money for the value of the benefits of which it had been wrongfully deprived. *On ordinary legal principles this constitutes a right of action for damages, but the Court prefers to base its award on the principle of 'unjust enrichment'* although in its opinion the money result is the same.[275] (emphasis added)

If the claim were based on breach of contract as such, the logical consequence would have been to grant a right of action for recovery of the claimant's expectation interest. So why did the tribunal choose to rely on unjust enrichment instead of the normal principle of expectation damages under contract? Arguably, this is a key to the underlying reasoning of the tribunal. What was material, it seems to suggest, was not so much the breach of contract as such, as the contribution of capital and resources to the state on the trust of that contract. Interpreted in this manner the reasoning thus hints at a concept of acquired rights based on reliance, rather than a stricter sanctity of contracts approach. First, it was the actual reliance by the company in making its investment that constituted the crucial and material factor of the state's enrichment. Secondly, the unjust enrichment argument suggests that the crucial reproach was not directed at the breach of contract as such, but against the essential appropriation by the state of the claimant's expectation interest for its own benefit. As I shall come back to in relation to damages below, this is a recurring element of the compensation standard relative to breach of contract claims cognisable under international law.

[274] *ibid*, 1094.

[275] *Lena Goldfields v Soviet Union* (Award, 1930), as reprinted in Nussbaum, 'The Arbitration between the Lena Goldfields, Ltd. and the Soviet Government' (1950–51) 36 *Cornell Law Quarterly* 31, 51.

On a closer scrutiny, and as is true also for the internationalisation argument described above, it is therefore arguable that the application of the traditional 'acquired rights' concept to contractual undertakings in respect of investments is not so much reminiscent of a strict sanctity of contracts approach as of a notion of legitimate expectations based on reliance, quite comparable to that seen in more recent investment treaty jurisprudence.

C. Internationalised Contracts and the Sovereign Act Requirement

As discussed above, the rationale of investment protection aims essentially at the exercise of state power. The existential rationale of international investment law is fundamentally to alleviate the risk that states may use government power to interfere with an investment.[276] As discussed elsewhere, this underlies what is a more or less recurring aspect of the interpretation of investment treaty standards, namely a requirement that the state, in breaching a contract, has acted in pursuance of its capacity as a state, ie a 'sovereign act' requirement. In this section, I argue that a comparable notion also lurks beneath the surface in cases adopting a strict sanctity of contracts or internationalisation approach based on general international law.

The doctrine of internationalisation as it is usually presented would appear initially to contradict this. A crucial aspect of the doctrine is precisely that it would make any breach of contract ipso facto into a breach of international law. This contrasts with the traditional customary law concept of acquired rights, which sees the contract as leading its essential existence under municipal law, and international law invoked only where it is substantially abrogated by a government act such as expropriation.[277] We may see this clearly reflected in the case leaning most towards a strict sanctity of contract approach based on the concept of acquired rights. Thus, in the *Aramco* case the tribunal held that public international law applied only when 'objective reasons lead it to conclude that certain matters cannot be governed by any rule of the municipal law of any state', among which it mentioned 'the responsibility of states for the violation of its international obligations'.[278] Implicitly, as also indicated elsewhere in the award,[279] this would seem precisely to point to a sovereign act requirement.

On a closer scrutiny, it may nevertheless appear that also the internationalisation approach yields to similar analysis. First, it is noteworthy

[276] See eg Guzman (1998) 639.

[277] See eg Brownlie, *Principles of Public International Law* (Oxford University Press, Oxford, 2003) 522–3; and Lalive (1965) 192.

[278] *Saudi Arabia v Aramco* (Award, 1958) 27 ILR 117, 172.

[279] *ibid*, 151–2.

that, with one notable exception, the described cases adopting the internationalisation theory all concerned contracts abrogated by government decree, the crucial issue in all cases being precisely whether this government action was illegal as a violation of contractual rights.[280] Secondly, both the underlying rationale of internationalisation and the substantive criteria under which it has been held to operate in practice support a basic limitation to government acts. As noted above, the relevant cases justified internationalisation based on the state's need to be able to commit irrevocably, irrespective of its legislative supremacy under municipal law.[281] It has also been inferred accordingly that the existence of a commitment by the state not to interfere with or modify the contract by subsequent government action (a stabilisation clause) is a fundamental criterion of internationalisation.[282] In other words, internationalisation is invoked precisely by virtue of the sovereign powers of the state.

The notable exception, where no sovereign act as such was involved, is the *Sapphire* case.[283] But tellingly also this case justified the internationalisation of the contract by reference to the need to insulate the contract from the legislative *fiat* of the state, and the mixed public and private character of the contract in question.[284] Moreover, it is noteworthy that the *Sapphire* case is one of those cases adopting the internationalisation scheme that did not in fact profess to be applying *international* law.[285] Instead the arbitrator purported to apply 'general principles of law', as a perceived autonomous contract law, apparently thought to differ both from municipal law and public international law.[286] Contrastingly, in both *Texaco v Libya* and *Saudi Arabia v Aramco*, the tribunals seemed to consider that private law matters were primarily governed by respectively Libyan and Saudi Arabian law, in combination with applicable 'general principles of law',[287] while prin-

[280] Cf especially *Texaco v Libya* (Award (Merits), 1977), (1979) 53 ILR 389, para 70; *BP v Libya* (Award, 1973), (1979) 53 ILR 297, 329; *Revere Copper v OPIC* (Award, 1978) 56 ILR 258, 285; *Himpurna v Persero* (Award, 1999), (2000) 25 *YbCA* 13, para 121.

[281] See especially *Texaco v Libya* (Award (Merits), 1977), (1979) 53 ILR 389, para 42; and *Revere Copper v OPIC* (Award, 1978) 56 ILR 258, 284.

[282] Leben (2003) 251.

[283] But see also *Petroleum Development v Abu Dhabi*, 18 ILR 144, *Petroleum Development Ltd v Ruler of Qatar*, 18 ILR 161; and *Ruler of Qatar v International Marine Oil Company Ltd*, 20 ILR 534.

[284] *Sapphire v NIOC* (Award, 1963) 35 ILR 136, 171.

[285] Compare also *Petroleum Development v Abu Dhabi*, 18 ILR 144, *Petroleum Development Ltd v Ruler of Qatar* 18 ILR 161; and *Ruler of Qatar v International Marine Oil Company Ltd*, 20 ILR 534.

[286] *Sapphire v NIOC* (Award, 1963) 35 ILR 136, eg at 175.

[287] *Texaco v Libya* (Award (Merits), 1977), (1979) 53 ILR 389, paras 49–52; and especially *Saudi Arabia v Aramco* (Award, 1958) 27 ILR 117, 169: 'Matters pertaining to private law are, in principle, governed by the law of Saudi Arabia, but with one important reservation. That law must, in case of need, be interpreted or supplemented by the general principles of law, by the custom and practice in the oil business and by notions of pure jurisprudence, in particular whenever certain private rights—which must inevitably be recognized to the to the concessionaire if the Concession is not to be deprived of its substance—would not be secured in an unquestionable manner by the law in force in Saudi Arabia'.

ciples of *international* law were reserved for application to the acts of the state in its sovereign capacity.[288]

In conclusion, this shows how the power of the state is the main element that justifies and conditions internationalisation, such as it has in fact been applied in arbitral practice. This arguably reflects the same considerations that underlie the 'government act' requirement in contemporary investment treaty jurisprudence; viz that the function of international investment law is primarily of a public law, as opposed to private law, nature.[289]

5.6 THE COMPENSATION STANDARD

A breach of contract which violates one of the standards addressed above incurs responsibility for the state concerned. State responsibility can be considered a term of art for the legal consequences incurred under international law when an international legal obligation is breached. In the terminology of the International Law Commission (ILC), international responsibility occasioned by a breach of 'primary obligations' invokes 'secondary obligations' of responsibility under international law. This is closely linked to what legal remedies may be invoked by the claimant. A point of confusion is that breach of contract, as a separate legal concept, invariably entails a precise set of consequences and secondary obligations also under municipal law. However, even though it may be the factual basis of responsibility in a specific case, breach of contract is not the relevant criterion of responsibility under international law. As a matter of principle, the consequences of breach of contract under international law must be deduced by means of what is the primary rule of international law upon which responsibility is based; in other words, what substantive standard has been breached.[290] Nevertheless, as we shall see in the following, arbitral practice in our context has developed a general compensation standard based on contractual expectation interest but conditioned by actual reliance. Significantly, practice seems to apply this standard irrespective of the substantive standard invoked. In the following I first discuss the relevance of general principles of state responsibility relating to this issue, I then examine arbitral practice concerning damages in relation to the common 'takings' standard, and then in relation to a more general 'legitimate expectations' standard.

[288] See especially *Saudi Arabia v Aramco* (Award, 1958) 27 ILR 117, 172; and *Texaco v Libya* (Award (Merits), 1977), (1979) 53 ILR 389, para 53 et seq; but contrast *BP v Libya* (Award, 1973), (1979) 53 ILR 297, where the arbitrator chose to apply general principles of law as a separate law applicable also to determine the validity of the annulment decree.

[289] See for a general discussion, Van Harten and Loughlin, 'Investment Treaty Arbitration as a Species of Global Administrative Law' (2006) 17(1) *EJIL* 121.

[290] See also Jagusch and Duclos, 'Compensation for the Breach of Relative Standards of Treaty Protection' (2009) 10(4) *JWIT* 515.

A. General Principles

The general rule is that state responsibility entails a secondary obligation to provide reparation for the breach.[291] This means that the claimant so far as possible ought to be put in the position in which he would have been had the breach not occurred. In the celebrated dictum of the Permanent Court of International Justice in the *Chorzow Factory case*, this was chiseled out as follows:

> [R]eparation must, so far as possible wipe out the consequences of the illegal act and re-establish the situation which would, in all probability, have existed if that act had not been committed. Restitution in kind, or, if this is not possible, payment of a sum corresponding to the value which a restitution in kind would bear; the award, if need be, of damages for loss sustained which would not be covered by restitution in kind or payment in place of it—such are the principles which should serve to determine the amount of compensation due for an act contrary to international law.[292]

The statement has subsequently been applied and confirmed in numerous instances as an authoritative statement of customary law.[293] The general principle of reparation undoubtedly applies also in theory to investor-state relationships since it is largely expressive of the very concept of responsibility in law, such as it was also conceived by the PCIJ in the *Chorzow Factory case* as a general principle of law.[294] The applicability of this as a general principle of state responsibility, such as it is conceptualised in the ILC Draft Articles on State Responsibility, is nevertheless not as straightforward in this context, for several reasons. The ILC draft itself expressly limits applicability to relationships between states.[295] This does not exclude the relevance of the ILC principles as expressions of more general ideas, but also this is a proposition to be applied with caution. A crucial point is that investor-state relationships invoke different structural considerations from what applies in inter-state relationships; hence the general principles of state responsibility cannot simply be assumed to

[291] See eg for a classical statement, *Case Concerning the Factory at Chorzów (Germany v Poland)* (Jurisdiction) (Judgment, 1927) PCIJ Series B No 3 (1927) 21: 'It is a principle of international law that the breach of an engagement involves an obligation to make reparation in an adequate form. Reparation therefore is the indispensable complement of a failure to apply a convention and there is no necessity for this to be stated in the convention itself'. See also the ILC Draft Articles on Responsibility of States for Internationally Wrongful Acts, Art 31, and commentary, in Crawford, *The International Law Commission's Articles on State Responsibility* (Cambridge University Press, Cambridge, 2002) 201.

[292] *Case Concerning the Factory at Chorzów (Germany v Poland)* (Indemnity) (Judgment, 1928) PCIJ Series A No 17 (1928) 47.

[293] See the Commentary to ILC Draft Art 31 in Crawford (2002) 201.

[294] *Case Concerning the Factory at Chorzów (Germany v Poland)* (Jurisdiction) (Judgment, 1927) PCIJ Series B No 3 (1927) 21.

[295] Cf art 33(2): 'This part is without prejudice to any right, arising from the international responsibility of a State, which may accrue directly to any person or entity other than a State'.

apply, even by analogy. Some aspects of this may be pointed to already here.

Under the ILC draft, the basic principle of 'full reparation' in Article 31 is set out to require 'restitution', primarily, and only secondarily, monetary 'compensation'. The main rule envisaged by the ILC, as also hinted at in the *Chorzow Factory case*,[296] is that state responsibility requires 'restitution in kind', in so far as it is claimed and is not materially impossible or unproportionally onerous:

> A State responsible for an internationally wrongful act is under an obligation to make restitution, that is, to re-establish the situation which existed before the wrongful act was committed, provided and to the extent that restitution: (a) is not materially impossible; (b) does not involve a burden out of all proportion to the benefit deriving from restitution instead of compensation.[297]

In the context of a breach of contract this might seem to echo a claim for specific performance, and even provide a separate basis for this under international law, at least if granted by the municipal law applicable to the contract. This could for instance involve the judicial affirmation of performance obligations of the state, such as rescinding an unlawful annulment or regulation of a contract or concession, granting a licence hitherto withheld in contravention of a contractual undertaking, or reinstating the claimant in possession of property taken in violation of an express contractual promise to the contrary. However, as we shall see, the main rule in investment arbitration is that reparation involves a duty of compensation.[298] This undoubtedly has something to do with the *non ultra petita* principle in international arbitration, which excludes an award of remedies not requested by the parties.[299] Most often the requested remedy naturally is compensation. But it is also, arguably, related to more fundamental concerns connected to internal sovereignty and the very purpose of investment law as complementary to such sovereignty. The fundamental notion that public power is inalienable, which is embedded in the general right of expropriation, suggests that orders for specific performance are generally excluded in investment arbitration.[300] Certain investment treaties also positively confine jurisdiction to damages awards.[301]

[296] See above n 291.

[297] ILC Draft Art 35.

[298] 'Compensation' is held by some to pertain only to lawful acts, whereas 'damages' is reserved for unlawful acts. This is however not the way the term is used by the ILC, and in the following I use the terms largely interchangeably. For more about the terminology and potential differences in common use of these terms, see Wälde and Sabahi, 'Compensation, Damages and Valuation in International Investment Law', Report to the ILA Committee on International Law on Foreign Investment (2006).

[299] Wälde and Sabahi (2006) 6.

[300] See further below Section 6.3.

[301] See NAFTA article 1135; US Model BIT (2004) Art 34; Canada Model BIT (2004) Art 44; and see generally OECD, 'Stocktaking' (2005) 11 (chart) and 70.

This means the relevant remedy in investment arbitration in any case usually will be an award of damages. Alternatively the tribunal may issue a declaratory award,[302] or what is more practical, a partial award, leaving the amount of damages to be decided at a later stage of the proceedings.[303]

When it comes to the measure of damages, the general principle of responsibility applicable is similarly that of full reparation in Article 31. This is spelled out as follows by the ILC Draft Article 36:

> 1. The State responsible for an internationally wrongful act is under an obligation to compensate for the damage caused thereby, insofar as such damage is not made good by restitution.
>
> 2. The compensation shall cover any financially assessable damage including loss of profits insofar as it is established.

Aside from its stipulated secondary status, this fails to give any direction on what 'damage interest' the claimant may seek recovered however. While the rule sets out a specific duty to compensate for lost profits, this clearly does not imply that disregard of a contractual undertaking in breach of a substantive investment standard must necessarily and in all cases involve a duty to cover lost profits (*lucrum cessans*). The issue for consideration is in any case what injurious consequences are causally related to the relevant breach; these constitute the damage or injury for which reparation is due. This again is necessarily intimately connected to the precise content of the primary rule. The crucial element in relation to a contract is of course the reliance on the contract by the claimant and the expectations created by the contract for the claimant. If the relevant primary rule can be construed to require respect for contractual expectations in a given situation, full reparation will consist in meeting those expectations; in other words, to grant the claimant his expectation interest.[304] If, however, the primary rule only requires a state not to make undertakings it cannot or will not hold, full reparation would consist in placing the claimant in the position in which he would have been if he had not relied on the undertaking; in other words, to grant the claimant his reliance interest. No conclusive guideline is provided by the general principles of responsibility. For this it is necessary to turn to the application of the substantive standards themselves.

[302] See eg *Saudi Arabia v Aramco* (Award, 1958) 27 ILR 117; and *Texaco v Libya* (Award (Merits), 1977) 53 ILR 389.

[303] See eg *CME v Czech Republic* (Partial Award, 2001); and *Eureko v Poland* (Partial Award, 2005).

[304] See for the classical discussion of this terminology and its relation to the economic objectives of contract law in common law, Fuller and Perdue, 'The Reliance Interest in Contract Damages' (Part I) (1936) 46 *Yale Law Journal* 52, and (Part II) (1937) 46 *Yale Law Journal* 373.

B. Contractual Damages under the 'Takings' Standard

The general criterion applicable to lawful expropriation under the classical 'takings' or expropriation standard is usually a requirement of 'prompt, adequate and effective' compensation, which in practice means compensation at the measure of the full economic value of the property taken. It may in general be assumed that the same criterion applies to unlawful or indirect expropriation.[305] While this criterion in itself is clear, it may nevertheless be difficult to apply, as there is no fixed criterion for what in fact constitutes full economic or market value.[306] Moreover, the 'full compensation' criterion was subject to fierce controversy, and momentarily disavowed by the NIEO movement in the 1960s and '70s.[307] At least in the opinion of some writers, this still casts some doubts on its status as customary law.[308] These issues in the abstract will not be further discussed here. In a contemporary setting, the 'full economic value criterion' will in practice constitute the applicable rule, whatever its exact basis, actual meaning, or possible modifications in the specific case.[309] This is for two reasons. First, most investment treaties expressly set this as the relevant criterion.[310] Secondly, as I come back to, it also has a relatively consistent basis in arbitral practice applying customary law,[311] at least as a general principle subject to modifications. The subject here is the specific application of this criterion in a contractual perspective. Two angles are conceivable: one perceiving the contractual right as a species of property, the other maintaining a contractual perspective.[312] I argue that arbitral practice displays a clear leaning towards the latter.

[305] In the *Chorzow Factory case*, the PCIJ distinguished lawful from unlawful expropriation in relation to the appropriate time of valuation, considering that property lawfully taken would be subject to valuation at the time of the taking, whilst compensation for an unlawful taking should also in principle take into account subsequent gains to the state, see *Case Concerning the Factory at Chorzów (Germany v Poland)* (Indemnity) (Judgment, 1928) PCIJ Series A No 17 (1928) 47. Where the property taken is a contractual right pursuant to a state undertaking, this distinction seems without consequence, since, as I show in the following, valuation in any case here is prospective and based on the claimant's expectation interest under the contract. See generally about the distinction between lawful and unlawful takings, Shepard, 'The Distinction between Lawful and Unlawful Expropriation' paper presented at Investment Arbitration and the Energy Charter Treaty, Conference, 9–10 June 2005 Stockholm.

[306] See eg Wälde and Sabahi (2006) 21.

[307] See eg Lowenfeld (2002) 407 et seq.

[308] See eg especially Sornarajah (2004) 435 et seq; but contrast the official Commentary to Article 36 of the ILC Draft Articles on State Responsibility, para 22, in Crawford (2002) 223–4; see also the general statement of the tribunal in *CME Czech Republic BV v Czech Republic* (Final Award, 2003) para 497; and see also Brownlie (2003) 509–11.

[309] See eg Wälde and Sabahi (2006); and Reisman & Sloane, 'Indirect Expropriation and its Valuation in the BIT Generation' (2003) 74 *BYIL* 115.

[310] Wälde and Sabahi (2006) 20.

[311] Sornarajah (2004) 457 et seq.

[312] See also, Sabahi, 'The Calculation of Damages for Breach of International Investment Contracts' Report prepared under the supervision of the Hague Academy of International Law, Centre of Studies and Research (2005) 4; and Wälde, 'Remedies and Compensation in International Investment Law' (2005) 2(5) *TDM* 71–2.

(i) The Property vs Contractual Perspective

A contractual right has a dual nature. It consists in a claim on another person (a right *in personam*), but as such it may also constitute an asset (a right *in rem*). This entails two possible but contrasting perspectives on valuation. From a property perspective, full value is the sale value; in other words, the prospective 'market price' if assigned to a third party. This would seem the approach prima facie applicable from an expropriation perspective, the very application of which is justified by the perception of the contractual right as a form of property. Valuing the contract as an item of assignable wealth, this would take into account any factor external to the contract that might influence its real value. Such factors might include whether it was a good or bad bargain for the claimant, or various risk factors such as the risk of breach, and in such case, the probability of successful recovery.[313] Where the state is not party to the contract this would seem to be the standard and reasonable approach to valuation.[314] But where the state *is* a party, this approach is problematic. The most significant value-influencing factor would then be the very risk of the state's own breach or cancellation of the contract. The alternative, and contractual approach, is to base compensation on the consideration that the undertaking ought to have been performed.[315] This considers the undertaking according to its value for the investor if actually discharged, setting the standard of compensation at the investor's expectation interest as defined by the applicable principles of contract of the applicable law.

The choice of perspective is usually addressed in arbitral practice as a choice between the present asset value of the investment committed on the trust of the contract (*damnum emergens*), and the additional value of lost profits that the contract probably would have incurred for the claimant if discharged (*lucrum cessans*). Commentators have criticised this distinction, rightly objecting that asset value in a free market is determined by means of its profit making potential.[316] Obviously, the investor cannot recover both asset value calculated on this basis[317] and lost profit, as this would provide for compensation twice for the same damage.[318] However, while this makes the distinction a somewhat theoretical one in many circumstances, it still points to a basic distinction between a property perspective and a contractual perspective. Whereas the former category would limit compensation strictly to the 'asset value' of the contract at the time of taking, the latter

313 Wälde (2006) 72.
314 Cf eg the *Norwegian Shipowners Claims* (1922) I RIAA 309, 339–40.
315 Wälde (2006) 72.
316 See Reisman and Sloane (2003) 137; and Sabahi (2006) esp 16 et seq.
317 Usually by means of a so-called 'discounted cash flow' analysis, see Sabahi (2006) 14.
318 Wells, 'Double-Dipping in Arbitration Awards? An Economist Questions Damages Awarded to Kahara Bodas Company in Indonesia' (2003) 19 *Arb Int'l* 471, esp 477.

would in principle set the value at the reasonable expectation interest, independent of market value.

(ii) The Contractual Perspective in Arbitral Practice

As I show in the following, it is the latter contractual approach that generally has been adopted by tribunals in cases concerning a plain taking of contractual rights by the state as party to the same contract. We see this as a consistent tendency already in early cases decided on the basis of customary law.[319] The *Shufeldt claim* is illustrative. It concerned a straightforward formal annulment of a resource extraction concession relied on by the investor to make a considerable investment in the territory of the state. As for the principle applicable to damages, the tribunal held that '[t]he *damnum emergens* is always recoverable, but the *lucrum cessans* must be the direct fruit of the contract and not too remote or speculative'.[320] In other words, the investor could recover his reasonable expectation interest as manifested by the contract.

The proposition as adopted in the *Shufeldt claim* was not novel; it could rely on several earlier cases as precedent.[321] Prior to this case, the proposition that a breach of contract entailed a right to recover lost profits was conspicuously adopted by the tribunal in the *Delagoa Bay Railway Company* case.[322] The tribunal held that the relevant acts of the government constituted a breach of the railway concession contract, and therefore justified a contractual perspective:

> Il resulte de toutes ces considérations que la question primordiale posée plus haut doit être résolue en ce sens que le décret de rescision et la prise de possession du chemin de fer n'ont pas été opérés en conformité du contrat de

[319] See generally, Whiteman, *Damages in International Law* (US Government Printing Office, Washington DC, 1943) 1643 et seq.

[320] *Shufeldt claim* (Award, 1930) II RIAA 1079, 1099.

[321] It relied specifically on the *May case (USA v Guatemala)* (Award, 1900) XV RIAA 47–75, which it cited as follows (*Shufeldt* II RIAA 1079, 1099): 'I cannot pretend to lay down the law concerning damages in clearer words than those of the advocate of Guatemala government who uses the following language in the counterclaim: "The law of Guatemala . . . establishes like those of all civilized nations of the earth, that contracts produce reciprocal rights and obligations between the contracting parties; that whoever concludes a contract is bound not only to fulfil it but also to recoup or compensate (the other party) for damages and prejudice which result directly or indirectly from the nonfulfilment or infringement by default or fraud of the party concerned and that such compensation includes both damage suffered and profits lost: *damnum emergens et lucrum cessans*"'. See also *Martini & Co (Italy) v Venezuela* (Award, 1903), as related by Whiteman (1943) 1669, 1671: 'It is the opinion of the umpire, several times expressed, that Venezuela is not to be held responsible for speculative profits, but the profits in the present case are not entirely speculative . . . if a clear measure of damages exists with respect to future business, it may be invoked'.

[322] *Delagoa Bay Railway Company case* (Award, 1900), La Fontaine, *Pasicrisie Internationale 1794–1900: Histoire Documentaire des Arbitrages Internationaux* (Martinus Nijhoff, The Hague, 1997) 398.

concession. Il n'est dès lors pas nécessaire de spécifier la nature juridique de ces actes. Du moment qu'ils ne peuvent se justifier pas des clauses mêmes de la concession et qu'on ne peut pas dire que le concessionnaire les ait encourus en vertu même de celle-ci, il ne reste plus qu'un seul principe de droit qui puisse être appliqué à la fixation de la 'compensation' à allouer par ce tribunal; ce principe ne peut être que celui des dommages et intérets, du *id quod interest*, comprenant d'après les règles de droit universellement admises, le *damnum emergens* et le *lucrum cessans*: le préjudice éprouvé et le gain manqué.[323]

The crucial aspect of this is that the right to recovery of the *lucrum cessans* was considered a direct consequence of the breach of contract. The contract was held to constitute the benchmark of what economic prospects could reasonably be relied on to determine the present-day value of the investment. The tribunal accordingly calculated lost profits on the basis of the length of the concession and its terms of redemption, effectively measuring compensation on the basis of the claimant's expectation interest under the contract.[324]

More recent arbitral practice confirms that the crucial aspects of this approach have stood the test of a century. The case of *AMINOIL v Kuwait* provides a clear and now classical example from the early modern era of foreign investment protection. The case concerned a (lawful) nationalisation of an oil concession granted by the State of Kuwait in its infant stages, in the form of a classic concession contract including both a stabilisation clause and the usual arbitration clause. As to the applicable standard of compensation, the tribunal invoked what it conceived as the 'fundamental equilibrium' of the contract as a guiding principle:

[W]ith reference to every long-term contract, especially such as involve an important investment, there must necessarily be economic calculations, and the weighing up of rights and obligations, of chances and risks, constituting the contractual equilibrium. This equilibrium cannot be neglected—neither when it is a question of proceeding to necessary adaptations during the course of the contract, nor when it is a question of awarding compensation. It is in this fundamental equilibrium that the very essence of the contract consists.[325]

The tribunal based this on a more basic notion of legitimate expectations in the context of foreign investment.[326] Particularly, it referred to the consideration that compensation ought to be calculated 'on a basis such as to warrant the upkeep of a flow of investment in the future'.[327] In this perspective, awarding the claimant its expectation interest was not a consequence of some natural law that set this as the only real and innate

[323] *ibid*, 402.
[324] *ibid*, 403–4, and see Whiteman (1943) 1699.
[325] *AMINOIL v Kuwait* (Award, 1982), (1982) 21 ILM 976, para 148.
[326] *ibid*, paras 146–50.
[327] *ibid*, para 147.

value of the contract, but a recognition and acceptance of the objective underlying an investment contract as a particular inducement for an investor to invest.

Other cases accepting *lucrum cessans* as the appropriate measure of damages can be seen in that light. Thus in the early ICSID case of *AGIP v Congo*, a contract had been entered into between the Italian oil corporation AGIP and the state of Congo regarding a transfer of 50 per cent of the shares of AGIP's local subsidiary in Congo to the state, as a solution to the state's nationalisation policies. The state subsequently carried through a full-scale nationalisation of the company, violating a number of its contractual undertakings. The tribunal held that the company as a result had a valid claim both for the recovery of the value of its shares in the company, and for its lost profits as a result of the breach of contract.[328] Although it only awarded a nominal sum of damages for lost profits, it still set out the claimant's expectation interest as the applicable measure of damages. In *LETCO v Liberia* a forestry concession contract was similarly terminated by the government in breach of various provisions of the contract, including a stabilisation clause. The tribunal held that damages were due in principle both for the actual investment lost, and for excess loss of profit that the contract would have earned for the claimant during its stipulated time frame.[329] While this case did not concern an outright expropriation, and the tribunal awarded damages essentially on the basis of Liberian law,[330] it clearly falls into the category of an essential taking of contractual rights, confirming as such the propensity to award damages in such cases based on the claimant's expectation interest. This is also attested to by several of the more typical 'de-nationalised contract' cases and other cases ostensibly decided on the basis of a municipal law, which have not invoked international law as such.[331] Finally, it is noteworthy

[328] *AGIP SpA v Govt of the Peoples Republic of Congo* (Award, 1979) 1 ICSID Rep 306. The tribunal reasoned as follows, notably disregarding the Congolese decree expressly annulling the agreement, but nevertheless referring to what it considered the applicable law of the contract, namely French law as incorporated by the law of Congo (paras 97–8): 'The tribunal recognizes that the present case is not limited to an act of nationalization but comprises also a series of repudiations by the by the Government of its contractual obligations, which are independent from the nationalization and have already been mentioned by the Tribunal. It considers, therefore, that AGIP is justified in presenting a claim for damages. With regards to the reparation for the material losses, according to the fundamental rule in Article 1149 of the French Civil Code both the loss suffered *(damnum emergens)* and the loss of profit *(lucrum cessans)* must be taken into account'.

[329] *Liberian Eastern Timber Corporation (LETCO) v Republic of Liberia* (Award, 1986) 2 ICSID Rep 343, 369–72.

[330] *ibid*, 372, the tribunal stating this as follows: '[B]oth according to international law and, more importantly, Liberian law, LETCO is entitled to compensation for damages for both its lost investment and its foregone future investments'.

[331] See *Sapphire v NIOC* (Award, 1963) 35 ILR 136, 185–6; and for more recent expressions. *Himpurna v Persero* (Award, 1999) (2000) 25 *YbCA* 13, para 291; *Kahara Bodas Co LLC v Pertamina* (Award, 2000) para 121 et seq; and *Autopista Concesionada de Venezuela (Aucoven) v Venezuela* (Award, 2003) para 351.

that even *LIAMCO v Libya*, the reported case that perhaps has gone furthest in accommodating the principle of permanent sovereignty over natural resources, also essentially accepted the principle of recovery of lost profits on the basis of the terms and length of the concession, although ultimately subject to a softer equity standard.[332]

Against this background it is not surprising that more recent investment treaty practice also leans towards a similar contractual approach to valuation, although there is not much practice addressing this as a plain issue. In *Middle Eastern Cement v Egypt* a licence that the claimant had relied on to build and operate a cement import and storage facility was held to have been expropriated pursuant to a subsequent prohibition of imports.[333] The tribunal based compensation on the claimant's lost opportunities as a result of the prohibition; in other words, on the claimant's expectation interest under the licence.[334] The bulk of 'breach of contract' cases in an investment treaty context concern takings of investments that are not in themselves merely contractual. Property rights in an investment deprived of value by subsequent regulation may be regarded as taken precisely for the reason that the regulation constituted a breach of previous undertakings.[335] In this context compensation will naturally be measured against the whole-value of the investment. Although concerned as such with a valuation of property, this implicitly adopts a contractual perspective. The point is that the deprivation of value is the investor's expectation interest, being compensable precisely for being based on a contractual (or comparable) undertaking. The case of *CME v Czech Republic* is illustrative. The basis of the tribunal's reasoning was that the claimant was illegally deprived of its investment because the actions of the Media Council infringed 'the legal basis' of the claimant's investment, a legal basis that was essentially contractual.[336] In this regard, the contractual interest of the claimant was precisely to retain the value of its investment despite the government's regulatory actions. This may be considered the perspective implicitly adopted by the tribunal, which held that the state was obligated to compensate the claimant 'by payment of a sum corresponding to the value which a restitution in kind would bear'.[337] This, it held, was constituted by 'the fair market value of the Claimant's investment as it was before consummation of the Respondent's breach of the Treaty'.[338]

On the basis of the above scrutiny of cases, it may be concluded that arbitral practice has adopted a distinct contractual perspective to valuation

[332] *LIAMCO v Libya* (Award, 1977), (1982) 62 ILR 141, esp 212–14.

[333] *Middle East Cement Shipping and Handling Co SA v Arab Republic of Egypt* (Award, 2002) para 107.

[334] *ibid*, para 112 et seq.

[335] See further below section 6.4.

[336] *CME v Czech Republic* (Partial Award, 2001) para 591 et seq.

[337] *ibid*, para 618.

[338] *ibid*, para 618.

of rights under the expropriation standard when applied to the state's own contracts. Compensation is measured according to the claimant's expectation interest, not against a more objective 'asset value'. This reflects the underlying normative structure of contractual commitment and protection of legitimate expectations shaping the interpretation of the expropriation standard in this context. The crucial point is that where a claim in reality is based on a breach of contract, it is only natural that the claimant's reasonable (contractual) expectation also comes to constitute the measure of compensation, even though the contractual right, in principle, should only be cognisable under the standard as a kind of 'reified' asset comparable to property.

C. The Legitimate Expectation Standard applied to Damages

While the criterion of compensation pursuant to a 'taking' is clear in principle, namely full 'market value', there is usually no similarly clear criterion of damages for a breach that does not amount to a taking, such as breach of the fair and equitable treatment standard or an umbrella clause.[339] Here I argue that the tendency is to award damages according to the same parameters as under the 'takings' standard, on the basis of the claimant's contractual expectation interest, conditioned in part by the requirement, express or implicit, that the claimant must have actually relied on that expectation.

(i) Full Reparation and the Contract Interest

Not many cases have addressed directly the applicable standard of damages for contractual violations that do not amount to a direct or indirect expropriation.[340] Lacking a clear criterion of damages in the standards themselves, the relevant tribunals have relied on the *full reparation* formula of the *Chorzow Factory case*,[341] or on a similar criterion of *causality*.[342] The most important point following from this is perhaps that the level of damages depends on what is the actual and crucial element of the breach. This is illustrated by *MTD v Chile*. The tribunal based damages for breach of fair and equitable treatment on the claimant's wasted expenditure in reliance on the contractual undertakings, in other words on the claimant's reliance interest.[343] This is, however, easily explainable, and should not be taken to mean that recovery of the claimant's expectation interest in

[339] See further Jagusch and Duclos (2009) 522.
[340] Sabahi (2006) 34.
[341] *CMS Gas v Argentina* (Award, 2005) para 400; and *MTD v Chile* (Award, 2004) para 238.
[342] *SD Myers Inc v Govt of Canada* (Second Partial Award, 2002) para 140 et seq.
[343] *MTD v Chile* (Award, 2004) para 237 et seq.

general is excluded. The actual breach in this case was held to be that the claimant was induced to invest in the first place, not that the undertakings on which it had relied were breached.[344]

Other cases, in contrast, have found the claimant entitled to damages on the basis of its expectation interest, essentially putting the claimant in the position it would have been if its reasonable expectation had been fulfilled. Most specific to this effect is *CMS Gas v Argentina* where the tribunal awarded damages for a breach of fair and equitable treatment, essentially on the basis of the government's revocation of a price adjustment formula in a gas transmission contract. The tribunal held that damages had to be awarded based on the likely situation if 'the license and regulatory environment remained unchanged'.[345] The claimant was accordingly awarded damages based on a consideration of the most likely discounted cash-flow value of its shares in the company, if the licence contract had been allowed to function and had been adjusted according to its own scheme during the stipulated time period.[346] In *Occidental v Ecuador*, the tribunal similarly held that a change in the applicable tax law, which withdrew a right for the investor to obtain reimbursements of VAT, constituted a breach of the investor's legitimate expectations as protected by the fair and equitable treatment standard.[347] The claimant was accordingly awarded damages based on VAT that it had actually paid, for the reason that it had a reasonable expectation to be reimbursed for such payments.[348] Moreover, in *CME v Czech Republic*, the tribunal applied the *Chorzow factory* formula to hold that the breach of the fair and equitable treatment involved an obligation 'to make full reparation'.[349] Since the relevant breach was the 'evisceration of the arrangements' relied on by the claimant, the tribunal held that the duty to make reparation could be equiparated to 'payment of a sum corresponding to . . . the fair market value of claimant's investment as it was before consummation of the Respondent's breach of the Treaty'.[350]

This at least provides some precedence for what would also seem to be the most structurally apposite proposition in relation to the concept of legitimate expectations; that the requisite level of damages is also set by the expectation interest in question. This would perhaps seem most obvious

344 *ibid*, para 188.

345 *CMS Gas v Argentina* (Award, 2005) para 419.

346 *ibid*, para 419: '[I]n order to arrive at a value loss, it is necessary to evaluate not only what the years 2000 to 2027 would have been like had TGN's license and regulatory environment remained unchanged but also to foresee what the future holds for TGN under the new (and not completely known) regulatory environment'. This at least seem to be most reasonable interpretation in light of the tribunal's reasoning elsewhere in the award, which emphasized the possibility of regulatory change within the scheme of the contract.

347 *Occidental v Ecuador* (Award, 2004) para 181.

348 *ibid*, para 205.

349 *CME v Czech Republic* (Partial Award, 2001) para 616.

350 *ibid*, para 618.

where the contract positively is set as the benchmark of the investor's legitimate expectation by virtue of an umbrella clause. Putting the investor in the position in which he would have been had the breach not incurred, in this context, means basically to transform the content of the state's contractual responsibility under municipal law into international responsibility. However, the cases cited also suggest that this constitutes the general rule where the standard breached is that of fair and equitable treatment, if the essential perspective is that the undertaking should have been fulfilled, and not merely that it should not have been given in the first place.[351]

(ii) Reliance and the Expectation Interest

As described above, the concept of legitimate expectations as applied by investment arbitral tribunals does not mean that contractual expectations are protected as such. As I have argued, the key factor is whether the investor has actually relied on the undertaking; contractual rights relating to investments are protected essentially because they have been relied on. In this section I argue that we see this also in relation to damages. Specifically, it is reflected in the reluctance of tribunals to award the claimant lost profits (*lucrum cessans*) that are merely 'speculative'.[352] Such lost profits, or the 'benefit of the bargain', is but another word for the claimant's reasonable expectation interests under a contract. On scrutiny, it may appear that the scepticism towards 'speculative' profits really converges with a potential inhibition in practice against awarding damages for 'naked' expectations, ie expectations not relied on.

The alleged rule excluding recovery of speculative profits is sometimes attributed to the *Shufeldt claim*, where the tribunal held that 'the *lucrum cessans* must be the direct fruit of the contract and not too remote or speculative'.[353] It seems clear that the tribunal here envisaged this essentially as a rule of remoteness and foreseeability, as it immediately subsequently qualified the criterion to require essentially that the loss should 'reasonably be supposed to have been in the contemplation of both parties as the probable result of the breach of it'.[354] At the same time, that case was

[351] See also, at least implicitly to this effect, *Tecmed v Mexico* (Award, 2003) para 188; and *Metalclad v Mexico* (Award, 2000) para 113; but contrast also *SD Myers v Canada* (Second Partial Award, 2002) paras 154–60. The latter tribunal rejected a contractual perspective as the most apposite analogy for the criterion of *causation* related to the compensation standard, invoking instead a comparison to the law of tort and delict.

[352] See eg *SPP v Egypt* (Award (ICC), 1983) 3 ICSID Rep 46; *Asian Agricultural Products Ltd (AAPL) v Democratic Socialist Republic of Sri Lanka* (Award, 1990) 4 ICSID Reports 245; *Metalclad v Mexico* (Award, 2000); *SARL Benvenuti & Bonfant v People's Republic of the Congo* (Award, 1979); and *Societe Ouest Africaine des Betons Industriel (SOABI) v Senegal* (Award, 1988).

[353] *Shufeldt claim* (Award, 1930) II RIAA 1079, 1099.

[354] *ibid*, 1099.

clearly an instance of a contract that had been relied on to commit a substantial investment for several years. Moreover, it is telling that this has been the case in nearly all cases where *lucrum cessans* have in fact been awarded as discussed above. Most interesting are nevertheless the few cases where this has actually been put to the test, and the 'benefit of the bargain' essentially has been claimed on the basis of a naked expectation. Two recent cases in particular are illustrating.

First, in *Himpurna v Persero*, as previously referred to, the claimant made a massive claim for lost profits on the basis of an energy sales contract, which obligated the state-owned company to buy electricity at fixed rates for a future period of 30 years. Based on notions of good faith and abuse of rights, the tribunal essentially held that the claimant could only recover lost profits on the basis of the contract for investments actually made.[355] The tribunal was clearly compelled towards this reasoning by the specific circumstances of the case, and especially the unfairness of the alternative, which was to award the claimant, from the treasury of a near bankrupt state, a return of, allegedly, more than US$2 billion on an investment of a little over US$300 million.[356] In relation to the general principle applicable, the tribunal actually stated that 'damages for the loss of a bargain may in principle be granted even when the victim of a breach has not yet incurred significant costs'.[357] However, more significantly, the tribunal then went on to justify its own applied exception to that principle in more general terms. It first referred to the particular function in which PLN (Persero) was acting when making the contract, emphasising its non-commercial and public purpose as 'an arm of governmental policy acting in pursuit of the public welfare'.[358] It then went on to justify the right to recover lost profits more narrowly than in an ordinary private contractual context, introducing to this effect the concept of *unjust enrichment*, borrowed from the early *Lena Goldfields case*,[359] as an underlying moderating rationale:

[355] *Himpurna v Persero* (Award, 1999), (2000) 25 *YbCA* 13, para 315 et seq, see especially para 330: '[I]t would be intolerable in the present case to uphold claims for lost profits from investments not yet incurred'; and para 343: 'To seek to apply [the contract] so as to permit the claimant to reap pure profit by reference to hypothetical future initiatives in pursuit of an agreement which has become an instrument of oppression would be like stepping on the shoulders of a drowning man. The Arbitral Tribunal finds that it would be insufferable and therefore an abuse of rights'.

[356] *ibid*, para 318: 'In such circumstances, it strikes the Arbitral Tribunal as unacceptable to assess lost profits as though claimant had an unfettered right to create ever-increasing losses for the State of Indonesia (and its people) by generating energy without regard to whether or not PLN had any use for it;'

[357] *ibid*, para 317.

[358] *ibid*, para 331: 'In reaching this conclusion, the Arbitral Tribunal is mindful of the status of PLN as an arm of governmental policy acting in pursuit of the public welfare. The [contract] itself was not directed to the narrow ends of profitable trading but must be seen, in the words of the *Aminoil* award, as "one of the essential instruments in the economic and social progress of a national community in full process of development"'.

[359] *Lena Goldfields Ltd v Soviet Union*, as reprinted in Nussbaum, 'The Arbitration between the Lena Goldfields, Ltd. and the Soviet Government' (1950–51) 36 *Cornell Law Quarterly* 31, 51.

> Although it is certainly true that the primary goal of monetary compensation in international arbitration is to make the victim whole rather than to prevent unjust enrichment, it seems justified to conclude that the prospect of unjust enrichment buttresses a claim for lost profits . . . whereas its absence has a moderating effect.[360]

Significantly, this meant the tribunal primarily confined the right to recover lost profits to situations where the breach of contract simultaneously constituted an appropriation by the state of expected future returns.[361]

The second and more recent case of *Aucoven v Venezuela* equally suggests how the customary reluctance to grant lost profits for hypothetical future investment represents a more fundamental concern. The case concerned an investment in a super-highway system in Venezuela, where the investor was to build and maintain a new viaduct on the highway system. The conditions of the investment were set down in an investment contract, promising a minimum return on the investment for a certain stipulated time period. Subsequently however, the investment was abandoned by the government; the viaduct was never built and no part of the substantial investment envisaged by the contract was made. The investor nevertheless brought a claim for damages based inter alia on its expected return on that investment. This was rejected by the tribunal, partly on the basis of an interpretation of the contract, but with a parallel argument based on international law.[362] The tribunal cited several ICSID decisions and inferred as a general characteristic that 'ICSID tribunals are reluctant to award lost profits for a beginning industry and unperformed work'.[363] On this basis it refused to grant recovery of expected returns on future investments;[364] moreover, it would seem, even if the probability of such returns could have been established with sufficient certainty.[365] The tribunal thus seemingly went even further in terms of principle than the *Himpurna* tribunal, stating as a quite general proposition that recovery of future profits would be limited to investments already made.[366] A particularly interesting aspect of the tribunal's reasoning in this respect is its more restrictive interpretation of two cases that have sometimes been held to reflect a liberal approach to the recovery of lost profits, the *Kahara Bodas*

[360] *Himpurna v Persero* (Award, 1999), (2000) 25 *YbCA* 13, para 342.

[361] *ibid*, para 338 et seq, the tribunal also relied on the following cases where recovery of lost profits was denied or substantially reduced to support this proposition; *SPP v Egypt* (Award, 1992); *SOABI v Senegal* (Award, 1988); and *AAPL v Sri Lanka* (Award, 1990).

[362] *Autopista Concesionada de Venezuela CA (Aucoven) v Republic of Venezuela* (Award, 2003) para 357.

[363] *ibid*, para 360.

[364] *ibid*, para 362.

[365] This would at least seem to be the implicit assumption of para 263.

[366] This tribunal also referred to the following cases as reluctant to 'speculative profits', in support of its more general proposition; *SPP v Egypt* (ICC Arbitration, 1983) 3 ICSID Rep 46; *AAPL v Sri Lanka* (Award, 1990) 4 ICSID Reports 245; *Metalclad v Mexico* (Award, 2000); *SARL Benvenuti & Bonfant v Congo* (Award, 1979); and SOABI v Senegal (Award, 1988).

and *Delagoa Bay Railway Company* cases.[367] It specifically referred to the fact that in both these cases the substantial part of the envisaged investment had been committed.[368]

While merely implicit, it is possible to consider this a crucial element of the applied rationale in the cases, suggesting precisely the application of a more flexible reliance standard in relation to damages. While lost profits in both cases were awarded on the basis of the envisaged investment as a whole, this expectation of profit could nevertheless be construed as an integral part of the reasonable expectation interest connected to the investment actually made. In other words, the requisite criterion of damages would not be what exact profits might be expected on the investment actually made, but what reasonable expectations the investor substantially relied on when making that investment. This suggests, in other words, a right to recover the expectation interest on the basis of a criterion of reliance, fundamentally buttressed by a concept of unjust enrichment. It may then also be asked, however, why it is that, if the crucial criterion is reliance, and it is, at least partly, justified by a concern to prevent unjust enrichment, it is not the claimant's reliance interest or restitution interest that should provide the requisite standard of damages. The answer is that a contractual perspective provides the only adequate protection of trust, conceived as a means to promote investment. In the *Himpurna* case, the rationale of an investor's right to recover 'the benefit of its bargain' in this context was explained compellingly as follows:

> [I]f recovery were limited to what a claimant has spent in reliance on a contract which has been breached, an incentive would be created which is contrary to contractual morality: obligors would generally find it in their interest to breach contracts which turn out to be valuable to their co-contractant. Parties do not enter into contracts involving risk in order to be repaid their costs. To limit the recovery of the victim of a breach to its actual expenditures is to transform it into a lender, which is commercially intolerable when that party was at full risk for the amount of investments made on the strength of the contract.[369]

The tribunal here justified the application of what it termed a 'contractual morality' in the investment field on the basis of a need to protect the function of contracts as incentives to invest. One might, in contrast, envisage a standard that only allowed investors recovery of their actual

[367] *Kahara Bodas v Pertamina* (Award, 2000); Delagoa Bay Railway Company case (Award, 1900), La Fontaine (1997) 398.

[368] *Aucoven v Venezuela* (Award, 2003) para 361: 'It bears emphasizing that the cases cited by Aucoven to support the proposition that "where future cash flows could reasonably be determined, tribunals have awarded lost profits even if the project had been only in its initial state" deal with fact situations in which a substantial part of the project had been realized. Specifically, the claimant in Kahara Bodas had invested US$ 93 million by the time the breach occurred and the claimant in Delagoa Bay had already completed 82 kilometers out of a total of a 90 kilometer railway project'.

[369] *Himpurna v Persero* (Award, 1999), (2000) 25 *YbCA* 13, para 291.

loss, ie the initial investment. This would provide an actual incentive for the state to breach its commitments, as a successful investment having gained in value could be appropriated by the state at initial cost value. To this effect it would provide a corresponding disincentive for investors to invest. The investor would effectively bear all commercial risks connected with the investment, without any certainty of being able to reap the commensurate returns. In other words, it would turn the investor into 'a lender', with no recognition and protection of its incentive to invest.

This shows how two essential elements can be seen to underpin, justify and moderate a contractual perspective on compensation, such that its rationale is largely embedded in and structured by practice itself. First, it preserves and ensures the character of state undertakings and specific expectations as *reliable* incentives for individual investors to invest and set up a commercial enterprise irrespective of the political risk element. Secondly, however, it also prevents unjustified enrichment of a state, in that it cannot appropriate an initial investment made into a profitable business without answering for the reasonable expectations initially relied on by the investor when the investment was made. This elemental rationale also contains its own limitation. Where no investment has been made, no enrichment is gained by the state and no actual trust is broken. This is reflected in practice, which generally refuses recovery for a naked expectation of profit pursuant to a promise not actually relied on. Where a particular undertaking has been relied on, by contrast, the particular risk element inherent in foreign investment is actualised and the consequent rationale of contractual commitment is invoked.

6

Contractual Restriction of Public Powers

6.1 SOVEREIGNTY AND COMMITMENT

TO CONTRACT WITH a state is to contract with a sovereign, with all the implications this has for the foreign investor in terms of structural inferiority and political risk . The reverse side of this is the state contracting away its sovereignty, which carries its own fundamental risk on the part of the state. The state may find that it needs to change its mind, and perhaps legitimately so. This dilemma lies at the heart of specific doctrines under municipal law relating to government contracts, in some countries considered part of administrative law with extended privileges for the state.[1] The separate response of international law to the same dilemma cannot escape being shaped by the way in which sovereignty itself is conceived under international law. Sovereignty is a fundamental concept of international law, separate and distinct from its municipal law counterpart.[2] Whereas under municipal law a concept of (democratic) sovereignty may constitute a unitary ideological justification underpinning the legal system as such, the comparable concept in international law is fundamentally schizophrenic, being in a sense both the basis and subject of a legal system composed of and concerned with co-sovereigns.[3]

[1] See generally Turpin, 'Public Contracts' in K Zweigert and K Drobnig (eds), *International Encyclopedia of Comparative Law* (Mohr Siebeck & Martinus Nijhoff, 1982), and see Rivero and Walline, *Droit Administratif* (Paris, 1998) 122: 'Le contrat privé met en contact deux volontés *autonomes*, libres, dans le cadre de la loi, de choisir les buts et les modalités de leur accord. Or la volonté de l'administration n'est jamais entièrement libre; l'intérêt général lui interdit de recourir au procédé contractuel pour l'exercice des attributions inhérentes à la souveraineté de l'État'.

[2] See eg *Antoine Goetz v Burundi* (Award, 1999) para 65: 'l'obligation pour la République du Burundi de respecter non seulement son droit national, mais aussi les dispositions de la Convention qu'elle a conclue avec l'Union belgo-luxembourgeoise, n'est pas autre chose que l'expression de sa souveraineté étatique au plein sens du terme'.

[3] This is a central aspect of Koskenniemi's structural critique of international legal argument, which has provided some inspiration for this chapter, see Koskenniemi, *From Apology to Utopia: The Structure of International Legal Argument (Reissue with new Epilogue)* (Cambridge University Press, Cambridge, 2006) especially 224–302.

A central objective of the book so far has been to flesh out the structural impact on the law of a perceived need for states, as sovereigns, to be able to commit definitively in order to attract capital and knowledge in a world of co-sovereignties, all of which are competing for the same uncommitted flow of capital. In this chapter I show how this concern is also tempered by an opposite structural component, namely the need to conceptualise sovereignty as a value-intensive function concerned with the exercise of power to manage public interests. The chapter may seem comparatively short. This may reflect the emphasis of the law and practice in this field on commitment and preservation of the status quo, as opposed to a focus on the more general legitimacy of public governance known from other fields.[4] This again is related to the purpose of investment arbitration as a remedy directed against change of policy and political risk in the face of specific undertakings. But this does not prevent law and practice in this field being increasingly shaped by a concern to defend the central functions of government against the demands of economic interests of preserving the status quo.[5]

In the following I first address the concept of sovereignty itself, as, in a way, the basic 'constitution' of international law, and therefore the concept theoretically and structurally underpinning investment arbitration. I argue however that this fundamental concept lacks clear normative import as a basis for internal authority, being perceived variably as both freedom of authority at any given time and as capacity to commit, the result of this being a lack of any similarly strong and confident response by international law to sovereign contracting as that provided by municipal legal doctrines (section 6.2). I then turn to the more specific principle of permanent sovereignty over natural resources, which I argue has emerged to reflect the concern of protecting internal authority, and to constitute an embryonic 'constitutional principle' preserving a certain core inalienability of public power in relation to sovereign contracting.[6] I particularly show how this in relation to state contracts has found a specific application in relation to stabilization clauses (section 6.3). In the

[4] See eg in relation to human rights, Delmas-Marty and Soulier, 'Restraining or Legitimating the Reason of State' in Delmas-Marty (ed), *The European Convention for the Protection of Human Rights: International Protection versus National Restrictions* (Martinus Nijhoff, Dordrecht, 1992) 7, and see especially, in the same collection, Delmas-Marty, 'The Richness of Underlying Legal Reasoning' (*ibid*) 319, 322 et seq; see also Emberland, *The Human Rights of Companies* (Oxford University Press, Oxford, 2006) 155, and especially at 188 et seq.

[5] There is not yet much literature on this, but see for recent contributions discussing various legal responses to these concerns eg Newcombe, 'The Boundaries of Regulatory Expropriation' (2005) 20(1) *ICSID Rev-FILJ* 1; and Wälde and Kolo, 'Environmental Regulation, Investment Protection and 'Regulatory Taking' in International Law' (2001) 50 *ICLQ* 811; and see also Paasivirta, 'Internationalization and Stabilization of Contracts versus State Sovereignty' (1989) 60 *BYIL* 315, especially 331 et seq; and Schrijver, *Sovereignty over Natural Resources* (Cambridge University Press, Cambridge, 1997), especially 278 and 285 et seq.

[6] See also Schrijver (1997) 285 et seq.

next section, I then examine the emerging concept of a right to regulate foreign investment. I examine how arbitral practice has relied on a concept of 'police powers', providing on the one hand a wide margin of appreciation for the state to enact changed policies according to its political discretion, but conditioned on the other hand by a notion of legitimate expectations where a distinct commitment has been made in respect of an individual investor or investment (section 6.4). Finally, I go on to examine the response of arbitral practice to interpretation of commitments restricting public power, discussing both how a notion of reserved powers has gained acceptance in arbitral practice and how a notion of changed circumstances may impact on such commitments (section 6.5).

6.2 THE NOTION OF SOVEREIGNTY

Sovereignty denotes the central characteristic of the international legal order, namely the independence of states from central authority, and the consequent repository of legal authority in individual states.[7] This does not detract from the fact that sovereignty is problematic, paradoxical and fundamentally ambiguous as a normative concept.[8] Its central role and importance is probably even the cause of this. The reason is that sovereignty signifies several functions, it being the denominator of respectively the ability of a state to commit itself to international obligations and create international law,[9] the characteristics of the state as a subject of international law,[10] and its function of constituting a government and the authority over a distinct territory and people.[11]

[7] Brownlie, *Principles of International Law* (Oxford University Press, Oxford, 2003) 287.

[8] See eg poignantly Henkin, *International Law: Politics and Values* (Martinus Nijhoff, Dordrecht, 1995), writing about 'the mythology of sovereignty' in international law (at 8): 'States are commonly described as sovereign, and sovereignty is commonly noted as an implicit, axiomatic characteristic of statehood. The pervasiveness of that term is unfortunate, rooted in mistake, unfortunate mistake. Sovereignty is a bad word, not only because it has served terrible national mythologies; in international relations, and even in international law, it is often a catchword, a substitute for thinking and precision. It means many things, some essential, some insignificant; some agreed, some controversial; some that are warranted and should not be accepted'.

[9] As it was expressed eg in the *Case of the SS 'Wimbledon'* (1923) PCIJ Series A No 1, 25: '[T]he right of entering into international engagements is an attribute of State Sovereignty'.

[10] See eg the classical position of the ICJ in *Reparation for Injuries suffered in the Service of the United Nations* (Advisory Opinion), [1949] ICJ Rep 174, 177: '[A] State can bring an international claim against another State. Such a claim takes the form of a claim between two political entities, equal in law, similar in form, and both the direct subjects of international law', and (at 180): '[A] State possesses the totality of international rights and duties recognized by international law'.

[11] See eg the *Island of Palmas case (Netherlands v USA)* (Award, 1928), 2 RIAA 829: 'Sovereignty in the relations between States signifies independence. Independence in regard to a portion of the globe is the right to exercise therein, to the exclusion of any other State, the functions of a State'.

Applied to contractual commitment, the problematic aspect of drawing meaningful normative consequences from sovereignty is that the ability to commit is, necessarily, always both a restriction and a manifestation of sovereignty.[12] This has nevertheless not prevented doctrine and practice from drawing such consequences. Indeed, this contradiction can be held to underlie the traditional controversy over internationalisation of state contracts, broached several times already by this book. The controversy revolves around the difficult substantive issue underlying the book as a whole, but posits it as a question mainly of applicability, in other words whether a state can become bound by making a solemn commitment that is expressly made subject to international law. As already alluded to, this has received two contradictory responses in international legal doctrine. One focuses on sovereignty as capacity and autonomy under international law, the other on sovereignty as fundamentally absolute and inalienable in relation to individuals.

The first response can be denoted the *Wimbledon* approach, after the famous judgment of the PCIJ by that name. The court here made the following much quoted statement on sovereignty as the fundamental ability to commit under international law:

> The court declines to see in the conclusion of any Treaty by which a State undertakes to perform or refrain from performing a particular act an abandonment of its sovereignty . . . [T]he right of entering into international engagements is an attribute of State Sovereignty.[13]

This exact proposition was relied on in *Texaco v Libya*, to suggest that sovereignty did not pose a problem for direct contractual commitment under international law in relation to the company.[14] Indeed, sovereignty

[12] Koskenniemi (2006) emphasises this fundamental duality of sovereignty as a central aspect of its ambiguity (244–5): 'From one perspective, undertaking obligations seems a limitation of the state's "sole right of decision" and in this sense its independence and sovereignty. From another perspective, the capacity to enter into such binding arrangements seems one without which a State could hardly be said to be truly sovereign at all. By arguing in this way, however, no solution can be found. The very problem-setting seems as frustrating as the little boys' dispute about whether God Almighty can create a stone so big He Himself cannot lift it up'.

[13] *Case of the SS 'Wimbledon'* (1923) PCIJ Series A No 1, 25.

[14] *Texaco Overseas Petroleum Co v Libyan Arab Republic* (Award (Merits) 1977) 53 ILR 389. See also *Saudi Arabia v Arab American Oil Co (Aramco)* (Award, 1958) 27 ILR 117, 168: 'By reason of its very sovereignty within its territorial domain, the State possesses the legal power to grant rights which it forbids itself to withdraw before the end of the Concession, with the reservation of the Clauses of the Concession Agreement relating to its revocation. Nothing can prevent a State in the exercise of its sovereignty, from binding itself irrevocably by the provisions of a Concession and from granting to the concessionaire irretractable rights'. A similar view was set forth by the sole arbitrator in ICC Case No 2321 (Preliminary Award, 1974), (1976) 1 *YbCA* 133, 134: 'I must admit that I have found some difficulties to follow a line of reasoning that a State, just because of its supreme position and qualities, should be unable to give a binding promise. The principle of *pacta sunt servanda* is generally acknowledged in international law and it is difficult to see any reason why it should not apply here. A sovereign State must be sovereign enough to make a binding promise both under international law and municipal law'. See also Koskenniemi (2006) 244.

was the fundamental premise by virtue of which such commitment was possible:

> The right of a State to undertake commitments under a treaty concluded with another State is unquestionable; this has always been recognised by international case law, in particular by the Permanent Court of International Justice in its judgment in the Wimbledon case . . . This observation has logically the same scope and significance in the case of an agreement entered into by a given State with a foreign private company . . . Under these two assumptions, the State, by entering into an international agreement with any partner whatsoever, exercises its sovereignty whenever the State is not subject to duress and where the State has freely committed itself through an untainted consent.[15]

This approach focuses, in short, on a normative conception of sovereignty as external autonomy.[16]

The opposite response adopts an equally normative conception of sovereignty, but seeing it instead fundamentally as independence and the unique repository of original authority over a given territory.[17] In relation to foreign investment, this approach typically finds its normative basis in ideas about sovereignty as *empowerment*, springing from the collective needs and acquiescence of the people over which power is exercised.[18] The best example of this position is the series of UN General Assembly Resolutions propounding a New International Economic Order in the 1970s.[19] This movement essentially sought to develop a notion of *absolute inalienability* as the main characteristic of sovereignty in the internal sphere. It posited internal economic sovereignty as a kind of reserved domain, an inherent authority over foreign investments and concessionary rights, unaffected by international commitment, by virtue of a kind of *jus cogens* character.[20] In practical terms, the material aspect was a supposed inalienable right to expropriate foreign owned enterprises and

[15] *Texaco v Libya* (Award (Merits) 1977) 53 ILR 389, paras 66–7.

[16] See especially Leben, 'La Théorie du Contrat d'État et l'Évolution du Droit International des Investissements' (2003-II) 302 *Recueil des Cours* 197, eg 329.

[17] As a classical contrast to its earlier Wimbledon approach another decision of the PCIJ may be cited for an example of this approach, see the *Austro-German Customs Union Case (Advisory Opinion)*, (1931) PCIJ Series A/B No 41, 36, 45: '[t]he independence of Austria, according to Article 88 of the Treaty of Saint-Germain, must be understood to mean the continued existence of Austria within her present frontiers as a separate State with sole right of decision in all matters economic, political, financial or other with the result that that independence is violated, as soon as there is any violation thereof, either in the economic, political, or any other field, these different aspects of independence being in practice one and indivisible'.

[18] This is one of the fundamental ideas behind the Human Rights system of the UN. It is set out in common article 1 of the International Covenants on Civil and Political Rights (1966), and Economic, Social and Cultural Rights (1966), see further below section 6.3.

[19] See in particular the Charter of Economic Rights and Duties of States from 1974 UNGA Res 3281 (XXIX), as well as UNGA Res 3171 (XXVIII) from 1973, and see generally, eg Brownlie, 'Legal Status of Natural Resources in International Law (Some Aspects)' (1979-I) 162 *Recueil des Cours* 245; and below Section 6.3.

[20] Brownlie (1979) 269–70.

concessions, that is, irrespective of contractual obligations to the contrary.[21] The position was set out as follows by a former president of the International Court of Justice:

> Contemporary international law recognizes the right of every State to nationalize foreign-owned property, even if a predecessor State or a previous government engaged itself, by treaty or by contract, not to do so. This is a corollary of the principle of permanent sovereignty of a State over all its wealth, natural resources and economic activities . . . The description of this sovereignty as *permanent* signifies that the territorial State can never lose its legal capacity to change the destination or method of exploitation of those resources, whatever arrangements have been made for their exploitation and administration.[22]

As the response and antidote to a sole focus on sovereignty as autonomy, this approach instead adopts a perspective on sovereignty as inalienable empowerment.

A crucial feature of both these perspectives is that they seem to preempt discussion, and point to a ready-made conclusion. It is close to absurd to hold that a state should not have the capacity to undertake private commitments. No state would then be able to engage in trade, borrow money in the marketplaces of the world, or instill trust in foreign investors to attract business. But it is equally problematic to hold that a state can contract away, or restrict unlimitedly, its sovereign powers by contracts with private persons and entities. A government could then theoretically subject huge tracts of territory, for an indefinite period of time, to individuals or corporations acting as feudal lords to people inhabiting that territory.[23] No government of any state can legitimately make that decision for the people it represents (or purports to represent). Both angles thus contain an important perspective. The problem is that the absolutism of sovereignty would seem to require that it is either/or, and both at the same time. From an absolutist perception of sovereignty, the perspectives seem mutually exclusive. Either a state has capacity to contract, or it has inalienable freedom of authority. It cannot have both. If the state has freedom to contract, it can make any contract it wants. If the state has inalienable freedom of power, it cannot contract it away in any part.

A reconciliation of these perspectives thus requires abandoning the notions of absolute freedom and autonomy. It is telling that both the positions related above give up the seemingly absolute claim of their initial stance, and in practice end up not too far apart. To adopt permanent,

[21] Sornarajah, *The International Law on Foreign Investment* (Oxford, 2004) 223.

[22] Jimenez de Aréchaga, 'International Law in the Past Third of a Century (General Course in Public International Law)' (1978-I) 159 *Recueil des Cours* 1, 297.

[23] A government may of course cede part of its territory, but then original authority and consequent accountability follows the cession and is conferred on the cessionary, see about this notion of permanent sovereignty as something attached to territory, Abi-Saab, 'Permanent Sovereignty over Natural Resources and Economic Activity' in Bedjaoui (ed), *International Law: Achievements and Prospects* (Paris (UNESCO), 1991) 597, esp 602 (para 25).

inalienable sovereignty as one's initial position does not exclude that the state may have a duty to pay compensation.[24] Conversely, to adopt commitment as one's initial position and starting point does not exclude a core-element of sovereignty which cannot be contracted away.[25] The problem is that this abandonment of the initial position undermines the seemingly confident normative significance drawn from that position in the first place.[26] The issue becomes one involving a balancing of policies and interests, or requiring a mere 'recourse to equity', where the formal concept of sovereignty in itself does not give any substantial direction.[27] This brings out the substantive question involved. In terms of policy and values, a government's repudiation of a contractual undertaking involves choosing between contractual stability and the regulatory need. This is a values-conflict with internal authority standing against contractual stability and predictability. However, to approach this in terms of law, and since sovereignty in itself does not resolve this conflict, we need a conceptual structure within or beneath sovereignty which conceptualises the normative significance of these values. While contractual stability and predictability are conceptualised as prerequisites of investment protection, as shown above, this does not necessarily mean that any and all contractual undertakings should necessarily be immune from regulation and government modification. The point here is that this requires a conceptualisation of internal authority as a value or function resisting restriction. If the normative rationale of internal sovereignty is left out of the equation in respect of a conflict pitting private rights against regulatory interests, there would seem to be no rational explanation for any government interference with established private rights.

[24] See eg, on the one hand, Jimenez de Aréchaga (1978) 307, after first having held that a stabilisation clause cannot 'deprive the host State of the power to put an end to the concession', he continues as follows on their purported legal significance: 'This does not mean that such stabilization clauses have no legal effect and may be considered as unwritten. An anticipated cancellation in violation of a contractual stipulation of such a nature would give right to a special right of compensation; the amount of indemnity would have to be much higher than in normal cases since the existence of such a clause constitutes a most pertinent circumstance which must be taken into account in determining the appropriate compensation. For instance, there would be a duty to compensate also for the prospective gains *(lucrum cessans)* to be obtained by the private party during the period that the concession still has to run'.

[25] See *Texaco v Libya* (Award (Merits), 1977) para 77. After having admitted the possibility of a core *jus cogens* element of permanent sovereignty as justification for repudiation, the tribunal reconciled such a potential basis of repudiation with the binding character of the concession contract in question as follows: 'It could only be a justification in those cases where a Government resorted to nationalization procedures in order to retract an effective alienation of its sovereignty, to which it or one of its predecessors had agreed. But this is not—or at least this is not necessarily—the significance of a petroleum concession. Particularly, when, as in the instant case, the State granting the concession has recognized in concession holders only rights limited in their scope and duration. The notion of permanent sovereignty can be completely reconciled with the conclusion by a State of agreements which leave to that State control of the activities of the other contracting party'.

[26] See Koskenniemi (2006) 245.

[27] *ibid*, 258 et seq.

6.3 PERMANENT SOVEREIGNTY AND THE RIGHT TO EXPROPRIATE FOREIGN INVESTMENT

A core element of a functional notion of government power, as usually conceived in municipal law, is its inalienability. It is not a private good, which may be traded as a commodity by the state, but a capacity bestowed on the government to defend and manage the interests of all. As shown above, the all-inclusive and ambiguous notion of sovereignty under international law proves a difficult basis upon which to structure a similar, conclusive response under international law. The embryo of a comparable functional-normative response is, however, provided by the principle of permanent sovereignty over natural resources. As the economic complement of a broader principle of self-determination,[28] this now forms an established part of general customary international law although the progress towards a relative consensus has been somewhat controversial, and the exact content of the principle remains debatable.[29] In the following I show how the principle of permanent sovereignty retains a core element of inalienability, which, applied in the specific context of foreign investment and foreign economic dominance over natural resources, provides a significant value-rationale for the undoubted right of states to expropriate foreign investment.[30] After discussing the general notion of permanent sovereignty and its basic rationale, I examine its impact on the right to expropriate foreign investment, before briefly discussing the principle as a possible basis for invalidation of contracts in exceptional cases.

A. A Core Concept of Inalienability

The best expression of the principle of permanent sovereignty, as a contemporary manifestation of customary law in relation to investment, is probably the 'compromise' Resolution 1803, adopted by the General

[28] See Brownlie (1979) 255 et seq; and Abi-Saab (1991) 597.

[29] The legal notion of permanent sovereignty over natural resources stands as the surviving end-result of the movement for a so-called 'New International Economic Order' (NIEO) in the 1960s and '70s. In short, this began with the widely accepted resolution 1803 on Permanent Sovereignty over Natural Resources, which was adopted by the UN General Assembly in 1962, and culminated with the adoption by the UN General Assembly, against the votes of most developed states, of a set of highly normative GA resolutions on national sovereignty over natural resources. The high point of this was the adoption of the so called Charter of Economic Rights and Duties of States in 1974 (GA Res 3281 (XXIX)), which sought to virtually exclude investment disputes from the domain of international law by, inter alia, subjecting the conditions of a legitimate taking, including payment of compensation, entirely to the discretion of the host state, and limit potential claims of investors to its courts. See further eg Lowenfeld (2002) 407 et seq.

[30] See also Brownlie (2003) 518.

Assembly in 1962, on 'Permanent Sovereignty over Natural Resources'.[31] While the lasting impact of the subsequent NIEO movement may have been less than it seemed at the time,[32] it at least served to strengthen and confirm the value rationale of the core principle of permanent sovereignty over natural resources,[33] accepted by developed and developing countries alike in the first resolution from 1962.

As to the content of the principle, it is best revealed by the 'consideranda' (preambular recitals) and subsequent stipulations of Resolution 1803. In the first consideranda it referred to 'the inalienable right of all States freely to dispose of their natural wealth and resources in accordance with their national interests'. It then clarified further the underlying rationale of this by setting out an apparent duty for governments:

> The right of peoples and nations to permanent sovereignty over their natural wealth and resources must be exercised in the interest of their national development and of the well-being of the people of the State concerned.[34]

In other words, the resolution envisaged a concept of internal power and authority conditioned by a notion of collective interest. This provides a value-rationale for perceiving internal authority as inalienable, which approaches the comparable concept in municipal constitutional and administrative law.

The notion of inalienability is further connected to the perception of permanent sovereignty as a fundamental human right. This is enshrined in common article 1 of the UN Conventions on Civil and Political Rights, and Economic Cultural and Social Rights:

> All peoples may, for their own ends, freely dispose of their natural wealth and resources without prejudice to any obligations arising out of international economic co-operation based upon the principle of mutual benefit, and international law. In no case may a people be deprived of its means of subsistence.[35]

The Human Rights formulation of the principle emphasises the collective interest element further, by connecting permanency to 'peoples' and not to

[31] UNGA Res 1803 (XVII) 14 December 1962 UN doc A/RES/1803 (XVII) (1962), the resolution was adopted by 87 votes to 2 (France and South Africa), with 12 abstentions (The Soviet-socialist block). In parts it was later widely confirmed in practice as an expression of customary law, see especially *Texaco v Libya* (Award (Merits), 1977) 53 ILR 389, 491–2; *Libyan American Oil Co (LIAMCO) v Libyan Arab Republic* (Award, 1977) 62 ILR 141, 188–9; *American Independent Oil Co (AMINOIL) v State of Kuwait* (Award, 1982), (1982) 21 ILM 976, para 90; *Revere Copper and Brass Inc v Overseas Private Investment Corp (OPIC)* (Award, 1978) 56 ILR 258, 279; see also Abi-Saab (1991) 601, and Lowenfeld (2002) 410.

[32] Lowenfeld (2002) 413, and Brownlie (2003) 517–19.

[33] See eg *LIAMCO v Libya* (Award, 1977) 62 ILR 141, 189.

[34] UNGA Res 1803 (XVII) para 1.

[35] International Covenant on Economic, Social and Cultural Rights (adopted by UN GA Res 2200A of 16 December 1966, entered into force 3 January 1976); International Covenant on Civil and Political Rights (adopted by UN GA Res 2200A of 16 December 1966, entered into force 23 March 1976) Art 1, para 2.

states,[36] reflecting the deep-structure and complexity of the principle. It cannot merely be thought of in terms of entitlement or right for the government to govern and control, but encompasses duties incumbent on governments towards their people. This complexity infuses territorial sovereignty with a deep-structure of value-intensive normativity, at the core of which is the fundamental notion that the authority to control and manage the 'means of subsistence' of peoples is inseparable from the interest and acquiescence of those peoples. Applied to contractual arrangements in relation to foreign investment, this suggests at a minimum that no government has capacity to permanently alienate its fundamental powers over exploitation and economic use of natural resources in its territory. This has been couched in the following terms by George Abi-Saab:

> The major characteristic of this power is the one designated from the beginning by the adjective 'permanent'. Its purpose is to indicate that sovereignty over natural wealth and resources is the rule, and any limitations on it are mere exceptions; that this sovereignty can be exercised at any time, and on a continuous basis, while limitations can only be ephemeral and circumscribed in scope and time.[37]

While the level of generality and abstraction of the principle prevents drawing definitive conclusions from it other than in the most extreme circumstances, it has at the same time been conceived in arbitral practice as a more or less decisive rationale for defending government authority and power against contractual restriction, as I will show in the next section.

B. The Right to Expropriate

The right to expropriate foreign investments did not develop as such with the principle of permanent sovereignty.[38] Expropriation of foreign property and assets has long been considered an inherent power of states, but subject to certain conditions of legality, most often held to include the following two: (i) it should be for a public purpose and not discriminatory

[36] Though what constitutes a 'people' for this purpose is debatable, see Crawford, 'The Rights of Peoples: Peoples or Governments?' in Crawford (ed), *The Rights of Peoples* (Clarendon Press, Oxford, 1988) 55.

[37] Abi-Saab (1991) 602. See also implicitly to this effect, *Texaco v Libya* (Award (Merits), 1977) 53 ILR 389, para 77

[38] See eg the famous note of State Secretary Hull, to the Mexican ambassador of 3 April 1940, subsequent to the Mexican expropriations during its agrarian reforms from 1917 and onwards: 'The Government of the United States readily recognizes the right of a sovereign State to expropriate property for public purposes . . . the right to expropriate property is coupled with and conditioned on the obligation to make adequate, effective and prompt compensation' (as reproduced in Lowenfeld (2002) 402).

or arbitrary;[39] and (ii) it should be combined with sufficient compensation, as I have already discussed in some detail in chapter five above. The significance of the concept of permanent sovereignty over natural resources is its re-invention of the value-rationale of expropriation. This has two main consequences for the substantive law: first, it underlies a potentially more flexible compensation standard; secondly, it suggests that the state cannot restrict its fundamental ability to exercise legal power and authority, eg, by agreeing to a stabilisation clause, as I come back to below.

At least before World War I and the Russian Revolution, there seems to have been general consensus on the principle that immediate and effective compensation was required for the full value of the property taken.[40] This was later expressed in terms of the so-called 'Hull formula' requiring 'prompt, adequate and effective compensation'.[41] This allegedly strict requirement of full compensation engaged one of the main thrusts of the NIEO movement, which sought to abolish a uniform *international* compensation standard.[42] While it is reasonably clear that this effort did not succeed as such, it confirmed that a strict standard might not in all circumstances be appropriate and supported by established consensus.[43] Here the more generally accepted principle of permanent sovereignty over natural resources is potentially significant as a conditioning rationale. This is related to the distinct value-rationale of the principle as discussed above; the inseparability of power and control over the natural wealth and 'means of subsistence' of a state from the interests of the people. It is conceivable that this, at least exceptionally, may provide a justification for giving less than the full value of an expropriated investment, on the condition that the essential purpose of the expropriation is a concerted effort to regain national control over resources of vital importance for the national economy.[44] The point is that a strict and absolute compensation standard would effectively undermine the ability of governments to exercise their right of expropriation in the circumstances where it is most

[39] This requirement is nevertheless usually considered subject to the virtually free discretion of the state, see eg *LIAMCO v Libya* (Award, 1977) 62 ILR 141, 194. What remains of this requirement is probably for most purposes that the expropriation must not be for a purpose considered illegal by international law, and not be wholly arbitrary, see eg Brownlie (2003) 520.

[40] See eg *Norwegian Shipowners' Claims* (1922) I RIAA 307, 334; and *Case Concerning the Factory at Chorzów* (Indemnity) PCIJ Series A No 17 (1928) 4, 47; see also generally Lowenfeld (2002) 395.

[41] See for citation n 38 above, and see further Lowenfeld (2002) 397 et seq.

[42] Higgins, 'The Taking of Property by the State: Recent Developments in International Law' (1982-III) 176 *Recueil des Cours* 259, 290.

[43] See also to this effect Lowenfeld (2002) 414–15; and Brownlie (2003) 519–20.

[44] To this effect, see eg Brownlie (2003) 519 as follows: 'Where major natural resources are concerned, cogent considerations of principle reinforced by the Declaration of 1962 and the Charter of Economic Rights and Duties of States, militate against the "prompt, adequate and effective" formula'.

needed. This would replace the strict requirement of 'prompt, adequate and effective compensation' with a somewhat more flexible fairness standard requiring 'appropriate',[45] 'fair',[46] or 'just',[47] compensation. As such, it would allow other circumstances than the strict and prospective value of an investment to be taken account of, such as the broader public interest and the necessity of the measure in question. The broader justice element would then require a balancing of such factors against the interest of the investor.[48]

Characteristically, however, not many cases decided by investment tribunals have adopted an approach perceptibly or clearly responsive to such a more flexible justice-based standard. One significant example is nevertheless provided by *LIAMCO v Libya*. The tribunal in this case applied a standard of 'equitable compensation',[49] which it especially held to be

> in complete harmony with the general trend of international theory and practice on the concepts of sovereignty, destination of national wealth and natural resources, nationalistic motivations in the attitude and behaviour of 'Third World' nations, the lawfulness and frequency of nationalization, and the recent declarations affirmed in successive United Nations Resolutions by the majority members of the General Assembly.[50]

Other cases have accepted in principle that the applicable standard is a broader justice standard, but have then proceeded to award full compensation on the basis of the facts. Thus, in *AMINOIL v Kuwait*, the tribunal

45 UNGA Res 1803 (XVII), item 4.

46 It may also be noted that this was the standard explicitly envisaged in the *Chorzow factory case* for *lawful* expropriation, see *Case Concerning the Factory at Chorzów* (Indemnity), PCIJ Series A No 17 (1928) 4, 47.

47 See also to this effect, the original 'Hull formula', elaborated by Secretary Hull in his letter to the Mexican ambassador of 21 July 1938 (as reproduced in Lowenfeld (2002) 398): 'The whole structure of friendly intercourse, of international trade and commerce and many other vital and mutually desirably relations between nations indispensable to their progress rest upon the single and hitherto solid foundation of respect on the part of governments and of peoples for each other's rights under international justice. The right of prompt and just compensation for expropriated property for expropriated property is a part of this structure. It is a principle to which the Government of the United States and most governments of the world have emphatically subscribed and which they have practiced and which must be maintained. It is not a principle which freezes the status quo and denies change in property rights but a principle that permits any country to expropriate private property within its borders in furtherance of public purposes. It enables orderly change without violating the legitimately acquired interests of citizens of other countries'.

48 This resembles the approach adopted under the ECHR, see eg *James and others v UK* (1986) Series A 98 para 54: '[T]he taking of property without payment of an amount reasonably related to its value would normally constitute disproportionate interference which could not be considered justifiable under Article 1 (P1-1). Article 1 (P1-1) does not however, guarantee a right to full compensation in all circumstances. Legitimate objectives of 'public interest' such as pursued in measures of economic reform or measures designed to achieve greater social justice, may call for less than reimbursement of the full market value'.

49 *LIAMCO v Libya* (Award, 1977) 62 ILR 141, 209–10.

50 *ibid*, 210.

accepted 'appropriate' compensation as the applicable standard, and seemingly held that this, in principle, required 'an enquiry into all the circumstances relevant to the particular concrete case'.[51] The tribunal nevertheless went on to award compensation on the basis of the full value of the enterprise expropriated.[52] Certain cases decided by the Iran-US Claims Tribunal similarly suggests that compensation, in principle, is subject to a standard of just or appropriate compensation rather than a strict and absolute full-value criterion.[53] But it is also reported that no case decided by the Tribunal has actually awarded less than full market value.[54]

Moreover, no investment treaty case seems to have awarded anything less than full compensation. In part this is no doubt a natural consequence of the common (though not uniform) stipulation in investment treaties of 'prompt, adequate and effective' and 'full market value', as the relevant compensation standard.[55] However, the Hull formula has also been considered the applicable standard without a clear stipulation in the treaty. In *CME v Czech Republic* the treaty merely provided for payment of 'just compensation', equivalent to the 'genuine value' of the investment taken.[56] The majority of the tribunal held that this had to be interpreted as a strict requirement of fair market value in accordance with the Hull formula.[57] The minority adopted a more lenient view, however, suggesting that the amount of compensation might be modified by a general legitimate expectation standard.[58] Two main inferences were drawn from this by way of

[51] *AMINOIL v Kuwait* (Award, 1982) (1982) 21 ILM 976, para 144.

[52] See also *Liberian Eastern Timber Corporation (LETCO) v Republic of Liberia* (Award, 1984) (1987) 26 ILM 647, para 34; and *Texaco v Libya* (Award (Merits), 1977) 53 ILR 389, para 87.

[53] See *Sedco Inc v National Iranian Oil Company (NIOC)* (1986) 10 Iran-US CT Rep 180, 187; *Amoco Int'l Finance Corp v Iran* (1987) 15 Iran-US CT Rep 189, paras 112–17; and especially *Ebrahimi v Govt of the Islamic Republic of Iran* (1994) 30 Iran-US CT Rep 170, para 88: 'The Tribunal believes that, while international law undoubtedly sets forth an obligation to provide compensation for property taken, international law theory and practice do not support the conclusion that the 'prompt adequate and effective' standard represents the prevailing standard of compensation . . . Rather, customary international law favors an "appropriate" compensation standard . . . The prevalence of the "appropriate' compensation standard does not imply, however, that the compensation *quantum* should be always "less than full" or always 'partial"'. And see also the separate opinion of Judge Lagergren in *INA Corp v Iran* (1985) 8 Iran-US CT Rep 373, 385, 386–7.

[54] Brower and Brueschke: *The Iran-United States Claims Tribunal* (The Hague, 1998) 491.

[55] See eg, with further references, Wälde and Sabahi, 'Compensation, Damages and Valuation in International Investment Law', Report to the ILA Committee on International Law on Foreign Investment (2006) available at: www.ila-hq.org/html/layout_committee.htm 20.

[56] The Netherlands-Czech Republic BIT (1991) Art 5.

[57] *CME Czech Republic BV v Czech Republic* (Final Award, 2003) para 497.

[58] *CME v Czech Republic* (Final Award, 2003), separate opinion of Brownlie, para 33: 'The treaty provisions make no explicit reference to a limitation placed upon the right to compensation based upon a reasonably rate of return or the legitimate expectations of the investor. However, it is clear that such a limitation forms an inherent part of the concept of investment and the principle of the "protection of investments" embodied in the treaty. The treaty is not related to the protection of "foreign property," but to the protection of "investments," all this in the context of the promotion of the economic development of the Contracting Parties'.

restrictions. First, that the host state had not accepted 'paying compensation at a level which would cause catastrophic economic consequences for the host State and its population'.[59] Secondly, that 'an investment carries the expectation that it will be profitable, but only on a basis of *reasonable* expectations'.[60] This primarily ruled out 'uncertain and speculative future benefits',[61] and an 'exclusively commercial' approach to valuation.[62] Instead the arbitrator reasoned that the compensation should encompass the value of the actual investments made, profits actually incurred, and 'foreseeable profits . . . compatible with a reasonable rate of return'.[63] This approach is clearly reminiscent of the equity-based approach of *LIAMCO v Libya*. While only a minority opinion, the reasoning is interesting because it suggests a potential restriction of the full-value criterion on the basis of the very purpose and function of investment protection. Thus, the more restrictive approach was held to be justified on the basis of two interrelated concerns: first, the treaty's specific purpose to promote economic development;[64] and secondly, its connection to the specific character and responsibilities of the state in relation to 'the well-being of its people'.[65] This reasoning points in the direction of something comparable to the rationale of permanent sovereignty, but is even more crucial for *combining* this with the function and purpose of investment protection in a distinct equity-based concept of legitimate expectations.[66] While it eventually failed to obtain a majority, this reasoning finds some support in other cases applying a legitimate expectation standard to damages.[67] It may, to this effect, suggest a potentially more flexible compensation standard also in an investment treaty context.[68]

[59] *ibid*, para 58.

[60] *ibid*, para 58 (my emphasis).

[61] *ibid*, para 69.

[62] *ibid*, para 74.

[63] *ibid*, paras 113–15.

[64] *ibid*, para 73.

[65] *ibid*, para 74: 'In this context, it is simply unacceptable to insist that the subject-matter is exclusively "commercial" in character or that the interests in issue are, more or less, only those of the investor. Such an approach involves setting aside a number of essential elements in the Treaty relation. The first element is the significance of the fact that the Respondent is a sovereign State, which is responsible for the well-being of its people. This is not to confer a privilege on the Czech Republic but only to recognize its special character and responsibilities. The Czech Republic is not a commercial entity'.

[66] *ibid*, paras 77–78.

[67] See especially *AMINOIL v Kuwait* (Award, 1982) (1982) 21 ILM 976, paras 146–7; and *Himpurna California Energy Ltd (Bermuda) v PT (Persero) Perusahaan Listruik Negara (Indonesia)* (Award, 1999), (2000) 25 *YbCA* 13, especially para 315 et seq.

[68] The circumstances in *CME v Czech Republic* may nevertheless be illustrative of the high threshold for applying such concerns. The case concerned a claim in the amount of US$495 million, compared with a gross national income of the Czech Republic of approximately US$54 billion (see the separate opinion of Brownlie, para 75). In fact, the difference between the majority and minority was somewhat less dramatic, the award being in the amount of approximately US$270 million, compared to the US$160 million suggested by the minority.

C. Stabilisation Clauses and the Right to Expropriate

Where a state expropriates, or exercises regulatory power in a manner requiring payment of compensation, the fundamental capacity to vest authority is still intact. The state is free to implement and change its policies, but must pay compensation for eventual harm to private investors. Such a duty can, at least formally, be reconciled with the notion that sovereignty is permanent and inalienable.[69] However, it may be that the state ostensibly has restricted also its capacity to regulate, or even expropriate. The question is whether the state literally may bind its powers in this manner. The typical instance is where the state has entered into a contract with a 'stabilisation clause',[70] ie an explicit promise not to alter the regulatory framework applicable to the contract.[71] The response of practice to such stabilisation commitments involves a confrontation and reconciliation of two—at the outset—equally applicable and contradictory perspectives; on the one hand the state's right to expropriate, and on the other hand the ability to commit contractually. First, it is clear that contractual rights constitute assets that can be expropriated for public use as a form of incorporeal property.[72] As a general rule, it is of no consequence that the state itself is a party to the contract which is expropriated. The only difference is that the state in that case annuls the contract to escape its own contractual obligations for a distinct public purpose, and

[69] See eg in relation to the original 'Hull formula', as formulated by Secretary Hull in his letter to the Mexican ambassador of 21 July 1938 (as reproduced in Lowenfeld (2002) 398, see also n 47 above for full quotation): 'It is not a principle which freezes the status quo and denies changes in property rights but a principle that permits any country to expropriate private property within its borders in furtherance of public purposes'.

[70] See eg Wälde and Ndi, 'Stabilizing International Investment Commitments: International Law versus Contract Interpretation' (1996) 31 *Tex Int'l LJ* 215; Paasivirta, 'Internationalization and Stabilization of Contracts versus State Sovereignty' (1989) 60 *BYIL* 315; Chatterjee, 'The Stabilization Clause Myth in Investment Agreements' (1988) 5 *J Int'l Arb* 97; and Weil, 'Les clauses de stabilisation et d'intangibilité insérées dans les accords de développement économique' in *Mélanges offerts à Charles Rousseau* (Pedone, Paris, 1974) 301.

[71] Such promises may be general so as to ostensibly cover any regulatory change affecting the contract, or specific so as to promise for instance a stable and favourable tax regime or that certain licenses will not be retracted. In any case the objective is to 'freeze' the applicable regulatory framework in order to ensure stability and predictability for the private investor, see further Wälde and Ndi (1996), eg 220 et seq. More modern contractual techniques to ensure the same may now more commonly be included in contracts between independent state companies and investors as risk allocation schemes, which place the economic risk of regulatory change on the state party, but obligates the investor to implement new and changing regulation, see further Wälde and Ndi (1996) 260 et seq, and see for the specific example of so called 'Change in Law' clauses in IPP contracts, Inadomi, 'Independent Power Projects in Developing Countries: Legal Investment Protection and Consequences for Development' (Phd thesis, University of Oslo, 2005, unpublished) 162 et seq.

[72] *Norwegian Shipowners Claims* (1922) I RIAA 307, esp 334 and 337, see also Brownlie (2003) 522 et seq.

not to reallocate performance under the contract to meet state purposes.[73] The value-rationale of permanent sovereignty and the general right to expropriate applies as much to contracts directly restricting the government's freedom of action as it does to property rights required for other public purposes. A state should, according to this rationale, be able to expropriate any private economic right, even a contractual right pursuant to a stabilisation clause. Secondly, it is equally clear that annulment of a state contract, or regulation in breach of a stabilisation clause, at least in an isolated, contractual context, may, and typically does, constitute a breach of contract.[74] This is especially so if the state explicitly has made a commitment not to expropriate, for instance in a concession contract relating to exploitation of a natural resource, where this may take the shape of an undertaking not to repeal or amend the concession for a certain period of time.[75] If such an undertaking is valid, a breach will incur the ordinary consequences of a breach of contract. These may include an obligation to pay damages and, potentially, to render specific performance, ie to actually perform the contractual obligation in question.

To give full effect to a contractual perspective would thus undermine the inalienability element of permanent sovereignty, while allowing annulment or expropriation in the face of an express undertaking to the contrary would inhibit the power of commitment of the state. This must proceed from a conceptual premise. The initial contractual claim must be distinguished from the investor's claim under international law. A regulatory change or annulment in breach of a stabilisation clause will typically take place within the applicable law of the contract (ie the host state's law, as the law of performance). The question before the tribunal is whether the relevant rule of international law protects the initial contractual position against the government interference. The position under international law is nevertheless independent of the breach of contract as such and its consequences under the applicable law of the

[73] Thus, in the *Norwegian Shipowners claims*, the US government expropriated a number of shipbuilding contracts between Norwegian shipowners and American shipyards, for use in the American war planning efforts, cf n 73.

[74] A potential perspective on this might be that the annulment, if by legislative decree, comes to constitute a part of the applicable law of the contract, and that no breach of contract in a strict sense therefore occurs. This disregards the fact that relevant investment protection standards may and will be directed at the initial contractual position, as a potentially protected interest defined by the contract as originally conceived under the applicable law.

[75] This was the case in most of the internationalisation cases concerning oil and mineral concessions, see eg cl 16 of the Libyan Oil Concessions at issue in the *Texaco, BP* and *LIAMCO cases*, as reproduced in *Texaco v Libya* (Award (Merits), 1977), 53 ILR 389, para 70 (extracts): 'The contractual rights expressly created by this concession shall not be altered except by mutual consent of the parties . . . This Concession shall throughout the period of its validity be construed in accordance with the Petroleum Law and the Regulations in force on the date of execution of the agreement of amendment by which this paragraph (2) was incorporated into the concession agreement. Any amendment to or repeal of such Regulations shall not affect the contractual rights of the Company without its consent'.

contract. Instead, this position depends on two interrelated questions: namely, whether a state may bind itself contractually not to regulate or expropriate with effect under international law, and what specific legal consequences are recognised by international law as a result of this. The position of practice with respect to the first question is that a state may, in principle, undertake a contractual obligation restricting its future exercise of power with effect under international law. This would seem initially to be dependent on the applicable municipal law and the interpretation of the contract. Concerns related to preservation of regulatory authority and freedom may suggest that a stabilisation commitment be interpreted restrictively or even as ultra vires under the applicable law.[76] However, if it is initially valid and effective under municipal law, such an undertaking will be recognised by international law in the same manner as other contractual undertakings. But beyond this, there is also a propensity to hold that a stabilisation commitment may have certain direct effects under international law as a basis of expectations reasonably relied on by an investor, irrespective of the position under municipal law. The internationalisation cases discussed above may be read in that light,[77] as may the more recent *Himpurna* case.[78] Certain cases decided under investment treaty standards tend in a similar direction. In the *CMS* case, the tribunal held that a stabilisation clause obligated the state not to legislatively alter the contractual regime, without any clear regard for the eventual capacity of Argentina to undertake such an obligation under its own law.[79] Other cases have assumed a stabilisation clause would have been effective to restrain subsequent regulation, by using the absence of such express stabilisation as a justification of regulatory change.[80]

That the state in this manner may bind itself contractually to exercise or not to exercise public authority in a certain manner is not necessarily problematic in relation to a core element of inalienability.[81] If the ultimate

[76] See eg *AMINOIL v Kuwait* (Award, 1982), (1982) 21 ILM 976, para 95, and Wälde and Ndi (1996) 238.

[77] See especially *AMINOIL v Kuwait* (Award, 1982), (1982) 21 ILM 976, para 90, where the tribunal considered a contractual limitation unproblematic in so far it concerned only a limited period of time, and *Revere Copper v OPIC* (Award, 1978) 56 ILR 258, 285, considering that initial invalidity under domestic law did not affect the position under international law.

[78] *Himpurna v Persero* (Final Award, 1999), (2000) 25 *YbCA* 13, esp para 41.

[79] *CMS Gas Transmission Co v Argentine Republic* (Award, 2005), para 151: 'The important question . . . is that concerning the right to benefit from stabilization clauses. This discussion is well known in international law and to the extent this dispute concerns the simultaneous operation of the License and protection under the treaty, the stabilization ensured a right that the Claimant can properly invoke'.

[80] *LG&E v Argentina* (Award, 2006) para 98; and *EnCana Corp v Republic of Ecuador* (Award, 2006) para 173.

[81] See eg *LIAMCO v Libya* (Award, 1977), 62 ILR 141, 213–14. The tribunal, which otherwise went far to accept the principle of permanent sovereignty, seemingly did not reject that the investor in principle had a right to 'equitable' or 'appropriate' compensation for lost profits, determined on the basis of the stipulated length of the concession.

right of the state to expropriate remains unaffected, protection of the contractual position pursuant to a stabilisation clause then merely requires compensation to be based on the terms of the contract. In other words, the state may still be able to lawfully cancel (ie expropriate) the right under the stabilisation clause, but against payment of compensation based on the contractual expectation of stabilisation.[82] Nevertheless, certain cases suggest that the consequences of a contractual commitment may go beyond that, entailing a duty of real performance. Two questions are seemingly interlaced relating to this issue. The first and general question is whether the state may in all cases lawfully extricate itself from a contractual undertaking, upon payment of compensation.[83] The second and real question is, however, whether unlawfulness may have as a consequence that the state is obligated to provide restitution in kind, in other words to perform the contractual obligation in question.

Several cases have positively held that annulment or breach of a stabilisation commitment is or would be 'illegal' under international law. Thus, both in *BP v Libya* and *Texaco v Libya*, the tribunals clearly held that the annulments were unlawful under international law.[84] In the latter case the tribunal even admitted that the measures in question were vested with 'formal regularity' under the applicable municipal law,[85] and that it had to consider the government 'as having acted in accordance with its own sovereign appreciation of the national interest'.[86] Similarly, in *AMINOIL v Kuwait* the tribunal held that the measures in question *were* lawful because they were not covered by the stabilisation clause, thus assuming that a specific commitment not to nationalise or expropriate for a limited period of time could have made a subsequent expropriation illegal.[87] This stands in some contrast to *LIAMCO v Libya*, where the annulment was considered lawful, but subject to a duty to pay compensation.[88] The tribunal here relied on 'a recent dominant trend of international opinion concerning the

[82] See eg *CMS Gas v Argentina* (Award, 2005) paras 419–20; and see also Jiménez de Aréchaga (1978) 307.

[83] The legal consequences of unlawfulness are in theory that other principles of responsibility apply, namely the duty of full reparation instead of a duty to pay compensation equivalent to the value of the property taken. This draws back to the *Chorzow factory case*, where the PCIJ held that the takings in question were unlawful and therefore in principle could be subject to higher compensation, or even restitution, depending on the general duty of full reparation, ie of placing the claimant state in the position it would have been if the breach had not occurred. See *Case Concerning the Factory at Chorzów* (Indemnity), PCIJ Series A No 17 (1928) 4, 46–7.

[84] *BP Exploration Co (Libya) Ltd v Libyan Arab Republic* (Award, 1973) 53 ILR 297, 329; *Texaco v Libya* (Award (Merits), 1977) 53 ILR 389, especially para 67, and para 97 et seq; and see also *AGIP SpA v Govt of the People's Republic of Congo* (Award, 1979), (1982) 21 ILM 726, para 37.

[85] *Texaco v Libya* (Award (Merits), 1977) 53 ILR 389, para 75.

[86] *ibid*, para 74, but contrast *BP v Libya* (Award, 1973) 53 ILR 297, 329.

[87] *AMINOIL v Kuwait* (1982) 21 ILM 976, paras 90 and 95 et seq.

[88] *LIAMCO v Libya* (1977) 62 ILR 141, 195–7.

sovereign right of States over their natural resources',[89] considering the right of nationalisation and expropriation to be an ever present power inherent in sovereignty. At the same time, the only case which actually ruled in favour of specific or real performance was *Texaco v Libya*, the tribunal quite extraordinarily holding that the annulments were *invalid*, ie without legal effect, under international law,[90] and that the company had a consequent right to *restitutio in integrum*, in other words, to be *reinstated* in the concession.[91] Contrastingly, in *BP v Libya*, the claim of the company 'to be restored to the full enjoyment of its rights under the BP concession',[92] was rejected by the tribunal, which held that the effective *validity* of the annulment had to be recognised, and that the investor could only claim damages. This was specifically justified on the basis of the nature of the measure in question, as an act of state power: 'an act of finality where a State has exercised its sovereign territorial power to expel a foreign enterprise and appropriate its property and other rights'.[93]

Newer investment treaty practice is inconclusive. Practice suggests that breach of a stabilisation commitment or similar undertaking in principle is 'illegal' under international law, as an indirect expropriation,[94] or a breach of either an umbrella clause or the general fair and equitable treatment standard.[95] The cases may nevertheless be read so as to suggest that what, in such cases, is illegal is the lack of sufficient compensation, and not the regulatory change or annulment as such. In such cases, the measures would have been legal if carried through as outright expropriations of the contractual rights in question.[96] It is telling that no case decided on the basis of an investment treaty has doubted the fundamental capacity of a state to regulate or expropriate in breach of contractual commitments, or suggested that a stabilisation commitment might be subject to a duty of real or specific performance.[97] This has potentially broader implications

[89] *ibid*, 189.

[90] *Texaco v Libya* (Award (Merits), 1977) 53 ILR 389, eg para 71, and paras 73–4.

[91] *ibid*, para 97 et seq.

[92] *BP v Libya* (1977) 53 ILR 297, 330.

[93] *ibid*, 353, and see also 354: 'A rule of reason therefore dictates . . . that, when by the exercise of sovereign power a State has committed a fundamental breach of a concession agreement by repudiating it through a nationalization of the enterprise and its assets in a manner which implies finality, the concessionaire is not entitled to call for specific performance by the Government of the agreement and reinstatement of his contractual rights, but his sole remedy is an action for damages'.

[94] See eg *Methanex Corp v USA* (Final Award, 2005) Part IV, Chapter D, para 7.

[95] *CMS Gas v Argentina* (Award, 2005) paras 302–3; and *CME v Czech Republic* (Partial Award, 2001) para 615.

[96] See eg *CMS Gas v Argentina* (Award, 2005) para 406 et seq, and *CME v Czech Republic* (Partial Award, 2001) para 618.

[97] See eg *CMS Gas v Argentina* (Award, 2005) para 406: 'In a situation such as that characterizing this dispute and the complex issues associated with the crisis in Argentina, it would be utterly unrealistic for the Tribunal to order the Respondent to turn back to the regulatory framework existing before the emergency measures were adopted'.

for the fundamental power of states to escape contractual obligations. If it is accepted, in principle, that the only possible or relevant remedy is compensation, this also means that the lawfulness or not of an annulment is largely irrelevant for practical purposes.[98] Compensation will in any case be based on the prospective economic position of the claimant under the commitment, since this represents its economic value for the claimant as an expropriated asset.[99] The crucial issue is thus whether specific performance or restitution in kind in principle is excluded in relation to a stabilisation commitment. With the notable exception of the *Texaco* case, this is precisely what is mostly suggested by case law, either by express reasoning to this effect,[100] or implicit assumptions about the 'lack of realism' of specific performance relied on by the tribunals.[101] For the purpose of legal consequences, this is largely equivalent to saying that a state may always expropriate, upon payment of compensation. It is possible to go beyond this, however, and see it as a normative implication of the rationale and function of public authority. This would suggest that the lawfulness of annulment and expropriation, even in the face of contractual commitments, may more naturally be explained as a consequence of a core element of inalienability, such as is suggested by the principle of permanent sovereignty.

Several cases have also, accordingly, held positively that contractual restrictions on government authority can always be abandoned lawfully as an inherent faculty of sovereignty, provided damages are paid. This is how the matter was conceived in *LIAMCO v Libya* as related above.[102] In *Framatome v Atomic Energy Agency of Iran*, the tribunal considered it 'undisputable' that the state by virtue of its 'national sovereignty' could 'modify its policy . . . to refuse specific performance of the agreements and contracts it freely concluded'.[103] In *Amoco International Finance Corporation v Iran*, the Iran-US Claims Tribunal similarly held that 'private parties who contract with a government are only entitled to fair compensation when measures of public policy are implemented at the expense of their contract

[98] Also to this effect, Sheppard, 'The Distinction between Lawful and Unlawful Expropriation' paper presented at Investment Arbitration and the Energy Charter Treaty, Conference 9–10 June 2005, Stockholm.

[99] In other words, full reparation under the *Chorzow Factory* formula, conceived as a duty to place the claimant in an economic position comparable to the situation if the breach had not occurred, is effectively and necessarily co-extensive with full compensation for contractual value, conceived under normal principles of contract as a right to be treated as though the contract had been performed.

[100] *BP v Libya* (Award, 1977) 53 ILR 297, 353–4.

[101] *CMS Gas v Argentina* (Award, 2005) para 406 et seq; and *CME v Czech Republic* (Partial Award, 2001) para 618.

[102] *LIAMCO v Libya* (Award, 1977) 195–7.

[103] *Framatome v Atomic Energy Agency of Iran* (Award, 1982), (published as *Company Z (Republic of Xanadu) and others v State Organization ABC (Republic of Utopia)* (1983) 8 *YbCA* 94 112.

rights'.[104] In the latter case this was justified by reference to the sovereignty of the state and the inherent public nature of the interests involved,[105] and held to entail that the expropriation ostensibly in breach of a stabilisation clause, nevertheless was lawful under international law.[106] Finally, in *LETCO v Liberia*, the tribunal held that a stabilisation clause would be effective to restrain government action, except if repealed by legislation justifying the criteria of legal nationalisation (ie expropriation) under international law.[107]

In conclusion, practice relating to stabilisation clauses exhibits a tendency more or less evidently responding to the concerns underlying the principle of permanent sovereignty, conceived as a minimum requirement of inalienability. This is either explicitly manifested as an inherent power to revoke previous commitments upon payment of compensation, or implicitly reflected in a routine-exclusion of specific performance relating to the exercise of state power. Welded into the form of a more principled rationale, this may suggest a more distinct principle of inalienability struggling to get free.[108] If it may be considered largely accepted that the only available remedy in the face of breach of a stabilisation commitment is compensation, it may be one could also say the state's power of expropriation is always retained as a lawful prerogative, both under investment treaties and customary law (in so far as nothing else is stipulated).

[104] *Amoco Int'l Finance Corp v Iran* (1987) 15 Iran-US CT Rep 189, para 178.

[105] *ibid*, para 178, referring to the rule that 'a state has the duty to respect contracts freely entered into with a foreign party', the tribunal then held: 'The quoted rule, however, must not be equated with the principle *pacta sunt servanda*, often invoked by claimants in international arbitrations. To do so would suggest that sovereign states are bound by contracts with private parties exactly as they are bound by treaties with other sovereign states. This would be completely devoid of any foundation in law or equity and would go much further than any State has ever permitted in its own domestic law. In no system of law are private interests permitted to prevail over duly established public interests, making impossible actions required for the public good'. Although see subsequently also para 179, where the tribunal seems to have contemplated the possibility that an express and specified commitment for a limited period of time could have made a subsequent expropriation unlawful, relying to this effect on *AMINOIL v Kuwait* (see above n 87).

[106] *ibid*, para 182.

[107] *LETCO v Liberia* (Award, 1986) 26 ILM 647, 667.

[108] See also to this effect, Higgins (1982) 338: '[G]overnments may indeed need to be able to act *qua* government and in the public interest. That fact will prevent specific performance (including restitution) from being granted against them. But that is not to liberate them from the obligation to compensate those with whom it has entered into specific arrangements. That is the reasonable place to strike the balance between the expectations of foreign investors and the *bona fide* needs of governments to act in the public interest'.

D. Avoidance of Prior Contractual Commitments—The Analogy of Odious Debts

Aside from providing a distinct value-rationale of the right to expropriate foreign investment, it has been suggested that the principle of permanent sovereignty may also provide a basis for 'subsequent scrutiny' of contracts concluded by the national government, and justify 'invalidation or avoidance, if these turn out not to have been in the interest of the population'.[109] Such avoidance of contracts entered into by a state involves the problem that a state (and with that, a people or nation) can only act legally through its government. As held by Crawford, the principle of permanent sovereignty could be 'dangerously double-edged'.[110] Instead of facilitating the empowerment of a legitimate government it could expand into an easy pretext for avoiding obligations entered into by a previous regime. To cast in doubt the legitimacy of policies and priorities underlying government undertakings could seriously undermine the reliability of such undertakings, and with that the very ability of states to commit.[111] In the long run this would not advance economic development and sensible resource management. To this is added that subsequent invalidation of a contract because it was entered into by an unrepresentative or dictatorial regime is not necessarily in the interest of what can reasonably be termed justice. The possibly reasonable and prima facie legitimate interests of the private contractants, which may have acted in good faith with what was the only, if not the ideal, government of the state in question, are also a part of the picture.[112] This suggests, at the outset, that a right of avoidance would have to be restricted to quite exceptional situations, such as where the collective interest aspect underlying the principle of permanent sovereignty is blatantly violated.

A certain restricted applicability in this manner is suggested by the law of state succession, where some support is entertained in literature and practice for lawful avoidance of *odious debts* contracted by a predecessor

[109] Crawford, 'The Rights of Peoples: Peoples or Governments?' in Crawford (ed), *The Rights of Peoples* (Clarendon Press, Oxford, 1988) 55, 64.

[110] Crawford (1988) 65.

[111] *ibid*, 64 (fn 18): '[W]holly exceptional situations apart, in the existing conditions of international relations, the State acts through its government, and if a State's acts are ever to be definitive so too must the government's be'.

[112] See to this effect the decision of the European Court of Human Rights in *Stran Greek Refinereries and Stratis Andreadis v Greece* (1994) Series A301-B. The Greek government claimed that the claims in the case derived from a 'preferential contract, prejudicial to the national economy, which had helped to sustain the regime and to give the impression at national and international level that it had the support of eminent figures from the Greek business world' (para 70). The court held that that this could not prejudice the right of the claimants under the convention to protection, since the contractual position had been validly established pursuant to an agreement with the legal government of the state, see decision, paras 72–4.

government. This supposed rule essentially suggests that a successor state does not bear responsibility for debts assumed contrary to the fundamental interests of the people of the predecessor state if the creditor acted in bad faith.[113] The idea is that a debt granted to a government against the needs and interests of its people cannot create obligations for the state.[114] This converges with the rationale of permanent sovereignty. It could potentially be seen as the reflection of a broader principle with somewhat wider application, being a general exception to the wider notion of acquired rights.[115] The criteria for avoidance ought therefore in principle also to converge.[116]

This may provide a basis for disputing clearly exploitative investment and concessionary contracts when it was or should have been relatively obvious to the private investor that the essential purpose of the contract was specific to the government, and at the expense of the rest of the population.[117] At the same time, however, no reported case (as far as I am aware) has relied on this proposition to effectively invalidate a contract.[118]

[113] See generally, and with further references, O'Connell, *State Succession in Municipal Law and International Law* (Cambridge University Press, Cambridge, 1967) vol I, 458 et seq; and see also Menon, *The Succession of States in Respect to Treaties, State Property, Archives, and Debts* (E Mellen Press, Lewiston (NY), 1991) 161–3.

[114] It would seem that this does not necessarily mean that the debt is illegal or invalid, which presumably requires a different test, but merely that it must be conceived as granted to the government in its personal capacity ('dettes de régime'), and not as the representative of the state in question, see O'Connell (1967) 458–9.

[115] O'Connell (1967) 459: 'An interest which a creditor possesses in a debt must, in order to constitute an acquired right protected by international law, be an interest in funds utilized for the needs and interests of the State. Any debt contracted for other purposes is a debt intrinsically hostile to the interests of the territory'. See also, for the notion of acquired rights as the fundamental basis of the law of state succession, Sack, 'La Succession aux Dettes Publiques d'État' (1928-III) 23 *Recueil des Cours* 145, 278.

[116] It has been suggested that the right must depend on three criteria; first, that the debt was undertaken without consideration for the interests of the population in question, secondly, that the creditors were aware of this, and thirdly, that the funds were not in fact used for the benefit of the population, cf Sack, *Les effets des transformations des États sur leurs dettes publiques et autres obligations financières* (Sirey, 1927), as cited by O'Connell (1967) 459.

[117] Given the strict criteria that would have to be fulfilled to justify avoidance, such a contract would conceivably in most cases also be tainted with corruption, which would then provide a more easily ascertainable and accessible legal basis of invalidity. There is a tendency of arbitral practice to the effect that invalidity due to corruption forms part of international public policy, see most recently in *World Duty Free Co Ltd v Republic of Kenya* (Award, 2006) para 137 et seq.

[118] But see the *Tinoco case* (Award, 1923) I RIAA 369. The case concerned two claims, one based on a concession contract entered into with the short lived *Tinoco* regime in Costa Rica, and another based on an alleged bank debt pursuant to a check drawn on the state and cashed in by the same regime. While the tribunal merely held that the concession was invalid as a violation of the Costa Rican constitution at the time (see 397–8), it held that the bank debt could not be construed as a debt of the state, since the bank must or ought to have known that the money was not for state use, but meant for the personal benefit of the regime, see 394.

6.4 'POLICE POWERS' AND PROTECTION OF LEGITIMATE EXPECTATIONS

Where the state formally appropriates or annuls rights underlying an investment, the rule of full compensation for expropriation applies as per definition. However, investments may, and typically will, rather, be affected by government measures which do not constitute outright appropriation or annulment. The most practical circumstance is that the investment is affected by new or changed more onerous regulation. The general rule now recognised is that such regulatory measures may and will nevertheless constitute a taking, subject to a duty to pay compensation, insofar as they must be considered equivalent in effect to a formal expropriation.[119] At the same time, it is increasingly considered a basic principle that states are entitled to regulate foreign investment within their jurisdiction even if it may have onerous or even injurious consequences for an investor. This 'right to regulate' has increasingly been conceptualised in investment jurisprudence as an inherent power of the state ('police powers'), which is defined through a distinction between legitimate non-compensable regulation and deprivatory regulation equivalent in effect to expropriation,[120] or a breach of, for example, the fair and equitable treatment standard in an investment treaty.[121] In the following I first examine the emergent concept of 'police powers' in arbitral practice, as a presumptive right to enact general regulatory measures, and then examine further how this is subject to a fundamental requirement of respect for legitimate expectations. Finally, I examine how this has been applied to contractual undertakings affected by regulatory change as a concept fundamentally balancing the opposing concerns of contractual commitment and regulatory need.

[119] In treaties, this is usually expressed through an extension of the rule to both direct and indirect expropriation, and as a requirement that the measures be tantamount to, or have similar effects, as expropriation, see eg NAFTA North American Free Trade Agreement (NAFTA) (signed San Antonio, 17 December 1992, entered into force 1 January 1994) art 1110, and the Energy Charter Treaty (Lisbon, December 1994) (1995) 34 ILM 360, Art 13.

[120] For relevant literature, see eg Fortier and Drymer, 'Indirect Expropriation in the Law of International Investment: I know It When I See It or Caveat Investor' (2004) 19(2) *ICSID Rev-FILJ* 293; Newcombe, 'The Boundaries of Regulatory Expropriation in International Law' (2005) 20(1) *ICSID Rev-FILJ* 1; Wälde and Kolo, 'Environmental Regulation, Investment Protection and 'Regulatory Taking' in International Law' (2001) 50 *ICLQ* 811; and see also the now classical study of Higgins, 'The Taking of Property by the State: Recent Developments in International Law' (1982-III) 176 *Recueil des Cours* 259, esp 322–54.

[121] See eg *EDF (Services) Ltd v Romania* (Award, 2009) para 215 et seq.

A. The 'Police Powers' Principle

As already examined in chapter five above, the main function of investment law is to protect established rights and expectations, relied on in the context of an investment, against unpredictable, arbitrary and abusive exercise of government authority. This assumes that normal exercise of government authority is justified, even though it may incidentally affect private rights and assets adversely.[122] Positive conceptualisation in modern investment law and practice is increasingly contained in the concept of 'police powers'.[123] Police powers denotes essentially, in this context, the right and duty of the state, under international as well as municipal law, to protect and manage the public interests through the exercise of regulatory (and executive) authority.[124]

It would be overly optimistic to see in this 'police powers' concept a clear and established meaning as a matter of in international law. In one sense it could be held to denote essentially all forms of legitimate exercise of public power, including expropriation with adequate compensation. However, it has become increasingly common to envisage police powers as denoting the justification of regulatory measures that cause harm to private rights and assets without being accompanied by compensation. Thus, the jurisprudence of arbitral tribunals generally recognises that regulation ordinarily does not constitute expropriation, even though it may adversely affect private rights and assets.[125] This recalls a long-held principle of customary law, which has gained new importance in an investment treaty context.[126] In the NAFTA case of *SD Myers v Canada*, the tribunal set this out as a general presumption, drawing on what it considered to be established precedent in arbitral case law:

> The general body of precedent usually does not treat regulatory action as amounting to expropriation. Regulatory conduct by public authorities is unlikely

[122] See eg for recent cases *EDF v Romania* (Award, 2009) para 217; and *Parkerings-Compagniet AS v Republic of Lithuania* (Award, 2007) para 332.

[123] 'Police powers' is commonly used in US Constitutional law to denote the inherent powers of the states of the union. In an international law context an early use of the concept is that of Higgins, in her 1982 study, to denote regulatory powers after the model of US law, see Higgins (1982) 330 et seq.

[124] See Newcombe (2005) 25 et seq; and Fortier and Drymer (2004) 298 et seq.

[125] Newer BITs expressly set this out as a general principle, see eg the Model BITs of the US and Canada.

[126] See eg *Restatement of the Law, third: foreign relations law of the United States* (the American Law Institute, 1987) section 712, comment g: 'A state is not responsible for loss of property or for other economic disadvantage resulting from bona fide general taxation, regulation, forfeiture for crime, or other action of the kind that commonly accepted as within the police power of states, if it is not discriminatory'. See also *Sedco v NIOC* (1985) 9 Iran-US CT Rep 248, 275: 'It is also an accepted principle of international law that a State is not liable for economic injury which is a consequence of a bona fide regulation within the accepted police power of states'.

to be the subject of legitimate complaint under Article 1110 of the NAFTA, although the tribunal does not rule out that possibility.[127]

The case concerned a PCB[128] waste disposal enterprise operated by an American company in Canada, which relied on transport from Canada to its facilities in the United States for the disposal of the waste. This operation was forced to temporarily close down pursuant to a Canadian ban on export of PCB waste, and the company claimed the ban constituted an unlawful expropriation of its interests in the enterprise. The claim was denied by the tribunal, which considered it a normal regulatory measure without the sufficient characteristics of an expropriation. A main consideration cited by the tribunal was the need to reduce the risk of governments being subjected to claims 'as they go about their business of managing public affairs'.[129]

Another important case is *Tecmed v Mexico*. The case concerned a landfill site for hazardous waste whose authorisation was withdrawn by Mexican authorities. This occurred after local resistance to the enterprise. The company held that it was de facto deprived of its rights in the landfill operation, and that a de facto or indirect expropriation therefore had taken place. The tribunal used the notion of police powers to distinguish *normal* regulatory measures from expropriatory regulation.[130] Crucially, it considered injury to private rights and assets in the former case as incidental to the regulation and therefore not subject to compensation. To this effect it set forth the following broad principle:

> The Principle that the State's exercise of its sovereign powers within the framework of its police power may cause economic damage to those subject to its powers as administrator without entitling them to any compensation whatsoever is undisputable.[131]

This notion of bona fide regulation is increasingly cementing itself as the general rule for evaluating regulatory measures in relation to investment treaty standards.[132] A considerable body of precedent now confirms that

[127] *SD Myers Inc v Govt of Canada* (First Partial Award, 2000) para 281.

[128] Polychlorinated Biphenyls.

[129] *ibid*, para 282: 'Expropriations tend to involve the deprivation of ownership rights; regulations a lesser interference. The distinction between expropriation and regulation screens out most potential cases of complaints concerning economic intervention by a state and reduces the risk that governments will be subject to claims as they go about their business of managing public affairs'.

[130] *Tecnicas Medioambientales (Tecmed) SA v United Mexican States* (Award, 2003) para 115.

[131] *ibid*, para 119.

[132] See for recent cases *Methanex v USA* (Final Award, 2005) Part IV, Chapter D, para 7; *Saluka Investments BV v Czech Republic* (Award, 2006) para 255; *International Thunderbird Gaming Corp v United Mexican States* (Award, 2006) para 208; *EnCana v Ecuador* (Award, 2006) paras 173–7; *Azurix Corp v Argentine Republic* (Award, 2006) paras 310–11; *LG & E v Argentina* (Decision on Liability, 2006) para 195; and *ADC Affiliate Ltd and ADC & ADMC Management Ltd v Hungary* (Award, 2006) paras 423–4.

ordinary regulatory measures do not create a duty to pay compensation even though foreign investment is affected adversely. The essential assumption is that economic damage resulting from new or changed regulation is generally not refundable; regulatory change is considered one of the ordinary hazards of business activity, along with fluctuating markets and the wider economic climate.[133] It is no different for foreign investors. In other words, in order for a regulation to create a legitimate expectation of compensation, it must be something out of the ordinary; some specific circumstances other than incidental loss or increased costs as a result of the regulatory change must be invoked. This notion of police powers, conceived as a right to regulate, and envisaged as an inherent capacity of the state function, necessarily inserts itself into any relevant standard of investment protection.[134]

B. Protection of Legitimate Expectations—Distinguishing bona fide Regulation from Indirect Expropriation

The right to regulate foreign investment is, however, conditioned on the equally established principle that regulatory measures are not exempt from the expropriation standard. In *Pope & Talbot v Canada*, the tribunal stated this as follows: '[A] blanket exception for regulatory measures would create a gaping loophole in international protections against expropriation'.[135] The main principle, accordingly, is that a measure is not exempt from the expropriation standard, merely because it is regulatory, if it is equivalent to an expropriation in substance and effect.[136] While this presumptively can be seen as a generally accepted rationale of the indirect expropriation standard, doctrine and precedent have remained divided in respect of what constitutes the applicable criterion of 'equivalence'. What is controversial is first and foremost the relevance of purpose, where two main theories stand out; one focusing solely on the effects of a regulation,

[133] See to this effect the vintage statement of the PCIJ in the *Oscar Chinn Case (UK v Belgium)*, PCIJ Series A/B No 63 (1934) 63, 88: 'Favourable business conditions and good-will are transient circumstances, subject to inevitable changes . . . Some industries may be able to make large profits during a period of general prosperity, or else by taking advantage of a treaty of commerce or of an alteration in customs duty; but they are also exposed to the danger of ruin or extinction if circumstances change'. And compare *MR Feldman Karpa v United Mexican States* (Award, 2002) para 112: 'Governments, in their exercise of regulatory power, frequently change their laws and regulations in response to changing economic circumstances or changing political, economic or social considerations. Those changes may well make certain activities less profitable or even uneconomic to continue'.

[134] See eg in relation to the fair and equitable treatment standard, *SD Myers v Canada* (First Partial Award, 2000) para 263: '[The] determination must be made in the light of the high measure of deference that international law generally extends to the right of domestic authorities to regulate measures within their own borders'.

[135] *Pope & Talbot Inc v Canada* (Interim Award, 2000) para 99.

[136] See eg *Tecmed v Mexico* (Award, 2003) paras 120–21.

the other adopting a more contextual approach with a focus on proportionality between purpose and effects.[137] In the following I argue that case law increasingly has moved towards the latter contextual approach, but fundamentally conditioned by a general principle of respect for legitimate expectations.[138]

The first and traditional approach is encompassed by the so-called 'sole effects' doctrine, which maintains that the sole criterion of whether a compensable taking has occurred is the effect of the regulation on the right or asset in question.[139] This excludes any assessment of purpose, public interests or necessity at the basis of the regulation.[140] If the regulation is substantially deprivatory in effect, this is held to engender a duty to pay compensation. This might seem most consonant with common treaty denotations of indirect expropriation, which usually extends the standard to measures with the same or similar effects as expropriation.[141] Moreover, in respect of a formal expropriation the duty of compensation does not depend on purpose; an expropriation is an expropriation no matter how laudable its purpose. The supposed rationale of the sole effects doctrine, accordingly, is twofold. One, it is based in the notion that expropriation is legal under international law, provided it is for a public purpose. The argument is that if public interest or purpose is a condition of legality for compensable expropriation, it cannot at the same time be a justification for non-compensation.[142] Two, it rests on a conception of the rationale of international investment law, as being concerned with protecting foreign rights and assets against deprivation for political purposes, notwithstanding the weight or quality of those purposes. The attitude is that of the detached and neutral arbitrator who will not meddle in the policies of a foreign government as long as compensation is paid. Two cases in particular can be cited to illustrate this approach.[143] In *Santa Elena v Costa Rica* the state had expropriated a large land property on the Costa Rican coast for use as a National Park. The respondent government had argued that it had an international obligation to protect the Santa Elena property and preserve its

[137] See also Dolzer and Bloch, 'Indirect Expropriation: Conceptual Realignments' (2003) 5(3) *Int'l L Forum* 155, 158.

[138] I am not the first to suggest this, see also eg Fortier and Drymer (2004) 306; and Wälde and Kolo (2001) 819.

[139] Fortier and Drymer (2004) 308.

[140] See eg Higgins (1982) 330–31.

[141] See eg the Energy Charter Treaty (1994) Art 13.

[142] This argument is made by Higgins (1982) 331; see also Fortier and Drymer (2004) 309.

[143] Other cases supporting an 'effects' or 'substantial deprivation' approach may include eg; *Biloune v Ghana Investment Centre* (Award, 1989), (1994) 19 *YbCA* 11, para 26; *Pope & Talbot v Canada* (Interim Award, 2000) para 102; *CME v Czech Republic* (Partial Award, 2001) para 591 et seq; *Middle East Cement Shipping and Handling Co SA v Egypt* (Award, 2002); *GAMI Investments v Mexico* (Award, 2004) para 126 et seq; *CMS Gas v Argentina* (Award, 2005) para 262; and *Eureko BV v Poland* (Partial Award, 2005) para 241; and see also among the extensive practice of the Iran-US Claims tribunal, especially *Phelps Dodge Corp v Iran* (1986) 10 Iran-US CT Rep 121, para 22; and *Starrett Housing Corp v Iran*, 4 Iran-US CT Rep 122, 154.

unique ecology. Nevertheless, the tribunal held the environmental purpose did not 'alter the legal character of the taking for which adequate compensation must be paid'.[144] Similarly, in *Metalclad v Mexico*, an environmental regulation effectively barring the future operation of a landfill site was considered a measure tantamount to expropriation, without any concern for the purpose of the regulation.[145] It was considered sufficient that the decree 'had the effect of barring forever the operation of the landfill'.[146] When this was established, the tribunal explicitly held that it 'need not decide or consider the motivation or intent of the adoption of the Ecological decree'.[147]

The second and contrasting approach adopts a more functional concept of regulatory necessity and a consequent focus on function and purpose as decisive factors.[148] Essentially, this approach maintains that government liability cannot be unaffected by the nature and urgency of the situation provoking the regulation. A basic rationale is that regulatory measures that are clearly deprivatory in effect may nevertheless be objectively required by circumstances intrinsically connected to the nature of a specific investment.[149] Thus, it could be discovered that an enterprise or land facility contaminates groundwater or freshwater supplies. A patented drug may be discovered to have lethal side effects. The government may place emission limits on cars, forcing certain manufacturers out of the market, or decide that electricity production plants based on coal or gas need to comply with certain emission quotas or limitations. In all such cases, the regulation may cause substantial injury and deprivation to private right-holders, but the deprivation will be caused by the loss of opportunity to continue an activity deemed harmful to society at large. This is not an interest normally deemed worthy of protection by the legal system.[150] It would seem to demand at least some sensitivity to the nature and purpose of the regulation in question.

[144] *Compañía del Desarrollo de Santa Elena, SA v Republic of Costa Rica* (Final Award, 2000) paras 71–2.

[145] This part of the award is an obiter dictum, as the tribunal also considered that the company had been divested of a separate right to operate the landfill, based on representations from the federal government.

[146] *Metalclad Corp v Mexico* (Award, 2000) paras 109–11.

[147] *ibid*, para 111.

[148] Fortier and Drymer (2004) 313.

[149] See also Newcombe (2005) 26–7.

[150] This has been recognised inter alia by the US Supreme Court under its so called 'inherent limitation analysis', applied to the comparable issue under the takings clause of the US constitution, see *Lucas v South Carolina Coastal Council*, 505 US 1003, 112 S Ct 2886 (1992) 2900, where it was held that regulation may wholly deprive an owner of the right to use property in ways harmful to others, or to society in general to the extent that such limitations 'inhere in the title itself, in the restrictions that background principles of the State's law of property and nuisance already place upon land ownership'. See also Newcombe (2005) 27.

A number of cases have adopted an approach more sensitive to the purpose and nature of the regulatory measures involved.[151] Particular attention may be called to two recent cases, which on the face of it would appear to stand in some contrast to the approach of the *Metalclad* tribunal related above. In *Methanex v USA*, the claim concerned a health and environment related California ban on a methanol-based gasoline additive, which caused the investor, a methanol producer, to lose a substantial part of its market base in California. One of the key disputed issues in the case was whether it could be established that the methanol compound had the harmful effects allegedly justifying the ban.[152] Having established that the policy decision to ban the compound 'was motivated by the honest belief, held in good faith and on reasonable scientific grounds, that MTBE contaminated groundwater',[153] the tribunal held that the investor had no legitimate and protected expectation to continue production and sale of a chemical substance deemed unsound and prohibited by the California authorities.[154] In *Tecmed v Mexico*, the situation was, quite comparably to the *Metalclad* case, that an existing permit to operate a landfill was revoked pursuant to environmental concerns and community pressure. Like in *Metalclad*, the tribunal deemed this comparable to an expropriation in terms of its effects,[155] but held that this did not by itself sufficiently establish that the decision could be deemed expropriatory. Instead, and drawing to this effect on ECHR jurisprudence, the tribunal held that the decisive factor was whether the measures were proportionate in view of their purpose and effects:

> [T]he Arbitral Tribunal will consider, in order to determine if they are to be characterized as expropriatory, whether such actions or measures are proportional to the public interest presumably protected thereby and to the protection

[151] In addition to the cases cited below, such an approach would seem more or less implicitly adopted in eg *SD Myers v Canada* (First Partial Award, 2000) para 280 et seq; *Olguin v Republic of Paraguay* (Award, 2001) para 84; *Lauder v Czech Republic* (Award, 2001) para 203; *Feldman v Mexico* (Award, 2002) para 129; and compare also the restrictive approach adopted in *Nykomb Synergetics Technology Holding AB v Republic of Latvia* (Award, 2003) 33.

[152] See *Methanex v USA* (Award, 2005) Part III, Chapter A.

[153] *ibid*, para 102.

[154] *ibid*, Part IV, Chapter D, para 9: 'Methanex entered a political economy in which it was widely known, if not notorious, that governmental environmental and health protection institutions at the federal and state level, operating under the vigilant eyes of the media, interested corporations, non-governmental organizations, and a politically active electorate, continuously monitored the use and impact of chemical compounds and commonly prohibited or restricted the use of some of those compounds for environmental and/or health reasons'.

[155] *Tecmed v Mexico* (Award, 2003) para 117: '[T]here is no doubt that in the future the Landfill may not be used for the activity for which it has been used in the past and that Cytrar's economic and commercial operations in the Landfill after such denial have been fully and irrevocably destroyed, just as the benefits and profits expected or projected by the Claimant as a result of the operation of the Landfill . . . As far as the effects of such Resolution are concerned, the decision can be treated as an expropriation under Article 5(1) of the Agreement'.

legally granted to investments, taking into account that the significance of such impact has a key role upon deciding the proportionality.[156]

This approach suggests a focus not on the nature or strength of a regulatory purpose as such, but on the proportionality or excessiveness of the individual loss or burden placed on specific investors *in view* of the purpose. It does not so much contradict as condition the traditional 'effects' approach, by suggesting that it is not the only decisive factor, albeit an important one.[157] The focus is still on effects, but not solely on whether the measures are substantially deprivatory, shifting instead to whether such deprivation causes the investor to bear 'an individual and excessive burden'.[158] It thus constitutes a development, not a refutation of the 'effects' (or 'substantial deprivation') approach in other cases.[159] While certain cases have adopted an even more restrictive approach, requiring an effective and deliberate appropriation of specific investments for the benefit of the state,[160] the tendency in more recent cases is to confirm and rely on the proportionality test of the *Tecmed* case.[161] This has two important corollaries, both of which are increasingly noticeable in recent case law. First, it entails a lenient attitude towards the legitimacy of the particular public interest or purpose underlying the regulatory measure in question. Secondly, it entails that compensation must be paid irrespective of the urgency or legitimacy of the measure in question, if it does in any case impose an individual and excessive burden.

This lenient attitude towards the legitimacy of purpose reflects an understanding that it is not the purpose of a government measure that primarily conditions its legitimacy, but whether it is a result of legitimate authority. Environmental restrictions applied to an established concession may be urgently required by a broad consensus of scientific evidence, but may also be enacted for mostly symbolic reasons, after arousal of public opinion, or pursuant to concerns of political prestige.[162] To conceive police powers in a functional sense, as actual power or authority to decide,

[156] *ibid*, para 122.

[157] *ibid*, para 121.

[158] *ibid*, para 122 (quoting the decision of the ECHR in the case of *James and others v UK*, Series A98 (1986) 19–20.)

[159] Compare especially the approach of the tribunal in *CMS Gas v Argentina* (Award, 2005) paras 262–3; with that of the tribunal in *Azurix v Argentina* (Award, 2006) paras 311–12, and 321–2.

[160] See *Olguin v Paraguay* (Award, 2001) para 84; *Lauder v Czech Republic* (Award, 2001) para 203; and *Nykomb v Latvia* (Award, 2003) 33. See also *Sea-Land Service Inc v Iran* (1984) 6 Iran-US CT Rep 149, 166; and see for a more general argument in favour of appropriation as a decisive criterion, Newcombe (2005) 7 et seq.

[161] See especially *Azurix v Argentina* (Award, 2006) paras 310–12; *EnCana v Ecuador* (Award, 2006) para 177; and *LG&E Int'l Inc v Argentine Republic* (Award, 2006) para 195; and see also *Saluka Investments v Czech Republic* (Award, 2006) para 271.

[162] Wälde and Kolo (2001) 820.

means that whether such restrictions are necessary or desirable remains for the government, as the competent authority, to decide. This suggests that governments in the exercise of their police powers must enjoy a wide 'margin of appreciation', a concept quite familiar from ECHR law[163] and increasingly other parts of international law.[164] It is clearly coming to be reflected as a general notion also in more recent investment treaty jurisprudence. The above-mentioned decision in *Methanex v USA* is illustrative. As already shown, the tribunal held that it would not review the concrete reasons behind the regulation any further than its appreciation of it being based on an 'honest belief, held in good faith, and on reasonable scientific grounds'.[165] Similarly, in *Tecmed v Mexico* the tribunal held it would not 'review the grounds or motives' of the measure in question,[166] and that the analysis of its potentially expropriatory character had to start at 'the due deference owing to the State when defining the issues that affect its public policy or the interests of society as a whole, as well as the actions that will be implemented to protect such values'.[167] In the recent case of *Saluka Investments v Czech Republic,* the tribunal took this a step further, stating that the state enjoyed 'a margin of discretion in the exercise of [its] responsibility' to regulate, and that the relevant decision of the Czech National Bank (CNB) had to be accepted 'in the absence of clear or compelling evidence that CNB erred or acted otherwise improperly in reaching its decision'.[168]

The complementary notion that compensation must be paid irrespective of the urgency or legitimacy of the measure in question if it does impose an individual and excessive burden, on the other hand reflects the public interest requirement underlying expropriation in general. If a measure is equivalent to expropriation in substance and effect, there is of course no

[163] See generally eg Yourow, *The Margin of Appreciation Doctrine in the Dynamics of European Human Rights Jurisprudence* (Kluwer, The Hague, 1996), and in the specific context of property protection see eg *James and others v UK* (1986) Series A98, para 46.

[164] See Shany, 'Toward a General Margin of Appreciation Doctrine in International Law?' (2005) 16(5) *EJIL* 907.

[165] *Methanex v USA* (Award, 2005) Part III, Chapter A, para 102.

[166] *Tecmed v Mexico* (Award, 2003) para 120.

[167] *ibid*, para 122; and see also to this effect, in relation to the fair and equitable treatment standard, *SD Myers v Canada* (First Partial Award, 2000) para 263.

[168] *Saluka Investments v Czech Republic* (Award, 2006) paras 272–3: 'The Czech State, in the person of its banking regulator, the CNB, had the responsibility to take a decision . . . It enjoyed a margin of discretion in the exercise of that responsibility. In reaching its decision, it took into consideration facts which, in the opinion of the tribunal, it was very reasonable for it to consider . . . In the absence of clear and compelling evidence that the CNB erred or acted otherwise improperly in reaching its decision, which evidence has not been presented to the Tribunal, the Tribunal must in the circumstances accept the justification given by the Czech banking regulator for its decision'. The case concerned a decision by the Czech National Bank, as the government organ responsible for regulation of the Czech banking sector, to place the privatised IP Banka (Investiãní a Poštovní banka) under forced administration to prevent a bank run, and consequent financial instability.

reason why it should not be compensable to the same extent. The reason expropriation must normally be compensated is not the lack of an urgent purpose, but because it appropriates an individual privilege for a public need, and therefore, if left uncompensated, requires an excessive sacrifice by the targeted individual for the benefit of society. The difficult question is, of course, what constitutes such an individual and excessive burden. Constituting in a way a development of the substantial deprivation criterion employed by the traditional 'sole effects' doctrine,[169] the novelty of recent investment treaty jurisprudence is to connect this with a fundamental criterion of legitimate expectations. In contrast to what was seen above, this may also act as a defence against a potential duty to compensate. A string of recent cases have held that no indirect expropriation could be established for the reason that the investor had received no definite commitment from the state, and therefore had no legitimate expectation that it would be exempt from regulatory changes.[170] Two cases are particularly illustrative, for being relatively explicit to this effect. In *EnCana v Ecuador*, the tribunal held that 'in the absence of a specific commitment from the host state', changes in the applicable tax regime did not violate any legitimate expectations of the investor.[171] Similarly, in *Methanex v USA*, the tribunal rejected the indirect expropriation claim explicitly for the reason that the regulation did not violate any 'commitments' or 'special representations' of the state that had been reasonably relied on by the investor.[172] Both these cases can be seen effectively to have relied on a strong presumption of non-compensability for general, regulatory measures incidentally affecting the value or profitability of an investment. In the *Methanex case*, the tribunal set this out as a general principle as follows:

> [A]s a matter of general international law, a non-discriminatory regulation for a public purpose, which is enacted in accordance with due process and, which affects, inter alios, a foreign investor or investment is not deemed expropriatory and compensable unless specific commitments had been given by the regulating government to the then putative foreign investor contemplating investment that the government would refrain from such action.[173]

Conversely, a number of cases have held that regulatory or comparable measures did constitute indirect expropriation, for the essential reason that specific commitments or expectations induced by the government

[169] See eg *CMS Gas v Argentina* (Award, 2005) para 262.

[170] See *Methanex v USA* (Award, 2005) Part IV, Chapter D, paras 7–10; *International Thunderbird v Mexico* (Award, 2006) para 208; *EnCana v Ecuador* (Award, 2006) para 173; *Azurix v Argentina* (Award, 2006) para 316; and *LG&E v Argentina* (Award, 2006) para 98.

[171] *EnCana v Ecuador* (Award, 2006) para 173.

[172] *Methanex Corp v USA* (Award, 2005) Part IV, Chapter D, paras 7–10.

[173] *ibid*, para 7.

clearly were broken.[174] The *Tecmed* and *Metalclad* cases are illustrative of the pervasiveness of this notion. The two tribunals held that government decisions not to renew or grant the necessary operating permits for the waste disposal facilities in question constituted indirect expropriation, for two main reasons it would seem. First, the decisions to reject the necessary permits were held to cause a substantial deprivation of the investments in question. The *Tecmed* tribunal held that the decision to reject the application 'fully and irrevocably destroyed' the enterprise.[175] Similarly, in *Metalclad v Mexico*, the tribunal held that the failure to grant a necessary construction permit 'effectively . . . prevented the Claimant's operation of the landfill',[176] and noted that together with a subsequent ecological decree, this had the effect of 'barring forever the operation of the landfill'.[177] Secondly, however, both tribunals seemed to indicate that the decisive reason why the decisions were deemed expropriatory was their violation of the reasonable expectations of the investors to continue operating the landfills, expectations which the investors had been induced to rely on by relevant government organs. Thus, in *Metalclad v Mexico*, the tribunal held that the expropriation consisted in the act of 'participating or acquiescing in the denial to Metalclad of the right to operate the landfill, notwithstanding the fact that the project was fully approved and endorsed by the federal government'.[178] A decisive factor was the investor's reliance on representations of the federal government, and that the subsequent circumstances leading to the denial of the permit did not justify a revocation of these representations:

> These measures, taken together with the representations of the Mexican federal government, on which Metalclad relied, and the absence of a timely, orderly or substantive basis for the denial by the Municipality of the local construction permit, amount to an indirect expropriation.[179]

In *Tecmed v Mexico*, the reasoning to this effect is more circumstantial. The tribunal essentially held that the investor had a reasonable expectation that the landfill would have a sufficient lifespan for it to recover the investment and generate a reasonable return. Its reasoning suggests this was considered to be an implicit understanding underlying the making of the investment, despite the absence of a formal agreement or government commitment to this effect. Read somewhat constructively, it would seem that the tribunal justified its finding of an indirect expropriation on three

[174] See eg *Revere Copper v OPIC* (Award, 1978), 56 ILR 258, 290; *Biloune v Ghana Investment Centre* (Award, 1989) para 29; *Metalclad Corp v Mexico* (Award, 2000) para 102 et seq; *CME v Czech Republic* (Award, 2001) para 428 et seq; and *Tecmed v Mexico* (Award, 2003) para 150.

[175] *Tecmed v Mexico* (Award, 2003) para 117.

[176] *Metalclad v Mexico* (Award, 2000) para 106.

[177] *ibid*, para 109.

[178] *ibid*, para 104.

[179] *ibid*, para 107.

interrelated grounds. First, the investor clearly expected the investment to last;[180] secondly, this was known to the government when it allowed the investment;[181] and thirdly, the reasons behind the decision not to renew the permit were not, in view of these expectations, proportionally justified by the environmental risks and complaints found to be associated with the landfill.[182] In relation to the latter ground, the tribunal appears to have held that the environmental concerns alleged to underlie the decision not to renew the permit were in reality mostly politically motivated[183] and based on sustained opposition from individual pressure groups.[184]

From this an evident concern and underlying rationale may be extracted. The decisive concern appears to have been that the state had first allowed the investments to be made and the facilities to be built, thereby clearly representing that they would be allowed to operate, only to revoke this for reasons without any substantial connection to subsequently manifested environmental risks or dangers that could conceivably have frustrated the investor's legitimate expectations. This may suggest that the legitimate expectation standard ought to be conceived according to a fundamental risk allocation scheme. Thus, if the state has encouraged and implicitly committed to an investment through its conduct or representations, it cannot then later disrupt the project for reasons unrelated to circumstances frustrating the reasonable expectations relied on by the investor. A key factor in this determination would seem to be the nature and extent of the state's commitment. In this respect an agreement clearly encompassing contractual commitments may obviously be of material importance.

[180] *Tecmed v Mexico* (Award, 2003) para 149: 'There is no doubt that, even if Cytrar did not have an indefinite permit but a permit renewable every year, the Claimant's expectation was that of a long-term investment relying on the recovery of its investment and the estimated return through the operation of the Landfill during its entire useful life'.

[181] *ibid*, para 150: 'This shows that even before the Claimant made its investment, it was widely known that the investor expected its investments in the Landfill to last for a long term and that it took this into account to estimate the time and business required to recover such investment and obtain the expected return upon making its tender offer for the acquisition of the assets related to the Landfill. To evaluate if the actions attributable to the Respondent—as well as the Resolution—violate the [BIT], such expectations should be considered legitimate and should be evaluated in light of the [BIT] and of international law'.

[182] *ibid*, paras 148–9: 'Cytrar's operation of the Landfill never compromised the ecological balance, the protection of the environment or the health of the people, and all the infringements committed were either remediable or remediated or subject to minor penalties . . . While the Resolution is based on some of these violations to deny the renewal of the permit, apparently through a literal and strict interpretation of the conditions under which the Permit was granted, it would be excessively formalistic, in light of the above considerations, the [BIT] and international law, to understand that the Resolution is proportional to such violations when such infringements do not pose a present or imminent risk to the ecological balance or to people's health'.

[183] *ibid*, para 127 et seq and para 140: 'As expressed by the respondent, the Landfill's proximity to Hermosillo's urban center and not concrete evidence that the Landfill's operation is harmful for the environment or public health is the issue that concentrates the opposition of the groups that are against the landfill'.

[184] *ibid*, paras 144–5.

6.5 RESERVED POWERS AS A PRINCIPLE OF INTERPRETATION

It follows from the above that a contractual commitment may be a primary factor affecting the legitimacy of future exercise of a state's regulatory powers. However, this interrelates with another issue, namely whether such a contract *itself* may be modified or affected by subsequent regulation. The general 'police powers' rule examined above would suggest that regulatory change may affect contractual arrangements to the same extent as other investments. This is not different merely because the state is a party to the contract. It is necessary to distinguish between the state as a contracting party and the state as a regulator. Imposition of new environmental or labour standards which affect an investment project conducted under an investment contract might make the contract unprofitable to the extent of deprivation. It follows from the above that this, at the outset, remains a normal business risk that the investor must accept, but subject to a proportionality requirement. At the same time, however, a contractual undertaking relied on to make an investment constitutes a prima facie basis for protected legitimate expectations. If the state has distinctly committed not to change the regulatory regime, a subsequent change will constitute a breach of the investor's legitimate expectations and, if deprivatory in effect, it will also be expropriatory in substance.[185] The crucial issue would thus seem to be whether the regulatory measure constitutes a breach of contract; in other words, whether it disregards a positive commitment of the state not to change the regulatory regime. Whether there is such a commitment is, however, subject to interpretation, where the fact of the state's regulatory power may influence what the investor could legitimately expect on the basis of the contract.[186] In the following I will show how an interpretative principle of reserved powers has been applied in arbitral practice to condition the expectations that may legitimately be inferred from state contractual commitments.[187] I show how this has two

[185] *Methanex v USA* (Award, 2005) Part IV, Chapter D, para 7.

[186] This is well known from municipal law applicable to government contracts, where it is often held that the state commitments restricting public power must be interpreted on the basis of a presumption against such restriction, or that the restriction must be explicit or 'appear in unmistakable terms', see *US v Winstar Corporation et al*, 518 US 839, 116 S Ct 2432 (1996) 2448.

[187] Deciphering the jurisprudence in this regard is complicated by the to some extent parallel applicability of international and municipal law. The relevant international law can, somewhat loosely, be conceptualised in a standard of legitimate expectations, which in principle sets out an independent standard of review. At the same time, the contractual right crystallising the legitimate expectation in question must be determined at the outset by reference to its applicable municipal law. A realistic approach is that investment law jurisprudence here reflects a quite autonomous appreciation of the conflicting interests and policies relevant to the general issue involved, viewed in the light of the particular objective of investment protection, and informed by the positive law constituted by relevant sources of municipal and international law. That is the approach I take in the following.

aspects. It may entail a general presumption to the effect that the state retains freedom to change its policies, and it may suggest a more extensive retention of powers in relation to a dramatic change of circumstances.

A. Change of Policy

It is intrinsic to the prerogative of public power and democratic majority rule that every government must have a large measure of freedom to change policies according to the attending circumstances and its own current priorities. For a government to undertake not to change policies in the future is tantamount to denying itself (or future governments) a fundamental attribute of government. This might suggest that such commitments should not be treated lightly, and, like other exceptional commitments, should be expressly and 'unmistakably' specified. In the context of foreign investment this stands against an opposing concern, however. A contract with the government is usually entered into precisely to ensure stability, and a 'stabilisation', or restriction on the government's ability to change its policies, may have been a fundamental pre-requisite for making the investment. In other words, a restriction on the government's ability to change policies in relation to a specific investment is not necessarily so exceptional.[188] This is reflected in a relatively distinct response of investment jurisprudence, mainly concerned with the interpretation of stabilisation clauses.[189] It holds that distinct commitments to refrain from regulatory change should not, as a rule, be interpreted restrictively, but that the state's ordinary right to regulate is preserved as a reserved power in the absence of a clear commitment in the contract.

This is first illustrated by *Saudi Arabia v Aramco*. The question was whether the concession included an exclusive right for the company to transport oil extracted by virtue of the concession, which would then have been violated when the government later granted an exclusive transport concession to the Greek shipowner Onassis. The question thus involved the authority of the state to regulate transport of oil extracted from its territory. The state accordingly claimed that the concession had to be interpreted restrictively, as a restriction on its sovereign powers. The tribunal rejected this, seemingly for the reason that it would not accept that there was a presumption *against* restriction of public power by

[188] Cf, eg *CMS Gas v Argentina* (Award, 2005) para 151: 'The important question . . . is that concerning the right to benefit from stabilization clauses. This discussion is well known in international law and to the extent this dispute concerns the simultaneous operation of the License and protection under the treaty, the stabilization ensured a right that the Claimant can properly invoke'.

[189] See also Nassar, *Sanctity of Contracts Revisited: A Study in the Theory and Practice of Long Term International Commercial Transactions* (Martinus Nijhoff, Dordrecht, 1994) 133 et seq.

contract: '[R]estrictions of its powers, which a State accepts by contract, are a manifestation of its sovereignty and States are bound to fulfill their obligations to the same extent as private persons'.[190] The tribunal held, accordingly, that whether the state had restricted its power depended on ordinary principles of contract interpretation. Since the concession expressly mentioned the company's right to 'transport, deal with, carry away and export' oil it extracted (although it did not expressly mention sea transport),[191] the tribunal held that the concession could not reasonably be interpreted so as to reserve a power to determine the means by which oil was to be 'transported, carried away and exported'.[192] However, the tribunal accepted at the same time that restrictive interpretation might be justified in relation to 'doubtful clauses of a contract', where 'interests of a general nature which cannot be defended otherwise' were concerned.[193] In other words, it suggested that such commitments had to be *clearly* ascertainable, displaying to this effect a more cautious attitude towards presuming that the state would have restricted its powers.

A clarity requirement is even more explicit in the older case of *Radio Corporation of America v China*.[194] Similar to the later *Aramco* case, the company claimed that an agreement entered into with the Chinese government gave it exclusive rights to operate radio communication between China and the United States. When the government later entered into a similar agreement with another company, the first company claimed that this constituted a violation of its contractual rights. Rejecting this claim on the basis of an interpretation of the contract,[195] the tribunal held that the government could not be presumed to have restricted its powers in this manner. On the contrary, it held that such an undertaking would have had to be 'effected in a clear and distinct manner',[196] and be ascertainable 'beyond reasonable doubt':

190 *Saudi Arabia v Aramco* (Award, 1958) 27 ILR 117, 192.

191 *ibid*, 175, reproducing Article I of the Concession Agreement of 1933 as follows: 'The Government hereby grants to the Company on the terms and conditions hereinafter mentioned, and with respect to the area defined below, the *exclusive right*, for a period of sixty years from the effective date hereof, to explore, prospect, drill for, extract, treat, manufacture, transport, deal with, carry away and export, petroleum, asphalt, naphta, natural gases, ozokerite and other hydrocarbons, and the derivatives of all such products. It is understood, however, that such right does not include the exclusive right to sell crude or refined products within the area described below or within Saudi Arabia'.

192 *ibid*, 179 et seq.

193 *ibid*, 192: 'Restrictive interpretation may only be justified when the sovereign rights invoked by the State concern interests of a general nature which cannot be defended otherwise than by disregarding the doubtful clauses of a contract'.

194 *Radio Corporation of America v National Govt of Republic of China* (Award, 1935) (1936) 30 *AJIL* 535.

195 It appears that the contract was interpreted partly on the basis of principles of law common to the parties (US and Chinese law), and partly on the basis of principles of international law, see eg *ibid*, 537, 540 and 542.

196 *ibid*, 540.

> The Chinese Government can certainly sign away a part of its liberty of action, and this also in the field of the establishment of international radio-telegraphic communications, and of its cooperation therein. It can do so as well in an implicit manner, if a reasonable construction of its undertakings leads up to that conclusion. It will, as any other party, be bound by law and by any obligations, legally accepted. *But as a sovereign government, on principle free in its action for the public interest as it sees it, it cannot be presumed to have accepted such restriction of its freedom of action, unless the acceptance can be ascertained distinctly and beyond reasonable doubt.*[197] (emphasis added)

This assumption that the state's powers are reserved, insofar as no distinct commitment to the contrary has been made, is also reflected in the classical discussion of stabilisation clauses. It may best be illustrated with the decision in *Texaco v Libya*, where it was discussed at length. The tribunal held that the contract in question could not be interpreted so as to reserve the state's powers, since it had expressly committed not to alter the rights of the company granted under the concession contract.[198] Essentially, the tribunal held that the inclusion of the stabilisation clause excluded the application of the administrative contracts doctrine (*contrat administratif*), which was otherwise part of Libyan law.[199] At the same time, the tribunal suggested that if the contract had not included a stabilisation clause, the state's powers would have had to be considered reserved.[200] It even expressly assumed that this, at the outset, would have

[197] *ibid*, 540 and contrast also *the Administration of Posts and Telegraphs of the Republic of Czechoslovakia v Radio Corporation of America* (Award, 1932), (1936) 30 *AJIL* 523.

[198] *Texaco v Libya* (Award (Merits), 1977) 53 ILR 389, paras 54–6; the clause in question (Cl 16 of the contract) read as follows, (see award para 3): 'The Government of Libya will take all steps necessary to ensure that the company enjoys all the rights conferred by this Concession—The contractual rights expressly created by this concession shall not be altered except by mutual consent of the parties . . . This concession shall throughout the period of its validity be construed in accordance with the Petroleum Law and the Regulations in force on the date of execution of the agreement of amendment when this paragraph was incorporated into this concession agreement. Any amendment to or repeal of such Regulations shall not affect the contractual rights of the Company without its consent'.

[199] *ibid*, para 56 (at 465): '[W]hat gives a contract entered into by a public or State legal entity its administrative character is the fact that it "confers on the administration rights and powers which are not usual in a civil contract, such as the power to modify, terminate or revoke the contract when the public interest requires it to do so", which is of course the most characteristic evidence that the parties have intended not to contract on a footing of equality—an administrative contract is essentially unequal. But when, as is the case in the present instance, the clause has an essentially negative import, the State or the administrative authorities undertaking not to use powers which are normally their powers, without the partner's agreement, it expresses on the contrary, the fact that the State intended to contract on a footing of strict equality with its partner: that it was the intention of the State, as under a civil contract, to deal on an equal basis with the contracting partner'.

[200] *ibid*, para 56 (at 466): 'Indeed, if the clause were not in the contract, one would have to presume that the State had intended to conserve intact, in respect of its contracting partner, the free and full exercise of its privileges and usual powers'.

made the contractually stipulated rights and obligations subject to subsequent regulatory change.[201]

Later cases have confirmed accordingly that clear and distinct commitments will have to be interpreted as creating a right for the investor to be exempt from subsequent regulatory change, irrespective of whether the commitment is general or specific.[202] In other words, practice displays little support for any presumption against commitments of regulatory stability, which in such case might have entailed a more general requirement of specificity. This reflects the consideration that a 'contractual immutability' commitment is not exceptional in such relationships; on the contrary, as held in a recent case, it is 'well known in international law'.[203] It may also fulfill an important and reasonable purpose as a means to ensure stability and predictability in a foreign investment transaction.[204] Conversely, it has been held that a requirement of specificity may apply to contractual restriction of particular prerogatives that would constitute an exceptional commitment, such as is the case with a restriction on the right to expropriate or nationalise.[205]

At the same time, the above suggests that state contracts at the outset are subject to regulatory change in the absence of a clear and distinct contractual commitment to the contrary. For instance, the state may impose a regulation fixing a maximum price for gas or electricity distribution, which may also contemplate application to any state contracts whereby the state or state-owned entities have contracted to buy energy from foreign-owned companies, possibly at a higher price regulated by a tariff adjustment scheme in the contracts themselves. The crucial question will be whether the tariff regulation in the contract also has to be interpreted as a commitment stabilising the regulatory regime. Since this requires, according to the practice related above, a distinct commitment, the presumption might seem

[201] *ibid*, 467: 'If the contract is silent, one can and should even accept the idea that the public authority intended to reserve the possibility of changing, by unilateral actions taken under normal conditions, certain of the contractual provisions and, in some cases, to abrogate the contract'.

[202] See eg *Revere Copper v OPIC* (Award, 1978) 56 ILR 258, 280; *AGIP v Congo* (Award, 1979) 21 ILM 726, para 84; *Petrola Hellas v Greece* (Award, 1986), (1986) 11 *YbCA* 105; *LETCO v Liberia* (Award, 1986) 26 ILM 647, 666–7; and *CMS Gas v Argentina* (Award, 2005) para 151.

[203] *CMS Gas v Argentina* (Award, 2005) para 151.

[204] See eg *LETCO v Liberia* (Award, 1986) 26 ILM 647, 666–7: 'This clause, commonly known as a "Stabilization Clause" is commonly found in long-term development contracts and, as is the case with notification procedures of the Concession Agreement, is meant to avoid the arbitrary actions of the contracting government. This clause must be respected, especially in this type of agreement. Otherwise, the contracting state may easily avoid its contractual obligations by legislation'.

[205] See *AMINOIL v Kuwait* (Award, 1982) (1982) 21 ILM 976, para 95: 'No doubt contractual limitations on the State's right to nationalize are juridically possible, but what that would involve would be a particularly serious undertaking which would have to expressly stipulated for, and be within the regulations governing the conclusion of state contracts; and it is to be expected that it should cover only a relatively limited period'. And see also to this effect *Amoco Int'l Finance Corp v Iran* (1987) 15 Iran-US CT Rep 189, para 179.

to be that it will not, and that the maximum price will apply. This comes with the caveat that it is still subject to the general proportionality test of the indirect expropriation standard. If, in other words, the regulatory change entails a substantial deprivation of a distinct contractual right, it may still be expropriatory and require compensation. Moreover, it is arguable that the impact of an umbrella clause could be to make all contractual obligations of the state immutable against subsequent regulatory change.[206]

B. Changed Circumstances (*rebus sic stantibus*)

To say that a contract is protected against a subsequent change of regulation, by a distinct 'stabilisation' or 'immutability commitment', as held above, is not to say that such a commitment is itself immutable.[207] No contractual undertaking is completely impervious to a change of circumstances or supervening events.[208] Given the potentially important public interests involved, and the function of public authority in this regard, it is conceivable that a commitment not to regulate could be more susceptible to changed circumstances than ordinary private law undertakings.[209] Moreover, as held above, a functional concept of police powers naturally encompasses a margin of appreciation, where the assessment of regulatory necessity due to changed circumstances would have to rest as a rule with the government. Combined with a liberal doctrine of changed circumstances, this could ensure that account would have to be taken of concerns specific to government contracts, in a manner not dissimilar to the comparable responses in municipal law. Such concerns are accommodated by the right of states to expropriate, as discussed above, and justify that a state may always lawfully annul a previous undertaking upon payment of compensation. However, this may also suggest that there is not much room for a liberal doctrine of changed circumstances beyond this. A stabilisation commitment, even if upheld as a contractual commitment, will not strictly restrain or prohibit regulatory change, but merely require payment of contractual damages. More than a prohibitive

[206] See above Section 5.3.

[207] See eg Nassar (1995) 136.

[208] This is a fundamental principle of contract law, deriving from Roman law and known to all modern legal systems. The considerable complexities and differences involved are beyond the scope of this book, but in general it would seem that one may distinguish between frustration of an undertaking by an unforeseen chain of events, and suspension of an obligation (or exemption of liability) through *force majeure* or hardship, see eg Zweigert and Kötz (eds), *An Introduction to Comparative Law* (Clarendon Press, Oxford, 1998) 517 et seq.

[209] See eg Friedmann, *The Changing Structure of International Law* (Stevens & Sons, London, 1964) 200–206, suggesting an analogy to the French legal doctrine of the *contrat administratif*. See also Maniruzzaman, 'State Contracts with Aliens: The Question of Unilateral Change by the State in Contemporary International Law' (1992) 9(4) *J Int'l Arb* 141, 159; and see also *LIAMCO v Libya* (Award, 1977), (1982) 62 ILR 141, 207.

restriction it should thus perhaps be conceived as an allocation of risk, ie as a promise by the state to bear the economic consequences of regulatory change.[210]

Conceived in this manner, the nature of a stabilisation commitment does not necessarily suggest that it must have any greater susceptibility to frustration by changed circumstances than other private undertakings.[211] This may also explain the quite restrictive line of arbitral practice to this issue. It would seem that no case has considered a distinct state commitment to have been frustrated by a change of circumstances, and a number of cases have held that even dramatic social and economic crises did not *exempt* the state from its contractual obligations. Two cases are illustrative. In *Himpurna v Persero,* the tribunal refused to consider an energy sales contract, pegged to US dollars, frustrated by the dramatic devaluation of the local currency.[212] A central concern seems to have been that the contract in question had already been relied on by the investor to make a substantial investment. To treat the contract as unwritten would thus have shifted the burden of the financial crisis onto the private investor:

> By its count, the claimant invested some US$ 289 million in the project. To argue that PLN may simply walk away from its contractual obligations, without any regard to these investments, and to say that this argument is based on considerations of good faith, is certainly unacceptable. PLN has never explained why the full brunt of the financial crisis should be deflected on to an innocent party which, moreover, is simply seeking to rely on a contract as it is written.[213]

Similarly, in *CMS Gas v Argentina,* a gas transportation licence was unilaterally amended by the government, as an emergency measure pursuant to the Argentine debt crisis in 1999–2002, and implemented without regard for the agreed tariff structure and stabilisation commitments in the contract. The tribunal held that the amendment could not be justified as an emergency measure required by a state of necessity under either Argentine law or international law,[214] nor could it be justified according to the contractual doctrine of *imprévision* which was a part of Argentine law.[215] A main concern seems to have been that the contract itself contained an elaborate tariff adjustment and renegotiation scheme,

[210] US law may provide an appropriate analogy in this regard, see eg *US v Winstar Corp et al*, 518 US 839, 116 S Ct 2432 (1996) 2452.

[211] Certain cases of the Iran-US Claims Tribunal nevertheless suggest that contracts related to particularly sensitive state functions may be frustrated by later events specifically connected with the government function, see especially *Questech v the Ministry of National Defence of Iran* (1985) 9 Iran-US CT Rep 107, which concerned contracts related to the intelligence services of Iran, held to have been frustrated by the Iranian revolution and the change of government.

[212] *Himpurna v Persero* (Award, 1999), (2000) 25 *YbCA* 13, para 181.

[213] *ibid*, para 191.

[214] *CMS Gas v Argentina* (Award, 2005) para 217, and para 315 et seq.

[215] *ibid*, para 221 et seq.

conceivably addressing the situation at hand. This meant the crisis could not be considered unforeseeable or even unforeseen, and therefore did not justify stepping outside the contractual framework.[216]

Only in the recent case of *LG&E v Argentina* has it been held that an emergency situation justified suspension of the state's obligation on the basis of a state of necessity.[217] As in the *CMS* case, the tribunal held that the Argentine emergency measures at the outset violated the BIT undertakings of the state to observe obligations under a number of gas distribution licences.[218] It nevertheless held that the measures were justified as emergency measures for a limited period of time,[219] both under the express 'necessity' exception in the BIT,[220] and under general international law as a 'state of necessity'.[221] At the same time, the tribunal merely held that the state's obligations were suspended for a very restricted period of time. It noted, moreover, the absence of a binding contractual agreement between the state and the claimant, holding that this *might* have 'allowed the parties to agree on stabilization clauses in the event of changes in certain circumstances'.[222] To this effect the case arguably *confirms* the restrictive tendency of practice in relation to changed circumstances, where a distinct commitment encompassing the circumstances at hand is involved.

This does not mean changed circumstances have no potential impact on state commitments. Nevertheless, recent arbitral case law evinces a concern to uphold the contractual relationship as such, and to accommodate changed circumstances *within* the contractual structure.[223] The

[216] *ibid*, paras 224–5.

[217] In contrast to the *CMS* case it would seem, the license arrangements in this case apparently were not contractual, and therefore not directly binding for the state, see *LG&E v Argentina* (Award, 2006), para 98, and contrast *CMS Gas v Argentina* (Award, 2005) para 123.

[218] *LG&E v Argentina* (Award, 2006) para 139, and para 175.

[219] *ibid*, para 226: 'In the judgement of the Tribunal, from 1 December 2001 until 26 April 2003, Argentina was in a period of crisis during which it was necessary to enact measures to maintain public order and protect its essential security interests'.

[220] *ibid*, para 204.

[221] *ibid*, para 257: 'The essential interests of the Argentine State were threatened in December 2001. It faced an extremely serious threat to its existence, its political and economic survival, to the possibility of maintaining its essential services in operation, and to the preservation of its internal peace. There is no serious evidence in record that Argentina contributed to the crisis resulting in the state of necessity. In this circumstances, and economic recovery package was the only means to respond to the crisis. Although there may have been a number of ways to draft the economic recovery plan, the evidence before the Tribunal demonstrates that an across-the-board response was necessary, and the tariffs on public utilities had to be addressed'.

[222] *ibid*, para 98.

[223] More generally, this is also a tendency reflected in new contractual techniques to ensure flexibility and the continuance of the relationship in the face of changed circumstances, through inclusion of quite sophisticated renegotiation and adjustment mechanisms in the contract. See generally about such a 'relational approach', Nassar (2005) 19 et seq; and see also Kröll (2004) 437 et seq.

decision in *AMINOIL v Kuwait* is illustrative. A main issue addressed by the tribunal was the potential impact of the passage of time and social development on a stabilisation commitment. Essentially, the tribunal held that the concession contract, and with it the stabilisation commitment, had undergone a fundamental change with the strong modernisation and economic development of Kuwait and the Kuwaiti state. Its changing context meant it became immersed in and subject to the same regulatory framework as a more ordinary government contract.[224] At the same time, this was not held to entail that the stabilisation commitment was devoid of effect.[225] The tribunal refused to adopt a more conventional analysis of changed circumstances as an excuse for non-performance or repudiation.[226] Instead it seems that it fundamentally adjusted the commitment in accordance with the change of circumstances. The actual consequence drawn from this was that the stabilisation clause had to be construed so as not strictly to *prevent* nationalisation, or conceivably other regulatory measures deemed necessary, but as a commitment to respect the economical equilibrium of the contract for the prescribed period.[227] The tribunal thus awarded compensation on the basis of a perceived contractual right to continue in operation of the concession for the prescribed period of time.[228]

This dual concern to uphold the economic balance of the contract, and accommodate changed circumstances within this structure, is evidenced also in cases confronting a more dramatic change of events. Again the *CMS* and *Himpurna* cases are illustrative. In *CMS Gas v Argentina*, as mentioned, the tribunal essentially held that the inherent flexibility of the contractual arrangement prevented the unilateral 'elimination' of the stabilised tariff-structure.[229] This did not mean that the claimant could insist on keeping the agreed tariff without adjustment, irrespective of the changed circumstances. The tribunal expressly assumed that an adjustment of the tariff would have been necessary to take account of the economic crisis.[230] The apparently crucial concern was, however, that the contractual arrangement itself contained the necessary adjustment mechanisms, which had been fundamentally disregarded by the state

[224] *AMINOIL v Kuwait* (Award, 1982) para 98: 'This Concession—in its origin a mining concession granted by a State whose institutions were still incomplete and directed to narrow patrimonial ends—became one of the essential instruments in the economic and social progress of a national community in full process of development . . . The contract of Concession thus changed its character and became one of those contracts in regard to which, in most legal systems, the State while remaining bound to respect the contractual equilibrium, enjoys special advantages'.

[225] *ibid*, para 89 and para 96.

[226] *ibid*, para 101.

[227] *ibid*, para 159.

[228] *ibid*, para 149, and paras 158–9.

[229] *CMS Gas v Argentina* (Award, 2005) para 162.

[230] *ibid*, para 154, and paras 165–6.

through the unilateral measures imposed.[231] Moreover, the tariff adjustment formula in the contract appears to have been intrinsic to the underlying financing of the project.[232] The tribunal accordingly held that the unilateral amendment of the tariff, which disregarded the company's financial costs, was irreconcilable with the general contractual requirement of a fair and reasonable tariff.[233] In other words, far from re-adjusting the contractual balance, the government measures were held to disrupt the economical balance of the contract. Conversely, in the *Himpurna* case, as also mentioned above, the tribunal similarly refused to hold the contract to have been frustrated by supervening events, as this would have pulled away the basic framework relied on by the investor to make its investment. At the same time, the tribunal relied on the concept of 'abuse of rights' to preclude recovery of lost profits on investments not yet made.[234] The reality of this was to allow government repudiation, in so far as the contract had not been relied on. The lack of reliance presented the tribunal with a very different situation to that confronting the tribunal in the *CMS* case. The devaluation of the local currency meant that the obligation of the Indonesian state entity to buy electricity at a price pegged to US dollars no longer corresponded with local demand. To uphold the initial bargain would thus have meant allowing the American investor to recover substantial windfall profits with no risk involved, on the basis of a contract fundamentally disrupted by a new economic reality. This presents the fundamental contrast to the *CMS* case. To hold that the government repudiation was justified to prevent an abuse of rights means nothing other than that it represented an adequate adjustment of the contract to a fundamental disruption of its original economic reality.

[231] *ibid*, para 238: 'The Tribunal can therefore conclude that if a rebalance of the contractual commitments was required because of changing economic circumstances and their effect costs and returns, the mechanisms to meet this objective were available under the law and the License. The necessary adjustments could be accommodated within the structure of the guarantees offered to the Claimant. This approach in turn would have made any unilateral determination by the Respondent unnecessary'.

[232] An important premise seems to have been that the stabilised tariff structure, pegged to US dollars, was meant to be relied on for the financing of the project, mostly dependent on debts denominated in US dollars, see *ibid*, para 171 et seq.

[233] *ibid*, para 181.

[234] *Himpurna v Persero* (Award, 1999), (2000) 25 YbCA 13, para 315 et seq.

7

Summary and Final Comments

7.1 INTRODUCTION

WHILE BEING OCCUPIED with a singular substantive legal issue, several disparate lines of reasoning have run through this book, all nevertheless related to a common theme, namely the transgression of traditional legal boundaries by a purpose-driven legal process directed towards certain distinct economic concerns and values, and involving states and (mostly) private companies as, in a sense, equal participants.[1] Two main angles have in particular been adopted and further explored in the book, the first being the conceptualisation of this process as a form of international law, followed by a closer examination into the substantive legal principles developed with respect to contractual claims against states. In this final chapter I shall attempt to draw together and briefly summarise further the main arguments and findings of the book in relation to these two overarching perspectives. I shall conclude by setting forth some thoughts and personal views on the nature and underlying concerns of the international arbitral process dealing with investment claims, as I believe have been illuminated by this study.

7.2 THE INTERNATIONAL LEGAL PROCESS OF CONTRACT CLAIMS—SUMMARY OF CHAPTERS TWO, THREE AND FOUR

Adopting the so-called 'process perspective', which has been a significant inspiration for me writing this book, meant in particular that the natural starting-point had to be the actual legal practice itself. In the first substantive chapter of the book (chapter two) I consequently address the roots and development of the present-day international arbitral process dealing with claims by private companies against states, partly through international commercial arbitration and partly through the now current mechanism of investment treaty arbitration. A particular aim of this chapter is to trace the development of international law on this subject as

[1] For a discussion of this concept and the process perspective in international law, see Higgins, *Problems and Process: International Law and How We Use It* (Oxford, 1994).

a response to certain shortcomings of the traditional doctrine of diplomatic protection in international law.

The chapter shows how the two distinct legal processes of mixed claims commissions and international commercial arbitration in parallel development came to share certain key characteristics in their dealings with investment claims, and in particular contract claims, against states. The most important common feature in this regard is what I have termed a hybrid perspective on the applicable substantive law, where the arbitral tribunals apply both international law and municipal law in one integrated legal process. I furthermore argue that this now has culminated in the development of modern investment treaty arbitration based on ICSID, where it is similarly a key feature and even explicitly provided for in Article 42 of the ICSID Convention.

In chapter three I then go on to approach this practice from the conceptual and theoretical framework of international legal doctrine. My point of departure in this regard is the conceptual challenge involved in dealing with contractual relationships between sovereign governments and private entities from the viewpoint of international law, traditionally conceived as a law consisting exclusively between states. The chapter describes how this was initially dealt with by what has been termed the theory of 'internationalisation', which, drawing on choice of law methodology, essentially attempted to justify the application of international law to state contracts as an intentional choice of law elevating the contract into the sphere of international law. I then show how this theory both side-stepped and provoked a more fundamental and underlying controversy between what I term, respectively, a monist and a dualist perspective on the nature and applicability of international law where private entities and interests are concerned. Following a scrutiny of this controversy and the substantive legal positions they presuppose, I argue in favour of a theoretical outlook that is on the one hand conceptually and formally open and 'monist'—in the sense that it does not acknowledge any fundamental characteristic of international law that would exclude its direct application to, say, a contractual undertaking made by a state towards a foreign investor. On the other hand, however, I argue that international law in its current form presupposes dualism as a substantive premise, structuring and co-ordinating the relationship between municipal and international law. This does not exclude in principle its application to individuals and private entities, but constitutes in a sense a rebuttable presumption to the effect that such matters are governed by municipal law. The essential argument that I then develop is that this theoretical approach both explains and justifies the hybrid perspective taken by international arbitral tribunals dealing with contract claims, as well as investment claims in general. This is followed by a surface analysis of the substantive norms applicable under international law to protect contractual and property interests, showing in this regard how both the real interests at which the norms are directed and the modality of their invocation clearly suggest that the rights at issue, at least from the moment they are relied on, must be deemed individual rights belonging to each individual investor, as distinct from 'collective' rights vested in the state. The final analysis developed in this chapter is that the 'applicability' of international law in a given case is a matter that depends both on the substantive applicability of the norms in question and on the competence of a relevant tribunal to take the norms into account. In other words, in order to apply international law, an arbitral tribunal must both ascertain that there is a rule or principle of international law claiming application to the case, and that it has been given jurisdiction to render a binding decision on the matter. A choice of law provision in a contract providing for application of international law may, according to this understanding, be construed as vesting the tribunal with competence to apply international law.

The latter issue of arbitral authority is also dealt with further in chapter four of the book, where I examine the question of jurisdiction over contract claims and how this has been dealt with in parallel by the 'contractual' process of international commercial arbitration and the more public international law based process of investment treaty arbitration. The chapter approaches this question from the perspective of arbitral practice, conceived in terms not merely of international law but as an international legal process dependent on interaction between municipal and international law. On the one hand, I show how the notion of international commercial arbitration, as an international remedy underlying and securing state undertakings, has been conceptualised by arbitral practice in terms of the private law concept of party autonomy, but modified and replanted in the fertile soil of international law to justify a legal authority independent of any particular municipal law. On the other hand, I show how similar concerns have driven the parallel process of investment treaty arbitration in a similar direction to encompass a wide scope of contractual claims, based on a flexible and open-ended notion of 'investment' and a strong notion of the primacy of international law over municipal law. This has justified a development where investment treaty tribunals increasingly have asserted jurisdiction over contractual claims irrespective of contractual jurisdiction clauses, and to this effect assumed powers otherwise vested in municipal courts and tribunals. The underlying concern seen to justify this is arguably, in the same manner as with the parallel practice of international commercial arbitration, the need to assert distance from the municipal law of the state concerned, in order to achieve an effective remedy upholding and securing state undertakings in the context of private investments.

Seen together, chapters two, three and four present a critical analysis of the contractual modality more or less openly adopted by the international arbitral process dealing with investment claims, also beyond the field of purely contractual claims. The analysis on the one hand shows how the 'contractual' process of international commercial arbitration constitutes the single most important procedural model for investment treaty arbitration. On the other hand, the analysis reveals that a purely contractual model contains severe limitations in terms of being able to adequately explain and conceptualise the arbitral process in terms of international law. The substantive aspect of this, dealt with in chapter three on the applicability of international law, is essentially that a substantive contract law perspective fails to take account of the nature and function of international law as applicable to the relationship between a state and a private investor, even where this is expressly based in a contract. It also has a procedural aspect, reflected especially in arbitral practice concerned with investment treaty jurisdiction over contract claims. A closer scrutiny clearly shows how the contractual model fails to account for the main features of this process as a unilateral claims procedure. At the same time, I show how the desire to uphold contractual undertakings remains a significant substantive concern of arbitral practice, and justifiably so in view of its underlying rationale to provide a remedy against state power. The paradox is, however, that this to some extent has lead to a tendency where investment treaty tribunals are increasingly assertive, even disregarding outright freely negotiated dispute resolution procedures in state contracts. This may give some thoughts for adjustment.

7.3 SUBSTANTIVE LAW AND TELEOLOGY—SUMMARY OF CHAPTERS FIVE AND SIX

In the second part of the book, chapters five and six, I address the substantive content of the law developed by arbitral practice in relation to contract claims. Chapter five first addresses the most relevant standards or principles under international law that protect, directly or indirectly, contractual rights and expectations. Specifically, I analyse arbitral practice dealing with contract claims in relation to three common treaty standards: the expropriation standard, the so-called 'umbrella' clause and the fair and equitable treatment standard. This is followed by an analysis of arbitral practice purporting to apply customary international law in relation to state contract claims, both in respect of so-called 'internationalised' contracts and on the basis of the customary international law principle of protection of acquired rights. The main analysis I develop on this basis is to identify a common undercurrent of concerns and values quite consistently reflected in arbitral practice dealing with state contract claims, and epitomised in a concept of respect for 'legitimate expectations'. As it has been applied and developed by arbitral practice I argue that this concept contains three main elements: first, a requirement of specific expectations being induced by a contractual or similarly concrete and binding commitment from the state; secondly, a requirement that these expectations have been relied on to make an investment; and thirdly, a requirement that the expectations have been frustrated by something comparable to a government act. The analysis presented shows how these elements may be more or less significant in respect of the relevant standards. Crucially, however, none are ever absent from consideration under any of the applicable standards. A good example is the analysis of the so-called umbrella clause. In this regard, the main controversy is whether the clause is breached only where a public or government act of some kind is involved, ie the third element identified above. Several cases do suggest this, although it is refuted by other cases and has no basis in the common wording of the clause. If the clause is seen as an expression of the more general 'legitimate expectations' standard, as I suggest, this provides an additional 'structural rationale' for considering such a government act requirement implicit in the clause—being an explicit requirement under both the expropriation standard and the fair and equitable treatment standard, and as I further show, a significant part of the rationale of applying international law to state contractual undertakings. This illustrates how a concept of 'legitimate expectations' constitutes an underlying structural context for the interpretation of different investment treaty standards, creating a basis for convergent interpretations. Another significant example of this is how arbitral practice has conceived the economical interest commonly held to be protected by the relevant standards—what may be denoted the 'compensation interest'. While I show in the chapter that one of the key elements in the 'legitimate expectation' standard is the investor's reliance on a promise or undertaking from the state, I also show that the level of compensation typically awarded is based on the investor's expectation interest where a breach of contract lies at the root of the claim. What this clearly shows is that arbitral practice perceives the relationship between state and investor from a 'transactional' perspective. While not surprising in the purely contractual context of international commercial arbitration—ie arbitral proceedings based directly on a contract between the state (or more commonly a state company) and the investor—it is interesting to note that the same perspective is adopted in respect of investment treaty standards as applied by investment treaty tribunals. In other words, investment treaty standards are also commonly interpreted to protect the contractual expectation interest as such, and not merely losses that the investor may have had by trusting a promise or an undertaking from the state. This is also an entirely logical approach in view of the underlying rationale of international investment law as a means to encourage the flow of foreign investment. If the relevant standards had only protected the capital committed (*damnum emergens*) and not lost profit (*lucrum cessans*), this would have constituted an implicit encouragement for states to expropriate profitable investments, and in practice leave the investor's prospects of return unprotected. The chapter thus shows how the underlying rationale of international investment law has inspired the development of a substantive law with an implicit contractual outlook, substantially limited to state undertakings and commitments relied on to make an investment.

In chapter six, I then examine further how this adopted contractual modality relates to the notion of state sovereignty and regulatory authority under international law. A main point of departure of this chapter is that the concept of public authority in international law lacks the normative deep structure it has under municipal law, where it usually coincides with the state's own political and constitutional source of legitimacy, eg the notion of democracy or popular sovereignty, as the basis of parliamentary authority. I nevertheless argue that a somewhat comparable normative core is found in international law through the notion of permanent sovereignty over natural resources, commonly affiliated with the increasing recognition of international human rights. I show how this principle has specific application in international investment law where it underlies a quite consistent recognition of expropriation as an inalienable state prerogative, ie a prerogative that cannot be restricted by contract at least in absolute terms. I especially show how this principle has been applied by international arbitral tribunals to justify a more lenient compensation standard, though with somewhat limited application in practice, and more practically to justify expropriation in spite of so called stabilisation clauses in state contracts. I then go on to show how a notion of public and regulatory authority has achieved recognition in international investment law mainly as a functional concept legitimising government control over private rights and investments. Analysis of practice shows that this is encapsulated primarily in a concept of 'police powers' conceived as a general right to regulate private investment, though in arbitral practice this is fundamentally held in check by a notion that previous commitments must be honoured. Pursuant to this, however, I also show how in interpretation of such commitments, arbitral practice has relied on a more or less implicit notion of reserved powers, which both (i) requires that a commitment placing restrictions on government authority must be clear and distinct and (ii) presumes a freedom of authority in case of a dramatic change of circumstances clearly calling for the exercise of government authority.

Chapters five and six taken together essentially show that arbitral practice dealing with contract claims against states has developed a substantive law containing all the elements of a doctrine of government contracts under international law, comparable, though not necessarily similar in content, to the doctrines that have developed on this issue under different municipal laws (eg and perhaps most prominently the doctrine of the *contrats d'état* in France).[2] The most noticeable feature is perhaps that

[2] See eg Turpin, 'Public Contracts' in K Zweigert and K Drobnig (eds), *International Encyclopedia of Comparative Law* vol VII (1982); and see also El Kosheri and Riad, 'The Law

the substantive law developed by international arbitral practice does not have the same degree of deference to government authority that is found in municipal law. In one sense, this is a natural consequence of the contractual modality underlying investment treaty arbitration, and the conception of it as a species of, or at least an outgrowth of, international commercial arbitration as further described in chapters two and four of this book. In another sense, this substantive legal response may, however, also be seen as something deeply rooted in the concerns and values embedded in the rationale of the arbitral process, and its essential justification as a remedy to facilitate the flow of foreign investment irrespective of different national legal traditions and legal uncertainty. It would thus be wrong to consider the strong contractual or 'transactional' perspective permeating international investment law as an accidental or haphazard development. On the contrary, the analysis presented in chapters five and six of this book may be seen to reveal the key notions recurring in arbitral practice in this respect to be both largely justified and limited by the primary concern to encourage reliance on state undertakings to invest in a foreign country.

On a more fundamental level, this analysis reveals a basic normative structure in the international law dealing with investment claims as it stands today, consisting in a sense of two main elements. The first is a fundamental requirement of respect for reasonable expectations relied on to make an investment ('legitimate expectations'), whereas the second is a functional concept of government authority as encompassing freedom to act or regulate in the public interest. The first element is related to the distinct rationale of the arbitral process, as a means to neutralise the structural inequality between states and investors, both being actors in a global marketplace where capital is the commodity, and states the demanders of that commodity. For states, this translates into a conceived need to be able to offer protection of the legitimate expectations of investors against various expressions of public power. Submitting to arbitration in an investment treaty or a contract with the investor constitutes a means for the state to 'tie itself to the mast', and makes the subsequent temptation to exploit its authority less alluring, or at least less 'threatening' from the investor's perspective.[3] The second element, standing opposed to this, concerns at heart significant public interests such as environmental and health concerns, human rights, minority interests, national control over the economy, financial stability, public welfare, cultural autonomy, social needs

Governing a New Generation of Petroleum Agreements: Changes in the Arbitration Process' (1986) 1 *ICSID Rev-FILJ* 257; Rivero and Walline, *Droit Administratif* (Paris, 1998) 122; Craig, *Administrative Law* (London, 2003) 541–4; Wade & Forsyth, *Administrative Law* (Oxford, 2004) 330–34; and Hadfield, 'Of Sovereignty and Contract' (1998–99) 467.

[3] Guzman, 'Why LDCs Sign Treaties That Hurt Them: Explaining the Popularity of Bilateral Investment Treaties' (1997–98) 38 *Va J Int'l Law* 639, 658.

and redistribution of wealth.[4] The analysis in chapter six reveals how such concerns in international investment law mostly are aggregated under a general public and government interest in freedom of authority at any given time. I argue that this may be seen as related to a functional concept of the state as the representative and defender of community interests, where the function of government authority is to perceive and determine the public interest constantly and at any given time, and if necessary enact measures appropriate to defend and maintain the public interest.

7.4 A CONCLUDING COMMENT

A main perspective of this book has been to describe investment treaty arbitration and international commercial arbitration as two related species of similar origin. Thus, I show how the function assumed by investment treaty arbitration was also foreshadowed by earlier developments related to state contracts and international commercial arbitration, and how investment treaty arbitration also draws on a distinctly contractual or transactional outlook. Drawing on some of the same observations, a recent critical analysis of the process of investment treaty arbitration has in contrast made it a focus of critique for being modelled according to the 'private law' and 'contractual' procedure of international commercial arbitration.[5] The focal point of the critique is that this form of ad hoc adjudication is inappropriate for dealing with the kind of 'public law' issues normally confronted in dealing with investment claims.[6] The preferred alternative suggested is a more traditional court-based procedure with a permanent international court consisting of tenured judges.[7]

In this book I have admittedly to a certain extent confirmed the underlying analysis of this critique, also going further to reveal the underlying contractual perspective adopted both in terms of procedure and substantive law by investment treaty arbitral practice. I have also exposed the severe limits of a pure contractual approach to the substantive issues involved, even where contractual undertakings are directly concerned, where these issues relate to the restriction of or exercise of government authority.

The analysis presented in this book nevertheless caters for an argument to the effect that the most significant elements of the arbitral system dealing with investment claims are in place for a reason, and would not appropriately be dealt with by a more formalised court procedure presided over by a permanent international court. Thus, a common theme running through

[4] See eg Sornarajah, *The International Law on Foreign Investment* (Cambridge, 2004) 59; and Muchlinski, *Multinational Enterprises and the Law* (Oxford, 1999) 95.

[5] Van Harten, *Investment Treaty Arbitration and Public Law* (Oxford, 2007).

[6] *ibid*, 58 et seq.

[7] *ibid*, 180 et seq.

this book has been how international commercial arbitration and investment treaty arbitration to some extent function in parallel in the international arbitral system, as alternative avenues for pursuing contractual claims. While this may be seen as an attestation to the contractual model underlying investment treaty arbitration, it may also say something about its required versatility as a legal remedy in order to be able to fulfill its underlying rationale. This is not meant to downplay the fact that current criticism of investment treaty arbitration and the broader system of international arbitration is a significant critique that needs to be taken seriously. It points to a lack of legitimacy of the existing system within significant interest groups, as further reflected in and acerbated by the ongoing attacks on the present system from NGO circles and reformist interests since the MAI controversy and before.[8] To share some of the concern underlying contemporary criticism of the system of investment treaty arbitration does not however necessarily mean that one has to agree with the cure.

Thus, it cannot be ignored at the outset that the primary and foremost concern underlying the international arbitral system, irrespective of whether it deals with investment claims or ordinary commercial contract claims, is to set in place an effective commercial remedial system for resolving and enforcing claims at the international level. In commerce, which of course is what international investment is all about, this includes not only a requirement of certainty with respect to eventually being able to get adjudicative assurance that one is right, but also and as important, a measure of certainty with respect to being able to enforce one's right in an effective manner. A further consideration, which may seem 'unprincipled' but nevertheless arguably represents a significant explanation of the present system, is that governments and private investors have a shared interest in downplaying the more fundamental aspects of matters forming the basis of investment claims. In terms of national politics, matters of money carry less prestige than matters of principle, and may therefore be easier to resolve and less likely to escalate into high-level political confrontations.[9] Moreover, it is easy to see that a permanent international court, enjoying the same authority as commercial arbitral tribunals to render binding judgments under the municipal law of the participating countries, would constitute a powerful international body vesting authority normally reserved for national courts subject to

[8] MAI stands for Multilateral Agreement on Investment, and was an iniative under the auspices of the OECD to negotiate and conclude a multilateral investment agreement that could replace the myriad of bilateral investment treaties now in place, and provide a unified framework for foreign investment worldwide. The negotiations were, however, abandoned in 1998 after fierce controversy.

[9] Cfr the point made in chapter two regarding the depoliticisation of investment disputes as one significant objective underlying the ICSID Convention, and see especially Shihata, 'Towards a Greater Depoliticization of Investment Disputes: The Roles of ICSID and MIGA' (1986) 1 *ICSID Rev-FILJ* 1.

constitutional control. Referring the same matters to ad hoc 'commercial' arbitral tribunals and framing them as 'commercial' may clearly appear less threatening from the viewpoint of national political authorities concerned to uphold national sovereignty.

For these reasons, there may be grounds for doubt as to whether a permanent international court would be able to fill the function today exercised by international arbitration to resolve investment claims. The practice of referring to arbitration in bilateral investment treaties is based on several of the same pragmatic considerations which explain the popularity of arbitration in commercial contracts between private companies. It is predictable, flexible and effective, and provides the parties with a measure of control over both the procedure and the composition of the tribunal. It is not an unlikely guess that if the current treaty practice of direct reference to ICSID subsided and instead was replaced by a permanent court, we would see an increase of references to ICSID by virtue of mutual consent of investors and states. The most undesirable consequence of this is perhaps that it would probably be a practice primarily confined to the most powerful of companies in their dealings with the weakest of states. Moreover, if this should turn out to be the preferred alternative for investors desiring effective investment protection, it would probably facilitate a legal process with a more clearly contractual perspective, lacking the moderating checks and balances built into public international law such as are today increasingly reflected in arbitral practice under bilateral investment treaties, NAFTA and the Energy Charter Treaty. Instead of advocating the replacement of the arbitral system with a permanent international court, a more realistically oriented reformist agenda might consequently be to furnish the existing arbitral system with further checks and balances to remedy some of its prime weaknesses. One such weakness is, arguably, precisely the lack of a permanent judicial authority subject to some form of political accountability, and responsible for the consistent development of the law. The solution to remedy this, however, is not necessarily the abolishment of the arbitral system altogether. One could envisage instead the creation of a form of permanent annulment body presiding over an annulment procedure similar to that found already in the ICSID Convention, but conceivably with strengthened and additional competences to review fundamental legal aspects of arbitral awards rendered in the first instance, ie not quite as an appellate body but with comparable though more limited powers.[10]

As a final afterthought, it should be noted that these considerations and the analysis presented in this book are premised on two initial assump-

[10] Van Harten also envisages the possibility of a two instance system with an initial arbitral process presided over by an appellate body, although he prefers a permanent international court that would not be dissimilar to the procedure under the European Convention on Human Rights, see Van Harten (2007) 180.

tions. The first is that foreign investment on the whole is seen to be desirable, and the second is that using arbitration as an effective remedy to uphold state commitments will indeed facilitate foreign investment. These assumptions are not wholly undisputed. The first controversy is nevertheless relatively easy to dispose of for the purposes of this analysis. While a critical approach to the desirability of foreign investment as such is bound to be a criticism of the very existence of a system of investment protection, it is sufficient to note here that a prevailing political consensus among relevant countries, capital-importing and capital-exporting alike, continues to support such a system based on the idea that increased investment is mutually beneficial. The controversy concerning the second assumption arguably raises a more acute objection. Based on available statistical data and surveys, it is difficult to prove with any great certainty that increased investment protection does in actual fact serve to facilitate a greater flow of foreign investment to countries in need of foreign capital.[11] Obviously, the availability of legal investment protection is only one factor in a multitude of other factors that will influence the 'investment climate' in a country, and the decisions of individual investors to invest there or not. A common sense approach nevertheless suggests that a framework that serves to strengthen the faith in legal commitments is positive, in so far as political risk is indeed considered a real impediment to making foreign investments. This critique against the effects (or lack of them) of the international system of investment protection then becomes one concerning the reliability and effectiveness of the arbitral process, and not its fundamental justification. It should also be borne in mind that faith in a legal process is something that develops over time and that cannot be established overnight. Besides providing an individual arrangement that can be relied on by concrete investors for protection, bilateral investment treaties are perhaps as important for opting into a legal system in the making, which has as its most important purpose to strengthen a general faith in legal commitments and international standards relating to foreign investment. It may be argued that it is this faith in the ascendancy of the rule of law and that individual commitments may be relied on, more than the individual arrangements themselves, which are likely to facilitate an increased flow of investment to countries in need of capital. The effect of individual treaties in this regard is not easily measured from one year to the next. As with the development of reliable legal institutions in the domestic sphere, it may be something that is only properly manifested over generations.

[11] See eg Neumayer and Spess: 'Do Bilateral Investment Treaties Increase Foreign Direct Investment to Developing Countries' (2005) 33(10) *World Development* 1567; and Hallward-Driemeier: 'Do Bilateral Investment Treaties Attract FDI? Only a Bit . . . and They Could Bite' World Bank Policy Research Working Paper 3121 (Washington DC, 2003).

Bibliography

Abi-Saab, G, 'Permanent Sovereignty over Natural Resources and Economic Activities' in Bedjaoui (ed), *International Law: Achievements and Prospects* (Paris (UNESCO), 1991) 597.

Aldrich, G, 'What Constitutes a Compensable Taking of Property? The Decisions of the Iran-United States Claims Tribunals' (1994) 88 *AJIL* 585.

Aldrich, GH, *The Jurisprudence of the Iran-United States Claims Tribunal* (Clarendon Press, Oxford, 1996).

Alexandrov, SA, 'Breaches of Contract and Breaches of Treaty: The Jurisdiction of Treaty-based Arbitration Tribunals to Decide Breach of Contract Claims in SGS v. Pakistan and SGS v. Philippines' (2004) 5(4) *JWIT* 555.

Al Faruque, A, 'The Rationale and Instrumentalities for Stability in Long-term State Contracts' (2006) 7(1) *JWIT* (2006) 85.

Allot, P, 'State Responsibility and the Unmaking of International Law' (1988) 29 *Harv Int'l LJ* 1.

Amerasinghe, CF, 'State Breaches of Contracts with Aliens and International Law' (1964) 58 *AJIL* 881.

—— *Local Remedies in International Law* 2nd edn (Cambridge University Press, Cambridge, 2004).

Andenæs, J, 'Er staten som lovgiver bundet av sine egne kontrakter?' (1977) *Lov og Rett* 435.

Andenæs, J and Fliflet, A, *Statsforfatningen i Norge 10. utgave* (Universitetsforlaget, Oslo, 2006).

Anzilotti, D, *Cours de Droit International* (Recueil Sirey, Paris, 1929).

Audit, B, 'Le caractère fonctionnel de la règle de conflit (Sur la 'crise' des conflits de lois)' (1984-III) 186 *Recueil de Cours* 219–398.

—— *Transnational Arbitration and State Contracts* (Hague Academy of International Law; Centre for Studies and Research, 1987).

Badr, GM, *State immunity—An Analytical and Prognostic View* (Martinus Nijhoff, The Hague, 1984).

Baldwin, E, Kantor, M and Nolan, M, 'Limits to Enforcement of ICSID Awards' (2006) 23(1) *J Int'l Arb* 1.

Barberis, D, *Negotiating Mining Agreements: Past, Present and Future Trends* (Kluwer, The Hague, 1998).

Barnett, H, *Constitutional and Administrative Law*, 4th edn (Cavendish, London, 2002).

Bederman, D, 'The Glorious Past and Uncertain Future of International Claims Tribunals' in Mark W Janis (ed), *International Courts for the Twenty-First Century* (Martinus Nijhoff, Dordrecht, 1992).

—— 'The United Nations Compensation Commission and the Tradition of International Claims Settlement' (1994–95) 27 *NYU J Int'l Law and Politics* 1.

Begic, T, *Applicable Law in International Investment Disputes* (Eleven International Publishing, Utrecht, 2005).

Bennouna, Preliminary Report on Diplomatic Protection (1998, A/CN.4/484).

Berg, B, *Almindelig forvaltningsret*, 2nd edn (Thomson, København, 2002).

Berlin, D, 'Contrat d'État', *Répertoire Dalloz de Droit International* (Dalloz, Paris, 1998).

Blessing, M, 'Choice of Substantive Law in International Arbitration' (1997) 14(2) *J Int'l Arb* 39.

Bodansky, D and Crook, J, 'Symposium: The ILC's State Responsibility Articles, Introduction and Overview' (2002) 96 *AJIL* 773

Böckstiegel, KH, *Arbitration and State Enterprises, a survey on the national and international state of law and practice: an international research study of the Institute of International Business Law and Practice of the International Chamber of Commerce* (Kluwer Law and Taxation Publishers, Deventer, 1984).

Borchard, EM, 'Basic Elements of Diplomatic Protection of Citizens Abroad' (1913) 7 *AJIL* 501.

—— *The Diplomatic Protection of Citizens Abroad* (The Banks Law Publishing Co, New York, 1916).

Bowett, D, 'Claims between States and Private Entities. The Twilight Zone of International Law' (1986) 35 *Catholic University Law Review* 929.

—— 'State Contracts with Aliens: Contemporary Developments on Compensation for Termination or Breach' (1988) 59 *BYIL* 49.

Broches, A, 'The Convention on the Settlement of Investment Disputes: Some Observations on Jurisdiction' (1966) 5 *Columbia Journal of Transnational Law* 261.

—— 'The Convention on the Settlement of Investment Disputes between States and Nationals of Other States' (1972-II) 136 *Recueil des Cours* 331.

Brower, CN and Brueschke, JD, *The Iran-United States Claims Tribunal* (Martinus Nijhof Publishers, Boston, 1998).

Brownlie, I, 'Legal Status of Natural Resources in International Law (Some Aspects)' (1979-I) 162 *Recueil des Cours* 247.

—— *Principles of Public International Law* (Oxford University Press, Oxford, 2003).

Brown Weiss, E, 'Invoking State Responsibility in the Twenty-First Century' (2002) 96 *AJIL* 798.

Brækhus, S, 'Lokaliseringsproblemer i internasjonal kommersiell voldgift' (1995) *Lov og Rett* 641.

Burdeau, G, 'Nouvelles perspectives pour l'arbitrage dans le contentieux économique intéressant les états' (1995) 1 *Revue de l'arbitrage* 3.

Caron, DD, 'The Nature of the Iran—United States Claims Tribunal and the Evolving Structure of International Dispute Resolution' (1990) 84 *AJIL* 104.

—— 'The ILC Articles on State Responsibility: The Paradoxical Relationship between Form and Authority' (2002) 96 *AJIL* 857.

Caron, DD and Crook, JR (eds), *The Iran-United States Claims Tribunal and the Process of International Claims Resolution* (Transnational Publishers, Ardsley (NY), 2000).

Caron, DD, Caplan, LM and Pellonpää, M, *The UNCITRAL Arbitration Rules* (Oxford University Press, Oxford, 2006).

Castberg, F, 'International Law in Our Time' (1973-I) 138 *Recueil des Cours* 1–26.

Cavers, DF, 'A Critique of the Choice of Law problem' (1933) 47 *Harv L Rev* 173.

Chatterjee, SK, The Stabilization Clause Myth in Investment Agreements, (1988) 5 *J Int'l Arb* 97.

Choudhury, B, 'Evolution or Devolution? Defining Fair and Equitable Treatment in International Investment Law' (2005) 6(2) *JWIT* 297.

Christie, CG, 'What Constitutes a Taking of Property under International Law?' (1962) 38 *BYIL* 307.

Collier, J and Lowe, V, *The Settlement of Disputes in International Law* (Oxford University Press, Oxford, 2000).

Cordero Moss, G, 'Contract or License? Regulation of Petroleum Investment in Russia and Foreign Legal Advice' (1998) 16 *Journal of Energy and Natural Resources Law* 186.

—— *International Commercial Arbitration—Party Autonomy and Mandatory Rules* (Tano Aschehoug, Oslo, 1999).

—— 'Can an Arbitral Tribunal Disregard the Choice of Law made by the Parties?' (2005:1) *Stockholm Int'l Arb Rev* 1.

Costamagna, F, 'Investor Rights and State Regulatory Autonomy: The Role of the Legitimate Expectation Principle in the CMS v. Argentina case' (2006) 3(2) *Transnational Dispute Management (available at www.transnational-dispute-management.com).*

Craig, P, *Administrative Law,* 5th edn (Sweet&Maxwell, London, 2003).

Craig, P and de Burca, G, *EU Law, Text Cases and Materials* (Oxford University Press, Oxford, 2003),

Craig LW, Park, WW and Paulsson, J, *International Chamber of Commerce Arbitration,* 3rd edn (Oceana Publications, Dobbs Ferry (NY), 2000).

Crawford, J, 'The Rights of Peoples: "Peoples" or "Governments" in J Crawford, *The Rights of Peoples* (Clarendon Press, Oxford, 1988).

—— 'International Law as an Open System' in *International Law as an Open System* (Cameron May, London, 2002) 17.

—— 'The ILC's Articles on Responsibility of States for Internationally Wrongful Acts: A Retrospect' (2002) 96 *AJIL* 874.

—— *The International Law Commission's Articles on State Responsibility* (Cambridge University Press, Cambridge, 2002).

Crawford, J and Sinclair, A, 'Application aux contrats d'Etat des principes UNIDROIT relatifs aux contrats du commerce international' (2002) *Bulletin de la Cour internationale d'arbitrage de la CCI,* Supplément spécial 59.

Chukwumerije, O, *Choice of Law in International Commercial Arbitration* (Quorum Books, Westport, 1994).

Crook, JR, 'Applicable Law in International Arbitration: The Iran-US Claims Tribunal Experience' (1989) 83 *AJIL* 278.

Currie, B, *Selected Essays on the Conflict of Laws* (Duke University Press, Durham, 1963).

De Beus, JG, *The Jurisprudence of the General Claims Commission, United States and Mexico* (Martinus Nijhoff Publishers, S-Gravenhage, 1938).

Delaume, G, 'State Contracts and Transnational Arbitration' (1981) 75 *AJIL* 784.

—— 'Recognition and Enforcement of State Contract Awards in the United States: A Restatement' (1997) 91 *AJIL* 476.

Delmas-Marty, M, 'The Richness of Underlying Legal Reasoning' in Delmas-Marty (ed), *The European Convention for the Protection of Human Rights:*

International Protection versus National Restrictions (Martinus Nijhoff, Dordrecht, 1992) 319.

Delmas-Marty, M, (ed), *The European Convention for the Protection of Human Rights: International Protection versus National Restrictions* (Martinus Nijhoff, Dordrecht, 1992).

Delmas-Marty, M and Soulier, G, 'Restraining or Legitimating the Reason of State' in Delmas-Marty, M (ed), *The European Convention for the Protection of Human Rights: International Protection versus National Restrictions* (Martinus Nijhoff, Dordrecht, 1992).

De Ly, F, *International Business Law and Lex Mercatoria* (North Holland, Amsterdam, 1992).

Dezalay, Y and Garth, BG, *Dealing in Virtue: International Commercial Arbitration and the Construction of a Transnational Legal Order* (The University of Chicago Press, Chicago, 1996).

Dicey & Morris, Collins, L (ed), *The Conflict of Laws,* 13th edn (Sweet & Maxwell, London, 2000).

Dolzer, R and Stevens, M, *Bilateral Investment Treaties* (Martinus Nijhoff Publishers, The Hague, 1995).

Dolzer, R and Bloch, F, 'Indirect Expropriation: Conceptual Realignments?' (2003) 5(3) *Int'l Law Forum* 155.

Douglas, Z, 'The Hybrid Foundations of Investment Treaty Arbitration' (2003) 74 *BYIL* 151.

—— 'Nothing if Not Critical for Investment Treaty Arbitration: Occidental, Eureko and Methanex' (2006) 22(1) *Arb Int'l* 27.

—— *The International Law of Investment Claims* (Cambridge University Press, Cambridge, 2009)

Dugard, JR, First report on diplomatic protection, Report to the International Law Commission on its 52nd session (2000) A/CN.4/506.

El Kosheri, AS and Riad, TF, 'The Law Governing a New Generation of Petroleum Agreements: Changes in the Arbitration Process' (1986) 1 *ICSID Rev-FILJ* 257.

Emberland, M, 'The Usefulness of Applying Human Rights Arguments in International Commercial Arbitration' (2003) 20 *J Int'l Arb* 355.

—— *The Human Rights of Companies: Exploring the Structure of ECHR Protection* (Oxford University Press, Oxford, 2006).

Fatouros, AA, *Government Guarantees to Foreign Investors* (Columbia University Press, New York, 1962).

—— 'International Law and the Internationalized Contracts' (1980) 74 *AJIL* 134.

Fauchald, OK and Schiøtz Thorud, K, 'Protection of Investors against Expropriation—Norway's Obligations under Investment Treaties' in *dog Fred er ej det Bedste . . . Festskrift til Carl August Fleischer* (Universitetsforlaget, Oslo, 2006) 113.

Feuerle, P, 'International Arbitration and Choice of Law under Article 42 of the Convention on the Settlement of Investment Disputes' (1977–78) 4 *Yale Studies of World Public Order* 89.

Fisher, L, *American Constitutional Law,* 4th edn (Carolina Academic Press, Durham (North Carolina), 2001).

Fitzmaurice, G, 'The General Principles of International Law Considered from the Standpoint of the Rule of Law' (1957-II) 92 *Recueil des Cours* 5.

—— 'Some Problems Regarding the Formal Sources of International Law' (1958) *Symbolae Verzijl* reprinted in Koskenniemi (ed), *Sources of International Law* (Ashgate, Aldershot, 2000).

Fleischer, CA, Tercero-saken og de obligatoriske kravs rettsvern ved ekspropriasjon, (1966) *Lov og Rett* 67.

—— Verdensbankens konvensjon om internasjonalt forliks- og voldgiftssenter for behandling av 'investment disputes' 1966 TfR 107.

—— Striden om Statens Kontrakter' (1978) *Lov og Rett* 367.

Fliflet, A, *Kongeriket Norges Grunnlov, Grunnloven med kommentarer* (Universitetsforlaget, Oslo, 2005).

Fortier, LY and Drymer, SL, 'Indirect Expropriation in the Law of International Investment: I know It When I See It, or *Caveat Investor*' (2005) 20(1) *ICSID Rev-FILJ* 1.

Fox, H, 'States and the Undertaking to Arbitrate' (1988) 37 *ICLQ* 1.

—— *The Law of State Immunity* (Oxford University Press, Oxford, 2002)

Franck, TM, *The Structure of Impartiality: Examining the Riddle of one Law in a Fragmented World* (The Macmillan Company, New York, 1968).

—— 'The Emerging Right to Democratic Governance' (1992) 86 *AJIL* 46.

—— *Fairness in International Law and Institutions* (Clarendon Press, Oxford, 1995).

Frick, JG, *Arbitration and complex international contracts* (Kluwer, The Hague, 2001).

Friedman, W, *The Changing Structure of International Law* (Steven & Sons, London, 1964).

Fuller, LL and Perdue, WR, 'The Reliance Interest in Contract Damages' (Part I) (1936) 46 *Yale Law Journal* 52.

—— 'The Reliance Interest in Contract Damages' (Part II) (1937) 46 *Yale Law Journal* 373.

Gaillard, E, 'Thirty Years of Lex Mercatoria: Towards the Selective Application of Transnational Rules' (1995) 10(2) *ICSID Rev-FILJ* 208.

—— 'Investment Treaty Arbitration and Jurisdiction over Contract Claims—The SGS Cases Considered' in T Weiler (ed), *International Investment Law and Arbitration: Leading Cases* (Cameron May, London, 2005) 325.

Gaillard, E and Banifatemi, Y (eds), *Annulment of ICSID Awards* (Juris Publishing, Huntinton (NY), 2004).

Gaillard, E and Savage, J (eds), *Fouchard, Gaillard, Goldman on International Commercial Arbitration* (Kluwer Law International, The Hague, 1999).

Gaja, G, 'Positivism and Dualism in Dionisio Anzilotti' (1992) 3 *EJIL* 123.

Gallus, N, 'The Influence of the Host State's Level of Development on International Investment Treaty Standards of Protection' (2005) 6(5) *JWIT* 711.

Gao, Z, *International Petroleum Contracts: Current Trends and New Directions* (Graham & Trotman, London, 1994).

Garcia-Amador, FV, 'State Responsibility in Case of Stabilization Clauses' (1993) 2 *Journal of Transnational Law and Policy* 23.

Garcia-Bolivar, OE, 'The Teleology of International Investment Law: The Role of Purpose in the Interpretation of International Investment Agreements' (2005) 6(5) *JWIT* 751.

Giardina, A, 'State Contracts: National versus International Law? (1980–81) *Italian Yearbook of International Law* 147.

Gill, J, Gearing, M and Birt, G, 'Contractual Claims and Bilateral Investment Treaties: A Comparative Review of the SGS Cases' (2004) 21(5) *J Int'l Arb* 397.

Gillis Wetter, J, *The International Arbitral Process: Public and Private* (Oceana Publications, Dobbs Ferry (NY), 1979).

Gillis Wetter, J and Schwebel, S, 'Some Little Known Cases on Concessions' (1964) 40 *BYIL* 83.

Goldman, B, 'Frontières du droit et lex mercatoria' (1964) *Archives de philosophie de droit* 177.

—— 'The applicable law: general principles of law—the *lex mercatoria*' in Lew (ed), *Contemporary Problems in International Arbitration* (Martinus Nijhof Publishers, Dordrecht, 1987).

Goldstajn, A, 'The New Law Merchant Reconsidered' in Fabricius (ed), *Law and International Trade: Recht und internationaler Handel/Festschrift für Clive M Schmitthoff zum 70 Geburtstag* (Frankfurt, 1973).

Goode, R, 'The Role of the Lex Loci Arbitri in International Commercial Arbitration' (2001) 17 *Arb Int'l* 19.

Gotanda, JY, 'Recovering Lost Profits in International Disputes' (2004) 36 *Georgetown Journal of International Law* 61.

Greenwood, C, 'State Contracts in International Law—The Libyan Oil Arbitrations' (1982) 53 *BYIL* 27.

Gunther, G and Sullivan, M, *Constitutional Law,* 13th edn (Foundation Press, Westbury (NY), 1997)

Guzman, AT, 'Why LDCs Sign Treaties That Hurt Them: Explaining the Popularity of Bilateral Investment Treaties' (1997–98) 38 *Va J Int'l Law* 639.

Hadfield, G, 'Of Sovereignty and Contract: Damages for Breach of Contract by Government' (1998–99) 8 *Southern California Interdisciplinary Law Journal* 467.

Hagstrøm, V, *Obligasjonsrett* (Universitetsforlaget, Oslo, 2003).

Hallward-Driemeier, M, 'Do Bilateral Investment Treaties Attract FDI? Only a Bit . . . and They Could Bite', World Bank Policy Research Working Paper 3121 (Washington, 2003).

Hambro, E, *Folkerettspleie* (Gyldendal, Oslo, 1956).

—— *Jurisdiksjonsvalg og lovvalg i norsk internasjonal kontraktsrett* (Universitetsforlaget, Oslo, 1957).

—— 'The Relations between International Law and Conflicts Law' (1962-I) 105 *Recueil des Cours* 1.

Hanotiau, B, 'What Law Governs the Issue of Arbitrability' (1996) 12(4) *Arb Int'l* 391.

Harris, JW, *Property and Justice* (Oxford University Press, Oxford, 2001).

Henkin, L, *International Law: Politics and Values* (Martinus Nijhoff, Dordrecht, 1995).

Higgins, R, 'The Taking of Property by the State: Recent Developments in International Law' (1982-III) 176 *Recueils de Cours* 259.

—— *Problems and Process: International Law and How We Use It* (Clarendon Press, Oxford, 1994).

Hobér, K, 'State Responsibility and Investment Arbitration', Draft Report submitted to the ILA Committee on Foreign Investment (2005), available at: www.ila-hq.org/html/layout_committee.htm.

Hochstrasser, D, 'Choice of Law and "Foreign" Mandatory Rules in International Arbitration' (1994) 11(1) *J Int'l Arb* 57.

Horn, N, 'Arbitration and the Protection of Foreign Investment: Concepts and Means' in Horn (ed), *Arbitrating Foreign Investment Disputes—Procedural and Substantive Legal Aspects* (Kluwer, The Hague, 2004).

—— **(ed),** *Arbitrating Foreign Investment Disputes—Procedural and Substantive Legal Aspects* (Kluwer, The Hague, 2004).

Hudson, MO, *International Tribunals: Past and Future* (Carnegie Endowment, Washington, 1944).

Hunter, M and Sinclair, A, '*Aminoil* revisited: Reflections on a Story of Changing Circumstances' in Weiler (ed), *International Investment Law and Arbitration: Leading cases from the ICSID, NAFTA, Bilateral Treaties and Customary International Law* (Cameron May, London, 2005) 347.

Hyde, JN, 'Economic Development Agreements' (1962-I) 105 *Recueil des Cours* 266.

Høgberg, AP, *Kontraktstolkning: særlig om tolkningsstiler ved fortolkning av skriftlige kontrakter* (Universitetsforlaget, Oslo, 2006).

Inadomi, H, 'Independent Power Projects in Developing Countries: Legal Investment Protection and Consequences for Development' (Phd thesis, University of Oslo, 2005, unpublished).

Jagusch and Duclos, 'Compensation for the Breach of Relative Standards of Treaty Protection' (2009) 10(4) *JWIT* 515

Jaksic, A, *Arbitration and Human Rights* (Peter Lang Publishing, Frankfurt, 2002).

Jennings, R, 'State Contracts in International Law' (1961) 37 *BYIL* 156.

—— 'Rules Governing Contracts between States and Foreign Nationals' in *Rights and Duties of Private Investors Abroad* (Matthew Bender, Albany (NY), 1965).

—— 'What is International Law and How Do We Tell It When We See It?' (1981) XXXVII *Schweitzerisches Jahrbüch für Internationales Recht* 60, as reproduced in *Collected Writings of Sir Robert Jennings* (Kluwer, The Hague, 1998).

Jessup, PC, 'Modernization of the Law of Contractual Agreements' (1947) 41 *AJIL* 378.

—— *A Modern Law of Nations* (Macmillan, New York, 1948).

—— *Transnational Law* (New Haven (CT), 1956).

Jimenez de Aréchaga, E, 'International Law in the Past Third of a Century—General Course in Public International Law' (1978-I) 159 *Recueil des Cours* 1.

Juenger, FK, *Choice of Law and Multistate Justice* (Nijhoff, Dordrecht, 1993).

Kaeckenbeeck, G, 'La Protection Internationale des Droits Acquis' (1937-I) 59 *Recueil des Cours* 317.

—— 'Arbitral Precedent: Dream, Necessity or Excuse' (2007) 23 *Arb Int'l* 357.

Kelsen, H, *General Theory of Law and State* (Harvard University Press, Cambridge, 1945)

Kinander, M, 'Sondringen mellom tinglige og obligatoriske rettigheter' (2003) 5 TfR 673.

Knoph, R, *Retslige Standarder: særlig Grunnlovens § 97* (Oslo, 1938).

Kokott, J, 'Interim Report on the Role of Diplomatic Protection in the Field of the Protection of Foreign Investment' in Conference Report 2002 International Law Association, Committee of Diplomatic Protection of Persons and Property, 21.

Kolo, A and Wälde, TW, 'Renegotiation and Contract Adaptation in International Investment Projects: Applicable Legal Principles and Industry Practices' (2000) 1 *JWIT* (2000) 5.

Koskenniemi, M, 'Letter to the editors of the Symposium' (1999) 93 *AJIL* 351.

—— **(ed)**, *Sources of International Law* (Ashgate, Aldershot, 2000).
—— *The Gentle Civilizer of Nations: The Rise and Fall of International Law 1870–1960* (Cambridge University Press, Cambridge, 2001).
—— *From Apology to Utopia: The Structure of International Legal Argument* (Reissue with New Epilogue) (Cambridge University Press, Cambridge, 2006).
Kröll, S, 'The Renegotiation and Adaptation of Investment Contracts' in Horn (ed), *Arbitrating Foreign Investment Disputes—Procedural and Substantive Legal Aspects* (Kluwer, The Hague, 2004) 425.
Kunoy, B, 'Singing in the Rain—Developments in the Interpretation of Umbrella Clauses' (2006) 7(2) *JWIT* 275.
Lafontaine, H, *Pasicrisie Internationale 1794–1900: Histoire Documentaire des Arbitrages Internationaux* (Martinus Nijhoff, The Hague, 1997).
Lando, O, 'The Conflict of Laws of Contracts' (1984-VI) 189 *Recueil des Cours* 225.
—— 'The Lex Mercatoria in International Commercial Arbitration' (1985) 34 *ICLQ* 747.
Lalive, JF, 'Contracts between a State or a State Agency and a Foreign Company' (1964) 13 *ICLQ* 987.
Lalive, PA, 'The Doctrine of Acquired Rights' in *Rights and Duties of Private Investors Abroad* (Matthew Bender, Albany (NY), 1965).
Lankarani El Zein, L, *Les contrats d'etat a l'epreuve du droit international* (Bruylant, Bruxelles, 2002).
Lauterpacht, H, 'International Law and the Law of the State' in E Lauterpacht (ed), *International law: being the collected papers of Hersch Lauterpacht* Vol I (Cambridge, 1970) 151.
—— *International Law and Human Rights* (Stevens & Sons, London, 1950).
—— 'The Grotian Tradition in International Law' in E Lauterpacht (ed), *International law: being the collected papers of Hersch Lauterpacht* Vol II (Cambridge University Press, Cambridge, 1975) 307.
—— 'The Subjects of the Law of Nations' in E Lauterpacht (ed), *International law: being the collected papers of Hersch Lauterpacht* Vol II (Cambridge University Press, Cambridge, 1975) 487.
—— 'Is International Law Part of the Law of England?' in E Lauterpacht (ed), *International law: being the collected papers of Hersch Lauterpacht* Vol II (Cambridge University Press, Cambridge, 1975) 537.
Leben, C, *Retour sur la notion de contrat d'Etat et sur le droit applicable à celui-ci, in Mélanges offerts à Hubert Thierry. L'évolution du droit international* (Pedone, Paris, 1998) 247.
—— *Quelque reflexions theoriques a propos des contrats d'Etats in Souveraineté étatique et marchés internationaux à la fin du 20ème siècle; Melanges en l'honneur de Philippe Kahn* (Litec, Paris, 2000) 119.
—— 'La théorie du contrat d'état et l'évolution du droit international des investissements' (2003) 302 *Recueil des Cours* 197.
Leboulanger, P, *Les Contrats entre Etats et entreprises étrangères* (Economica, Paris, 1985).
Lew, J, *Applicable Law in International Commercial Arbitration* (Oceana, Dobbs Ferry (NY), 1978).
—— **(ed)**, *Contemporary Problems in International Arbitration* (Martinus Nijhof Publishers, Dordrecht, 1987).

Lillich, R, 'The law Governing Disputes under Economic Development Agreements: Reexamining the Concept of Internationalization' in Lillich and Brower (eds), *International Arbitration; Towards Judicialization and Uniformity* (Transnational, Irvington (NY), 1994) 61.

—— *The Human Rights of Aliens in Contemporary International Law* (Manchester University Press, Manchester, 1984).

Lillich, R and Weston, B, *International Claims: Their Settlement by Lump Sum Agreements* (University Press of Virginia, Charlottesville, 1975).

Lloyd Jones, D, 'The Iran-United States Claims Tribunal: Private Rights and State Responsibility' (1983–84) 24 *Va J Int'l Law* 259.

Lowe, V, 'The Role of Equity in International Law' (1988–89) 12 *Australian Yearbook of International Law* 54.

Lowenfeld, AF, *International Litigation and the Quest for Reasonableness* (Clarendon Press, Oxford, 1996).

—— 'Lex Mercatoria: an Arbitrator's View' in TE Carbonneau (ed), *Lex Mercatoria and Arbitration* (Juris Publishing, Yonkers (NY), 1998) 71.

—— *International Economic Law* (Oxford University Press, Oxford, 2002).

MacCormick, N, *Legal Reasoning and Legal Theory* (Clarendon Press, Oxford, 1978).

Manciaux, S, 'The Notion of Investment: New Controversies' (2008) 9(6) *JWIT* 443.

Maniruzzaman, AFM, 'State Contracts with Aliens: The Question of Unilateral Change by the State in Contemporary International Law' (1992) 9(4) *J Int'l Arb* 141.

—— 'Choice of Law in International Contracts—Some Fundamental Conflict of Laws Issues' (1999) 16(4) *J Int'l Arb* 141.

—— 'State Contracts in Contemporary International Law: Monist versus Dualist Controversies' (2001) 12(2) *EJIL* 309.

—— 'The Relevance of Public International Law in Arbitrations concerning International Economic Development Agreements' (2005) 6(2) *JWIT* 263

Mann, FA, 'The Law Governing State Contracts' (1944) 21 *BYIL* 11.

—— 'State Contracts and State Responsibility' (1960) 54 *AJIL* 572.

—— '*Lex facit arbitrum*' in *Liber Amicorum for Martin Domke* (Nifhoff, The Hague, 1967) 157.

—— 'State Contracts and International Arbitration' (1967) 42 *BYIL* 1.

—— 'The Theoretical Approach towards the Law Governing Contracts between States and Private Persons' (1975) *Rev B Dr Int'l* 562.

—— 'British Treaties for the Promotion and Protection of Investments' (1982) 52 *BYIL* 241.

—— 'England Rejects Delocalized Contracts and Arbitration' (1984) 33 *ICLQ* 193.

Marks, S, *The Riddle of All Constitutions: International Law, Democracy and the Critique of Ideology* (Oxford University Press, Oxford, 2000).

Mayer, P, 'La neutralisation de pouvoir normatif de l'Etat en matière de contrats d'Etat' (1986) *J Dr Int'l* 5.

—— 'Le mythe de "l'ordre juridique de base" (ou grundlegung)' in *Le droit des relations économiques internationales. Etudes offertes à Berthold Goldman* (Litec, Paris, 1982).

McNair, A, 'The General Principles of Law Recognised by Civilized Nations' (1957) 33 *BYIL* 1.

Meidell, A, *An Anational Approach to International Contracts* (Cappelen, Oslo, 2007).

Menon, PK, *The Succession of States in Respect to Treaties, State Property, Archives, and Debts* (E Mellen Press, Lewiston (NY), 1991).

Mestad, O, 'The Ekofisk Royalty Case: Construction of Regulations to Avoid Retroactivity' (1987) 2(2) *ICSID Rev-FILJ* 139.

—— *Om force majeure og risikofordeling i kontrakt* (Universitetsforlaget, Oslo, 1991).

Moore, JB, *Arbitrations* (Government Printing Office, Washington, 1898).

—— International Law Digest (Government Printing office, Washington, 1906).

Muchlinski, PT, *Multinational Enterprises and the Law* (Blackwell Publishers, Oxford, 1999).

Mustill, Lord Justice (hon), 'The New Lex Mercatoria: The First 25 Years' (1988) 4 *Arb Int'l* 86.

Mæland, HJ, *Voldgift* (Universitetsforlaget, Oslo, 1988).

Nassar, N, *Sanctity of Contracts Revisited—A Study in the Theory and Practice of Long-Term International Commercial Transactions* (Martinus Nijhoff, Dordrecht, 1994).

—— 'Internationalization of State Contracts: ICSID the Last Citadel' (1997) 14 *J Int'l Arb* 183.

Neumayer, E and Spess, L, 'Do Bilateral Investment Treaties Increase Foreign Direct Investment to Developing Countries?' (2005) 33(10) *World Development* 1567.

Newcombe, A, 'The Boundaries of Regulatory Expropriation in International Law' (2005) 20(1) *ICSID Rev-FILJ* 1.

Nijman, J, *The concept of international legal personality: an inquiry into the history and theory of international law* (TMC Asser Press, The Hague, 2004).

Norum, M, 'The Fair and Equitable Treatment Standard in International Investment Treaties' (Masters Thesis, University of Oslo, 2005, Unpublished).

Nussbaum, A, 'The Arbitration between the Lena Goldfields Ltd and the Soviet Government' (1950–51) 36 *Cornell Law Quarterly* 31.

Nygh, PE, 'The Reasonable Expectations of the Parties as a Guide to the Choice of Law in Tort and in Contract' (1995) 251 *Recueil des Cours* 269.

O'Connell, DP, *State Succession in Municipal Law and International Law* (Cambridge University Press, Cambridge, 1967).

O'Connell, ME, 'New International Legal Process' in S Ratner, S and AM Slaughter (eds), 'Symposium on Method in International Law' (1999) 93 *AJIL* 334.

OECD (Note by the Secretariat), *Stocktaking of Developments in Investment Agreements,* Directorate for Financial and Enterprise Affairs Investment Committee, 1 September 2005, (DAF/INV/WD(2005)10).

Oppenheim (Lauterpacht (ed)), *International Law: A Treatise,* 8th edn (Longmans, London, 1955).

Oppenheim, LFL (with Jennings and Watts), *Oppenheim's International Law,* 9th edn (Longman, Harlow, 1992).

Orrego VicuÀa, F, *Interim Report on the Changing Law of Nationality of Claims,* First Report of the Committee on Diplomatic Protection of Persons and Property, International Law Association (2000) 28.

—— 'Regulatory Authority and Legitimate Expectations: Balancing the Rights of the State and the Individual under International Law in a Global Society' (2003) 5(3) *Int'l Law Forum* 188.

—— 'Of Contracts and Treaties in the Global Market' (2004) 8 *Max Planck Yearbook of United Nations Law* 341.

—— *International Dispute Settlement in an Evolving Global Society—Constitutionalization, Accessibility, Privatization* (Cambridge University Press, Cambridge, 2004).

Paasivirta, E, 'Internationalization and Stabilization of Contracts versus State Sovereignty' (1989) 60 *BYIL* 315.

—— *Participation of States in International Contracts* (Lakimiesliiton Kustannus, Helsinki, 1990).

—— 'The Energy Charter Treaty and Investment Contracts: Towards Security of Contracts' in Wälde (ed), *The Energy Charter Treaty—An East-West Gateway for Investment and Trade* (Kluwer, London, 1996) 349.

Paulsson, J, 'Arbitration Unbound: Award Detached from the Law of its Country of Origin' (1981) 30 *ICLQ* 358.

—— 'Delocalisation of International Commercial Arbitration: When and Why it Matters' (1983) 32 *ICLQ* 53.

—— 'May a State Invoke its Internal Law to Repudiate Consent to International Commercial Arbitration?' (1986) 2(2) *Arb Int'l* 90.

—— 'Arbitration without Privity' (1995) 10 *ICSID Rev-FILJ* 232.

Paulsson, J and Douglas, Z, 'Indirect Expropriation in Investment Treaty Arbitrations' in N Horn (ed), *Arbitrating Foreign Investment Disputes—Procedural and Substantive Legal Aspects* (Kluwer, The Hague, 2004).

Ralston, JH, *International Arbitration from Athens to Locarno* (Stanford University Press, London, 1929).

Redfern, A and Hunter, M (with Blackaby, N and Partasides, C), *Law and Practice of International Commercial Arbitration*, 4th edn (Sweet & Maxwell, London, 2004).

Reinisch, A, 'Expropriation', Report to the ILA Committee on Foreign Investment 2006, available at: www.ila-hq.org/html/layout_committee.htm.

Reisman, WM & Sloane, RD, 'Indirect Expropriation and its Valuation in the BIT Generation' (2003) 74 *BYIL* 115.

Rigaux, F, 'Des dieux et des héros—Réflections sur une sentence arbitrale' (1978) *Rev Cr Dr Int'l Privé* 435.

—— 'Souverainité des Etats et arbitrage transnational' in *Le droit des relations économiques internationales. Etudes offertes à Berthold Goldman* (Litec, Paris, 1982) 261.

Rivero, J and Walline, J, *Droit Administratif*, 17th edn (Dalloz, Paris, 1998).

Rogers, A and Launders, R, 'Separability—The Indestructible Arbitration Clause' (1994) 10(1) *Arb Int'l* 77.

Ross, A, *Om Ret og Retfærdighet* (Nyt Nordisk Forlag, København, 1966).

Rosendahl, RW, 'Political, Economic and Cultural Obstacles to Effective Arbitration of Foreign Investment Disputes' in N Horn (ed), *Arbitrating Foreign Investment Disputes—Procedural and Substantive Legal Aspects* (Kluwer, The Hague, 2004).

Rubins, N, 'The Notion of "Investment" in International Investment Arbitration' in N Horn (ed), *Arbitrating Foreign Investment Disputes* (Kluwer, The Hague, 2004) 283.

Sabahi, B, *The Calculation of Damages for Breach of International Investment Contracts*, Report prepared under the supervision of the Hague Academy of International

Law, Centre of Studies and Research, 2004 (pt unpublished, copy on file with author).

Sack, AN, 'La Succession aux Dettes Publiques d'État' (1928-III) 23 *Recueil des Cours* 145.

Scelle, G, *Précis de droit des gens: Principes et Systématique première partie* Vol I (Recueil Sirey, Paris, 1932).

—— *Précis de droit des gens: Principes et Systématique deuxième partie* Vol II (Recueil Sirey, Paris, 1934).

Schmitthoff, CM, 'International Business Law: A New Law Merchant' in Cheng (ed), *Clive M Schmitthoff's Select Essays on International Trade Law* (Martinus Nijhoff Publishers / Graham & Trotman, Dordrecht, 1988).

Schreuer, CH, *State Immunity: Some Recent Developments* (Grotius Publications, Cambridge, 1988).

—— *The ICSID Convention: A Commentary* (Cambridge University Press, Cambridge, 2001).

—— 'Travelling the BIT Route: Of Waiting Periods, Umbrella Clauses and Forks in the Road' (2004) 5(2) *JWIT* 231.

—— 'Fair and Equitable Treatment in Arbitral Practice' (2005) 6(3) *JWIT* 357.

—— *The Concept of Expropriation under the ETC and other Investment Protection Treaties,* (paper submitted to Investment Arbitration and the Energy Charter Treaty Conference 9–10 June 2005 in Stockholm, available at: www.univie.ac.at/intlaw/pdf/csunpublpaper_3.pdf.

—— 'Diversity and Harmonization of Treaty Interpretation in Investment Arbitration' (April 2006) 3(2) *TDM* .

Schrijver, N, *Sovereignty over Natural Resources: Balancing Rights and Duties* (Cambridge University Press, Cambridge, 1997).

Schwarzenberger, G, *International Law as Applied by International Courts and Tribunals* Vol I (Stevens & Sons, London, 1957).

—— *A Manual of International Law,* 4th edn (Stevens & Sons, London, 1960).

Schwebel, SM, *International Arbitration: Three Salient Problems* (Grotius Publications, Cambridge, 1987).

—— *Justice in International law: Selected writings of Stephen M Schwebel* (Cambridge University Press, Cambridge, 1994).

—— 'The Law Applicable in International Arbitration: Application of Public International Law' in Van den Berg (ed), *Planning Efficient Arbitration Proceedings—The Law Applicable in International Arbitration* (Kluwer, The Hague, 1996).

Schønberg, SJ, *Legitimate Expectations in Administrative Law* (Oxford University Press, Oxford, 2000).

Seidl-Hohenveldern, I, 'The Abs-Shawcroft draft convention to protect private foreign investment: Comments on the Round Table' (1961) 10 *Journal of Public Law* 100.

—— 'The Theory of Quasi-International and partly International Agreements' (1975) *Revue Belge de Droit International* 567.

—— *International Economic Law* (Kluwer, The Hague, 1999).

Sereni, AP, 'International Economic Institutions and the Municipal Law of States' (1959-I) 96 *Recueil des Cours* 129.

Shany, Y, 'Toward a General Margin of Appreciation Doctrine in International Law?' (2005) 16(5) *EJIL* 907.

Sheppard, A, 'The Distinction between Lawful and Unlawful Expropriation, paper presented at Investment Arbitration and the Energy Charter Treaty', Conference 9–10 June 2005 in Stockholm, (copy on file with author).

Shihata, IFI, 'Towards a Greater Depoliticization of Investment Disputes: The Roles of ICSID and MIGA' (1986) 1 *ICSID Rev-FILJ* 1.

—— 'The Institute of International Law's Resolution on Arbitration between States and Foreign Enterprises—A Comment' (1990) 5(1) *ICSID Rev-FILJ* 65.

Shihata, IFI and Parra, AR, 'Applicable Substantive Law in Disputes between States and Private Foreign Parties: The Case of Arbitration under the ICSID Convention' (1994) 9 *ICSID Rev* 183.

—— The Experience of the International Centre for Settlement of Investment Disputes' (1999) 14 *ICSID Rev-FILJ* 299, 308.

Simma, B, 'The Contribution of Alfred Verdross to the Theory of International Law' (1995) 6 *EJIL* 1.

Sinclair, A, 'The Origins of the Umbrella Clause in the International law of Investment Protection' (2005) 20(4) *Arb Int'l* 411.

Sornarajah, M, 'The Myth of International Contract Law' (1981) *Journal of World Trade Law* 187.

—— Power and Justice in Foreign Investment Arbitration, (1997) 14(3) *J Int'l Arb* 103.

—— *The Settlement of Foreign Investment Disputes* (Kluwer, The Hague, 2000).

—— *The International Law on Foreign Investment*, 2nd edn (Cambridge University Press, Cambridge, 2004).

Spiermann, O, *Enten & eller: studier i suverænitetsbegreper* (Jurist og Økonomforbundets Forlag, København, 1995).

—— 'Individual Rights, State Interests and the Power to Waive ICSID Jurisdiction under Bilateral Investment Treaties' (2004) 20(2) *Arb Int'l* 179.

—— *Applicable Law*, Draft Report to the ILA Committee on Foreign Investment 2006, available at www.ila-hq.org/html/layout_committee.htm.

Stern, B, 'Trois arbitrages, un même problème, trois solutions' (1980) *Rev Arb* 3.

Stuyt, AM, *Survey of International Arbitrations 1794–1989* (Martinus Nijhoff, Dordrecht, 1990).

Summers, LM, 'The Calvo Clause' (1932–33) 19 *Va L Rev* 459.

Tesón, F, 'State Contracts and Oil Expropriations: The Aminoil-Kuwait Arbitration' (1983–84) 24 *Va J Int'l Law* 323.

Teubner, G, 'Breaking Frames: Economic Globalisation and the New Lex Mercatoria' (2002) 5(2) *European Journal of Social Theory* 199.

Toope, S, *Mixed International Arbitration, studies in arbitration between states and private persons* (Grotius Publications, Cambridge, 1990).

Triepel, 'Les Rapports entre le Droit Interne et le Droit International' (1923-) 1 *Recueil des Cours* 82.

Turpin, C, 'Public Contracts' in K Zweigert and K Drobnig (eds), *International Encyclopedia of Comparative Law* (Mohr Siebeck & Martinus Nijhoff, 1982).

UNCTAD: World Investment Report 2006.

Van den Berg, AJ, *The New York Arbitration Convention of 1958: towards a uniform judicial interpretation* (Kluwer Law and Taxation Publishers, Deventer, 1981).

—— 'Recent Enforcement Problems under the New York and ICSID Conventions' (1989) 5 *Arb Int'l* 2.

Vandevelde, KJ, The Economics of Bilateral Investment Treaties, 41 *Harv Int'l Law J* (2000) No 2 469.

Van Harten, G, *Investment Treaty Arbitration and Public Law* (Oxford University Press, Oxford, 2007)

Van Harten, G and Loughlin, M, 'Investment Treaty Arbitration as a Species of Global Administrative Law' (2006) 17(1) *EJIL* 121.

Van Hecke, G, 'Les accords entre un Etat et une personne privée étrangère', Rapport à l'Institut de droit international, session d'Oslo 1977, Ann IDI, vol 57.

Van Houtte, H, 'Article 52 of the Washington Convention—A Brief Introduction' in E Gaillard and Y Banifatemi (eds), *Annulment of ICSID Awards* (Juris Publishing, Huntinton (NY), 2004).

Vasciannie, S, 'The Fair and Equitable Treatment Standard in International Investment Law and Practice' (1999) 70 *BYIL* 99.

Vattel, E, *Le droit des gens—ou principes de la loi naturelle appliqués a la conduite et aux affaires des nations et des souverains,* Nouvelle Édition 1863 (Librairie de Guillaumin, Paris, 1863).

Veeder, VV, 'The *Lena Goldfields* Arbitration—The Historical Roots of Three Ideas' (1998) 47 *ICLQ* 747.

Verdross, A, 'Quasi-International Agreements and International Economic Transactions' (1970) *Yearbook of World Affairs* 739.

—— 'Protection of Private Property under Quasi-International Agreements' in *Varia Juris Gentium, Liber Amicorum to JP François* (Sijthoff, Leiden, 1959) 355.

Verhoeven, J, 'Droit international des contrats et droit des gens' (1978–79) *Rev B Dr Int'l* 209.

—— 'Arbitrage entre États et entreprises étrangères: des regles specifique?' in 'Hommage à Jean Robert' (1985) *Rev Arb* 609.

Vernon, R, 'Economic Sovereignty at Bay' (1968–69) 47 *Foreign Affairs* 110.

—— *Sovereignty at Bay: the Multinational Spread of US Enterprises* (Basic Books, New York, 1971).

Voigt, C, 'From Climate Change to Sustainability: An Essay on Sustainable Development, Legal and Ethical Choices' (2005) 9(1) *Worldviews* 112.

Von Mehren, AT, 'Arbitration between States and Foreign Enterprises: The Significance of the Institute of International Law's Santiago de Compostela Resolution' (1990) 5(1) *ICSID Rev-FILJ* 54.

Von Mehren, AT and Jimenez de Aréchaga, E, Arbitration between States and Foreign Enterprises (Draft Report to the *Institut de droit international*) in (1989) 63-I *Ann IDI* 100.

Von Mehren, RB and Kourides, PN, 'International Arbitrations between States and Foreign Private Parties—The Libyan Nationalization Cases' (1981) 75 *AJIL* 476.

Wade, W and Forsyth, C, *Administrative Law,* 9th edn (Oxford University Press, Oxford, 2004).

Wälde, TW, 'Investment Arbitration under the Energy Charter Treaty' (University of Dundee (CEPMLP), Dundee, 1997).

—— 'The "Umbrella" Clause in Investment Arbitration: A Comment on Original Intentions and Recent Cases' (2005) 6(2) *JWIT* 183.

—— 'Remedies and Compensation in International Investment Law' (2005) 2(5) *TDM* 71.

Wälde, TW and Hobér, K, 'The First Energy Charter Treaty Award' (2005) 22(2) *J Int'l Arb* 83.

Wälde, TW and Kolo, A, 'Environmental Regulation, Investment Protection and "Regulatory Taking" in International Law' (2001) 50 *ICLQ* 811.

Wälde, TW and Ndi, G, 'Stabilizing International Investment Commitments: International Law versus Contract Interpretation' (1996) 31 *Tex Int'l LJ* 215, 220.

Wälde, TW and Sabahi, B, 'Compensation, Damages and Valuation in International Investment Law', Report to the ILA Committee on International Law on Foreign Investment (2006), available at: www.ila-hq.org/html/layout_committee.htm

Warbrick, C, 'Diplomatic Representations and Diplomatic Protection' (2002) 51 *ICLQ* 723.

Weil, P, 'Problèmes relatifs aux contrats passés entre un État et un particulier' (1969-III) 128 *Recueil des Cours* 95.

—— 'Les clauses de stabilisation et d'intangibilité insérées dans les accords de développement économique' in *Mélanges offerts à Charles Rousseau· la communauté international* (Pedone, Paris, 1974) 301.

—— 'Droit international et contrats d'Etat' in *Mélanges offerts à Paul Reuter: le droit international, unité et diversité* (Pedone, Paris, 1981) 549.

—— 'Principes généraux du droit et contrats d'Etat' in *Le droit des relations économiques internationales. Etudes offertes à Berthold Goldman* (Litec, Paris, 1982) 387.

—— 'Towards Relative Normativity in International Law' (1983) 77 *AJIL* 413.

—— 'Le droit international en quête de son identité' (1992-VI) 237 *Recueil des Cours* 9–370.

—— 'The State, the Foreign Investor, and International Law: The No Longer Stormy Relationship of a *Ménage À Trois*' (2000) 15(2) *ICSID Rev-FILJ* 401.

Weiler, T, 'The Treatment of SPS Measures under NAFTA Chapter 11: Preliminary Answers to an Open-Ended Question' (2003) 26 *BC Int'l & Comp Law Rev* 229.

—— 'Saving Oscar Chinn: Non-Discrimination in International Investment Law' in N Horn (ed), *Arbitrating Foreign Investment Disputes—Procedural and Substantive Legal Aspects* (Kluwer, The Hague, 2004)

—— **(ed),** *International Investment Law and Arbitration: Leading cases from the ICSID, NAFTA, Bilateral Treaties and Customary International Law* (Cameron May, London, 2005).

Weiner, AS, 'Indirect Expropriations: the Need for a Taxonomy of Legitimate Regulatory Purposes' (2003) 5(3) *Int'l Law Forum* 166.

Wells, LT, 'Double-Dipping in Arbitration Awards? An Economist Questions Damages Awarded to Kahara Bodas Company in Indonesia' (2003) 19 *Arb Int'l* 471.

Wengler, W, 'Les accords entre états et entreprises étrangères, sont ils des traités de droit international?' (1972) *Rev G Dr Int'l Privé* 313.

Whiteman, MM, *Damages in International Law* (US Government Printing Office, Washington, 1943).

Wilson, RR, 'Some Aspects of the Jurisprudence of National Claims Commissions' (1942) 36 *AJIL* 56.

Wolff, M, 'Some Observations on the Autonomy of Contracting Parties in the Conflict of Laws' (1959) 35 *Transactions of the Grotius Society* 143.

Yala, F, 'The Notion of 'Investment' in ICSID Case Law: A Drifting Jurisdictional Requirement?' (2005) 22(2) *J Int'l Arb* 105.

Yourow, HC, *The Margin of Appreciation Doctrine in the Dynamics of European Human Rights Jurisprudence* (Kluwer, The Hague, 1996).

Zillman, D, Mestad, O and Laitos, J, 'Constraints on Legislative Actions Affecting Natural Resources Development' in *Energy Law '88* (Graham & Trotman, London, 1988) 268.

Zweigert, K and Kötz, H, *An Introduction to Comparative Law* (Clarendon Press, Oxford, 1998).

Index

www.ingramcontent.com/pod-product-compliance
Ingram Content Group UK Ltd.
Pitfield, Milton Keynes, MK11 3LW, UK
UKHW020237290926
15470UKWH00002B/580

9 781841 136578

AF342265

Cybersicherheit für Dummies

Schummelseite

SCHÜTZEN SIE SICH SELBST UND IHRE FAMILIE IM INTERNET

Um sich und Ihre Familie zu schützen, sollten Sie dafür sorgen, dass jeder Einzelne verstanden hat, dass er oder sie ein Ziel ist. Wem klar ist, dass Hacker in den eigenen Computer und das Smartphone eindringen und dass Kriminelle die eigenen Daten erbeuten wollen, handelt anders als jemand, der das alles für Humbug hält.

Wer diesen Gedanken verinnerlicht, verhält sich anders – oft völlig unbewusst.

Die folgenden Tipps helfen Ihnen, Ihre Daten und sich und Ihre Familie vor Internetbetrügereien zu schützen.

- ✔ **Schützen Sie Ihre Geräte.** Lassen Sie mindestens einmal täglich eine Sicherheitssoftware über die Geräte laufen, mit denen Sie auf sensible Daten zugreifen. Konfigurieren Sie Ihre Geräte so, dass sie sich automatisch bei Nichtbenutzung sperren, und vergeben Sie ein starkes Passwort, um sie zu entsperren. Lassen Sie Ihre Geräte nicht an unsicheren Orten liegen und installieren Sie Software nur aus vertrauenswürdigen Quellen, beispielsweise aus den offiziellen App-Stores und von den Websites der Hersteller.
- ✔ **Schützen Sie Ihre Daten.** Verschlüsseln Sie alle sensiblen Daten und erstellen Sie häufige Backups. Wenn Sie sich unsicher sind, ob Sie etwas verschlüsseln sollten, tun Sie es. Wenn Sie nicht sicher sind, ob Sie häufig genug Backups erstellen, tun Sie es vermutlich nicht – und sind damit (leider) in guter Gesellschaft.
- ✔ **Nutzen Sie sichere Verbindungen.** Greifen Sie nie auf sensible Informationen über ein öffentliches WLAN zu und vermeiden Sie es überhaupt, sich mit einem Gerät, auf dem Sie sensible Aufgaben erledigen oder auf sensible Daten zugreifen, auf diese Weise im Internet zu bewegen. Die Datenleitung Ihres Mobilfunkanbieters ist höchstwahrscheinlich sehr viel sicherer als jedes öffentliche WLAN-Netzwerk.
- ✔ **Nutzen Sie eine gute Authentifizierung und Passwörter.** Jeder, der auf ein wichtiges System zugreift, sollte über seine eigenen Anmeldedaten verfügen. Teilen Sie keine Passwörter für Onlinebanking, E-Mail-Konten oder Social-Media-Dienste mit Ihren Kindern oder Ihrem Partner. Erstellen Sie für jeden ein eigenes Login. Nutzen Sie starke und einzigartige Passwörter für Ihre kritischen Systeme.
- ✔ **Geben Sie nicht zu viel über sich preis.** Seien Sie nicht allzu freigiebig mit Ihren Daten in den sozialen Netzwerken oder auf anderen Plattformen. Betrüger durchkämmen diese Netzwerke nach Daten, mit denen sie das Verhalten von Menschen manipulieren können, das sogenannte Social Engineering.

Cybersicherheit für Dummies

Schummelseite

VERMEIDEN SIE HÄUFIGE FEHLER BEI DER CYBERSICHERHEIT

Es gibt Fehler, die immer wieder begangen werden und die Hacking und die Begehung von Cyberverbrechen erleichtern. Hier sind sie:

- **Sie gehen davon aus, dass es Ihnen selbst nicht passieren kann.** Jede Privatperson, jedes Unternehmen, jede Organisation und jede Behörde ist potenziell im Visier von Hackern. Wer davon ausgeht, dass er für Hacker uninteressant ist oder nichts bei ihm zu holen ist, handelt oft unvorsichtig und erfährt schnell, wie falsch er damit liegt.
- **Sie verwenden schwache Passwörter.** Trotz allgegenwärtiger Warnungen, es nicht zu tun, verwenden viele immer noch schwache Passwörter, wie zum Beispiel *123456* oder *passwort*. Dies zeigen Listen kompromittierter Passwörter, die nach einem Datenleck im Internet veröffentlicht wurden. Wenn Sie ein schwaches Passwort verwenden oder auf einer sensiblen Seite dasselbe Passwort verwenden, das Sie auch an anderer Stelle nutzen, laufen Sie große Gefahr, dass eines Ihrer Konten beeinträchtigt wird.
- **Sie nutzen keine Zwei-Faktor-Authentifizierung, obwohl sie verfügbar ist.** Alle großen Social-Media-Plattformen, Google, Amazon und die meisten großen Finanzinstitute bieten in irgendeiner Form eine mehrstufige Authentifizierung an. Die Zwei-Faktor-Authentifizierung kann dafür sorgen, dass Ihr Konto geschützt bleibt, selbst wenn Ihr Passwort abgegriffen wurde. Und trotzdem nutzt nur ein Bruchteil der Nutzer diese Funktion.
- **Sie setzen keine angemessene Sicherheitssoftware ein.** Moderne Sicherheitssoftware erhöht Ihre Sicherheit ungemein und kann eine Vielzahl möglicher Cybersicherheitsgefahren abwehren, unter anderem Schadsoftware, Hacker-Angriffe, Spam und vieles mehr. Trotzdem benutzen viele gar keine auf ihren Geräten (einschließlich Laptops, Tablet-Computer und Smartphones) und viele andere halten sie nicht auf dem neuesten Stand. Sie untergraben damit die Fähigkeit der Software, sie gegen die neuesten (und oft gefährlichsten) Gefahren zu verteidigen.
- **Sie halten Software nicht auf dem aktuellsten Stand.** Viele Betriebssystem- und Software-Updates schließen Sicherheitslücken, die von IT-Experten (oder Hackern) in früheren Versionen entdeckt wurden. Wenn Sie Ihre Software nicht aktuell halten, sind Ihre Geräte anfällig für Angriffe. Sobald der Hersteller öffentlich die geschlossene Schwachstelle benennt, kann es vorkommen, dass Kriminelle Skripte schreiben, um nach Geräten zu suchen, bei denen die Lücke noch nicht geschlossen wurde – und um diese dann anzugreifen.
- **Sie schalten den gesunden Menschenverstand aus.** Das schwächste Glied in der Cybersicherheitskette ist fast immer der Mensch. Sei es das Klicken auf einen Link, der nicht hätte angeklickt werden sollen, das Versenden von Geld an einen Betrüger, der sich in einer fingierten E-Mail als der Vorgesetzte ausgegeben hat, die Installation einer gefährlichen App, dem Herunterladen einer Film-Raubkopie oder irgendeine

andere unvorsichtige Aktion – menschliches Versagen öffnet oft die Büchse der Cyber-Pandora und ermöglicht es Kriminellen, noch viel mehr Schaden anzurichten, als unter anderen Umständen möglich gewesen wäre.

- **Sie lernen nicht die Grundlagen.** Wer an einer schweren Krankheit leidet, informiert sich in der Regel selbst viel über diese Krankheit, um zu verstehen, ob er richtig und passend behandelt wird. Beim Thema Cybersicherheit verhalten sich viele jedoch völlig gleichgültig und denken aus irgendeinem Grund, dass es sie schon nicht treffen wird, wenn Sie so tun, als gäbe es keine Gefahren.
- **Sie engagieren keinen Experten.** Wenn ein ernster Cybersicherheitsvorfall eintritt, versuchen viele (meist Privatpersonen oder Inhaber kleiner Unternehmen), die Probleme selbst zu lösen. Das ist ungefähr genauso schlimm, als wenn Sie bei einer schweren Erkrankung nicht zum Arzt gehen oder wenn Sie sich bei Gericht selbst verteidigen und keinen Anwalt zurate ziehen. Hacker, Malware-Entwickler und andere Cyberschurken verfügen über enormes Wissen. Wenn Sie schon in den Cyberring steigen müssen, sollten Sie sich auch einen Profi an Ihre Seite holen.

VERBREITETE CYBER-BETRUGSMASCHEN BEIM ONLINEKAUF

Es gibt ein paar sehr verbreitete Betrugsmaschen, die Cyberkriminelle nutzen, um Sie beim Online-Einkauf abzuziehen, aber Sie können sich recht einfach vor diesen Internetbetrügern schützen.

Eine sehr einfache Vorgehensweise kann Sie vor all diesen Betrugsmaschen schützen. Wenn Ihnen ein Händler oder sonst irgendwer von einem tollen Angebot schreibt, das Sie sich unbedingt anschauen sollten, klicken Sie auf keinen Link in der Nachricht und öffnen Sie keine Anhänge. Starten Sie Ihren Webbrowser, gehen Sie auf die Website des angeblichen Absenders, suchen Sie nach den Kontaktdaten und fragen Sie ihn auf diesem Wege direkt, was es mit der Nachricht auf sich hat.

Das sind ein paar der beliebtesten Betrugsmaschen, mit denen Sie in Berührung kommen könnten:

- **»Es gibt ein Problem mit Ihrer Bestellung«:** Kriminelle verschicken häufig Massenmails (oder Massen-SMS), die so aussehen, als stammten sie von einem Online-Händler und in denen den Empfängern mitgeteilt wird, dass der Händler die Bestellung aufgrund eines Problems nicht verschicken kann und dass der Empfänger etwas unternehmen muss, um die Ware zu erhalten. Diese E-Mails enthalten in aller Regel einen Link zu einer fingierten Website, die – mindestens – die Anmeldedaten (Benutzername und Passwort) abgreift. Diese Betrugsmails sind meist nicht zielgerichtet. Sie imitieren einfach große Online-Händler. Die Gauner gehen davon aus, dass viele, die die Mail erhalten, vor nicht allzu langer Zeit eine Bestellung bei besagtem Händler aufgegeben haben.

Schummelseite

- **»Es gibt ein Problem mit Ihrer Zahlungsart«:** Diese E-Mails oder SMS ähneln der ersten Betrugsmasche aus dieser Liste. Kriminelle versenden massenhaft E-Mails, die scheinbar von einem Online-Shop stammen und die allen Empfängern mitteilt, dass es ein Problem mit der Zahlungsart für diese Bestellung gegeben hat. Dazu erhält der Empfänger Anweisungen, wie er neue Zahlungsdaten über eine Webseite eingeben kann. Wenn Sie bei diesem Händler gerade kürzlich eine Bestellung aufgegeben haben, werden Sie von einer derartigen Nachricht womöglich kalt erwischt und klicken sich bis zum Ende durch. Die Seite, die Ihre neuen Zahlungsdaten sammelt – manchmal sogar zusammen mit den Anmeldedaten zum Online-Shop –, ist natürlich einfach nur ein Tool, mit dem die Gauner Kreditkarten- und Bankdaten stehlen.
- **Zustellprobleme:** Kriminelle verschicken E-Mails, die so aussehen, als kämen Sie von einem Lieferdienst, der Sie darüber informiert, dass es mit der Zustellung ein Problem gegeben hat und Sie dazu auffordert, etwas zu unternehmen, damit ein erneuter Zustellversuch unternommen wird. Natürlich verbreiten diese Nachrichten entweder Schadsoftware über E-Mail-Anhänge oder leiten die Empfänger auf Phishing-Seiten oder Malware-verseuchte Websites weiter. Auf diese Weise erhalten Sie sicherlich keine Warenlieferung.
- **Fingierte Angebote, Social-Media-Beiträge oder Weblinks:** Cybergauner verschicken gerne E-Mails oder veröffentlichen Beiträge in den sozialen Netzwerken, in denen sie allerlei tolle Angebote anpreisen, die meist zu gut sind, um wahr zu sein. Ein nagelneues Samsung-Smart-TV für 100 Euro! Ein brandneues Apple-MacBook für 200 Euro!? Manche dieser Angebote sind vielleicht seriös – und wenn sie von den großen Händlern beworben werden, können Sie das schnell auf der Website nachprüfen –, die überwältigende Mehrheit ist es allerdings nicht. Wenn das Angebot von einem großen Händler zu stammen scheint, aber nicht echt ist, führt Sie der Link vermutlich entweder auf eine fingierte Website oder Sie fangen sich Malware ein. Wenn das Angebot von einem Händler stammt, von dem Sie nie ein Sterbenswörtchen gehört haben, könnte der gesamte Shop ein Fake-Shop sein. Die kassieren das Geld, verschicken die Waren jedoch nie oder versenden defekte oder gestohlene Güter.
- **Gefälschte Rechnungen:** Kriminelle verschicken häufig E-Mails mit angeblichen Rechnungen von Online-Händlern für Bestellungen in beträchtlicher Höhe und vermerken dann, dass die Kreditkarte des Empfängers mit diesem Betrag belastet wurde. Diese Fake-Rechnungen sollen Ihnen Angst einflößen und Sie glauben machen, dass Sie unabsichtlich eine Bestellung aufgegeben haben, Ihnen mehr für eine Bestellung berechnet wurde oder Ihre Kreditkarte sonst in irgendeiner Form für Betrug verwendet wurde. Sie als Empfänger sollen dann auf den Link klicken, der praktischerweise in der Mail enthalten ist, um den Händler zu kontaktieren. Dieser Link führt Sie allerdings auf eine Seite, die Ihre Daten abfängt, Malware installiert oder beides tut. Manchmal werden die Rechnungen gleich mit als Anhang zur E-Mail verschickt und enthalten – Sie ahnen es! –Schadsoftware.

Cybersicherheit für Dummies